Games and Sanctuaries in Ancient Greece

GAMES AND SANCTUARIES IN ANCIENT GREECE

Olympia, Delphi, Isthmia, Nemea, Athens

Panos Valavanis

Translated by
Dr. David Hardy

Foreword by
Sir John Boardman

THE J. PAUL GETTY MUSEUM   LOS ANGELES

INTRODUCTION

Athletics and Religion

From the gods stem all the virtues of mortals.
The gods endow men with the strength of their hands.
It is they who grant grace of speech and wisdom.

Pindar

2

A predominant feature of ancient Greece was the presence of the gods in every aspect of daily life. All activities, from the simplest, such as eating, to the most complex, such as performances of drama, were pervaded and animated by the presence of the divine. Athletic games, too, were not autonomous events, as they are today, but were invariably held in the context of religious festivals in or near sanctuaries, along with other celebrations in honour of the gods, such as sacrifices, processions, prayers, hymns and libations. The ancient Greeks believed that the gods honoured in this way were present and enjoyed the noble competition of well-built bodies and the display of ability by the athletes, who competed first for the gods, and only then for their native city and themselves. Finally, it was believed that the victors in the games did not distinguish themselves solely through their own outstanding ability, but because they enjoyed divine favour.

Although the religious character of the games became blurred with the passage of time, it never ceased to exist. Down to the end of the ancient world, minor and major games were never held as autonomous events. It is no exaggeration to claim that the entire ideological structure of ancient Greek athletics had its roots in the worship of the gods and was based on the profound religiosity of the ancients. This close relationship between athletics and religious and cult procedures is clearly illustrated by the following extract from *De gymnastica* by Philostratos, in reference to the early period of the Olympic games:

'After this they placed the sanctified pieces [of the sacrificed animals] on the altar, on which, however, they had not yet ignited a fire. The runners were a *stade*, [i.e., 600 ancient Greek feet] away from the altar. In front of them stood a priest, who gave the starting signal with a torch. The victor lit the fire for the sanctified pieces and thus departed as Olympic victor.'

Initially, then, the foot-race was held to produce a victor, who had the honour of lighting the sacrificial fire. In essence, then, the contest was a way of selecting the strongest, the best, the most worthy mortal to communicate with the god by lighting the fire on his altar.

1. A victor in the torch race prepares to light the sacrificial fire at an altar. He is approached by a winged Victory, who will tie a ribbon of honour on his body. Attic red-figure bell-krater by the Nikias Painter (410 BC). London, British Museum.

2. Gold wreath of the Hellenistic period. Athens, Benaki Museum.

The Prehistory of Athletics

Athletics is not a Greek invention. Its beginnings lie in a spontaneous tendency amongst human beings of all periods to compete and stand out from others. Its roots go back to remote prehistoric times and are associated with the activities of our ancestors, who were obliged to be continually on the move and always fully prepared not only to secure their food, but also to avoid falling prey to some other stronger human or animal.

Organised athletics makes its first appearance later, at the beginning of the 3rd millennium BC, in the first urban civilisations of Mesopotamia and Egypt. Documents and artistic representations reveal that these peoples practised archery, rowing, wrestling, boxing and equestrian events on various occasions, and entertained themselves by engaging in exercises with balls and acrobatics. The depictions on Egyptian temples and tombs of the Pharaohs and officials throughout Egypt are highly impressive. There is a particularly interesting group of about 400 relief depictions of wrestling at Benni Hassan, dating from about 2000 BC. The detailed representations of the holds reveal a long tradition in the event. However, it cannot easily be established whether athletics was practised in a military or a cult environment.

3

4

There was also considerable athletic activity in Minoan Crete in the 2nd millennium BC. Many scenes in Minoan art reveal the Minoan love for boxing, a characteristic example being the famous wall-painting from Thera dating from the 16th c. BC. The famous 'Prince with the Lilies' has recently been reinterpreted very convincingly as a boxer, with a slight change in the position of the arms. The great passion of the Minoans was for events involving bulls – the famous acrobatic bull-leaping contests, which were probably held in the courtyards of the Minoan palaces. Slender, very fit young individuals ventured the dangerous jump either at festivals in honour of the gods or as a rite of passage on attaining adulthood or access to the social hierarchy.

The Mycenaeans adopted athletic events as part of the great influence exercised on them by the Minoans, and added a further two: the foot-race and the

3. Reconstruction drawing of a relief found in a tomb at Benni Hassan in Egypt (ca. 2000 BC), depicting various phases of a wrestling match.

4. One of the earliest scenes of a boxing match. Two young boys wear loincloths and jewellery (earrings, necklaces, bracelets and anklets), with gloves only on their right hands. The scene probably has ritual character and renders the playful movements of the young bodies skillfully and sensitively. Wall painting from Akrotiri on Thera (16th c. BC). Athens, National Archaeological Museum.

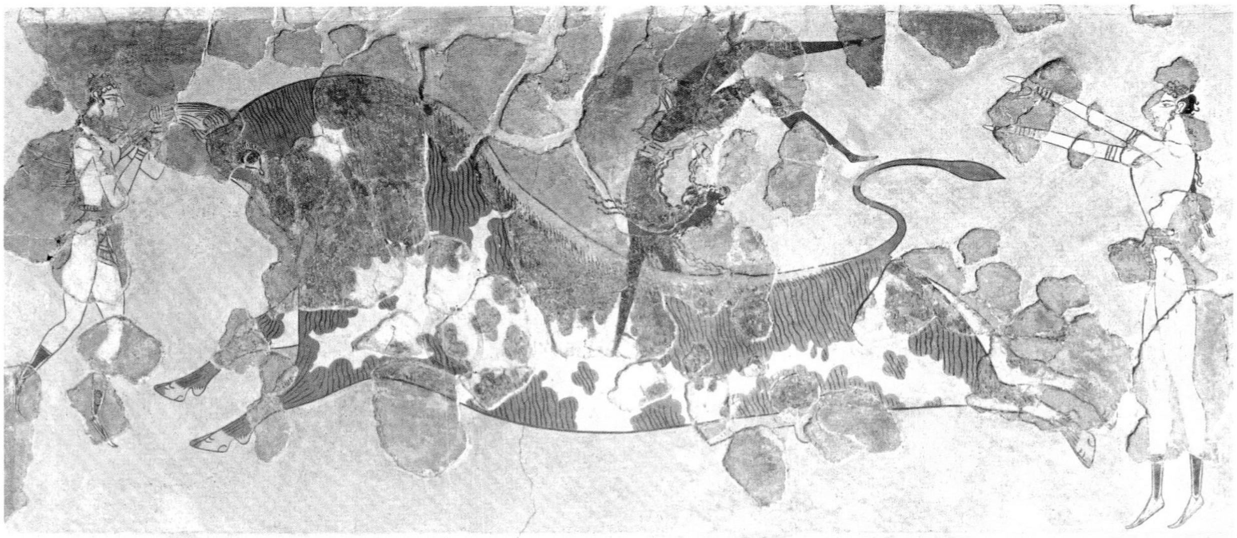

5

5. Bull-leaping scene. The athletes grasp the animal by the horns and leap over its back. Wall painting from the palace at Knossos (middle of the 15th c. BC). Heraklion, Archaeological Museum

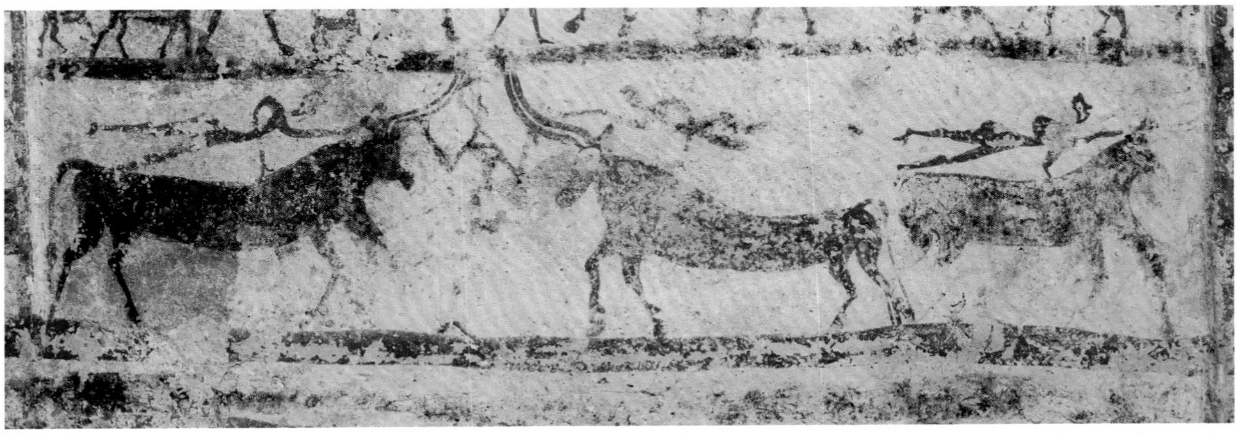

6

6. A funerary larnax depicting three male figures leaping over bulls. Bull leaping took place here with other contests during funeral games. From chamber tomb 22 at Tanagra, Boeotia (first half of the 13th c. BC). Thebes, Archaeological Museum.

chariot-race, which are unambiguously depicted for the first time on Mycenaean vases dating from the 13th c. BC. Recent interpretations of cuneiform documents originating from the Hittite kingdom, which developed in Asia Minor at the same time as Mycenaean civilisation, argue that many of the athletic events to which Homer alludes in the games in honour of the dead Patroklos are also found in similar funeral games held by the Hittites in the 2nd millennium BC. This observation does not necessarily imply Hittite influence on the early stages of Greek athletics, for athletic events are known to have formed part of the funeral rituals of the Mycenaeans, as is evident from the representations on both sides of a coffin from Tanagra dating from the first half of the 13th c. BC.

It appears, therefore, that the competitive ethos of the Indo-European tribes that lived in Greece, combined with the long athletic tradition of the peoples of the eastern Mediterranean, prepared the ground for the major athletics revolution that took place later in Greece, after a period of cultural 'silence' in the early historical period.

Great Festivals and Games

In ancient Greece there were hundreds of games, extending like a huge network to every area of the Mediterranean in which Greek culture flourished. All cities and small communities and most of the sanctuaries took care to ensure that their religious festivals were accompanied by contests, not only to honour their gods, but also to secure prestige for themselves, while at the same time reaping all of the political and economic advantages attendant upon organising such games. As we shall see below, athletics and games formed one of the most important and complex institutions in ancient Greece, the influences and ramifications of which extended throughout the entire period of Greek antiquity.

7

Wreath of wild olive
Olympic Games, 776 BC

Laurel wreath
Pythian Games, 582 BC

Pine wreath
Isthmian Games, 582 BC

Wreath of wild celery
Nemean Games, 573 BC

Olive wreath
Panathenaic Games, 566 BC

8

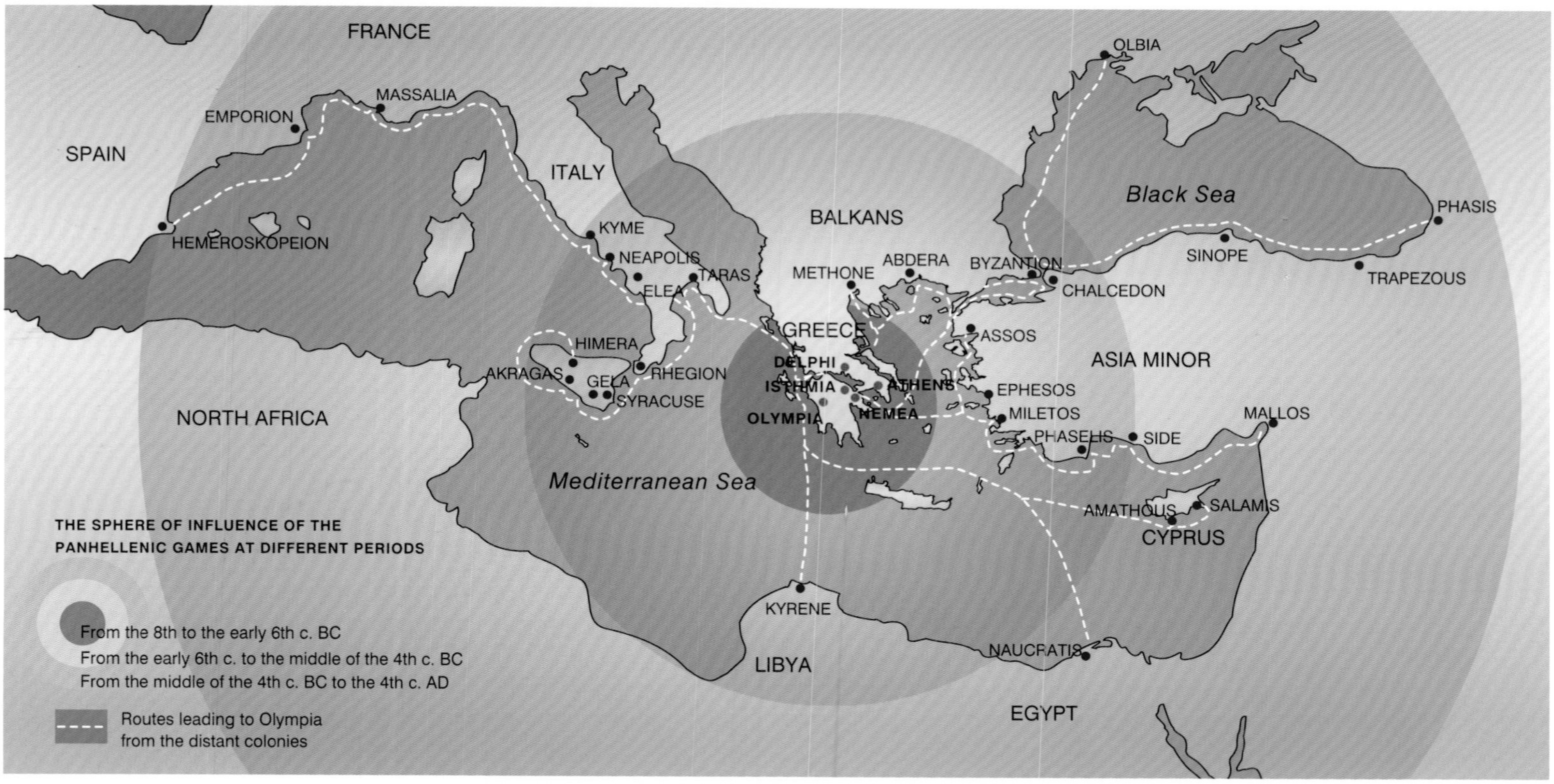

7. Drawings of the wreaths awarded at the most important festivals in antiquity. Each wreath was made of the plant sacred to the god in whose honour the games were held. Traditional foundation dates are also provided.

8. Map of the Mediterranean region showing the sphere of influence of the panhellenic games at different periods and the routes leading from the Greek colonies to Olympia.

9. Modern engraving with a scene of the deification of Diagoras at Olympia in 448 BC. The wreaths and palm branches were tokens of victory.

10. The sequence of the panhellenic games was fixed and formed a 'circuit.' The table illustrates, by way of example, the sequence of the panhellenic games and the Panathenaia for the four years 480-476 BC.

Of the vast number of games, several transcended their narrow, local bounds and became more widely known. Four of them attained the status of panhellenic games and later, in Roman imperial times, of international games, influencing the history of humankind to a greater degree than most ancient institutions. These were the Olympic games, held at Olympia in honour of Zeus, the Pythian games, which took place at Delphi at the festival of Apollo, the Isthmian games, at the sanctuary of Poseidon at Isthmia, and the Nemean games, celebrated in the sanctuary of Zeus at Nemea. All four were *stephanitai* games – that is, games at which the prize awarded to the victor was a simple wreath taken from the sacred tree or plant of the appropriate god. The Panathenaic games, held in Athens at the festival of the Panathenaia, were another major festival, though they never attained the status of panhellenic games, despite the prestige and authority enjoyed by the cultural capital of the ancient world.

The oldest and most important of these games were those at Olympia, the fame and splendour of which surpassed those of all the rest. They were founded as early as the 8th c. BC, while the others came into being only in the 6th c., and throughout the history of the ancient world they took the lead in introducing changes and innovations. The laws of athletics and the regulations and rules for the conduct of the events were all instituted at Olympia and were not only copied by the other games, both inside and outside Greece, but were also respected throughout the ancient world by rulers and states, even by mighty Rome.

The four panhellenic games formed what was called the 'circuit' (*periodos*), a closed group into which no other athletic celebration was able to break. The time at which they were held was so arranged that no festival conflicted with another. The first two, the Olympian and Pythian games, were held every four years, separated by a two-year interval. The other two, the Isthmian and Nemean games, took place every two years, but the Isthmian were held in the spring of the year of the summer Olympic games and thus acted as a prelude to them. No other contests occurred in the year of the Nemean games.

9

TABLE SHOWING THE DATES AT WHICH GAMES WERE HELD

480 BC	April	ISTHMIAN GAMES
480 BC	August	75th OLYMPIC GAMES
479 BC	August	NEMEAN GAMES
478 BC	April	ISTHMIAN GAMES
478 BC	August	PANATHENAIC GAMES
478 BC	September	PYTHIAN GAMES
477 BC	August	NEMEAN GAMES
476 BC	April	ISTHMIAN GAMES
476 BC	August	76th OLYMPIC GAMES

10

OLYMPIA

The Site

The finest place in Greece.

Lysias

Olympia: a verdant, fertile area surrounded by hills and low mountains spreading loosely at the confluence of two rivers, the majestic, serene, silver-eddying Alpheios and the small, gushing Kladeos.

Outstanding natural beauty, the first, magical image that meets people's gaze, was attributed, naturally, to the favour of the gods. Sanctuaries were accordingly founded in beautiful areas in an attempt to honour and repay the gods. Something of this kind would have occurred at Olympia. The place-name, moreover, is derived from Mount Olympos, the home of the gods, and was originally an epithet applied to a female deity of the region, probably Hera. Kronios, the pine-clad conical hill that dominates the plain at the north and lends the little place particular grandeur, is also a very ancient name.

In addition to the landscape, Olympia had another important natural feature: its location in a level, open area to which the inhabitants of many of the villages in the surrounding mountains used to descend, and from which they could find their way to the Ionian Sea, 18 km. away, by way of the Alpheios, which was navigable in ancient times. From the outset, therefore, Olympia was the most important communications node of the surrounding area, in this small part of the western Peloponnese.

11. Pelops drives his chariot with the beautiful Hippodameia, detail (see fig. 36).

12. Map showing the natural features of Olympia, particularly the position of the Kronios hill to the north of the sanctuary and the courses of the Alpheios and Kladeos rivers.

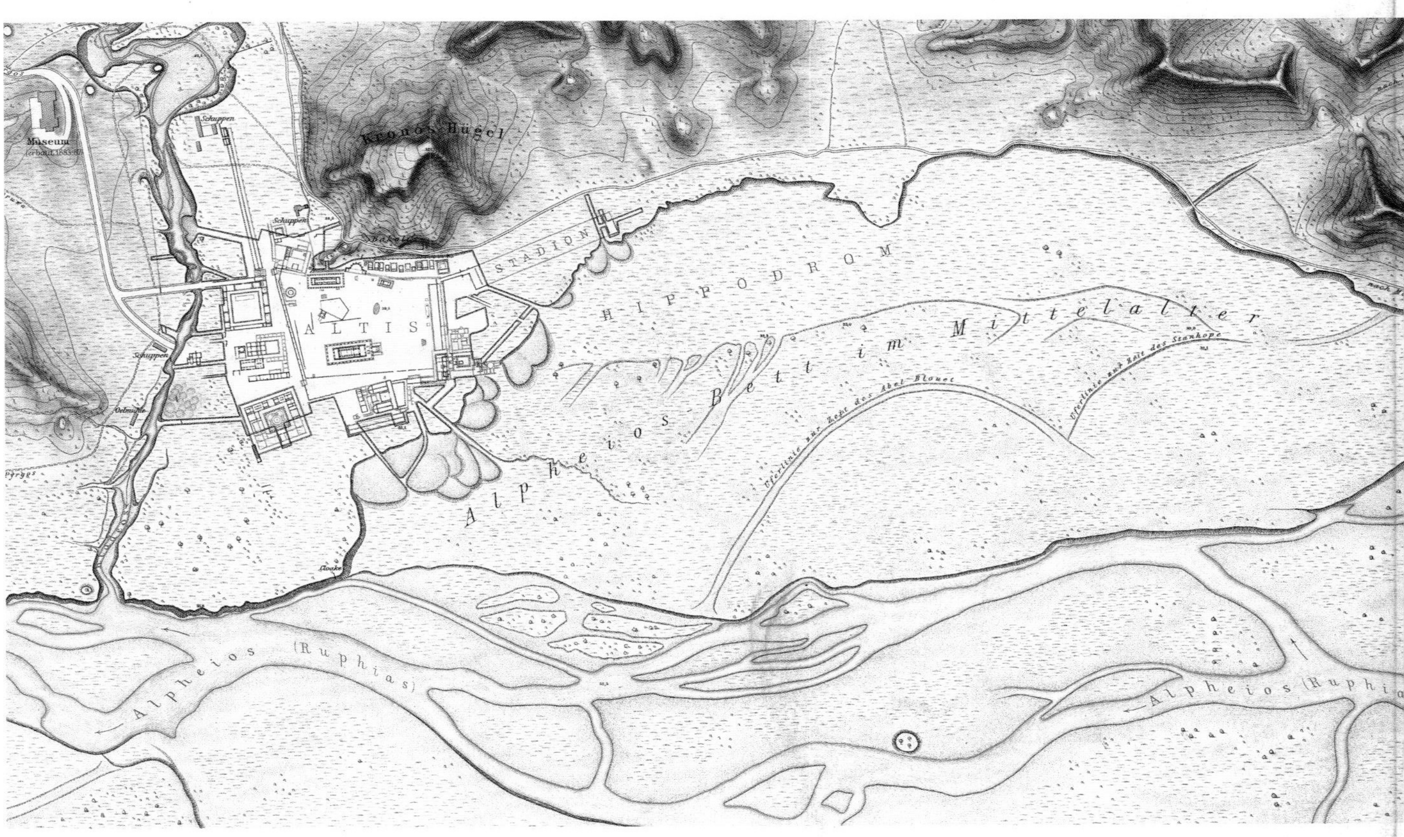

12

13. A contest winner raises his prize, a bronze tripod. He is accompanied and assisted by four youths wearing wreaths. Attic black-figure amphora (ca. 540 BC). Copenhagen, National Museum.

14. The enthroned Zeus holds a thunderbolt in his right hand; a sceptre, no longer preserved, was in his left. The bronze statuette copies the chryselephantine statue of Zeus at Olympia (1st-2nd c. AD). Paris, Louvre Museum.

13

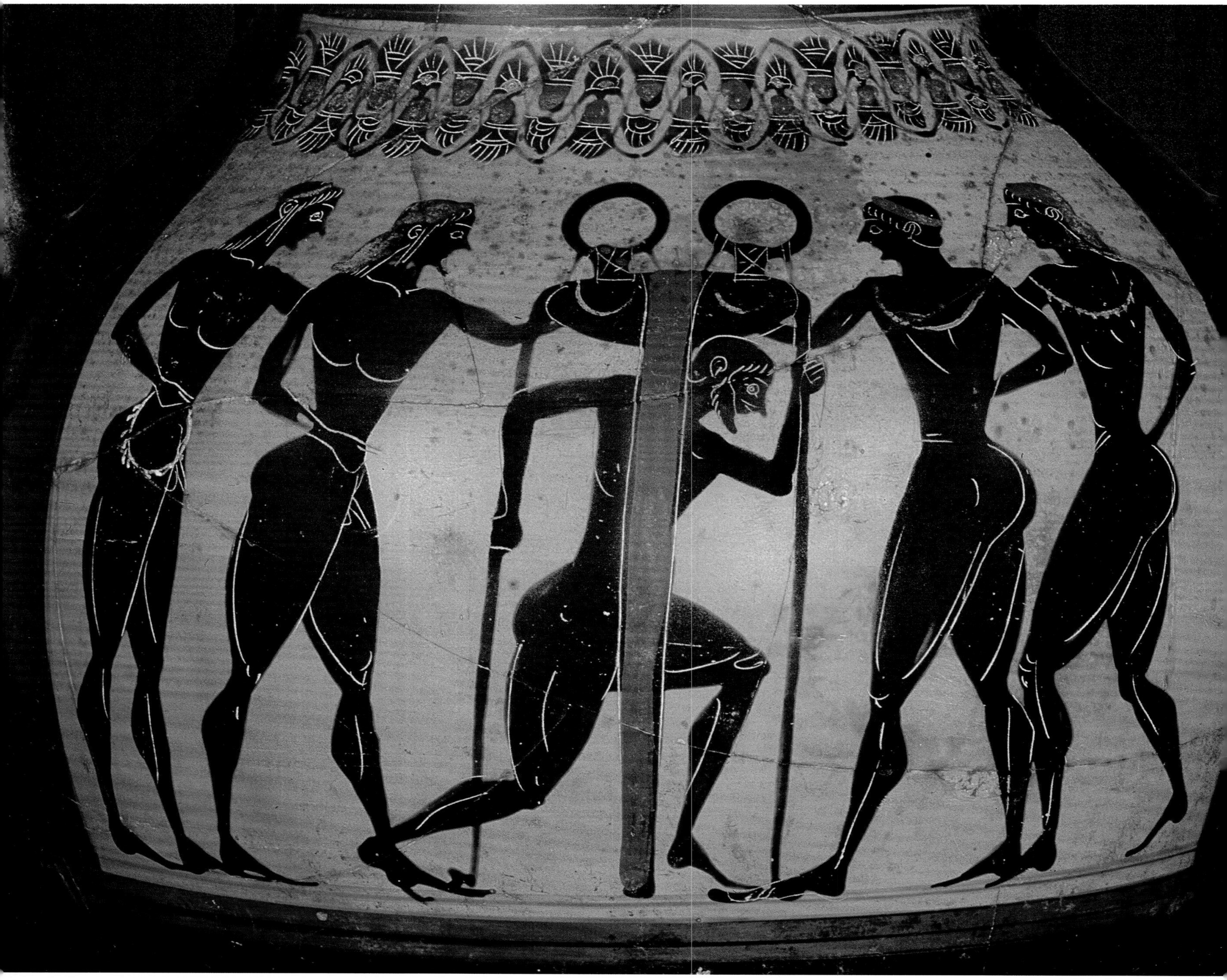

Olympia and the Olympic Games

By day do not seek a bright star more brilliant than the sun in the deserted heavens, nor a contest more famous to sing than that at Olympia.

Pindar

It is no coincidence that Olympia is one of the most important historical sites in the world, both on account of its archaeological interest and because it is the starting point and reference point of the world history of sport.

It was at Olympia that organised contests were first held and developed gradually to become one of the most important institutions of the ancient world, one that lasted from 776 BC to AD 393. During this period of 1,169 years, there were 293 Olympiads.

The Olympic games, deeply rooted in the consciousness of the ancient Greeks, not only played a profound role in shaping and influencing life, society, education, celebrations, politics and art, but they also transcended some of the major changes in ancient history. Moreover, their power was so great and the archetypal ideals they expressed so strong, that they have been revived in modern times and are now an institution just as important as the ancient games, despite the enormous differences that exist between ancient and modern society.

Zeus

Zeus is air, Zeus is earth, Zeus is the sky,
Zeus is everything, and whatever exists superior to it.

Aeschylus

The god in whose honour the festival at Olympia and the Olympic games, and also the festival at Nemea, were held was Zeus, father of gods and men, the personification of authority and order according to Indo-European patriarchal beliefs. At the same time, he had won his position as absolute lord through hard struggles, and it was he who took decisions that determined the fate of the world. The Greeks therefore depicted him either as a warrior, holding a spear or a thunderbolt in his raised right hand, or as a king seated on a throne, with the symbols of authority next to him. In the former guise, he is known from the earliest dedications at Olympia, indicating that, from the beginning of the sanctuary's life, this was his main capacity – the capacity that provided the first great impulse to the development of the cult.

Zeus was depicted in the form of a god wielding a thunderbolt in the Bouleuterion, too, the place where athletes, trainers and judges swore the oath to preserve and abide by the rules of the games. Here, as Zeus Horkios (god of the oath), he was ready, with thunderbolts in both hands, to smite those who broke their oath, again championing obedience to rules and order. A different depiction of Zeus, still holding a thunderbolt but now tranquil, adorned the middle of the east pediment of the great temple, on which was depicted the foundation myth of the Olympic games: the preparations for the mythical chariot-race between Pelops and Oinomaos. Here, too, Zeus, standing between the two competing pairs, is the final judge of the outcome, not only of this particular confrontation, but of all conflict on earth, whether in war or in a period of peace.

He was presented in another, more peaceful form by the great Athenian sculptor Pheidias in the statue that stood in the cella of his temple, the most famous chryselephantine work of ancient art. The god sat majestically on his throne, holding a figure of Victory in his right hand and his sceptre in his left. The throne and its base were adorned with relief and painted scenes from mythology, worked in gold, ebony and precious stones.

The impact made by this sculpture, owing partly to the materials and partly to the great art of its creator, quickly made it so famous that it was considered one of the seven wonders of the ancient world. Those who had the good fortune to see the Olympian god were enchanted, and in Roman times special journeys were arranged for its viewing. These visits to Olympia were probably the earliest examples of organised cultural tourism in history, since before this time organised tours had solely the character of pilgrimages. We are told by ancient authors that those who saw the statue could not meet with an unhappy death – another example of the beneficial influence of great art on the human soul.

The influence exercised by the resplendent statue was not confined to Olympia, however: The Romans adopted the figure of the enthroned god for the depiction of their own heavenly god, Jupiter Optimus Maximus, which in turn influenced the image of God the Father in western Christian iconography.

14

MVR DE TERRASSE SVD
AVTEL DE ZEVS

Chemin des Processions
asse Svd

Olympia Over the Centuries

3rd and 2nd millennia BC
Prehistoric Elis and Olympia

17

16. View of the plain of Olympia from the northeast. At the top left is the river Alpheios and at the bottom right the Kronios hill, which with the river Kladeos formed the natural boundaries of the site. To the right can be seen the sacred buildings of the Altis with part of the stadium at the bottom.

17. Pithoid vase from an Early Helladic apsidal house at Olympia (2100-2000 BC). Olympia, Archaeological Museum.

18-19. Pebble with Linear B symbols from Kaukania in Elis, the earliest example of the Linear B script from mainland Greece (ca. 1650 BC). Olympia, Archaeological Museum.

20. Vases from Late Mycenaean tombs found around the area of Olympia (13th-11th c. BC). Olympia, Archaeological Museum.

The antiquity of the site as recorded in the mythological traditions is confirmed archaeologically by recent excavations.

The earliest remains of human activity on the site of the sanctuary at Olympia consist of pottery of the Late Neolithic period, found to the north of the stadium, which suggests that there was a Neolithic village or at least a temporary dwelling place on the southeast slope of the Kronios hill at the end of the 4th millennium BC. Of greater importance is a circular enclosure 27-30 m. in diameter, made of large river boulders forming a tumulus above a natural rise in the ground at the exact centre of the sanctuary, beneath the Classical shrine of Pelops. It dates from the Early Helladic II period (2600-2500 BC), but nothing has been found inside (e.g., a grave) that might clarify its function; whatever this was, however, it was of great importance in the foundation of the sanctuary, about 1,500 years later, as we shall see. About 2100 BC, a small settlement of houses with apsidal ground-plans was built to the northeast of the enclosure, to be abandoned a few centuries later, probably when the area was flooded by the waters of the Kladeos.

18

19

For many hundreds of years there are no traces of occupation in the region, but a recent excavation find has added a new dimension to the role played by the site in the Mycenaean period. This is a pebble incised with symbols of Linear B script, found in an early Mycenaean level (about 1650 BC) at Kaukania, a small village 7 km. north of Olympia. This find has provided fresh stimulus to the investigation of the period during which this script was created and adopted by the inhabitants of mainland Greece. The predominant scholarly view is that this Minoan script was adopted by the Mycenaeans after they made themselves masters of Crete in the 14th c. BC. The new find indicates that Linear B must have been invented in mainland Greece and thus supports earlier scholars, who claimed that it was inconceivable that the development of the Mycenaean palace civilisation in the 16th century, as evidenced by the finds of the two Grave Circles at Mycenae, was not accompanied by a knowledge of writing.

The great prosperity of the area of Olympia and the whole of Elis in the Mycenaean period is revealed mainly by the excavation of cemeteries of this early date, while the rich chamber tombs of the Late Mycenaean period (13th-12th c. BC) beneath and around the modern museum in Olympia, suggest that there was a flourishing settlement nearby, possibly at Pisa, the birthplace of the mythical king Oinomaos.

This picture of prosperity is completely reversed after the collapse of the Mycenaean civilisation, when the general abandonment and the survival of only a few settlements, observable throughout the whole of southern Greece, is also to be noted in Elis.

11th - 8th c. BC

The establishment of the sanctuary and the early period

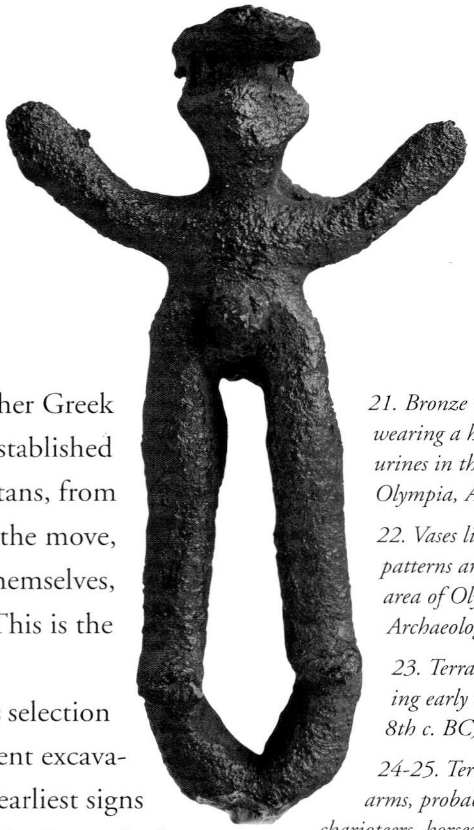

21

In the following period, the 11th and 10th centuries, other Greek tribes crossed from Aitolia to the Peloponnese and established themselves in Elis, driving the earlier inhabitants, the Pisatans, from the area of Olympia. Gradually, the peoples that were on the move, due to the 'Dorian Invasion,' settled down and organised themselves, building new settlements and founding new sanctuaries. This is the dawning of the Greek civilisation of historical times.

The first major event in the history of Olympia was its selection as the site of a sanctuary. According to the evidence of recent excavations, this probably happened before 1000 BC, when the earliest signs of religious activity make their appearance at Olympia, in the form of a few large clay kylikes of a definite cult character. Other vases indicate that collective dinners were attended by believers, a phenomenon common to all early sanctuaries. Olympia appears never to have ceased to be the most important meeting and communication point, and possibly a trade centre, for the inhabitants of the surrounding area, and this role seems to have been one of the reasons for its selection as the foundation of a supralocal sanctuary that belonged to no particular city but to all the surrounding settlements.

21. Bronze Geometric figurine of a naked man or god wearing a head cover, one of the earliest votive figurines in the sanctuary (first half of the 9th c. BC). Olympia, Archaeological Museum.

22. Vases like this submycenaean kylix with geometric patterns are the earliest evidence for worship in the area of Olympia (11th c. BC). Olympia, Archaeological Museum.

23. Terracotta Geometric bull figurines, representing early offerings in the sanctuary of Zeus (9th-8th c. BC). Olympia, Archaeological Museum.

24-25. Terracotta human figurines with outstretched arms, probably representing worshippers. Figurines of charioteers, horses and parts of chariots were the most characteristic dedications in the sanctuary in the Geometric period (9th-8th c. BC). Olympia, Archaeological Museum.

22

23

The pretext for the establishment of the sanctuary in this particular location could be found in the round prehistoric tumulus that was probably still visible in the area 1,500 years after its construction. This was the tumulus that the new inhabitants, in an attempt to consolidate their presence, sought to associate with the tombs of their ancestors; later the legend would be cultivated that it stood above the tomb of Pelops, the mythical founder of the games at Olympia. However, the main god worshipped by the new inhabitants was Olympian Zeus, who accordingly became the dominant deity in the new sanctuary. The most important feature to emerge from recent investigations, which may well account for the importance of Olympia at so early a date in Greek history, is the fact that, along with Dodona, we here have one of the earliest, if not the earliest, examples of the cult of Zeus in Greece.

This first sanctuary at Olympia was a small, open-air one and would have been marked off from the surrounding area only by a simple enclosure fence. Inside it were many trees, including wild olives, from which the sacred tree was later chosen for the wreaths worn by victors. These trees formed a sacred grove (*alsos*), from which appears to derive the cognate word in the Eleian dialect Altis, used of the most sacred part of Olympia. The only 'architectural' features

24

25

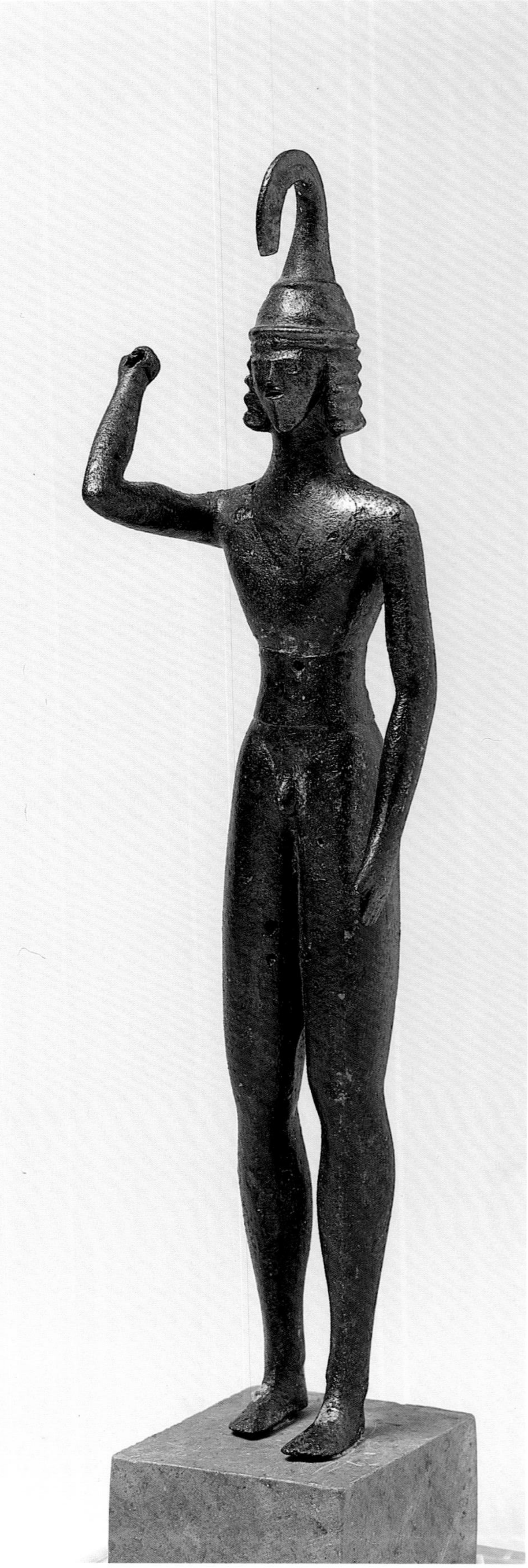

were associated with the double cult practised here. One was the tumulus of Pelops, at which some form of hero cult would have been practised, and the other was a high heap of earth and ash, an 'altar of ash' as it was called, that formed gradually as the result of the sacrifices and other cult rituals carried out here in honour of Zeus.

Beginning already in the early 9th century, Olympia gradually became known to the surrounding area and throughout the Peloponnese and central Greece, from where the worshippers came. They would stand and pray around the altar, make sacrifices to Zeus, and dedicate their offerings, either throwing them on the altar or hanging them from trees. The nature of the offerings found in the excavations – the many thousands of terracotta and bronze figurines of men (about 6,000 of them, of which 4,000 are bronze and 2,000 terracotta), bulls, horses, rams, deer and birds – indicates that the adorants placed themselves and their property (that is, their hunting animals and flocks) under the protection of the god.

There are several figurines of charioteers with their chariots (about 100), possibly depicting the wealthy farmers and stock-raisers who travelled in them to Olympia, though they conceivably had a military character, since chariots were used only in warfare in the contemporary Homeric poems. These warrior figurines, whether they represent the god himself or their dedicators, reflect Zeus's character as a military god in the early period. Another kind of dedication made by the faithful at Olympia consisted of bronze cauldrons, a sacred vessel of great value at the period. Fragments of more than three hundred of

26

27

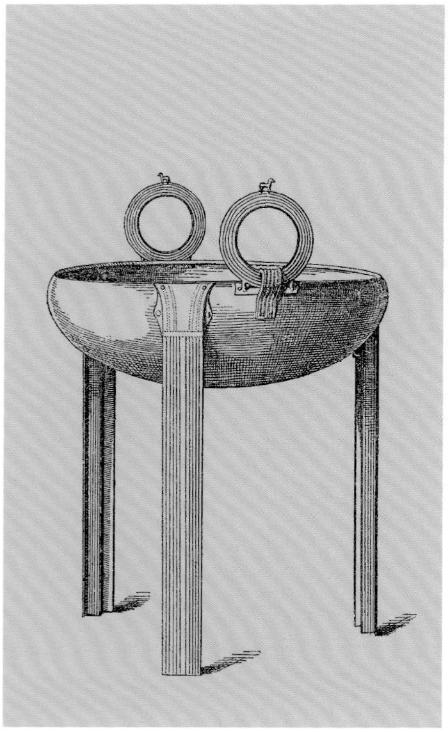

28

29

30

26. *Bronze statuette of a warrior wearing a helmet and holding a spear in his right hand and, probably, the reins of a horse in his left. By dedicating such figures, warriors placed their life under the protection of the god (680-670 BC). Olympia, Archaeological Museum.*

27. *Reconstruction drawing of the handle of a bronze cauldron with the figurines of a warrior and a horse attached to the top. Many bronze figurines were used as attachments for the handles of cauldrons (first half of the 8th c. BC). Drawing: E. Kunze.*

28. *Drawing of a bronze tripod cauldron. Cauldrons, vessels that originally had a household use, became the most common dedications in the sanctuary. Drawing: A. Furtwängler.*

29. *Group of bronze Geometric animal figurines. Thousands of these were found in the ash of the early altar. Like terracotta figurines, they served as substitutes for sacrificial animals (9th-8th c. BC). Olympia, Archaeological Museum.*

30. *Charioteer standing on a chariot, part of a bronze group from a dedication of the Geometric period (second half of the 8th c. BC). Olympia, Archaeological Museum.*

31. *Bronze Geometric horse figurines from Olympia (8th c. BC). Olympia, Archaeological Museum.*

31

these have been found, some of them as high as 3 m. Since there were very few enclosed rooms, these were probably displayed in the open air, amongst the trees and possibly around the altar.

At this early period of the sanctuary, then, from the 10th to the 8th c. BC, Olympia should be imagined as an open-air sacred grove with a few light timber structures; the main cult features were the tumulus of Pelops and the ash altar of Zeus, while the area around them was full of large tripod cauldrons.

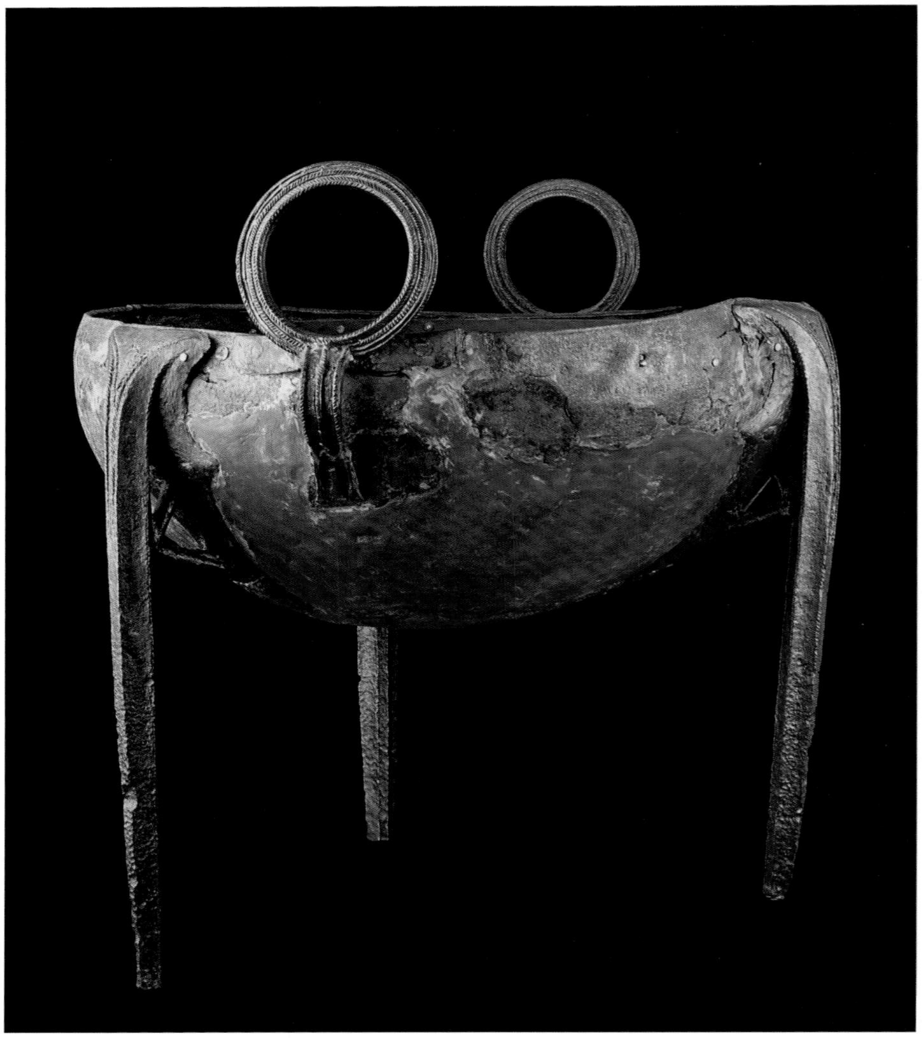

32

33

32. Bronze cauldron with a hammered body and cast legs and handles, one of the earliest cauldrons from the sanctuary of Zeus (9th c. BC). Olympia, Archaeological Museum.

33. Bronze leg of a Cretan tripod cauldron dedicated at Olympia, with a depiction of two heroes or gods fighting for a tripod (late 8th c. BC). Olympia, Archaeological Museum.

34. Cast handle of a bronze tripod cauldron with a horse figurine attached to the top (8th c. BC). Olympia, Archaeological Museum.

8th c. BC

The foundation of the Olympic games

34

We learn from the ancient literary sources that the establishment of the Olympic games occurred in 776 BC. The date was already disputed in ancient times as a 'fabrication' of the Eleian sophist Hippias, who, at the behest of his place of origin, undertook in about 400 BC to compile the first list of Olympic victors and, for reasons unknown to us, assigned the beginning of the games to that year. The archaeological evidence deriving from recent excavations, however, precludes any athletic activity before 700 BC, and assigns the great moment of the foundation of the games to about this period.

It was at this time that Olympia entered a new and important period, a development that must have been occasioned not only by the economic prosperity and intellectual flowering observable throughout Greece, but also by the need then felt by the city-states for new religious centres to serve as cohesive agents binding together their peoples and the centres of power that were coming into being. The small area of the sanctuary was apparently not large enough to meet the needs of the ever-increasing numbers of pilgrims. The priests must have decided to expand and comprehensively remodel the sanctuary by levelling the low natural and artificial elevations to the south of the Kronios hill. All the earlier structures were destroyed, apart from the tumulus of Pelops. Even the ash from the conical altar of Zeus, along with the dedications, was spread throughout the sacred area to fill the depressions. It is characteristic that a black layer full of dedications and animal bones was found over a great area, extending from the Philippeion to the stadium and from the Heraion, the temple of Hera, to the Temple of Zeus.

At the same period, there was a change in the nature of the dedications, namely, a steady reduction in the number of figurines and tripods and a corresponding increase in weaponry. This fact points to a great change: whereas figurines were individual dedications and had an agricultural and stock-breeding character, weapons were collective dedications by cities, of a military-political character. All the available evidence thus points to the turn of the 8th to the 7th c. BC as a period of great change at Olympia.

Foundation Myths and Traditions

Already in antiquity a large number of different myths were in circulation that attributed the foundation of the games to gods, heroes and even historical figures, in an endeavour to fill the gaps in historical memory and provide interpretations for events that were already very ancient and the starting point of which had been forgotten. Another reason for the existence of different versions lay in the efforts of many cities to usurp the grandeur of Olympia and the games by attributing their inception to 'their own' god, hero or historical figure. The paternity of the sanctuary and the games was claimed mainly by the two cities closest to Olympia, Pisa and Elis, though the two major Peloponnesian powers, Sparta and Argos, never disguised their indirect claims.

Let us begin with the ancient literary sources, however, which are the most immediate sources and those closest in time to the period when the games were founded. Homer makes no mention of Olympia, but does speak of chariot races held at the palace of Augeias, the king of Elis (*Iliad* XI, 697-701). Though some scholars believe this reference probably represents an oblique reference to the games by Homer, many impressive athletic competitions are described in the Homeric poems. In the *Iliad*, Achilles organises spectacular games in honour of the dead Patroklos, and in the *Odyssey*, Odysseus, while the guest of Alkinoos, is honoured with a display of athletic feats by the Phaiakian youth.

After this, [they say] that Pisos and Pelops, and also Herakles, were the first to institute the games at Olympia.

Phlegon

35. Depiction of the chariot race organised by Achilles during the funeral games in honour of his friend Patroklos. Detail from the Attic black-figure François krater (570 BC). Florence, Archaeological Museum.

36. Pelops drives his chariot with the beautiful Hippodameia during his contest against Oinomaos. Attic red-figure amphora (late 5th c. BC). Arezzo, Archaeological Museum.

37. Reconstruction drawing of the complete scene from the Attic red-figure amphora, showing the four-horse chariot of Pelops and Hippodameia. The olive trees in the background suggest the landscape of Olympia.

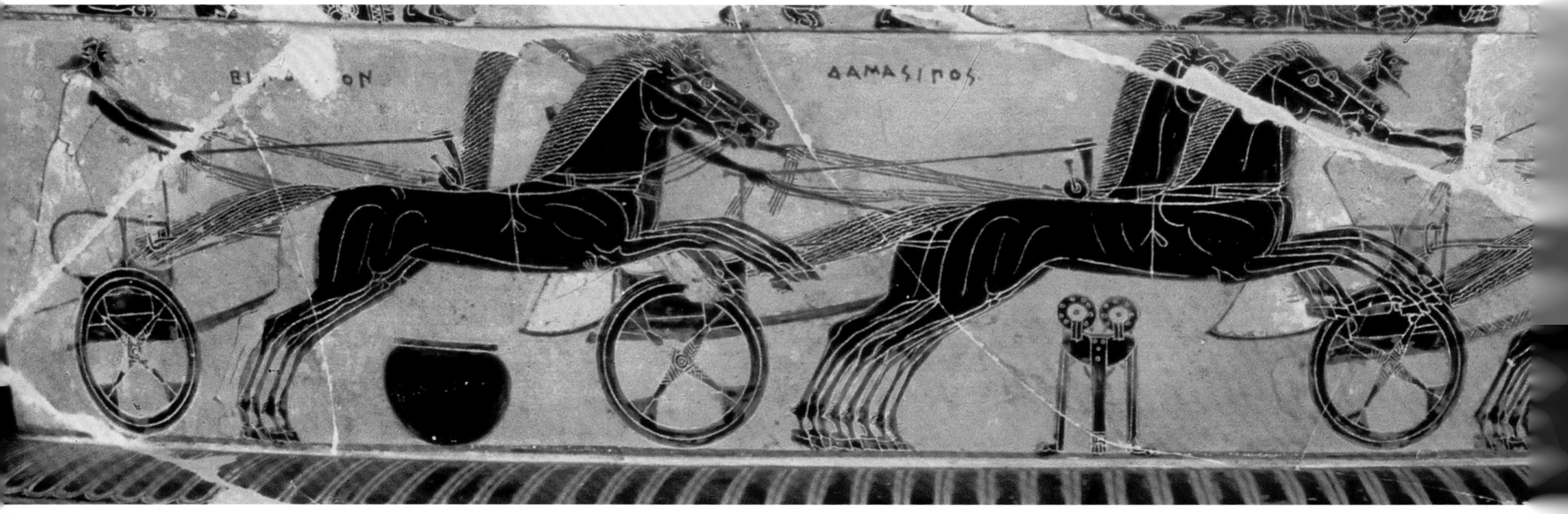

35

The earliest and strongest ancient tradition relating to the foundation of the Olympic games is to be found in the Hesiodic poem *Eoiai* (Catalogue of Women), which is generally thought to be later than the poet but not after the 6th c. BC. In this poem, the games are said to have been founded by Pelops, a prince from Phrygia: aspiring to the hand of the daughter of Oinomaos, the king of Elis, he defeated the king in a chariot race, killed him, took his daughter Hippodameia as his wife, and became king of the region, giving his name to the entire Peloponnese. Pelops founded the Olympic games in order to give thanks to Zeus for his victory or, according to another legend, to secure expiation for the murder of Oinomaos.

36

Another version, mentioned for the first time by Pindar in the first half of the 5th c. BC, attributes the foundation of the games to the great hero Herakles, after his victorious campaign against Augeias, the king of Elis, who had refused to pay him the agreed fee for cleansing his stables.

Later authors, particularly in Roman times, claim that the games were founded by Zeus or Apollo. Pausanias attributes the institution of the games to Idaean Herakles, born in Crete, who competed with his four brothers in the first foot-race and established the first prize of wild olive. Of greater interest are the attempts to attribute the great honour to 'historical' persons, mainly to prehistoric kings of Pisa or Elis, such as Oxylos and Iphitos, since these two cities, both close to Olympia, vied for the right to organise the games.

The ancient Greeks themselves approached the views in circulation with some reservation. Writing at about the time of Jesus, Strabo (8.3.30) expressed considerable scepticism, urging his contemporaries (and perhaps ourselves as well?) not to believe anything they hear on this subject: 'We should abandon all the old views about the building of the sanctuary and the foundation of the games . . . since they are told in various versions, but are by no means credible.'

37

THE HISTORICAL BEGINNINGS OF THE GAMES

Modern research has so far failed to solve the problem of the historical beginnings of the games, despite the vast amount of evidence and despite new data emerging from the excavation of the early phases of the sanctuary, mentioned above. Various theories have been advanced regarding the origins of the Olympic games, which can be divided into two groups: those that trace them back to religious-ritual practices and those that propose a secular origin.

The first group associates the beginning of the games with funeral games, that is, with the ceremonies and contests held to honour important dead kings or heroes. This view cites as the most characteristic example the games organised by Achilles in honour of the dead Patroklos, described by Homer in the *Iliad*. A more practical variant of this theory interprets these games as a means of distributing the property of the deceased, which was awarded to the victors

38. Scene of a chariot race, from the funeral games organised by Achilles in honour of Patroklos. The spectators, sitting in a tiered stand, gesture vigorously and cheer the competitors as they pass in front of them. The painted inscriptions identify the subject, the artist, and the position of Achilles. Fragment of an Attic black-figure dinos by Sophilos (580-570 BC). Athens, National Archaeological Museum.

39. Achilles harnessing the horses to his chariot. Fragment of an Attic black-figure kantharos by Nearchos (570-560 BC). Athens, National Archaeological Museum.

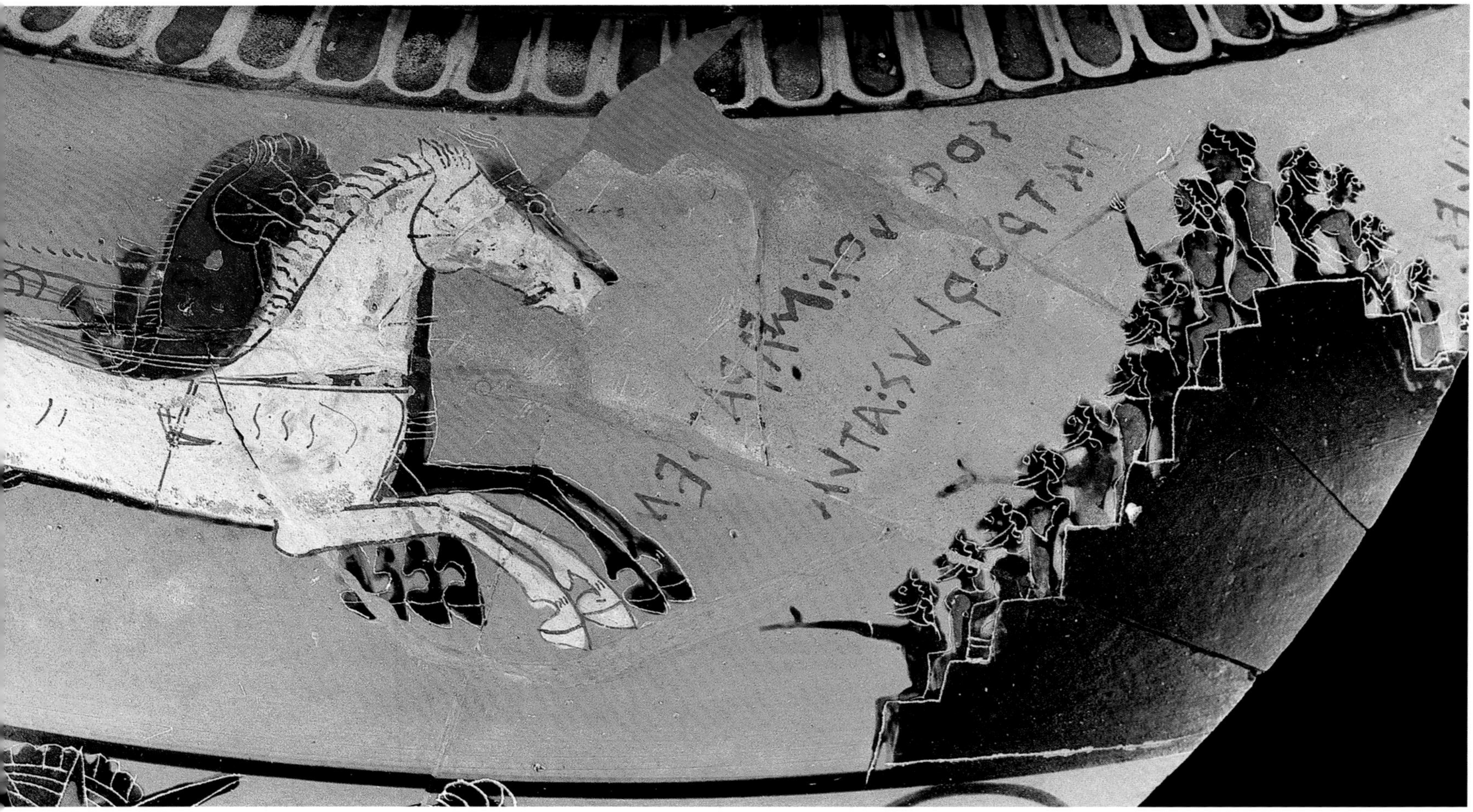

38

in the form of prizes. A related view is that the games were simply a competition to decide the successor to the throne after the death of the king.

In the same group are those who assert that the games derive from fertility rituals held as part of a rural cult. These rituals culminated in a sacred marriage between the priestess of the fertility goddess and the victor of the contest, a parallel for which we have seen in the myth of Pelops and Hippodameia. The main evidence adduced here includes the existence at Olympia of many cults of fertility deities, the nature of the prizes in the games (wreaths made of shoots of plants), and the importance at Olympia of the priestess of the rural goddess Demeter Chamyne, the only woman allowed to watch the games inside the Olympic stadium.

Scholars who claim that the games had secular roots trace their beginnings back to prehistoric hunting methods that, with the passage of time, assumed a ritual character, or to military training designed to prepare hoplites for war. Others consider them to be the relics of rites of passage – ordeals through which young men were admitted to adulthood and which were very common in the ancient world. These scholars assert that the incorporation of the games into religious celebrations was a subsequent development, following the precedent of earlier periods when religious festivals were the only occasions of peace and calm in which men could gather together to relax by taking part in various kinds of competition.

39

Regardless of the theories advanced on the origins of the games, what is of particular importance for Olympia is their starting point – whether 776 BC according to tradition, or about 700 BC according to the archaeological record, the priesthood at Olympia decided to incorporate competitive events into the cult. The decision was the result of certain historical events that, though obscure because of their early date, are well worth investigating.

Interestingly, Greeks in the Hellenistic and Roman periods connected the beginning of the games with two events. Pausanias, the Roman traveller of the

2nd c. AD, describing the history of Elis (5.4.5-6) writes: 'After a time, Iphitos, . . . who was a contemporary of Lykourgos, . . . organised the Olympic games and established the festival at Olympia once more, from the beginning, and also the sacred truce that had ceased for I don't know how long. Since Greece was then suffering great destruction as a result of internecine war and plague, Iphitos thought of consulting the Delphic god on the way to be rid of the disasters. And they say that the Pythia ordered Iphitos and the Eleians to renew the Olympic games.' According to this passage, the occasion for the founding of the games was an oracle by Delphi, to which the king of Elis, Iphitos, had resorted to discover how the Greeks could be free of wars and disasters.

40. The plain of Olympia before the start of the excavations in 1875. Detail of a drawing by A. Boetticher.

41. Reconstruction drawing of the area to the north of the Temple of Zeus, with the altar of ash that was the centre of the cult at Olympia. Special interpreters predicted the outcome of a battle or a war from the flames of the fire on the altar. Drawing: F. Adler.

40

Another important event noted by the ancient Greeks at the same time as the instituting of the games was the establishment of the sacred truce, which was achieved by an agreement between the king of Elis, Iphitos, the king of Pisa, Kleosthenes, and the Spartan lawgiver Lykourgos. These three agreed that a cessation of all hostilities between belligerents should be imposed at every Olympiad and that Olympia should be proclaimed a place of peace. The agreement was recorded on a bronze disk that was later placed in the Temple of Hera, which was seen by Aristotle himself, and was later described by Pausanias.

Despite the fact that some modern scholars dispute the historical nature of these events, on the grounds that they are only recorded by later authors, the reports of wars and misfortunes appear to correspond fully with the situation in Greece in the late 8th and early 7th century. It might be claimed, therefore, that these statements contain a kernel of historical truth. On this basis, I attempt below to trace some aspects of the beginning and early history of the Olympic games.

THE ORACLE OF OLYMPIA

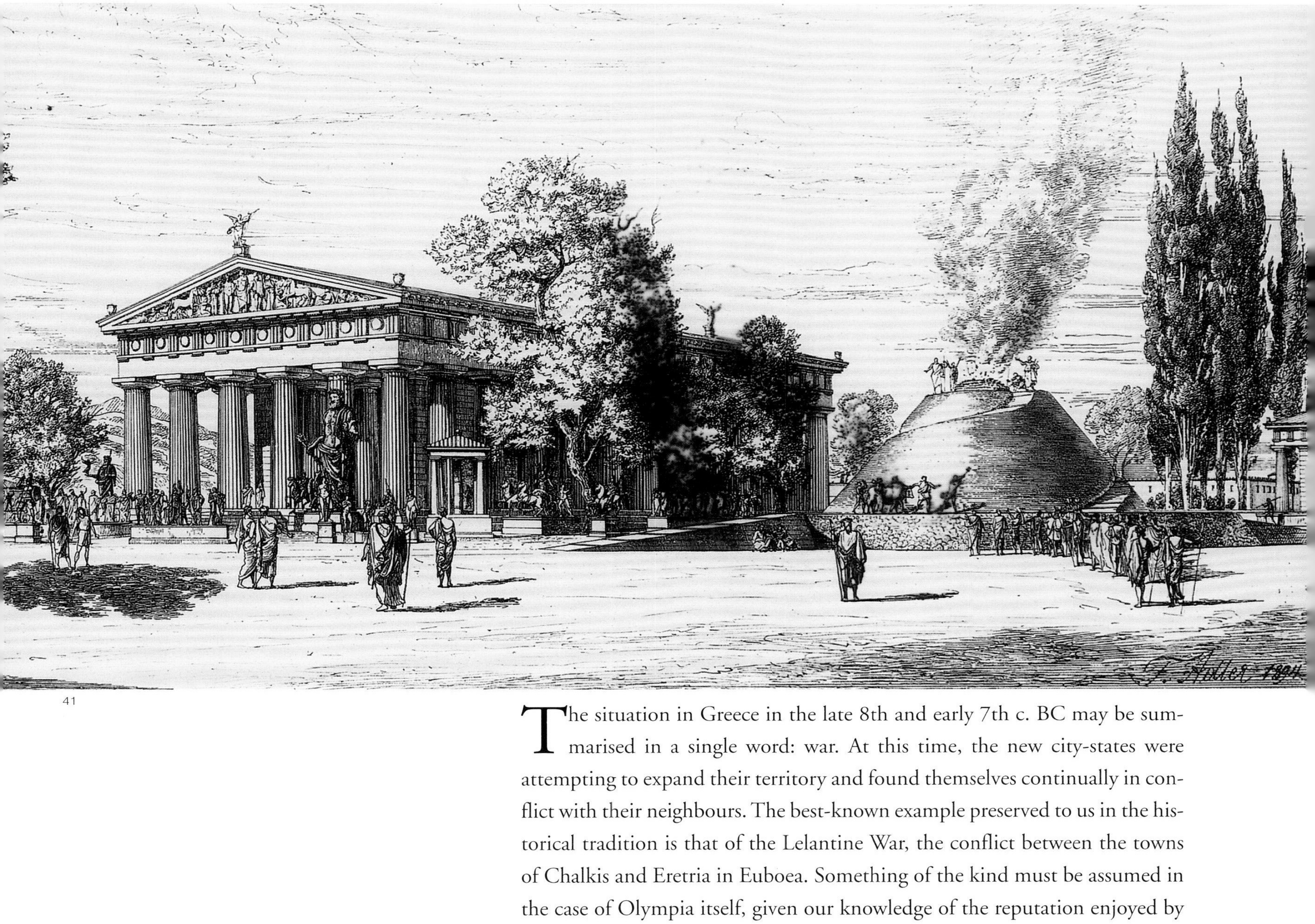

41

The situation in Greece in the late 8th and early 7th c. BC may be summarised in a single word: war. At this time, the new city-states were attempting to expand their territory and found themselves continually in conflict with their neighbours. The best-known example preserved to us in the historical tradition is that of the Lelantine War, the conflict between the towns of Chalkis and Eretria in Euboea. Something of the kind must be assumed in the case of Olympia itself, given our knowledge of the reputation enjoyed by the sanctuary already at this time, as well as the continual later rivalry between the Elians and the Pisatans.

It is also interesting that, in the eyes of the ancient Greeks, the beginning of the games was associated with the cessation of hostilities and the imposition of a truce. The sacred truce, however, was not imposed by the priesthood, but was the result of a political decision taken by secular rulers in the Peloponnese, who placed their decision under the protection of the sanctuary. The reason that this decision was taken at Olympia is connected not only with the need to put an end to the conflict concerning the sanctuary and to place the area under divine protection, as has been conjectured, but also with the role of the sanctuary in the military conflicts of the period.

According to Strabo (8.3.30) Olympia owed its initial rise to prominence, long before the games, to the existence there of an oracle connected with the ancient cult of Gaia (Earth). As a result of the military character of the early Zeus, the oracle at Olympia began to specialise in questions related to war. We also learn from Herodotus that many generations before his time, prophets from Olympia served in belligerent Greek cities, often accompanied armies on distant campaigns in order to make sacrifices before battles, and even provided advice on military strategy, invoking the will of Zeus. About the same time as Herodotus, Pindar referred to Olympia in his 8th Olympian Ode as mother of the games and mistress of the truth, through prophecy: 'O mistress of golden-crowned games and truth.' That is, he considered games and prophecies to be equally important at Olympia.

At Olympia itself, moreover, representatives of Greek cities sought advice on the favourable circumstances for beginning a campaign (Xenophon, *Hellenika*, 4.7.2). This accounts for the existence of so many military dedications made by Greek cities: these were erected in the sanctuary in the form of trophies to give thanks to Zeus for his aid in victories. It also explains the many dedications in the form of statues of Victory, in this case, Victory associated with military rather than athletic success.

42

42. Bronze corselet with a representation of gods. At the centre are Zeus and Apollo with his lyre. The ancient Greeks decorated even purely functional objects, such as weapons (650-625 BC). Olympia, Archaeological Museum. Drawing: Olympia Bericht *IV, pl. 59.*

43

43. The oldest photograph of the site at Olympia, immediately after the beginning of excavations in 1875. Athens, German Archaeological Institute.

44-45. Reconstruction of the two akroteria with the figure of Victory. Drawing: A. Moustaka.

46. Torso of a terracotta akroterion with a figure of Victory, from one of the treasuries. Two winged Victories, only parts of which are now preserved, adorned the corner akroteria of a composition that had the goddess Athena (see fig. 69) at the centre (500-490 BC). Olympia, Archaeological Museum.

44

This oracular activity is known from inscriptions to have continued until the 3rd c. AD as a secondary function of the sanctuary, hidden in the shadow cast by the brilliance of the games. The actual place where the prophecies were issued was the altar of Zeus and the divine signs were 'read' from the shape and intensity of the flames of the sacrificial pyre; as in the case of oracles elsewhere, the experts in this reading were members of two old families of the region, the Iamidai and the Klytiadai, who traced their descent back to the mythical prophets Apollo and Amphiaraos. All this evidence suggests that, long before the games, the military aspect of Zeus was the primary element in the cult at Olympia, and that the oracular function in association with warfare was the reason for the prestige enjoyed by the sanctuary throughout Greece at such an early date.

Gradually, with the passage of time, this oracular role at Olympia declined in importance, due in part to the rise of the Delphic oracle, which later usurped the paternity of many panhellenic institutions. As the prestige and influence of the games became primary at Olympia, the oracle connected with the beginning of the games was attributed to Delphi, and the naïve myth was invented of the visit by the Eleian king Iphitos to seek a prophecy. The prophecy relating to the foundation of the games was in fact issued by the oracle at Olympia, which is clear not only from the reference to the cessation of local wars between the city-states who contested control of the sanctuary in question, but also from the 'material competence' of the oracle of the warlike Zeus to provide a solution to the pressing problem of wars that are attested in southern Greece in the late 8th and early 7th c. BC, the period to which the beginnings of the Olympic games are dated.

45

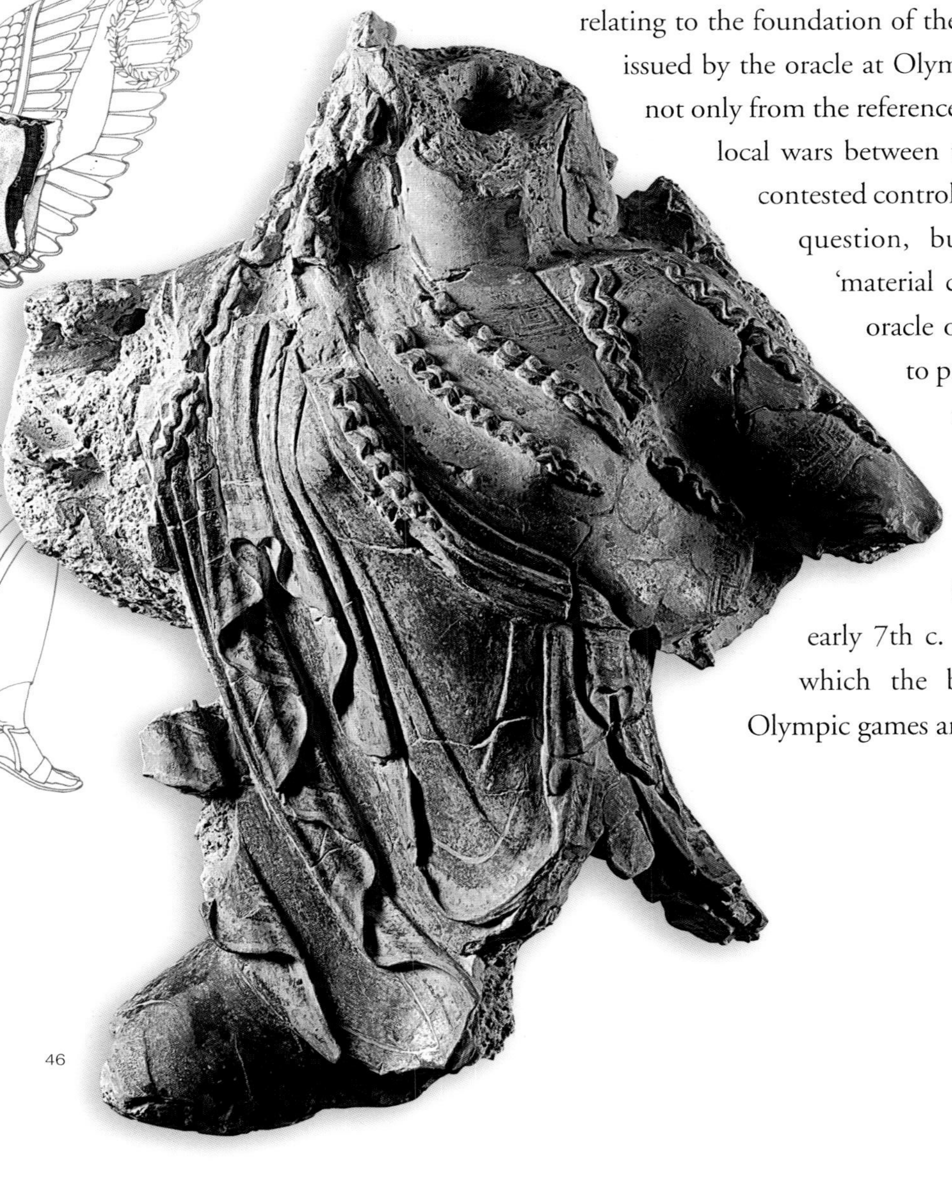

46

Games and Hero Worship

The athletic contests that were incorporated in the cult at Olympia already existed before they made their first appearance in the 8th c. BC, not as an institution, of course, but as individual athletic events, either in the form of military exercises or as a performance designed to entertain the ruling class. Three elements point to this conclusion. The first, mentioned above, is the existence of athletic events in the prehistoric cultures of the Near East and the Aegean. The second is the statement in the ancient sources that the games at Olympia were not held for the first time at this date, but were revived after being suspended for a long period. The third is the many references in Homer to games in which his heroes participated, involving a large number of events of great importance, above all the games held in honour of the dead Patroklos. These contain all the elements of hero worship that was developing at this period.

This last accords very well with the hero worship practised from the start at Olympia in honour of Pelops, who was regarded as the mythical founder of the games. The importance of hero worship in the founding of the games is also indicated by the fact that when other cities and sanctuaries founded their own games 200 years after the Olympic games were instituted, these, on analogy with Olympia, were addressed to local heroes and incorporated into an original local hero cult.

We are faced with the conclusion that the games were not something completely new, introduced for the first time at Olympia, but that they derive from

47. Reverse of the larnax in fig. 6, showing a chariot race, one of the events during funeral games. From chamber tomb 22 at Tanagra (first half of the 13th c. BC). Thebes, Archaeological Museum.

48. Shield emblem, made of a hammered bronze sheet with engraved details. The composite daemonic figure (wings, a fish's tail, lion's paws, and the face of a Gorgon) was intended to strike fear into the enemy (second half of the 6th c. BC). Olympia, Archaeological Museum.

49. Hammered bronze sheet with the figure of a female griffin suckling its young, probably a decorative appliqué for wooden furniture (630-620 BC). Olympia, Archaeological Museum.

50. Plan of the archaeological site at Olympia immediately after the completion of the first phase of excavations in 1881. Athens, German Archaeological Institute.

47

an earlier custom of hero worship that survived after the collapse of Mycenaean civilisation. This custom, transmitted in epic poems and oral tradition, was revived again at the end of the 8th or the beginning of the 7th century, along with other elements of the cult at Olympia (processions, sacrifices, oracle, etc.). The Olympic games, like most of the major events and institutions in Greece during the early historical period, were thus a revival of earlier, possibly Mycenaean, customs, now integrated into a later religious, ideological and political context.

TABLE SHOWING THE DATE AT WHICH EVENTS WERE INTRODUCED INTO THE OLYMPIC GAMES

OLYMPIAD	YEAR	EVENT
1st	766 BC	*stadion*
14th	724 BC	*diaulos*
15th	720 BC	*dolichos*
18th	708 BC	pentathlon and wrestling
23rd	688 BC	boxing
25th	680 BC	chariot race for four horses
33rd	648 BC	horse race and pankration
37th	632 BC	boys' foot race and pankration
38th	628 BC	boys' pentathlon (held only once)
41st	616 BC	boys' boxing
65th	520 BC	race in armour
70th	500 BC	*apene* (race for mules, held until 444 BC)
71st	496 BC	*kalpe* (race for mares, held until 444 BC)
93rd	408 BC	*synoris* (chariot race for two horses)
96th	396 BC	contests for trumpeters and heralds
99th	384 BC	chariot race for foals
128th	268 BC	*synoris* (chariot race for two foals)
131st	256 BC	horse race for foals
145th	200 BC	boys' pankration

48

Recent research at Olympia tends to underplay the role of the hero cult in the foundation of the games, and asserts that the cult of Pelops was not introduced before 600 BC. Whatever the case, the official recognition of the games was accompanied by the expansion of the competitive programme, since there was a rapid increase in the number of events at Olympia at this period, as is evident from the following table.

49

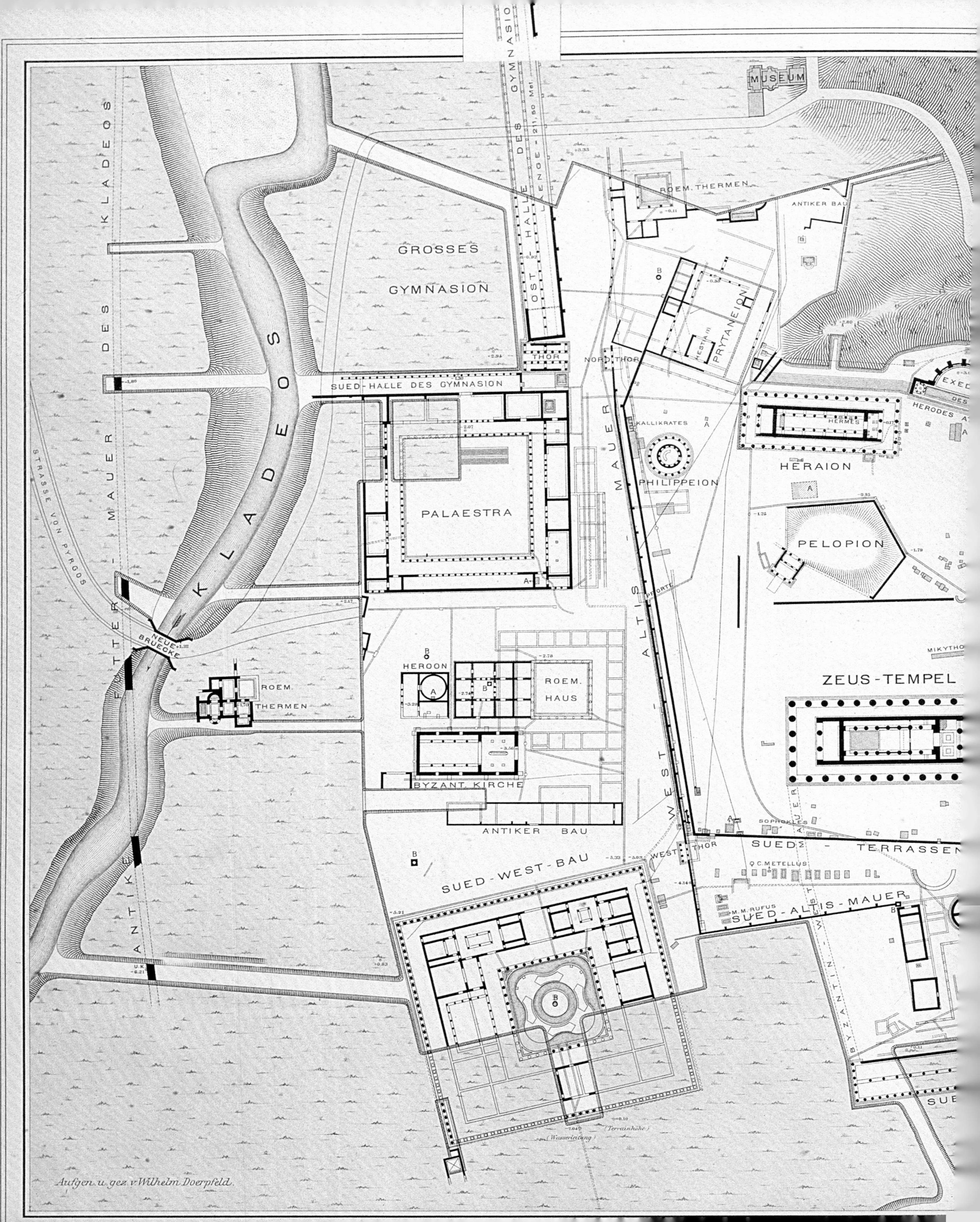
MUSEUM
OST-HALLE DES GYMNASION
LAENGE - 21,50 Met.
ROEM. THERMEN
ANTIKER BAU
GROSSES GYMNASION
PRYTANEION
HESTIA
NORD THOR
THOR
SUED-HALLE DES GYMNASION
KLADEOS
FUTTER-MAUER DES KLADEOS
ANTIKE
STRASSE VON PYRGOS
NEUE BRUECKE
ROEM. THERMEN
PALAESTRA
KALLIKRATES
PHILIPPEION
HERAION
HERMES
HERODES
EXED
PELOPION
PFORTE
MIKYTHO
ZEUS-TEMPEL
HEROON
ROEM. HAUS
BYZANT. KIRCHE
ANTIKER BAU
WEST - ALTIS - MAUER
WEST THOR
SUED - TERRASSEN
SOPHOKLES
Q.C.METELLUS
M.M.RUFUS
SUED-ALTIS-MAUER
BYZANTIN. WEST
SUED-WEST-BAU
SUE
(Wasserleitung)
(Terrainhöhe)
Aufgen. u. gez. v. Wilhelm Doerpfeld.

an earlier custom of hero worship that survived after the collapse of Mycenaean civilisation. This custom, transmitted in epic poems and oral tradition, was revived again at the end of the 8th or the beginning of the 7th century, along with other elements of the cult at Olympia (processions, sacrifices, oracle, etc.). The Olympic games, like most of the major events and institutions in Greece during the early historical period, were thus a revival of earlier, possibly Mycenaean, customs, now integrated into a later religious, ideological and political context.

48

Recent research at Olympia tends to underplay the role of the hero cult in the foundation of the games, and asserts that the cult of Pelops was not introduced before 600 BC. Whatever the case, the official recognition of the games was accompanied by the expansion of the competitive programme, since there was a rapid increase in the number of events at Olympia at this period, as is evident from the following table.

TABLE SHOWING THE DATE AT WHICH EVENTS WERE INTRODUCED INTO THE OLYMPIC GAMES

OLYMPIAD	YEAR	EVENT
1st	766 BC	*stadion*
14th	724 BC	*diaulos*
15th	720 BC	*dolichos*
18th	708 BC	pentathlon and wrestling
23rd	688 BC	boxing
25th	680 BC	chariot race for four horses
33rd	648 BC	horse race and pankration
37th	632 BC	boys' foot race and pankration
38th	628 BC	boys' pentathlon (held only once)
41st	616 BC	boys' boxing
65th	520 BC	race in armour
70th	500 BC	*apene* (race for mules, held until 444 BC)
71st	496 BC	*kalpe* (race for mares, held until 444 BC)
93rd	408 BC	*synoris* (chariot race for two horses)
96th	396 BC	contests for trumpeters and heralds
99th	384 BC	chariot race for foals
128th	268 BC	*synoris* (chariot race for two foals)
131st	256 BC	horse race for foals
145th	200 BC	boys' pankration

49

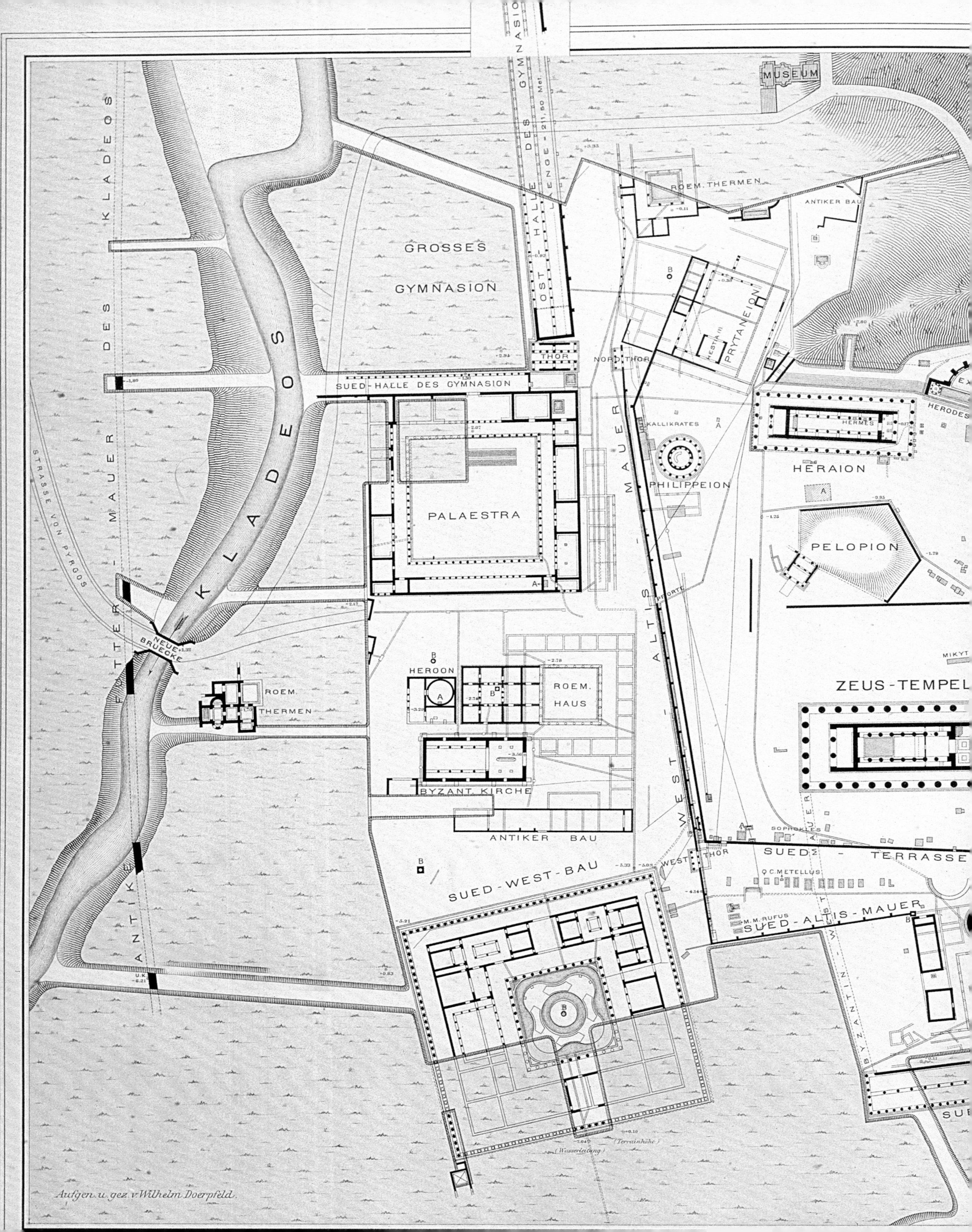

MUSEUM
GYMNASION
OST-HALLE DES GYMNASION
LÄNGE - 21,50 Met.
ROEM. THERMEN
ANTIKER BAU
GROSSES
GYMNASION
PRYTANEION
HESTIA
NORD THOR
THOR
SUED-HALLE DES GYMNASION
KLADEOS
FUTTER-MAUER DES KLADEOS
ANTIKE
STRASSE VON PYRGOS
KALLIKRATES
PHILIPPEION
HERMES
HERAION
HERODES
PALAESTRA
PELOPION
PFORTE
WEST - ALTIS - MAUER
NEUE BRUECKE
HEROON
ROEM. HAUS
ROEM. THERMEN
ZEUS-TEMPEL
BYZANT. KIRCHE
ANTIKER BAU
SOPHOKLES
SUED - TERRASSE
WEST THOR
SUED-WEST-BAU
Q.C.METELLUS
M.M.RUFUS
SUED-ALTIS-MAUER
BYZANTIN. - WEST
(Wasserleitung)
(Terrainhöhe)
Aufgen. u. gez. v. Wilhelm Doerpfeld.

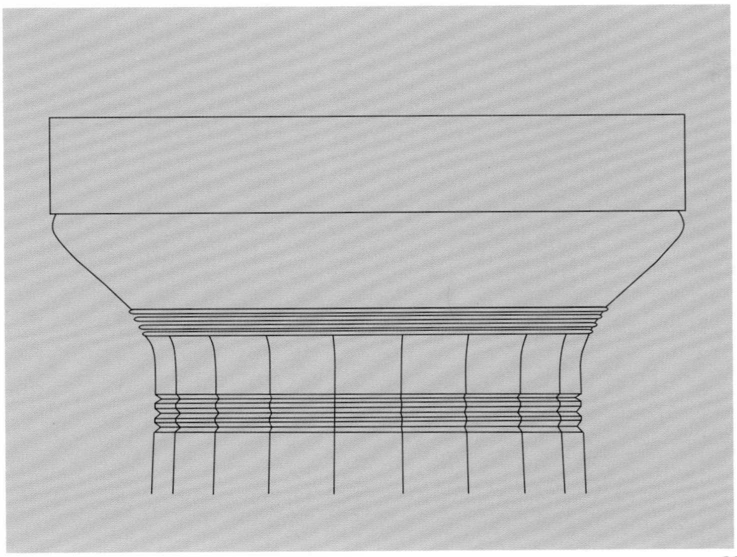
82

83

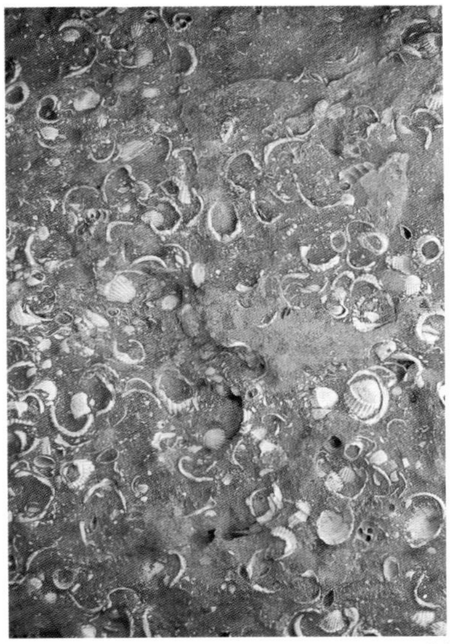
84

85

and opisthodomos, the roof tiles and the sima (water spout, often animal-headed, on the upper part of the cornice).

The central akroterion above the pediment at the east end of the temple was a large, gilded Victory by the sculptor Paionios, who also made the corresponding marble figure. (See discussion of the statue on page 113.) The corner akroteria were gilded tripod cauldrons.

The pronaos, closed by an iron grill, was full of many and various dedications, either of a political character, such as the statue of the mythical king of Elis, Iphitos, being crowned by Ekecheiria (personification of the sacred truce), or of an athletic nature, since the Olympic victors were awarded their wreaths in front of the pronaos on the last day of the games. Precious votives were also dedicated inside the cella of the temple, while the opisthodomos had a stone bench around the walls and became a place for lectures. The entire floor of the colonnade was covered with pebbles, which were used to form representations of Tritons in the pronaos. In Roman times this floor was covered by another that consisted of a composition of hexagonal slabs of coloured marble.

87. The hexagonal stone slabs with which the floor of the pronaos of the Temple of Zeus was paved in the Roman period.

88. Drawing of a section of the pronaos of the Temple of Zeus, showing the position of six marble metopes depicting six of the labours of Herakles. The other six were rendered in the corresponding positions on the opisthodomos.

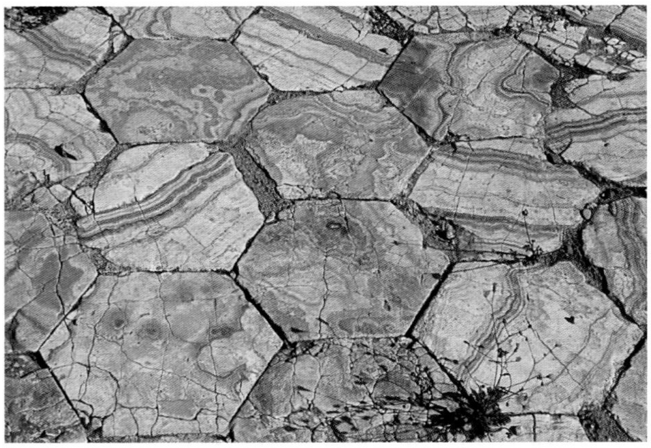

87

88

90. Central part of the composition on the east pediment of the Temple of Zeus. At the centre is the figure of Zeus, now headless; to his right are Oinomaos and Sterope, and to his left Pelops and Hippodameia. At the edges are the two four-horse chariots with charioteers and maidservants.

THE EAST PEDIMENT

The most impressive features of the temple were the sculptural compositions on the triangular pediments on the east and west sides. Within these pediments, measuring 26.5 m. in length and 3.5 m. in height, a sculptor whose name is unknown to us exploited the axes of the building and skilfully placed in position a large number of sculptures. In the process, this undoubtedly great artist created the most characteristic example of early Classical architectural sculpture and one of the most important compositions of Greek art. On the east pediment is depicted the most common of the foundation myths associated with the sanctuary, the chariot race between Oinomaos and Pelops. The scene chosen was not from the race itself, but a moment during the preparations for it:

89. Reconstruction drawing of the east facade of the Temple of Zeus. The composition on the pediment depicts the preparations for the chariot race between Oinomaos, king of Pisa, and Pelops, the claimant to the throne. The contest was judged by Zeus, depicted at the centre of the composition. In this old drawing, the positions of the two pairs of figures on either side of Zeus differ from the current museum reconstruction. Athens, German Archaeological Institute.

89

91

91. Seated figure from the right side of the east pediment, thought to be the seer of the palace of Oinomaos. His face is etched with an agonised expression, for he can foresee the tragic outcome of the contest for his master.

92. The reclining human figure in the right corner of the east pediment, sometimes identified as Alpheios, one of the two rivers at Olympia. Together with the corresponding figure in the left corner, perhaps depicting Kladeos, it may denote Olympia, the place in which the events were unfolding.

the centre of the composition is dominated by the figure of Zeus holding a thunderbolt in his left hand, the god who was not only the judge of the race but also the eternal arbiter of all human actions. On either side of Zeus stand the two couples involved in the race: Oinomaos and Sterope and Pelops and Hippodameia. Next on either side come the four-horse chariots being prepared by the servants, two prophets seated on the ground, and, reclining near the corners, two figures identified as the river gods Alpheios and Kladeos. The entire composition is pervaded by a silent, tragic quality personified in the figure of the prophet on the right, whose gesture indicates that he already foresees the tragic outcome. This was a highly charged scene that brought to life before the eyes of spectators the plot of a tragedy, similar to the works performed in Athens at this period.

92

THE WEST PEDIMENT

93. A Lapith woman, lying in the left corner of the west pediment, fearfully awaits the outcome of the battle with the Centaurs. It is one of two statues carved in the Roman period as replacements for the originals, which collapsed after an earthquake.

94. The head of Apollo, the central figure on the west pediment. In his mien can be detected a majestic divine tranquillity, which is underscored by the way his right hand is extended decisively in the direction of the combatants. The rendering of his profile and coiffure have a clear affinity with the slightly earlier Blond Boy in the Akropolis Museum.

In contrast with the static, linear composition on the east pediment, the one on the west is characterised by intense movement, arising from the subject itself: the battle between the Lapiths and the Centaurs. According to the myth, this battle was provoked when the Centaurs got drunk at the wedding of Perithoos, the king of the Lapiths, to which they had been invited, and attacked the women. Peirithoos, with the aid of his friend Theseus, eventually managed to drive them away. The impressive features of the composition are the intertwining of the figures, the constantly intersecting axes of the human limbs, and the contrast between the sensual figures of the women and the wild, primitive, bestial forms of the Centaurs. At the centre of the composition is

93

95. Group of Lapiths and a Centaur from the west pediment. The Centaur is attacked from the right by a Lapith, who pierces his breast with a sword. The dynamism of the composition is emphasised by the diagonal axes of the figures. Note the contrapposto, with the movement of the Lapith woman's left leg as she struggles to escape the grip of the Centaur who seeks to restrain her. The Centaur's taut veins form a realistic contrast with the youthful elegance of the woman's leg.

96. Eurytion, king of the Centaurs, attempts to abduct the newly married Deidameia, wife of Peirithoos.

98. A Centaur struggles to break free of the grasp of a Lapith by biting his arm. The rough, ugly features of the Centaur and his contorted face contrast with the tranquil, noble personality of the Lapith, whose pain is subtly indicated by the lines in his brow. The struggle has the dimensions of a clash between two worlds.

95 96

a group consisting of three male figures. Apollo stands erect and lordly in the middle, his right arm outstretched to direct the battle and exercise complete control over the outcome of the struggle. On either side of him, the two balanced protagonists, Theseus and Perithoos, fight to save the women from abduction by the Centaurs.

There has been considerable scholarly debate on the choice of this myth for the west pediment, since the Centauromachy does not appear to be related to the mythology of the area. Generally speaking, the battle between the Lapiths and Centaurs was a very popular subject in the religious iconography of the period. In Attic art in particular it denoted the struggle of the Greeks against the Persians. According to some scholars, it may here indicate the victory of the Elians over the Pisatans. With regard to the presence of Apollo, the dynamic figure of the god is generally believed in this instance to represent the power of divine forces and their control over the history of the world. Other scholars, however, see in the presence of Apollo an indirect allusion to the oracular character of the sanctuary, while the strong projection of the Athenian hero Theseus is thought to transmit a political message relating to the democratisation of the Eleian

97. The figures from the west pediment of the Temple of Zeus, as restored in the Archaeological Museum at Olympia. The subject was the Centauromachy, the mythical clash between the Centaurs and the Lapiths of Thessaly at the wedding of the Lapith king Peirithoos and Deidameia. Twenty-one figures were placed on a pediment 26.4 m. long in a composition of outstanding harmony.

From left to right: Two Lapith women at the edge of the composition watch the battle in terror.

A young Lapith man seizes a Centaur who has captured a young Lapith woman, whom he holds by the hair.

99

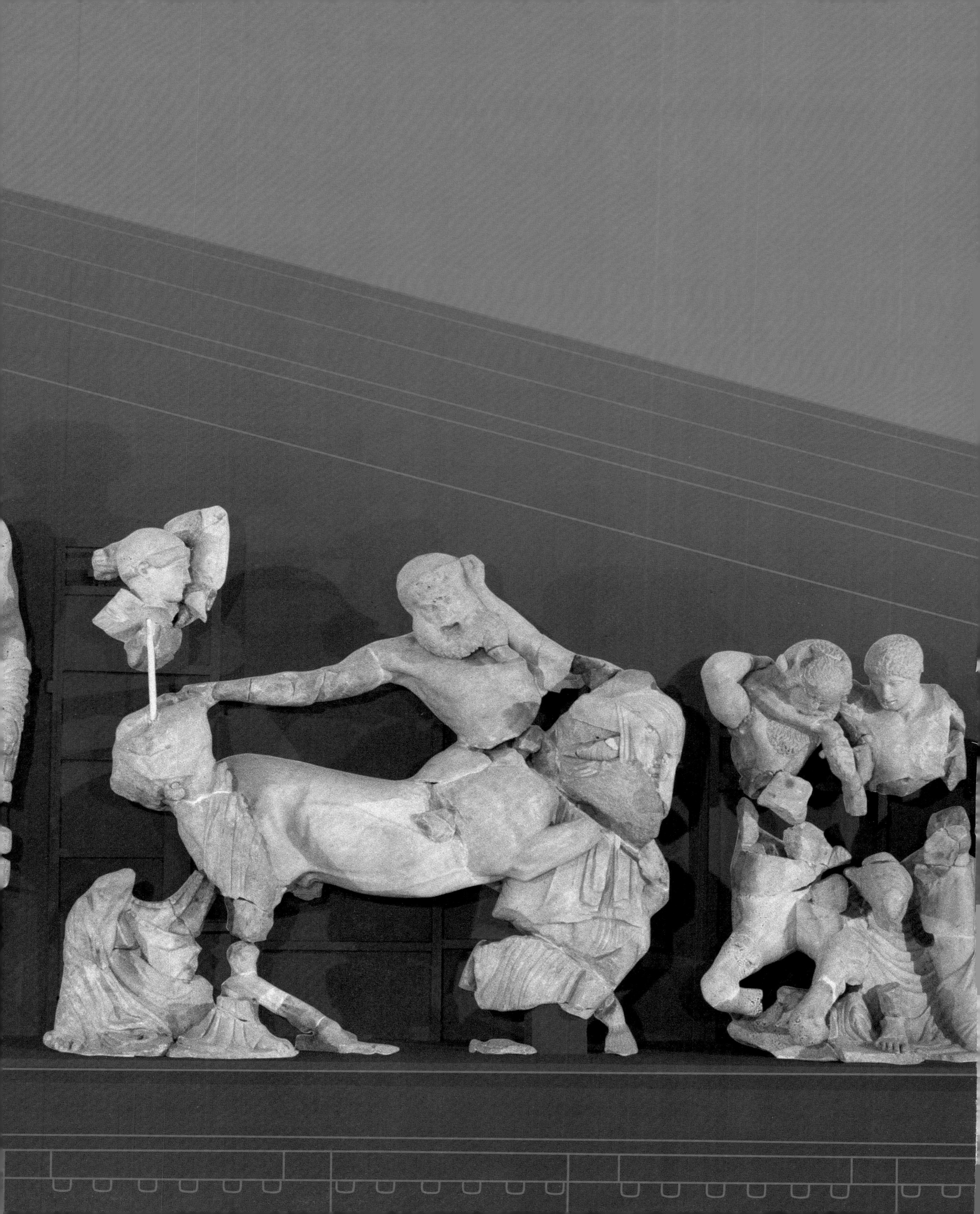

A group that includes the Centaur king Eurytion and Deidameia and, to their right, the head and part of the body of Peirithoos, raising his sword to strike the Centaur and free his young wife.

In the centre of the composition Apollo, larger than the other figures (3.1 m. high), stretches out his hand to impose order.

The Athenian hero Theseus, the friend of Peirithoos, rushes with drawn sword against a Centaur who has seized a Lapith woman, who is fighting him off with both hands.

A Centaur struggles to free himself from the arms of a young Lapith.

A Lapith woman and a seated Centaur, who is attacked by a Lapith on his right.

Two Lapith women in the right corner of the pediment watch the battle in terror.

state a few years earlier, based on the Athenian model and with the involvement of Themistokles himself. This hypothesis is strengthened by certain sculptural resemblances, namely, between the figure of Apollo and the 'Blond Boy' from the Athenian Acropolis and between the two protagonists, Theseus and Perithoos, and the statues of the Tyrannicides, Harmodios and Aristogeiton, which had been erected in the Athenian Agora a few years previously (480 BC). These resemblances, however, could also be due simply to the proximity in time of the works and carry no ideological implications. The placing of the Centauromachy and Apollo on the west pediment has also been interpreted as an artistic expression of the existence at Olympia in the first half of the 5th c. BC of an international court of arbitration for disputes between states.

It should be stressed, however, that the central divinities on the two pediments, Zeus on the east and Apollo on the west, do not take an active part in and are not directly connected with the myths depicted alongside them. They are placed here in a position that could only be occupied by gods in order to project the importance of their sovereign and undisputed presence not only in the sanctuary but also in the lives of men.

THE METOPES

100

101

The sculptural decoration of the Temple of Zeus was continued inside the temple. Reliefs on the six metopes of the pronaos and opisthodomos narrated the twelve labours of Herakles, the other founder of the games, a popular hero with all Greeks and the ideal model of an athlete. This was the first time in history that all twelve labours were depicted together. Indeed, since they are also mentioned for the first time, by Pindar, as a group of twelve, it is believed that it was in this period that the labours of Herakles were established as a single corpus. In these works, the same great artist who executed the pedimental sculptures captured the essence of each myth in an uncluttered, clear fashion while attempting a variety of formulations. The two-figure or three-figure scenes, each measuring 160 by 150 cm., show the hero in his labours. His patron, Athena, appears four times. Hermes also appears twice, and Atlas and Eurystheus, the king of Argos who imposed the labours on Hercules, are depicted once each.

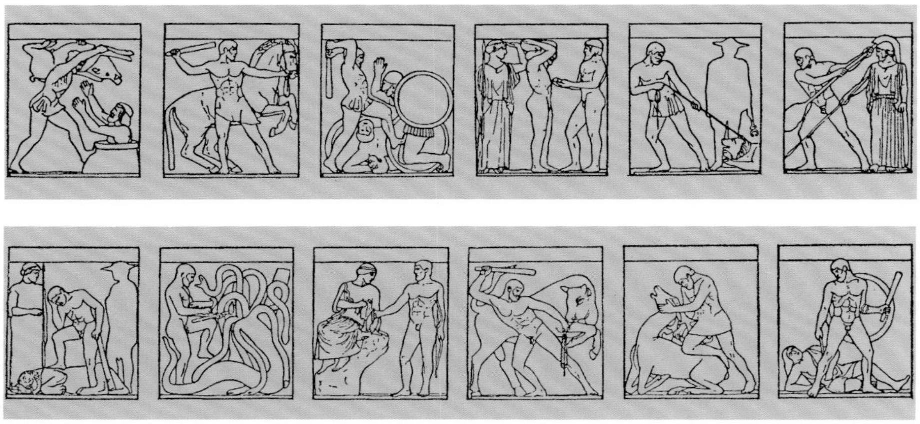

102

99. The metope depicting Herakles and Atlas is the best-preserved metope from the Temple of Zeus. The hero is shown in the centre holding up the sky, with a cushion on his neck to give him relief from the weight. His patron, Athena, helps him, supporting the sky with one hand, while Atlas holds out the apples of the Hesperides.

100. The metope with the Stymphalian birds. Herakles held in his left hand a bronze bow, made separately, while offering the dead birds to Athena with his right.

101. The metope with the cleansing of the stables of Augeias. Herakles, following the instructions of Athena, uses a crowbar to shift the course of the river to wash away the accumulated dung. This, the only local myth depicted in the metopes, was created partly under the influence of the great stock-raising activity in the area.

102. Reconstruction drawing of the twelve marble metopes depicting the labours of Herakles, from the pronaos and opisthodomos of the Temple of Zeus.

THE CHRYSELEPHANTINE STATUE OF ZEUS

The finest of all the statues that exist in the world [the Zeus of Olympia] and the most dear to the gods.

Dion Chrysostom

The back of the three-aisled cella of the temple was dominated by the cult statue of Zeus fashioned by the Athenian sculptor Pheidias. After completing the design of the building project on the Athenian Acropolis and making the statue of Athena Parthenos, in 438 BC, Pheidias was invited by the priesthood at Olympia to execute the chryselephantine statue of the god. The name refers to the materials that went into its making: gold (Greek *chrysos*) and ivory (*elephas*). It was a sculpture worthy to stand in the great temple. The choice of artist was not fortuitous: Pheidias was already famous for his work in Athens and was in general regarded as the supreme maker of statues of gods, the only sculptor who could transmit the essence of the divine to the figures he modelled. In fact the statue was so majestic that the ancient Greeks wondered whether Pheidias had not ascended to Olympos to copy the figure of the god, or whether the god himself had not appeared on earth. The great sculptor inscribed his name secretly underneath the god's feet, indicating the relationship between the sculptor and his work: ΦΕΙΔΙΑΣ ΧΑΡΜΙΔΟΥ ΥΙΟΣ ΑΘΗΝΑΙΟΣ Μ' ΕΠΟΙΗΣΕΝ ('Pheidias son of Charmides of Athens made me').

This rare masterpiece of ancient Greek sculpture could be seen at a distance from the entrance, and it was also possible to ascend staircases to the gallery above the side aisles of the cella in order to get a more immediate view of the face. The statue itself has not survived. It stood in the temple for about 800 years, suffered much damage and was repaired from time to time, on one occasion by the Messenian sculptor Damophon in the 2nd c. BC. In the end, it perished along with the ancient religion it represented: in the early 4th c. AD it was carried off to Constantinople, together with other works of art, to adorn the new capital of the Roman empire, and was destroyed by fire in 475. The figure of the god can be reconstructed on the basis of the detailed description of the statue by the traveller Pausanias and depictions of it on coins of Elis.

Although he was depicted seated on a throne, the great god was 12.4 m. high. His head must have reached to just beneath the ceiling of the temple. In his extended right hand he held a figure of Victory and in his left the sceptre, which was crowned by an eagle. The statue itself consisted of a wooden core, to

103

104

105

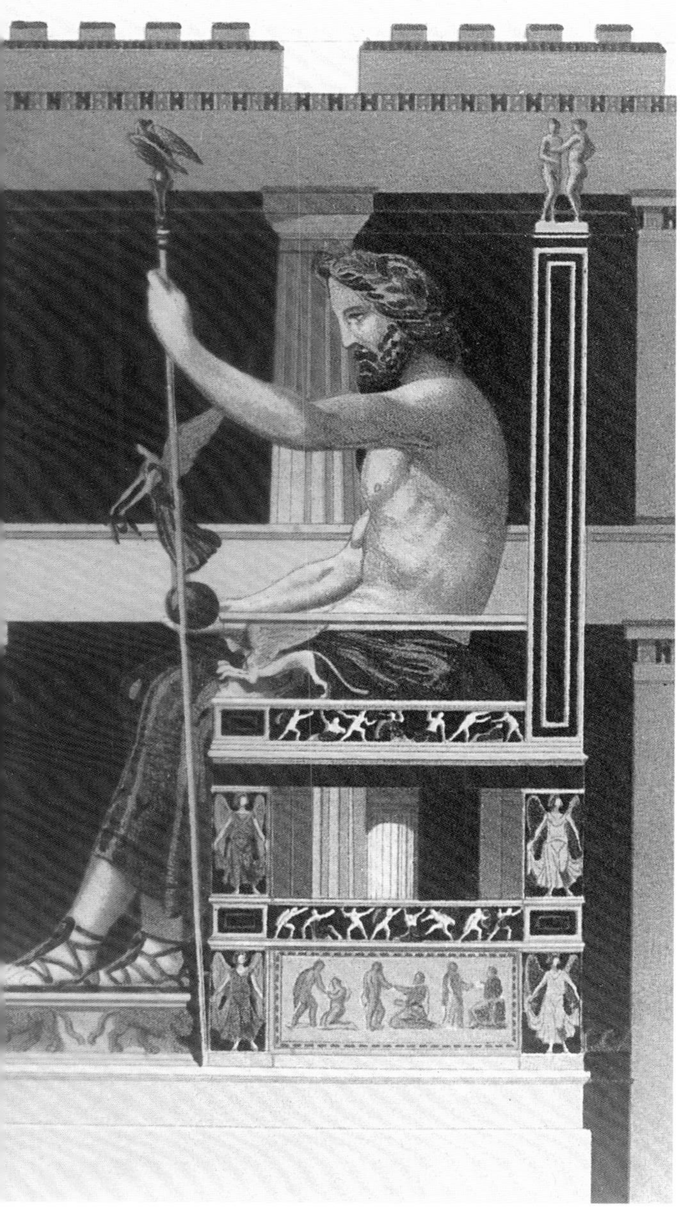

106

103-104. Drawing and photograph of a bronze coin of Elis dating from Roman times, depicting the chryselephantine statue of Zeus. Athens, National Archaeological Museum.

105-106. Proposed reconstruction of the front and side of the chryselephantine statue of Zeus inside the temple. The god holds a winged Victory in his right palm and a sceptre topped by an eagle in his left hand. Athens, German Archaeological Institute.

which were attached the ivory plaques representing the exposed parts of the body (face, upper torso, arms and feet) and gold sheet for the hair, beard, sandals and himation. There were also many decorative inlays of glass paste and precious stones.The shallow pool filled with oil that Pheidias placed in front of the statue, to prevent the ivory from becoming corroded by the humid climate of Olympia, reveals the care shown by the ancient Greeks for their works of art. There was also a team of experts, called *phaidryntai* (cleaners), whose task it was to ensure that the statue was always perfectly clean.

It is striking that a purple curtain that was seized from the Temple of Solomon in Jerusalem by the king of Syria, Antiochos IV Epiphanes, was placed in front of the statue about 165 BC.

107

THE WORKSHOP OF PHEIDIAS

The excavation of Pheidias's workshop added a new dimension to our knowledge of how the statue of Zeus was made. The workshop was situated to the west of the temple, outside the boundary of the Altis. Here were found pits and waste from the work, and the room in which the statue was assembled was also preserved: it was exactly the same size as the cella of the temple and was the second tallest building at Olympia. In the area of the workshop should be imagined not only houses in which a large, specialised team of artists and craftsmen lived for about 10 years but also workshop facilities in the open air or beneath makeshift wooden shelters or tents. In the earth deposits excavated to the south of the workshop was found debris that had been swept from the workshop after cleaning: tools and remains from the finishing of a statue, waste pieces of bronze, iron, lead, bone, amber, rock crystals, and ivory, as well as clay moulds containing remnants of glass paste used to create the drapery of the garments and the jewellery. Although it is not absolutely

107. The workshop of Pheidias in the form it assumed after its conversion into a Christian church in the 5th c. AD. The outdoor workshop facilities were set up in the flat area in front, while the initial assembling of the sculpture was carried out inside the building.

108. Plan of Pheidias's workshop, which was the same shape and size as the cella of the Temple of Zeus. Drawing: Ol. Forsch. V, plate 9.

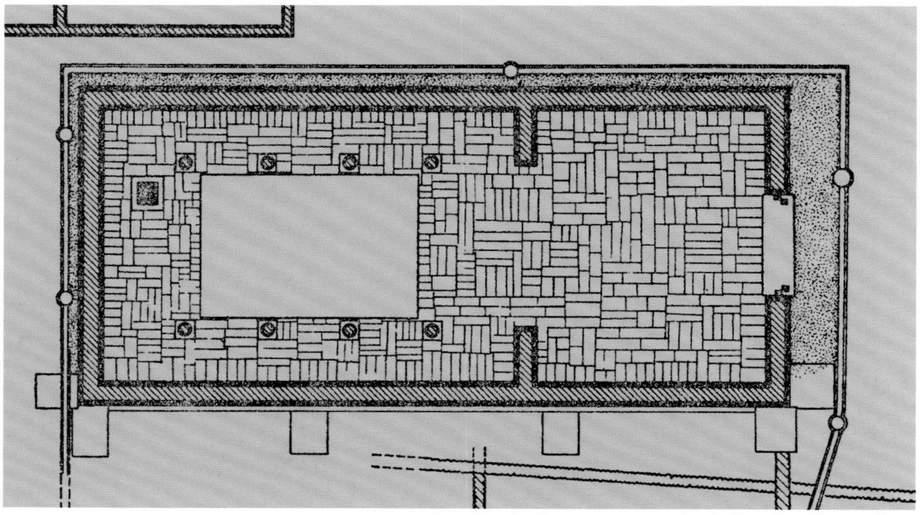
108

certain whether these were associated with Pheidias's statue of Zeus, for they date from a little later and may belong to some other work, they nevertheless provide very important evidence for the technique of chryselephantine sculptures.

The building that is now called Pheidias's workshop, then, is the place in which the individual parts of the statue were assembled prior to its erection in its final position inside the temple. It had an entrance on the east side and was divided into two rooms. The vestibule would have been used as a storage area for materials and for carrying out delicate manual work. The main room had the necessary infrastructure for constructing the enormous statue, including very high scaffolding and pulleys. The most moving find from the excavation of the workshop, however, is the cup from which the great sculptor drank. It is a simple black vessel with vertical ribbing on the outside and the inscription ΦΕΙΔΙΟ ΕΙΜΙ ('I belong to Pheidias') on the base, presumably scratched by the hand of the master himself. After the Classical period, the building was converted into a place of worship, with an altar common to all the gods, and later into a Christian church.

109

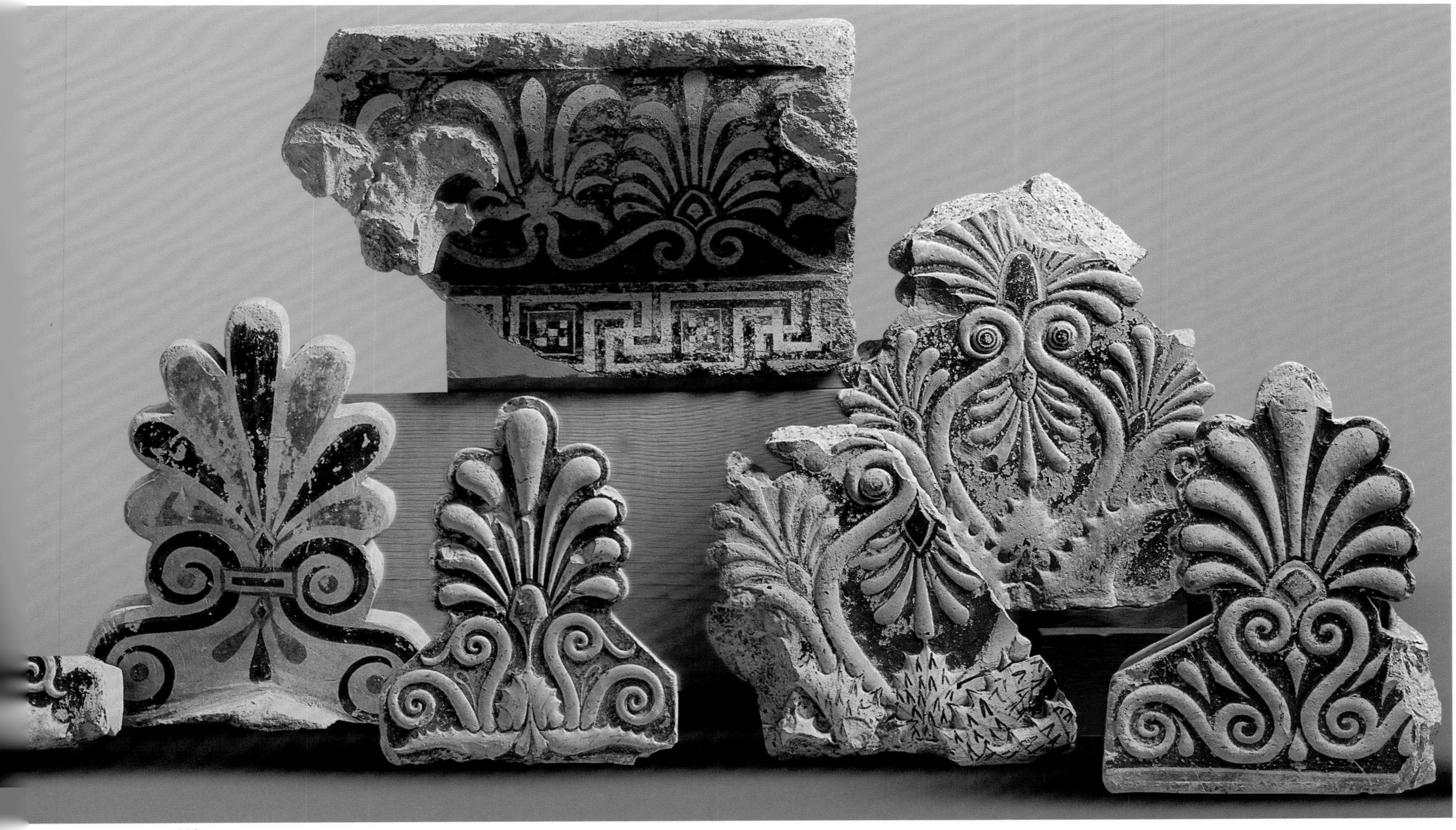

110

109. Small black-glaze cup bearing the name of Pheidias, inscribed at the bottom in his own hand (ca. 430 BC). Olympia, Archaeological Museum.

110. Terracotta sima fragment and six antefixes from the roof of Pheidias's workshop and other Classical buildings in the sanctuary (5th c. BC). Olympia, Archaeological Museum.

THE BATHS

Nothing at all has survived of the Classical gymnasium and palaestra, very simply designed areas in which athletes trained and practiced. That they existed, however, is thought to be certain on the basis of the athletes' bathhouse preserved to the west of the sanctuary near the bank of the Kladeos. This is one of the earliest bath facilities in Greece, and included a circle of eleven individual bathtubs and an open-air 'swimming pool' – a rectangular cistern measuring 16 by 24 m. and a depth of 1.6 m., filled directly with water from the river and in which the athletes could unwind after the fierce intensity of the contest. This baths complex was renovated on many occasions in later periods. In the 1st c. BC, indeed, the first hot baths of Roman type were established here, shortly after their invention in Campania.

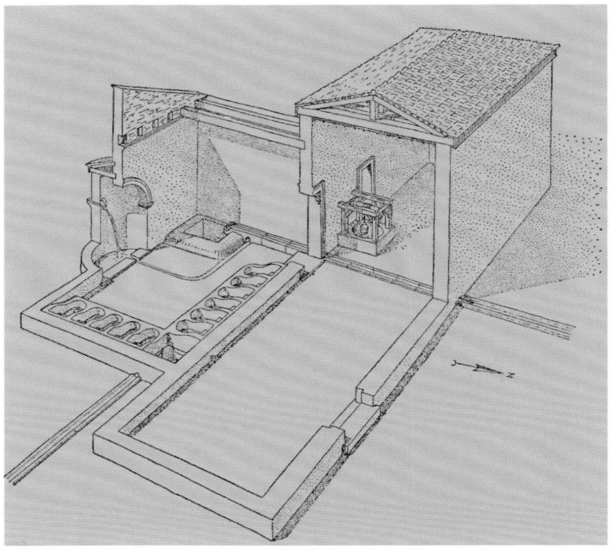

111

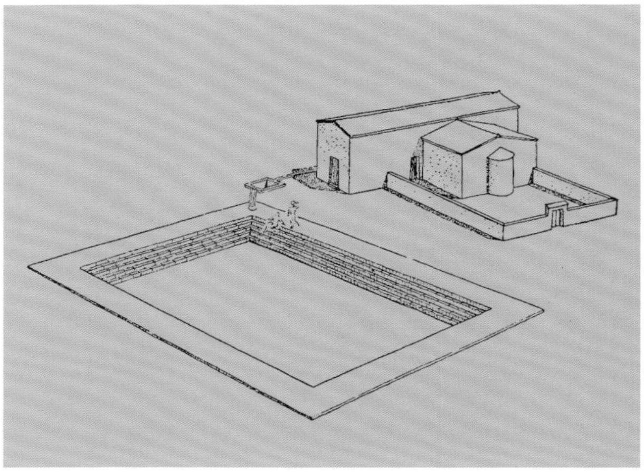

112

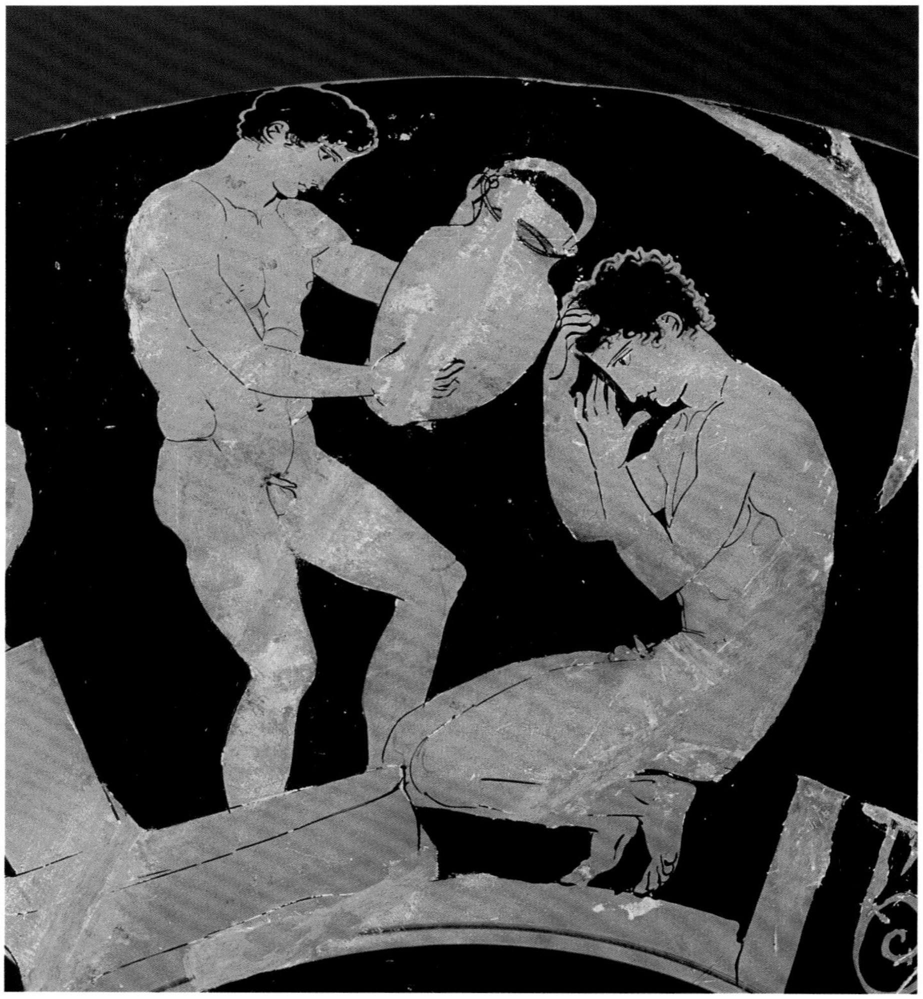

113

111. Reconstruction drawing of the Classical bathhouse at Olympia with the eleven bathtubs, the well, and the rectangular changing room. Drawing: H. Schleif.

112. Reconstruction drawing of the exterior of the Classical bathhouse, with the large rectangular 'swimming pool.' Drawing: H. Schleif.

113. An athlete helps a fellow athlete to rinse his hair next to a bathtub in a gymnasium. Attic red-figure kylix (475-450 BC). London, British Museum.

THE STADIUM

The constantly growing prestige and reputation of Olympia throughout the entire world led during this period to a large increase in the number of pilgrims and by extension of spectators at the games. After the addition of a number of events, the games now lasted for five days, while the radical redesigning of the stadium resulted in improved organisation and facilities for the spectators. In order to free space for the needs of the sanctuary and make it possible to create larger embankments for spectators, the stadium was moved 75 m. to the east and 12 m. to the north, to occupy the position in which it can now be seen. The earth track also received its final form: its length was 212 m. and the distance covered by the runners between the stone starting posts and the

114

115

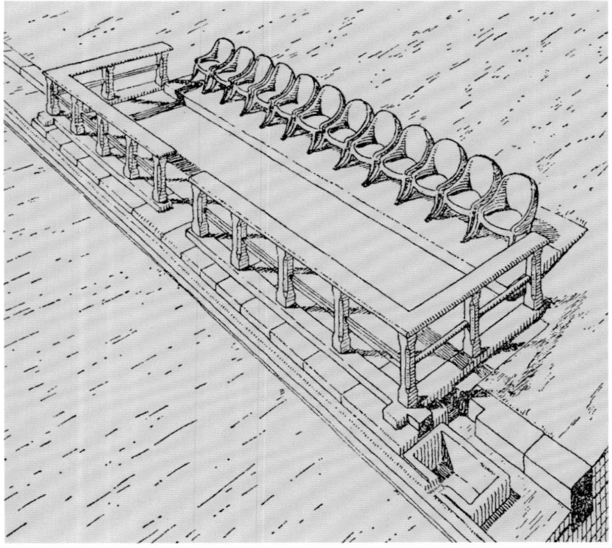

116

finish was 600 Olympic feet, that is, 192.28 m. This distance, the longest of all the Greek stadia, is due to the length of the Olympic foot, .32 m. larger than that used in the measuring systems of all other Greek regions. This circumstance may be the reason the construction of the stadium at Olympia was attributed to Herakles who, according to legend, defined the length of the stadium by measuring out the length of his enormous feet 600 times.

The starting and finishing points of the foot races were marked by a continuous row of marble slabs on which the athletes placed their feet, and there are signs that some form of mechanical device was used to prevent false starts (*hysplex*).

The present form of the stadium, which was restored after the end of the modern excavation, presents a picture of the site in the 4th c. BC. The stadium is now entered by way of the *krypte stoa*, a vaulted passageway of 32 m., the

114. The starting line for the foot races, at one end of the stadium. It consists of marble slabs with two parallel grooves, and could accommodate up to 20 competitors.

115. The remains of the exedra of the Hellanodikai, the Elean magistrates, during excavation. They reflect the form of the monument in the Roman period. Athens, German Archaeological Institute.

116. Reconstruction drawing of the exedra of the Hellanodikai in its original form of the 4th c. BC. Drawing: H. Schleif.

117. Excavation activity in the stadium in 1958. Athens, German Archaeological Institute.

118. View of the stadium of Olympia from the west. The starting line can be seen in the foreground, with the altar of Demeter Chamyne at the middle left and the exedra of the Hellanodikai at the middle right.

117

118

119

roof of which is preserved only at the west end. The sides of the entrance were adorned with Corinthian columns. The small statues of Nemesis placed here, now on display in the museum at Olympia, were a final reminder to the athletes of the goddess who punished overweening behaviour and cheating. In ancient times, only the athletes, priests and games officials entered the stadium through this passageway; the spectators ascended the north embankment from the terrace of the treasuries and the south embankment from the Echo Stoa.

The earth embankments of the stadium provided room for about 40-45,000 spectators to watch the games. In the middle of the south embankment is preserved the exedra on which were the seats of the Hellanodikai, the Elean magistrates who oversaw the games and also served as judges. Directly opposite this were places for official guests (*theoroi* from the cities, kings, etc). The embankments of the stadium at Olympia were never equipped with stone seats like those known from other stadia. At some point during the final repair of the stadium in the 2nd-3rd c. AD, they seem to have been fitted with wooden benches.

The altar of Demeter Chamyne, of Roman date, has been restored in the middle of the north side of the stadium. The priestess of this goddess was the only woman allowed to watch the games.

120

119. Aerial view of the stadium of Olympia, restored in the form it would have had in the 4th c. BC. At bottom left are the foundations of the treasuries and the Metroon.

120. The Lancelloti Diskobolos. Roman copy dating from the Antonine period of the bronze original by Myron, ca. 450 BC. Rome, Vatican Museum.

THE HIPPODROME

121

To the same building programme should be assigned the remodelling of the hippodrome, with artificial embankments for the spectators that extended south of the stadium as far as the banks of the Alpheios.

The hippodrome was an enormous oval structure, the north side of which was bounded by the south terrace of the stadium. On the south and east sides was earth, and the west side was closed by a long building, the Stoa of Agnaptos. On the basis of the detailed descriptions provided by Pausanias, attempts have been made by scholars to make a reconstruction drawing of the hippodrome. According to the most recent, and most probable, reconstruction, the length of the arena was about 5 stades, that is, about 900 m., with a width of 64 m. Of the total length, the first two stades were devoted solely to the starting procedure. The course covered the remaining three stades and had to be completed twice, from the start and back, making the unit length of the race 6 stades, or 1,152 m. Depending on the individual event, the distance to be covered by the horses or chariots was from 3 to 12 times.

The most impressive feature of the hippodrome at Olympia was the starting mechanism for the horses, the *hippaphesis*, the configuration of which can be compared to the prow of a ship. The horses took up positions obliquely behind each other. By using a complicated mechanical system, the last contestants set off first, followed by the ones immediately in front of them, and so on. When all the animals were in a straight line, a trumpet signaled the official start of the race.

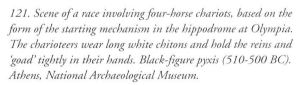

121. Scene of a race involving four-horse chariots, based on the form of the starting mechanism in the hippodrome at Olympia. The charioteers wear long white chitons and hold the reins and 'goad' tightly in their hands. Black-figure pyxis (510-500 BC). Athens, National Archaeological Museum.

122. Plan and dimensions of the hippodrome at Olympia, based on the most recent evidence. The hippodrome, swept away by the river Alpheios, can be reconstructed from the detailed description by Pausanias. Drawing: J. Ebert.

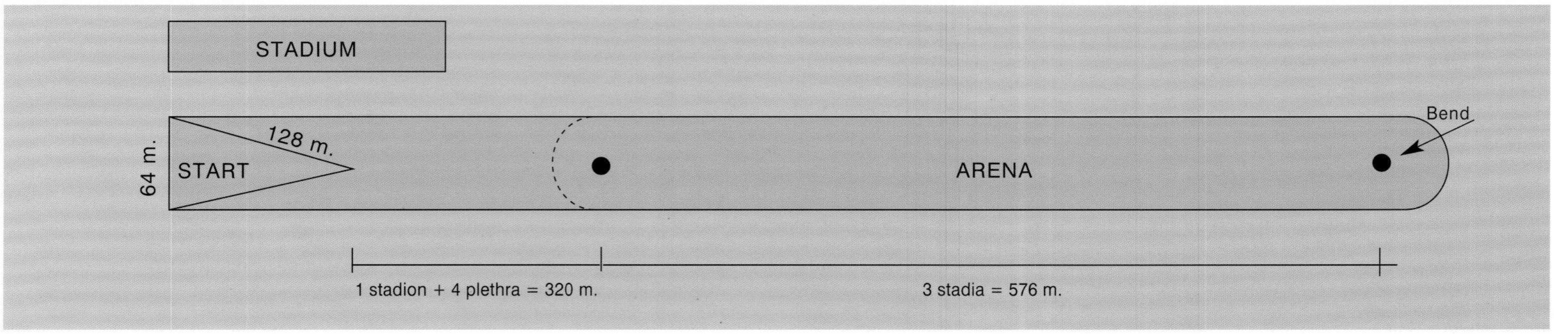

122

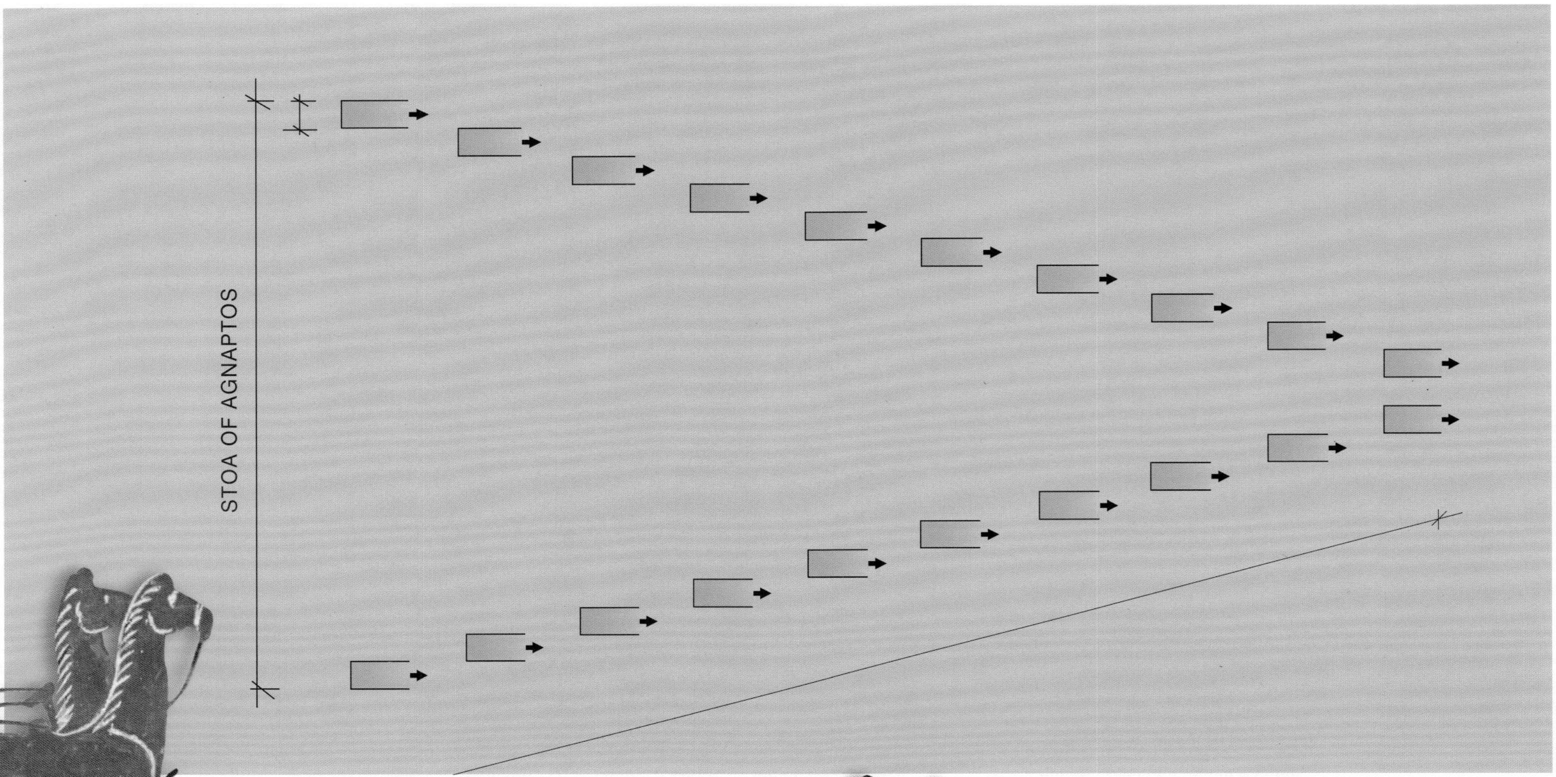

123

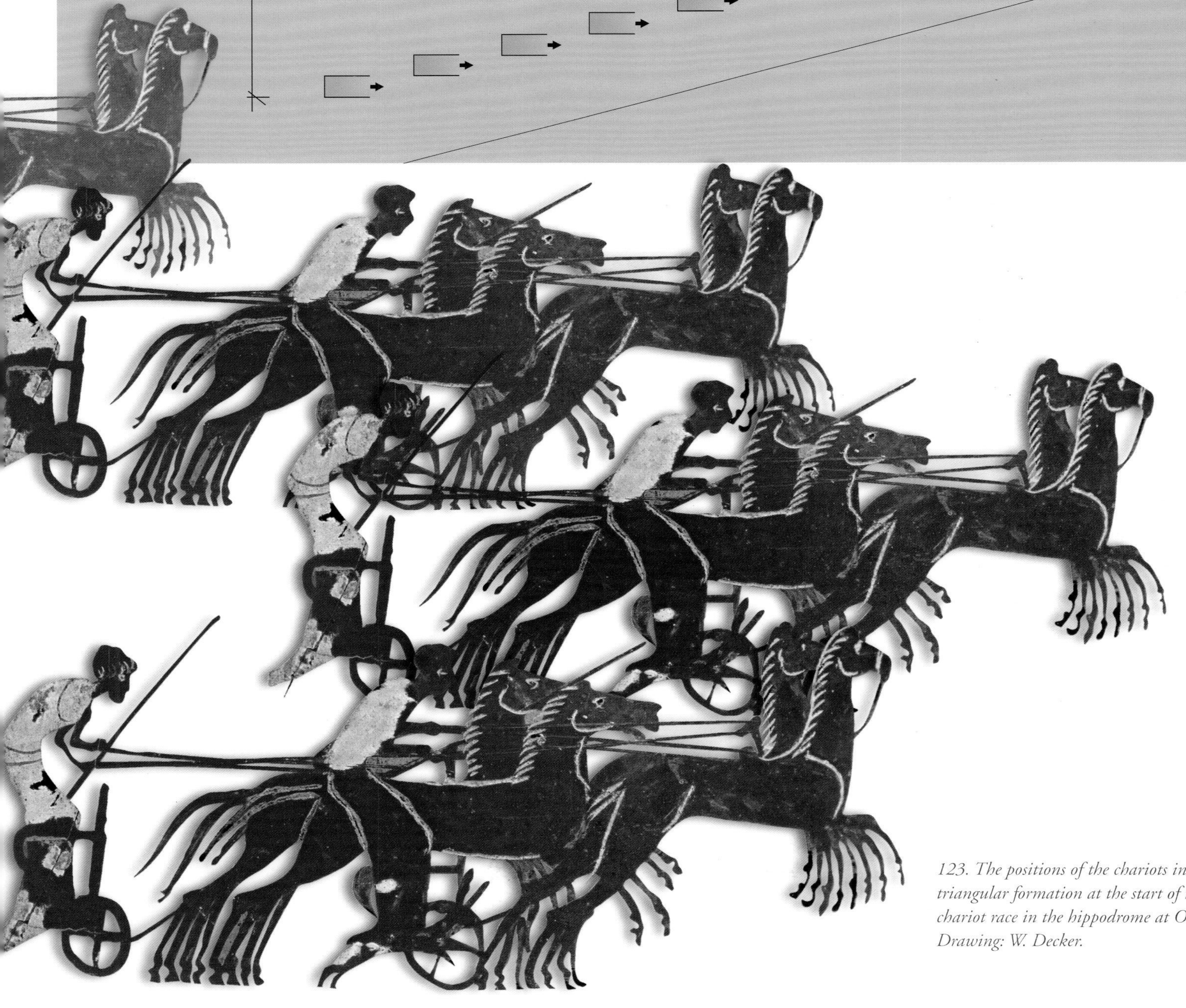

123. *The positions of the chariots in triangular formation at the start of the chariot race in the hippodrome at Olympia. Drawing: W. Decker.*

124. Athletes practising the discus, javelin and jumping, to the accompaniment of the flute. Attic red-figure kylix (515-510 BC). Los Angeles, J. Paul Getty Museum.

125. Two athletes practising boxing. The referee, at the left, holds a rod. Attic black-figure amphora (ca. 500 BC). Munich, Staatliche Antikensammlungen.

126. Scene of a four-horse chariot driven by winged Victory. The four horses (one of them pure white) are very successfully arranged in perspective. With their forelegs raised, they give a fine impression of galloping. Attic red-figure kalyx krater (370-360 BC). Athens, National Archaeological Museum.

127. Inscription found on the altar in the middle of the circular room in fig. 129, which led to the identification of the building as the Heroon.

128. Drawing of an inscription on an unused marble roof tile from the Temple of Zeus with a list of names of officials of the sanctuary at Olympia in the years 28-24 BC. Olympia, Archaeological Museum.

129. The Heroon, in which the cult of an unknown hero was practised in the Late Hellenistic and Roman period.

124

125

126

OTHER BUILDINGS

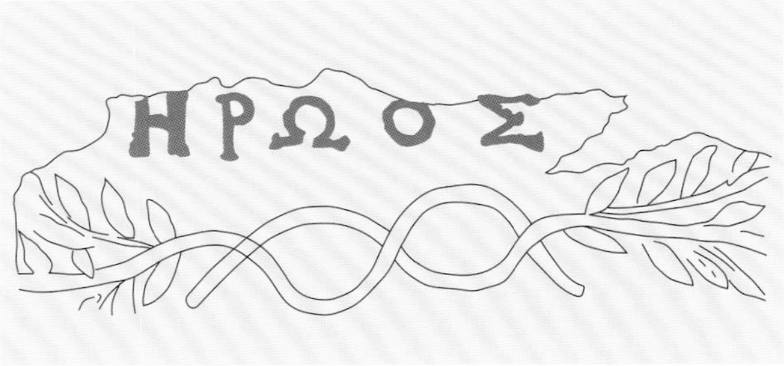

127

The so-called Theokoleon to the north of Pheidias's workshop, the residence of the permanent staff of the priesthood, the *theokoloi*, may also be identified with the headquarters of the sanctuary administration. According to inscriptions on a tile in the Temple of Zeus, the staff of the priesthood consisted of three theokoloi, who were chosen every Olympiad from eminent families in Elis; three *spondophoroi*, (libation bearers); two to four seers; a secretary; an *alytarches* (musician); an *epimeletes* (who kept order during the festival); a *theotropos*, to interpret dreams; and an *exegetes*, to conduct guided tours. Besides a special staff for the sacrifices (*auletai*, *kathemerothytes*, a woodcutter for the wood for the sacrifice, a head cook and cooks), there were also bakers, one to five *kleidouchoi* ('keyholders'), an architect, and a *steganomos*, who maintained the buildings, and also a doctor.

A smaller building, one room of which was circular, was excavated to the west of the Theokoleon. An altar inside bore an inscription containing the word ΗΡΩΟΣ ('of the hero'). Hence, the Heroon, a building probably connected with the cult of an unknown hero, possibly Iamos, founding father of the famous clan of the Iamidai, who were seers at Elis, or of some great athlete heroised after his death.

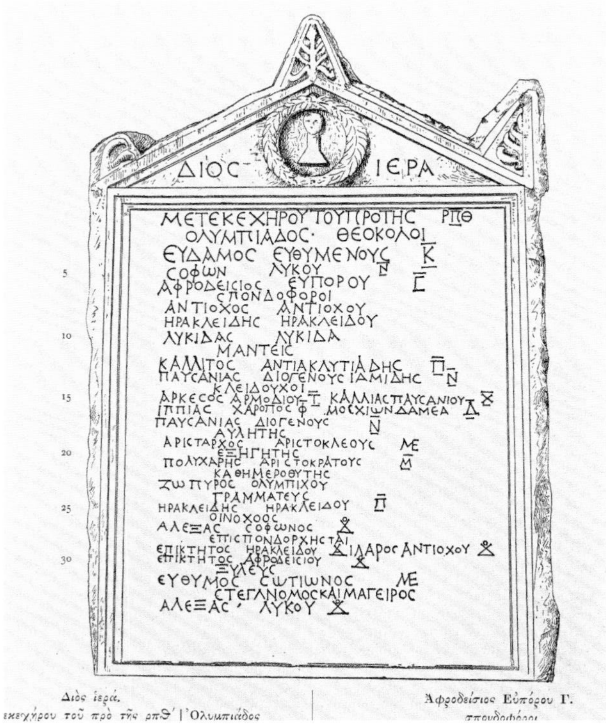

128

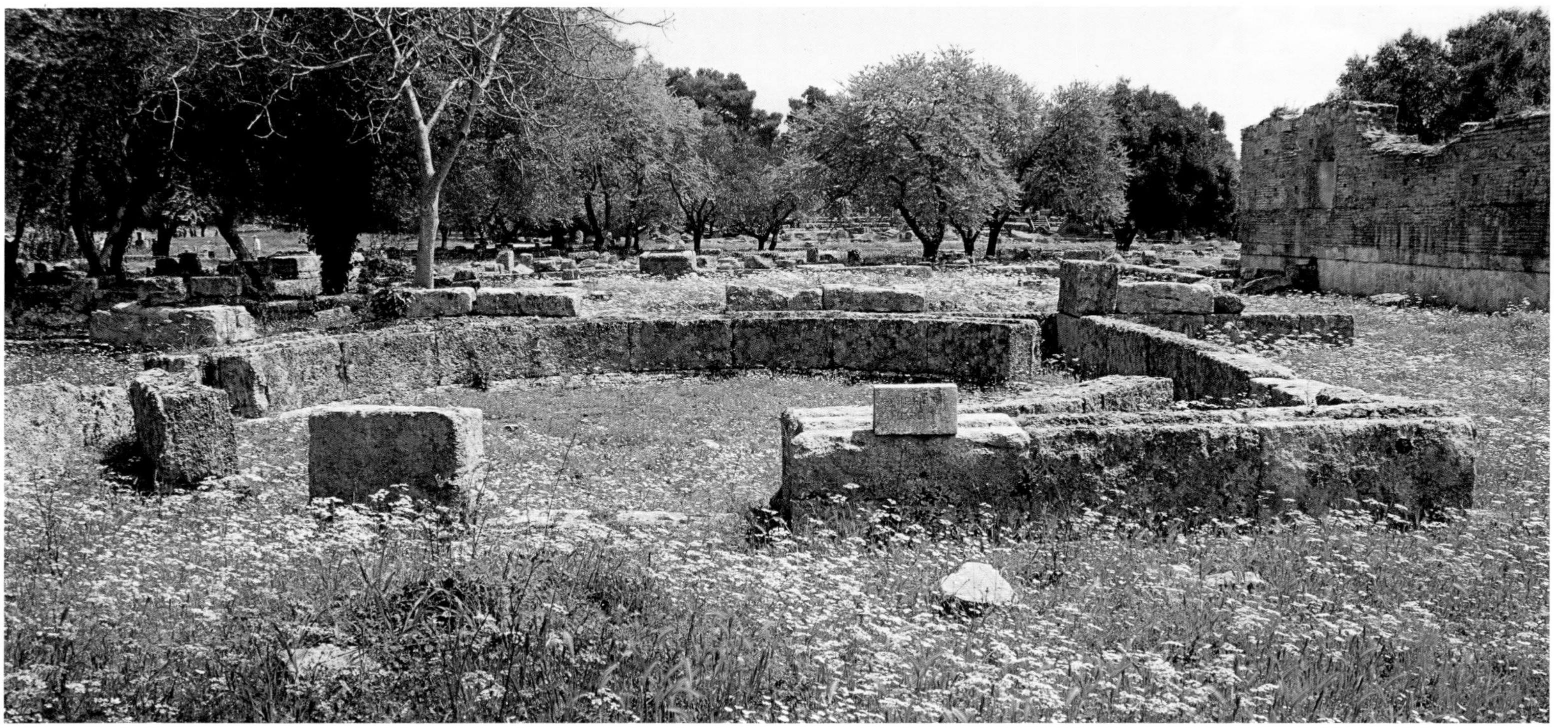

129

THE PRYTANEION

The Prytaneion, near the sanctuary of Hestia, was very important: not only was it the headquarters of the officials of the city of Elis (the *prytaneis*), but it was also the place in which the Olympic victors were entertained with dinner after they had received their victory wreaths on the final day of the festival and in which music, songs and hymns could be heard all around. This building had an interior peristyle courtyard with banquet rooms around it, and the eternal flame of the hearth of the Eleian community burned at a central point.

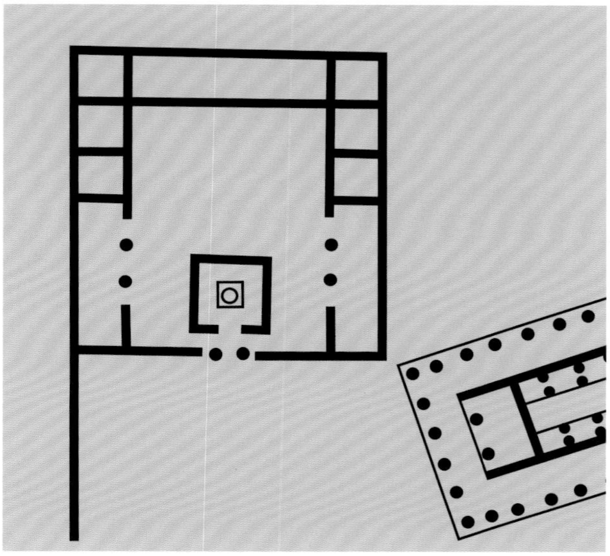

130

130. Plan of the Prytaneion at Olympia, with the Heraion at the lower right.

131. Five youths dance to the sound of the double flute, filling their kylikes with wine from a krater. Red-figure kylix (500-475 BC). London, British Museum.

132. Young men at a banquet amuse themselves drinking wine from skyphoi and kylikes. Victory in the games was an excellent excuse for a banquet. Attic red-figure kylix (480-470 BC). London, British Museum.

131

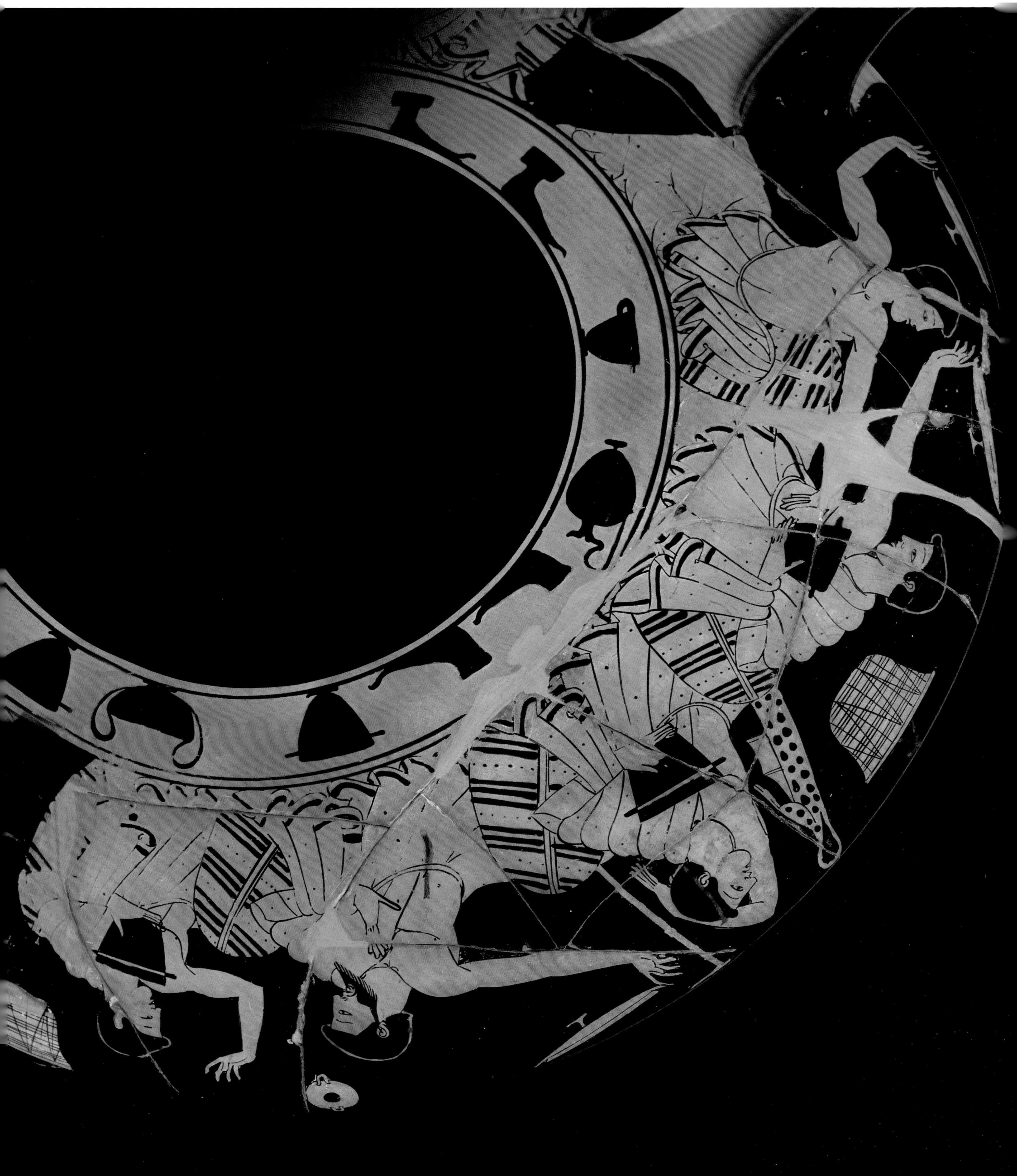

DEDICATIONS

The old custom of dedicating military trophies was suspended in the 5th c. BC, and the sanctuary was filled with a large number of notable votives, some of them statues of Olympic victors and others sculptures dedicated by cities to give thanks to Zeus for great victories over their foes. The statues, usually of bronze, were by the great sculptors of the day – Onatas, Kalamis, Myron, Pythagoras, and Polykleitos – though all that now survives of them are references in Pausanias, a few tresses of hair, fragments of limbs, and a number of inscribed bases that usually recorded the names of the dedicator and the artist. The works themselves were either melted down to be recast in later periods or were carried off to Rome, like many works of art from other sanctuaries. Of the second category of votives, those associated with war, the majority were statues of Zeus or Victory and were erected in the open area around the temple. They were usually large-scale, to match the magnitude of the victory and the spoils seized from the enemy by the victorious dedicators. Pausanias mentions a statue of Zeus, 4 m. high, dedicated by the Spartans after the Messenian wars, and another of 5.4 m. erected by the city of Kleitoria in Arkadia. An idea of the dedications may be gained from the surviving bases and from small-scale copies.

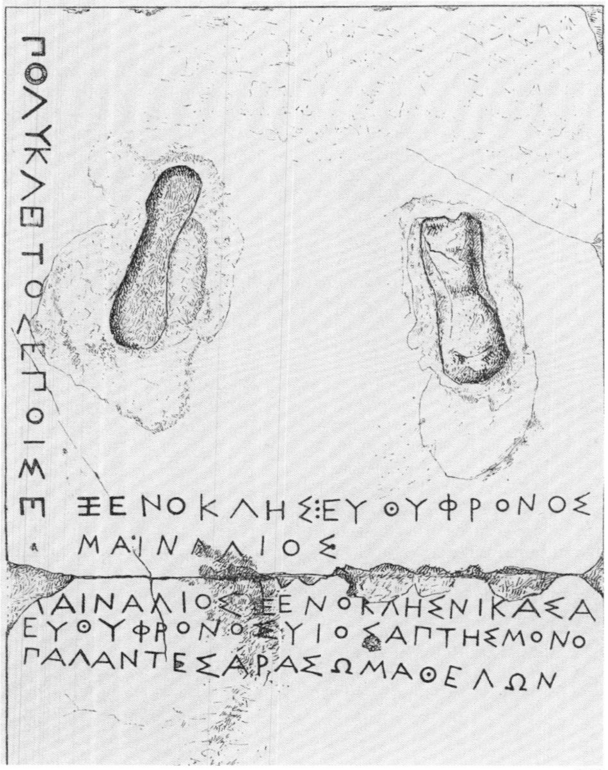

133

134

133. Drawing of the base of a statue dedicated to the athlete Xenokles of Mainalon. Xenokles won the wrestling competition and, according to the inscription, the statue was made by the sculptor Polykleitos (middle of the 5th c. BC).

134. Inscribed base of a statue dedicated to an athlete.

135. Bronze statue of Zeus holding a thunderbolt in his right hand. Statues of Zeus were commonly dedicated in the sanctuary (first half of the 5th c. BC). Athens, National Archaeological Museum.

136. Bronze statuette of a horse from a four-horse chariot, dedicated in the sanctuary of Zeus by a winner in the chariot race. The details of the harness are impressive. The meticulous rendering of the mane, the severe outlines, and the solid structure of the body suggest an Argive workshop (ca. 470 BC). Olympia, Archaeological Museum.

137. A bronze stele dating from the 3rd c. BC, inscribed with a decree passed by the Eleians in honour of Demokrates of Tenedos. Stelai bearing the texts of interstate treaties and decrees erected in the sanctuary may be regarded as dedications. Olympia, Archaeological Museum.

135

136

137

THE VICTORY OF PAIONIOS

138-139. The Victory of Paionios, dedicated by the Messenians and Naupaktians in the sanctuary of Zeus about 420 BC, as restored and reconstructed by the contemporary sculptor Michalis Tombros in a smaller plaster copy. Olympia, Archaeological Museum.

140. Reconstruction drawing of the Victory of Paionios and the high triangular pedestal on which the statue stood.

141. The inscription naming the dedicators and creator of the Victory on the base of the statue, carved about eye level to make it easy to read.

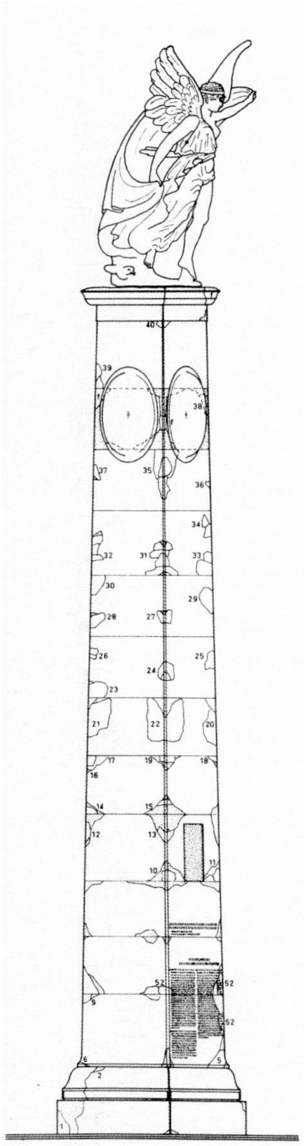

139

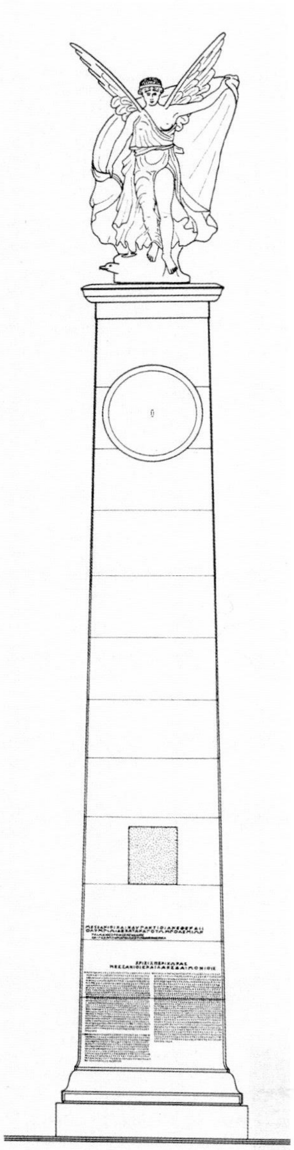

140

It is a major piece of good fortune that a notable marble votive of the Classical period has been preserved almost intact, together with its base, on which is carved an inscription giving the names of the dedicators and the creator of the sculpture – a very rare combination. This is the Victory by Paionios, dedicated by the Messenians and Naupaktians, according to the votive inscription, after a victory over the Spartans, about 420 BC: ΜΕΣΣΑΝΙΟΙ ΚΑΙ ΝΑΥΠΑΚΤΙΟΙ ΑΝΕΘΕΝ ΔΙΙ ΟΛΥΜΠΙΩ ΔΕΚΑΤΑΝ ΑΠΟ ΤΩΝ ΠΟΛΕΜΙΩΝ ('the Messenians and

141

Naupaktians dedicated to Olympian Zeus a tithe from the enemy'). The expression 'from the enemy' is interesting: the enemy is probably not named because the dedicators feared reprisals from the powerful Spartans.

The statue of Victory is 2.1 m. high. It stood on a triangular pillar, 9 m. high, in front of the Temple of Zeus, where it competed with another, similar statue of Victory by the same sculptor, the akroterion that crowned the pediment at the east end of the temple. We also learn from the inscription on the pillar that Paionios of Mende in Chalkidiki undertook the execution of these Victories, as well as the central akroterion on the west facade of the temple, after winning an artistic competition organised by the priesthood: ΠΑΙΩΝΙΟΣ ΕΠΟΙΗΣΕ ΜΕΝΔΑΙΟΣ. ΚΑΙ ΤΑΚΡΩΤΗΡΙΑ ΠΟΙΩΝ ΕΠΙ ΤΟΝ ΝΑΟΝ ΕΝΙΚΑ ('Paionios of Mende made this. And, making the akroteria on the temple, he was victorious'). Competitions were common, not only for works of art but for all public works in the ancient world.

Paionios's statue of Victory is one of the masterpieces of ancient sculpture. The figure, carved from a single block of marble (a 3-meter cube), descends, flying, to earth. With her raised left hand she holds her himation; she probably had a palm branch in her right. An eagle beneath her feet gave an immediate effect of height, while the sense of flight is assisted by the astonishing artistic treatment of all the elements of the composition: the dress clings to the body at the front, revealing the beauty of the flesh, and at the same time billows out behind, creating an ideal background. The movement of the garments,

142. Part of a marble votive relief with winged Victories crowning a victor (ca. 410 BC). Athens, Akropolis Museum.

143. Marble head of an athlete. Roman copy drawing inspiration from the Doryphoros of Polykleitos, ca. 450 BC. Corinth, Archaeological Museum.

144. A seated, bearded official crowns a victor, behind whom is borne the tripod prize. Attic black-figure amphora (540-530 BC). Washington, D.C., National Museum of Natural History, Smithsonian Institution.

142

143

combined with the postures of the arms and wings, explodes the work to every part of the blue sky that was its natural background. The piece is a landmark in the history of art for the completely original way that the artist captures the sense of flight.

Besides artists, Olympia and the other sanctuaries were frequented by many men of letters and writers. Foremost amongst them were poets, for, to immortalise their achievement, the victors not only had statues erected but also turned to a poet for a paean, a victory hymn, known as an Olympian, Pythian, Nemean or Isthmian ode, depending on the games it celebrated. Accordingly, Pindar of Thebes and Bacchylides and Simonides of Kea, the most famous composers of this kind of hymn, often attended the games at Olympia. Philosophers, too, like Thales of Miletos, writers like Herodotos, and politicians such as Alkibiades did not miss the opportunity of appearing before the crowds at Olympia, which consisted of the ruling classes of the Greek city-states, to present a new work or simply to air their views on some subject.

It can therefore be claimed without hesitation that the great ancient sanctuaries, especially Olympia during its games, formed ideal places for the development of literature and the arts, and were at the same time melting pots for new ideas and views. With the many works of art housed there, the sanctuaries were also living museums covering the complete development of ancient Greek architecture, sculpture, and painting. Finally, the dedication of the spoils of war and other votives, invariably accompanied by inscriptions, made them living archives of ancient Greek history.

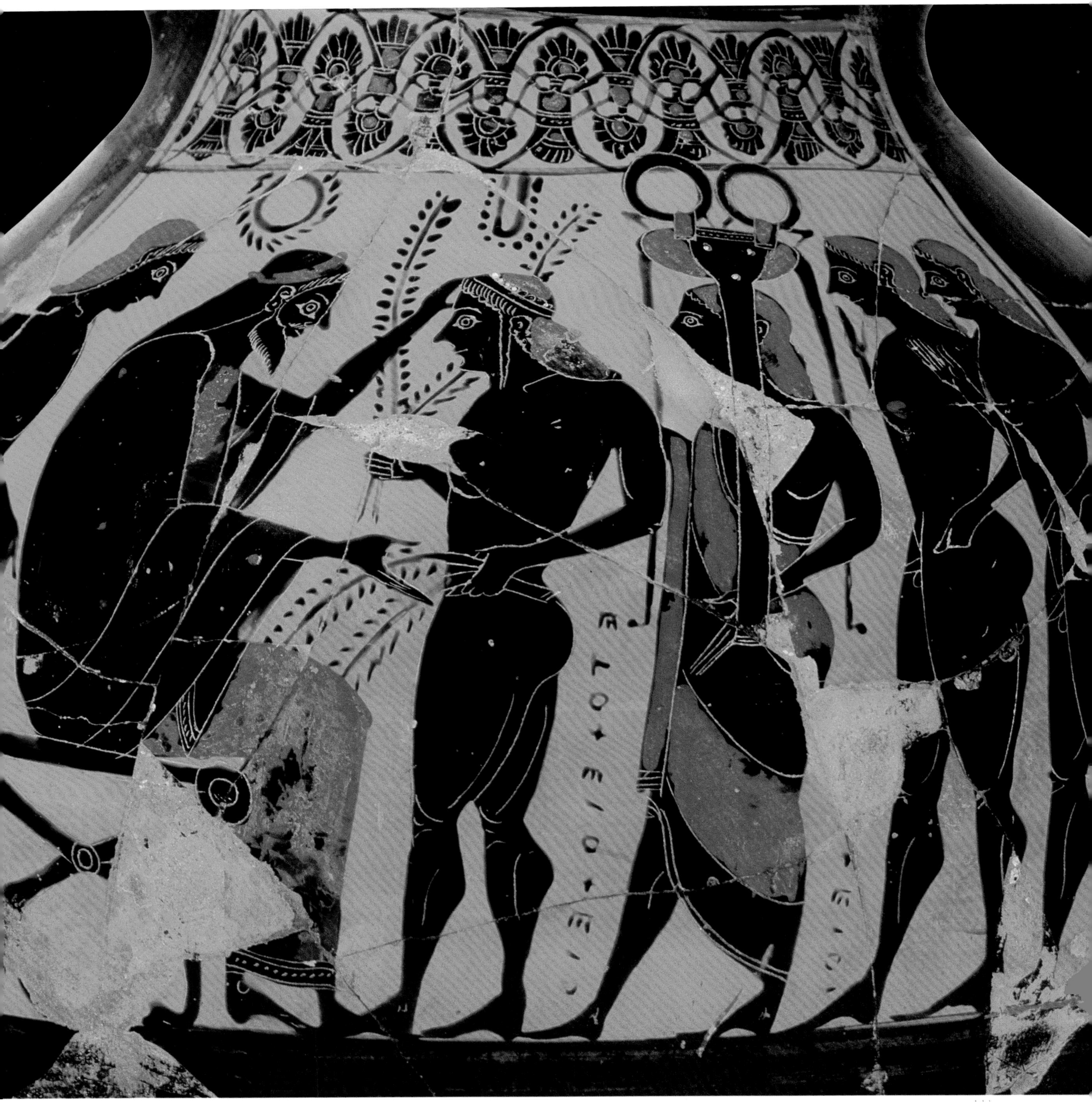

144

4th c. BC
The Late Classical period

THE METROON

Olympia continued to flourish in the 4th c. BC. Just after 400 BC, the Metroon, the third temple in the sanctuary, was erected in honour of Rhea, mother of the gods, who had probably been worshipped at Olympia from ancient times. It was a Doric temple with an external colonnade of 6 by 11 columns. About the same time, a new pentagonal enclosure was created in the sanctuary, between the Zeus Temple and the Heraion. This was the Pelopeion, a shrine dedicated to Pelops, a mythical founder of the games, and was entered from the southwest through a Doric porch. The embankments of the stadium were also extended, creating seats for about 40,000 spectators and giving the structure the form that we see today. The first exedra of the Hellanodikai was also created at this time, in about the middle of the south embankment, though it was renovated at a later date.

An unprecedented event occurred at Olympia in 364 BC, known from the description by Xenophon, and constituted the most serious infringement of the sacred truce in the history of this institution. The Pisatans had expelled the Eleians and assumed sole responsibility for organising the 105th Olympiad, with the aid of a corps of the Arkadian army deployed next to the sanctuary. In an attempt to recapture Olympia, the Eleians invaded the sanctuary during the games, but were repelled by the Arkadians. Defensive trenches, detected during the excavations, were dug between the Bouleuterion and the stadium, but even more striking is the fact that the thousands of spectators who had gathered for the games watched the whole military operation, after which the games resumed and the victors were announced. Another astonishing circumstance connected with this battle is reported by Pausanias, who, during his visit to Olympia about AD 170, was told by a guide that, during a repair to the roof of the Heraion a few years earlier, he had been present at the discovery of the skeleton of a dead hoplite in the space between the ceiling and the roof of the temple. The hoplite had presumably sought refuge there and died, after being wounded and considered 'missing' in the battle about 500 years earlier.

After the battle, the Eleians regained control of the sanctuary and the games and in thanks dedicated to Zeus a bronze statue over 8 m. high, the largest piece of sculpture at Olympia. Finally, the 105th Olympiad was not recognised as a regular one but was declared Anolympias (a 'non-Olympiad'); this had happened twice previously in the history of the games, in 748 and 644 BC, again on occasions when they had been organised by the Pisatans.

145. North part of the sanctuary at Olympia, reconstruction by Victor Laloux, 1883. In the centre is the Metroon. Paris, École Nationale Supérieure des Beaux-Arts.

146. View from the southeast of the foundations of the Metroon. Rhea, the Mother of the gods, was worshipped in this building.

146

146

THE PHILIPPEION

147

The intervention of the Macedonians in the politics of southern Greece found expression in the personal interest taken by Philip II in entering his horses in the chariot race and horse races of the Olympiad of 356 BC. The architectural expression of this interest was the Philippeion, a building constructed at a vital point within the Altis. It is a circular building with a diameter of 15.3 m., surrounded by 18 Ionic columns. Inside were 8 Corinthian half-columns, in front of which were placed five chryselephantine statues by the sculptor Leochares, depicting members of the Macedonian royal family, including Philip himself, his wife, Alexander the Great, and Philip's parents. Construction of the building began after the Battle of Chaironeia (338 BC) and was probably completed by Alexander himself, after Philip's death in 336 BC. Philip and Alexander's dedications at Olympia, like those at other sanctuaries, were intended to project the Macedonian king not as a conqueror, but as a leading exponent of the panhellenic ideal, of which the panhellenic sanctuaries were the preeminent representatives. A head of Alexander, found in the village of Alpheiousa near the mouth of the river Alpheios, is also represented in the museum at Olympia.

147. Silver tetradrachm of Philip II, king of Macedonia.

148. The Philippeion, a building begun by Philip II to promote the Macedonian dynasty (340-330 BC).

149. Marble portrait head of Alexander the Great, from Alpheiousa near Olympia. Roman copy of a Hellenistic original rendering the personal features of the king. Olympia, Archaeological Museum.

150. Reconstruction drawing of the Philippeion, the only round building erected at Olympia. It was in the Ionic order and adopted many architectural innovations that became established features of Hellenistic architecture. Drawing: H. Schleif.

151. Reconstruction drawing of the plan and architectural members of the Philippeion: Ionic capital, Corinthian half-column, coffers and entablature. Athens, German Archaeological Institute.

148

149

150

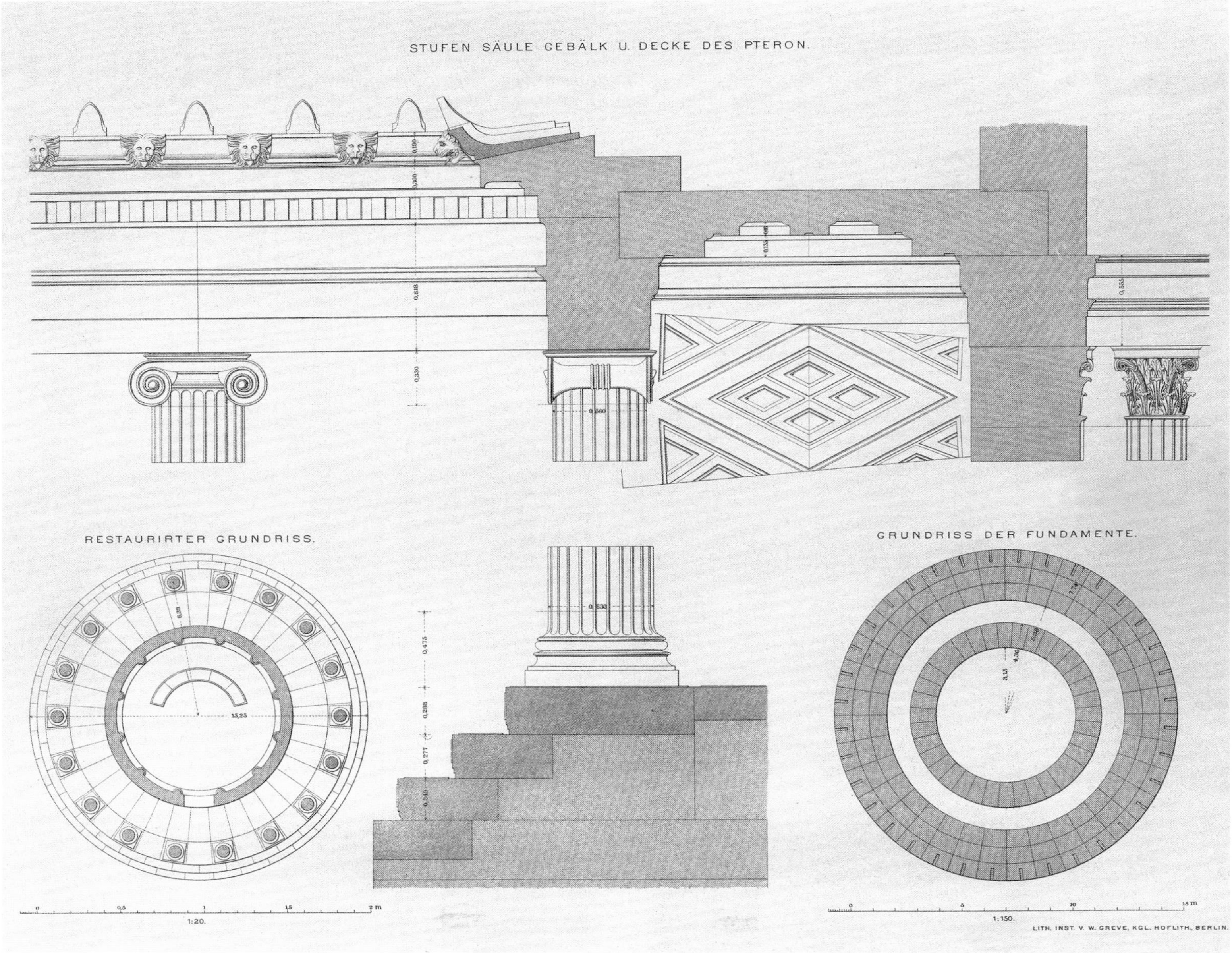
STUFEN SÄULE GEBÄLK U. DECKE DES PTERON.
RESTAURIRTER GRUNDRISS.
GRUNDRISS DER FUNDAMENTE.
1:20.
1:150.
LITH. INST. V. W. GREVE, KGL. HOFLITH, BERLIN.

151

THE LEONIDAION

From the 4th century on, the main building activity concerned the construction of secular buildings designed to improve facilities for pilgrims. A large guest-house was created to the south of Pheidias's workshop. Funded and designed by the wealthy Naxian Leonides, it was therefore known as the Leonidaion. The inscription on the architrave proudly proclaims the name of the dedicator and builder: ΛΕΩΝΙΔΗΣ ΛΕΩΤΟΥ ΝΑΞΙΟΣ ΕΠΟΙΗΣΕΝ ('Leonides son of Leotos of Naxos made'). The building, which measures 75 by 81 meters and is more than 6,000 square meters in area, was the largest roofed structure at Olympia. It was enclosed by an exterior colonnade of 138 Ionic columns, while the interior courtyard had a Doric peristyle of 44 columns. The building had a large number of rooms in which to entertain over one hundred wealthy, eminent visitors, as well as dining rooms for official banquets.

152. Drawing of the elevation and section of the Leonidaion, with details of the interior Ionic and exterior Doric colonnades. Athens, German Archaeological Institute.

153. The Leonidaion, a large guest-house for distinguished visitors to the Olympic games, was erected in 330 BC. It consisted of a continuous colonnade around the outside, a series of rooms, and a square open-air courtyard at the centre.

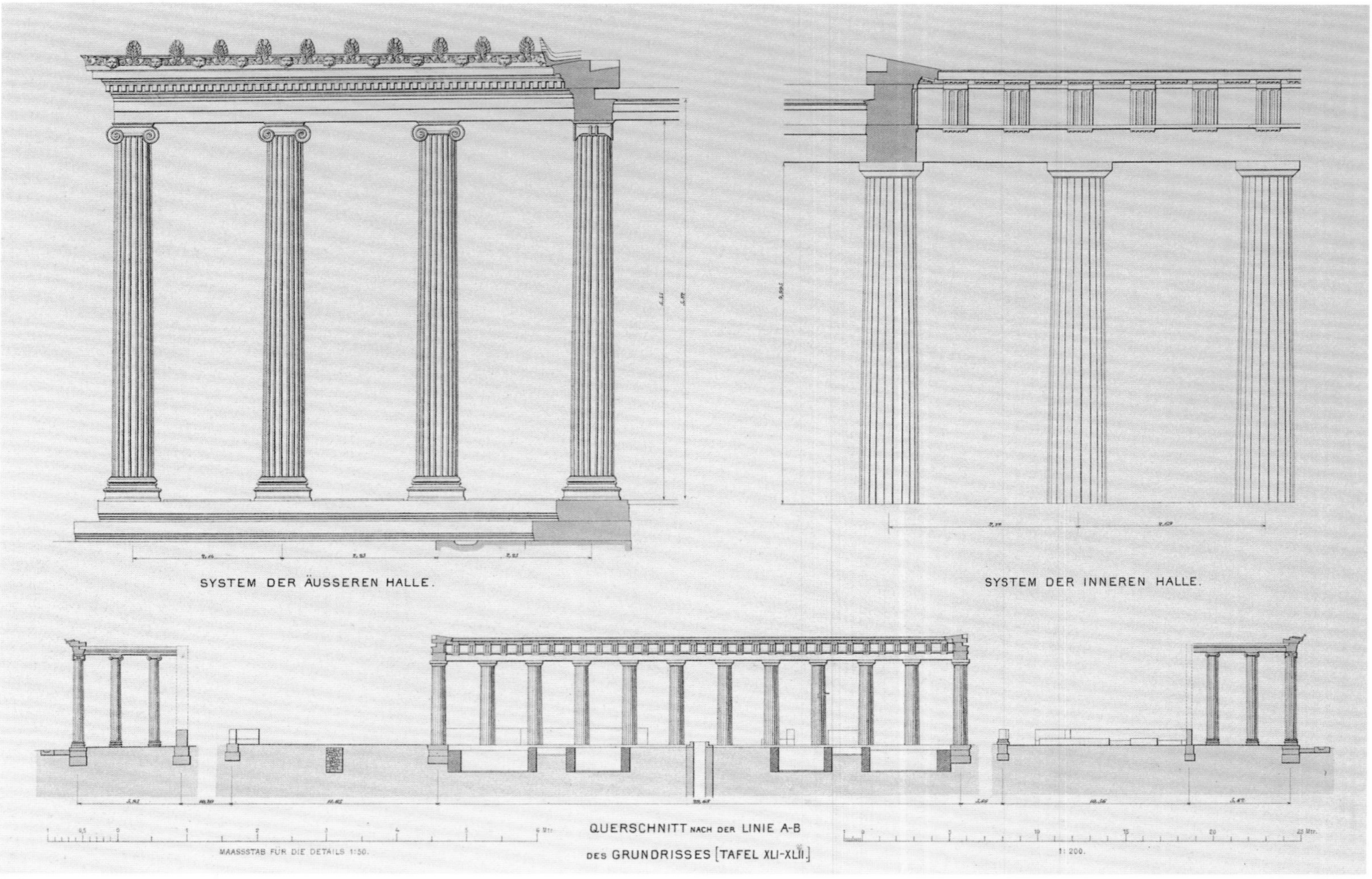

152

153

THE STOAS

Three long stoas were built in the 4th c. BC. The Doric South Stoa had an interior colonnade in the Corinthian order. Its situation on the sacred way and the existence of a projecting porch suggest that it was used to view the official procession, or its official reception, when it arrived at the Altis from Elis on the first day of the festival. The Echo Stoa next to the stadium, 98 m. long, was so called, according to Pausanias (5.21.17), because a shout in it would be echoed seven times. Study of its architectural details has revealed that it was the work of the same designer who worked on the Philippeion; it is not impossible, therefore, that it was yet another donation by the Macedonian kings. The Stoa of Agnaptos was erected in the middle of the 4th c. by the architect of this name in front of the hippodrome, possibly for the charioteers and horses. No trace of it has survived, however. All these large stoas were multipurpose buildings at the service of visitors: besides providing shelter in case of bad weather, for example, they were also decorated with wall paintings and housed dedications. The most impressive was the dedication erected in 270 BC in front of the Echo Stoa: two columns 9 m. high, bearing gilded statues of the king of Egypt, Ptolemy II Philadelphos, and his sister and wife, Arsinoe.

154. Reconstruction drawing of the Echo Stoa. In front is the dominating dedication by Ptolemy II and his wife, Arsinoe. Drawing: W. Hoepfner.

155. Reconstruction drawing of the South Stoa (360-350 BC). Drawing: H. Schleif.

156. The Apoxyomenos, a marble statue of an athlete scraping the dust from his body with a strigil. Roman copy of an original by the sculptor Lysippos (330-320 BC). Rome, Vatican Museum.

157. Bronze head of a boxer, perhaps from the statue of the famous Olympic victor Satyros by the sculptor Silanion, one of the few surviving original statues of Olympic victors (middle of the 4th c. BC). Athens, National Archaeological Museum.

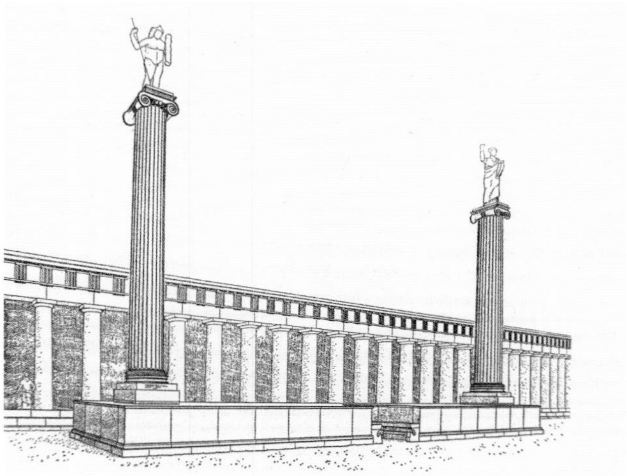

154

155

DEDICATIONS

STATUES OF OLYMPIC VICTORS

Olympia was adorned with many other works of art, mainly statues of Olympic victors, of which a few bases have survived, such as that of the statue of the pankratiast Polydamas from Skotoussa in Thessaly. This was the work of Lysippos and was probably made about 70 years after the event. Polydamas was one of the most important athletes in the ancient world and used to imitate the labours of the great hero Herakles. A bronze head of a boxer has also survived, which may have belonged to a statue by the Athenian sculptor Silanion of the Eleian athlete Satyros.

156

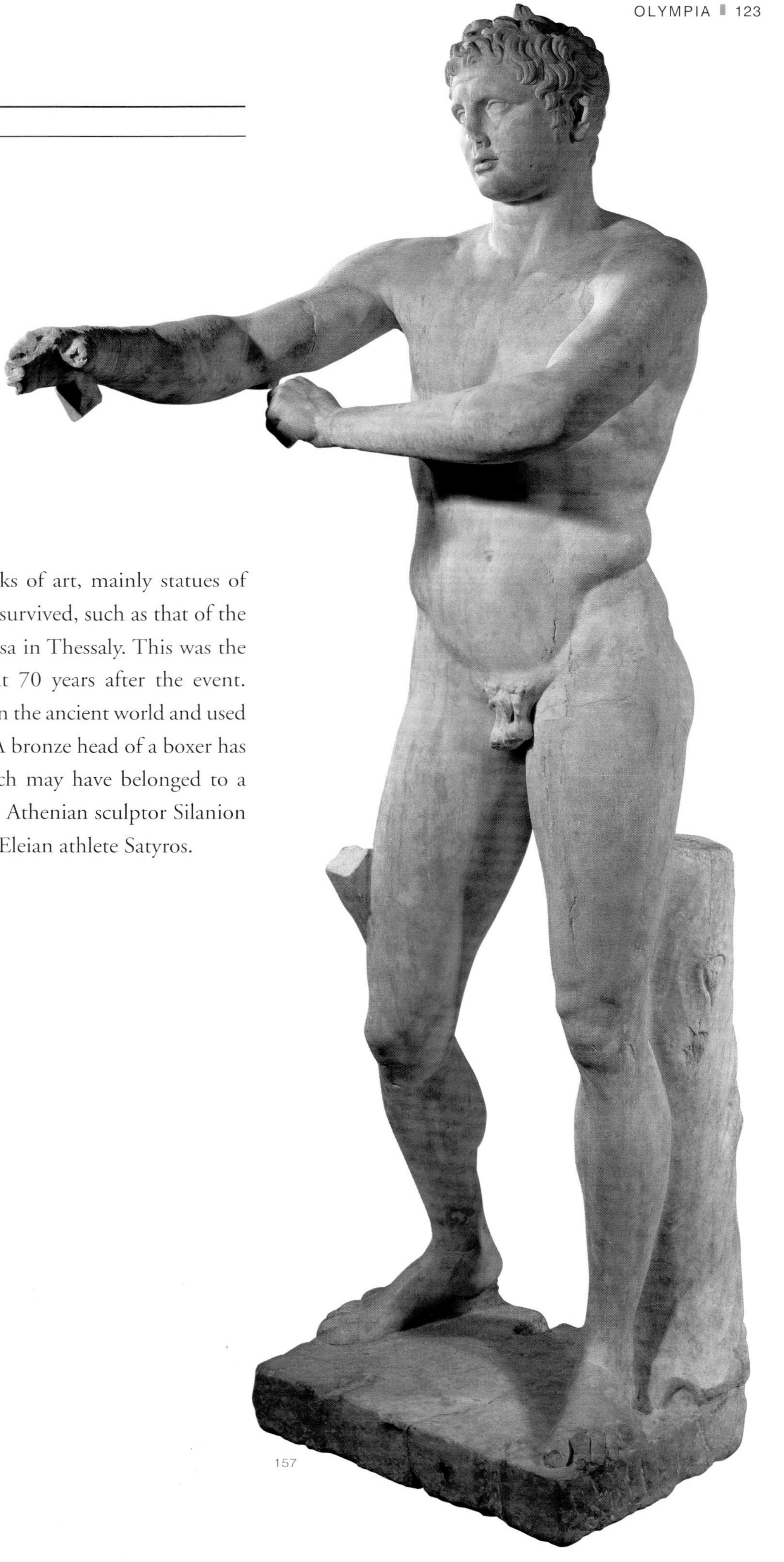

157

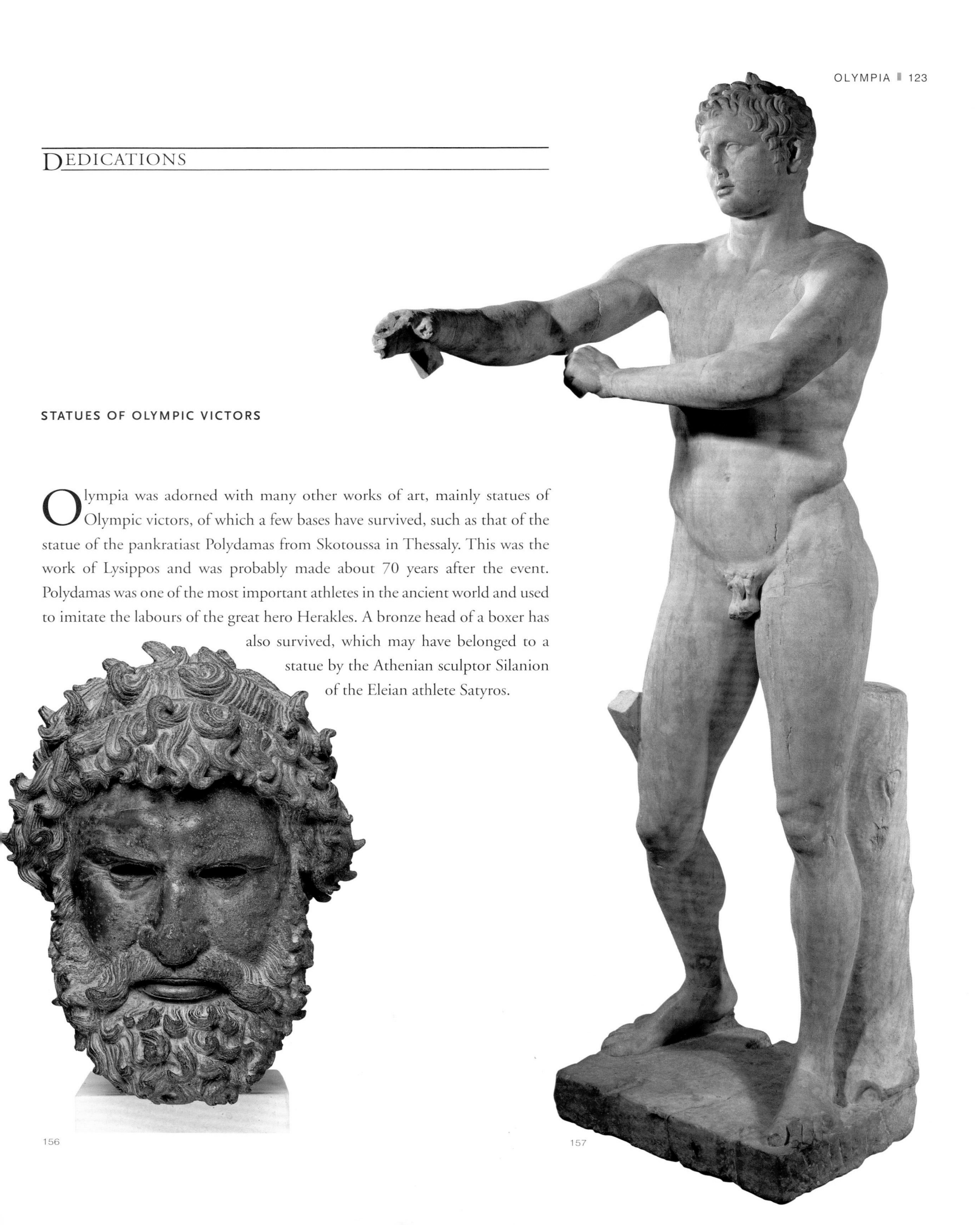

THE HERMES OF PRAXITELES

By great fortune, another notable statue of the period has been preserved: the Hermes of Praxiteles, which Pausanias (5.17.3) saw in the cella of the Heraion: *Ερμῆν λίθου, Διόνυσον δὲ φέρει νήπιον, τέχνη δέ ἐστι Πραξιτέλους* ('Hermes in stone, carrying the infant Dionysos; and the art is that of Praxiteles'). The statue of Hermes, found in spring 1877 by German excavators at Olympia, is one of the few original marble works in the round preserved from ancient times. In addition to the great art of Praxiteles, one of grace and beauty, the statue reveals something of the tranquil majesty and Olympian calm with which the gods of the Classical period were portrayed. There is no evidence indicating why the statue was dedicated at Olympia. Its dating to about 340 BC and the connection between Hermes, the god of Arkadia, and Dionysos, the god of Elis, suggest that it was erected to mark the treaty between the Arkadians and the Eleians concluded in 343 BC.

It is not known whether this statue was originally erected in the Heraion or whether it was transferred there during the Roman imperial period, when the temple was converted into a repository of important works of art, possibly after the destruction of the buildings in which they had been housed up to that time. According to Pausanias's description, valuable heirlooms of the sanctuary were also kept there, such as the disk of Iphitos, on which the treaty concluding the first sacred truce was inscribed, and the larnax of Kypselos, a large wooden chest with mythological scenes dedicated 800 years earlier by Kypselos, the tyrant of Corinth. In the Heraion, Pausanias also saw 21 statues, mainly of gold and ivory, two of which were from the Philippeion, and the gold and ivory table by the sculptor Kolotes was also stored here. The olive wreaths were placed on this table during the ceremony at which the victors were crowned in the Temple of Zeus.

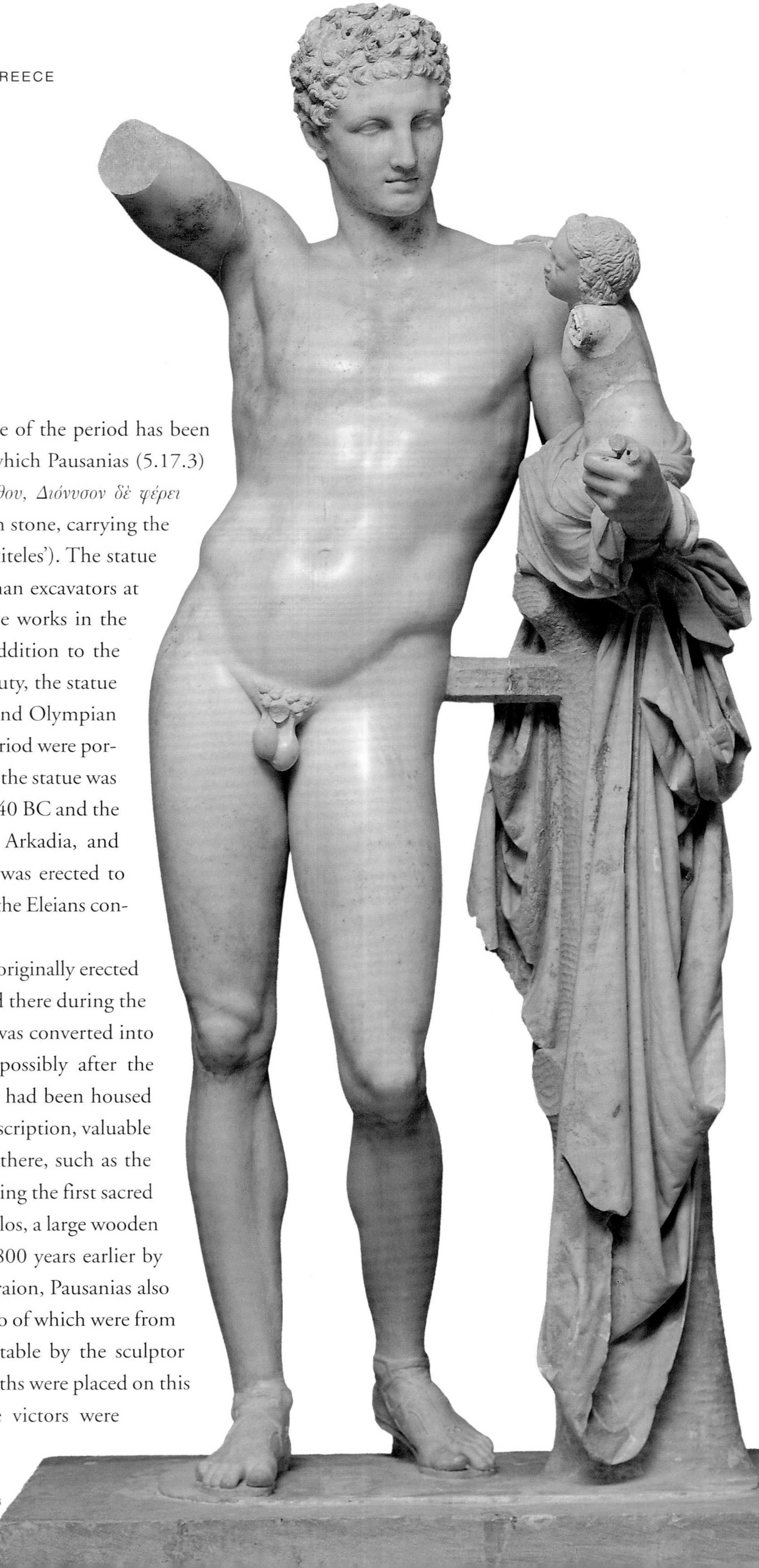

158

Praxiteles, who imbued his stone statues with the passions of the soul.

Diodorus Siculus

159

158. Hermes with the infant Dionysos. In his raised right hand the god probably held a bunch of grapes, toward which the baby is turned. Hermes wears only his sandals, showing off his beautiful youthful body. The willowy posture foreshadows the languid, coquettish expression adopted by sculpture in the Hellenistic period. This marble masterpiece was found in the Heraion and, based on the description of Pausanias, is often thought to be an original by Praxiteles (340 BC). Olympia, Archaeological Museum.

159. Detail, head of Hermes. The Olympian god is portrayed as completely calm, with a faint smile.

160-163. Heads based on the Hermes of Praxiteles. The drawing shows the holes in which the ivy wreath was fixed, as in the restored plaster copy of the head. Drawing: A. Asher, 1897.

160

161

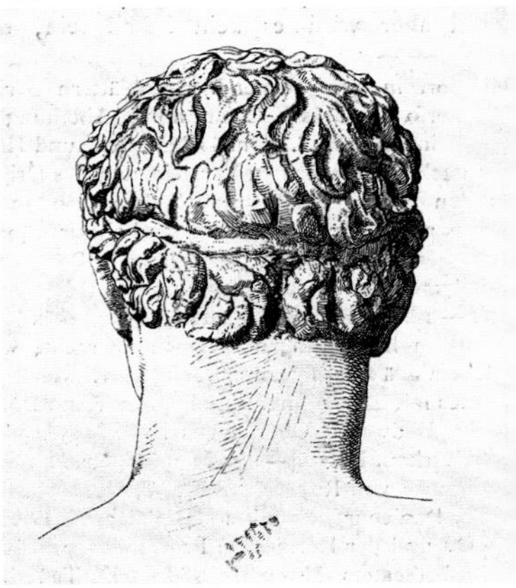

162

163

THE ZANES

In the 4th c. BC, another type of statue of Zeus made its appearance at Olympia. There were sixteen such bronze statues, which were known as Zanes (plural of Zeus), all of them financed from fines imposed on athletes who had violated their oath and infringed the rules of the games, mostly by attempting to bribe their opponents. The statues stood in a row beneath the stepped terrace of the treasuries, so that athletes could see them as they entered the stadium. The presence of these statues and the didactic epigrams carved on the bases served as a deterrent to the human tendency toward such infringements: for instance, *οὐ χρήμασιν ἀλλὰ ὠκύτητι τῶν ποδῶν καὶ ὑπὸ ἰσχύος σώματος ὀλυμπικὴν ἐστιν εὑρέσθαι νίκην* ('Victory at Olympia is to be won not by money but by swiftness of foot and strength of body').

The first six Zanes were erected in 388 BC with fines paid by Eupolos of Thessaly and three boxers who had been bribed by him. Six more were erected after the 112th Olympiad in 332 BC, when it was discovered that the Athenian pentathlete Kalippos had resorted to bribery. Kalippos was unable to pay the fine himself and it had to be paid for him by his native city. The Athenians, however, refused to do so and sent the orator Hypereides to appeal against the judges' decision. The appeal was rejected by the Eleians, who sought the assistance of the Delphic oracle; this announced that it would never again issue a prophecy for the Athenians if they did not pay the fine, which was duly paid. The familiar solidarity of the sanctuaries proved highly effective once again. The last Zanes were erected in AD 125, according to Pausanias.

It is worth noting at this point the role played by Olympia in the maturing of the panhellenic idea – that is, the perception of the Greeks as a unified 'race.' This idea began to mature in the 4th century, when the first signs of crisis were emerging in the city-state as an institution, and it is no coincidence that the leading figures of the day came to Olympia to proclaim their views on the subject. The orator and sophist Gorgias made a fiery speech in 388 BC in which he urged the Greeks to desist from their internecine wars and unite in the face of the Persian threat, as their ancestors had done a hundred years earlier. The same views were expressed a few years later by two more representatives of the panhellenic idea, Lysias, who delivered his *Olympian* oration here, and Isocrates with his *Panegyric*.

164. Base of one of the bronze Zanes. An inscription with the name of the sculptor Daidalos is preserved.

165. The sixteen bases of the Zanes standing along the street leading to the stadium reminded the athletes of the price to be paid for failure to observe the rules of the games.

164

165

Their orations were reactions to the difficulties southern Greece faced in the 4th c. BC: civil conflict, the interventions of Philip II, and the appearance of signs of political decay, all of which led the sensitive intellectuals, especially those who were also fine orators, to write speeches and deliver them before large audiences in the presence of the ruling class of Greece. Despite their attempts to change the situation, history could not be turned back.

3rd - 2nd c. BC
The Hellenistic period

During this period, a great impulse was given to the development of Olympia, as of most of the major cities and sanctuaries throughout Greece, by the rulers of the Hellenistic kingdoms of the East. They sought in this way to cement and project their ties with their Greek roots. Building activity continued undiminished outside the Altis with the construction of new secular buildings, most of them bathhouses and guest-houses, and buildings in which the athletes stayed and prepared for the games.

166. Plan of the archaeological site at Olympia in the Hellenistic period. Athens, German Archaeological Institute.

167. View of the palaestra, a characteristic Hellenistic building, amidst trees and flowers at Olympia.

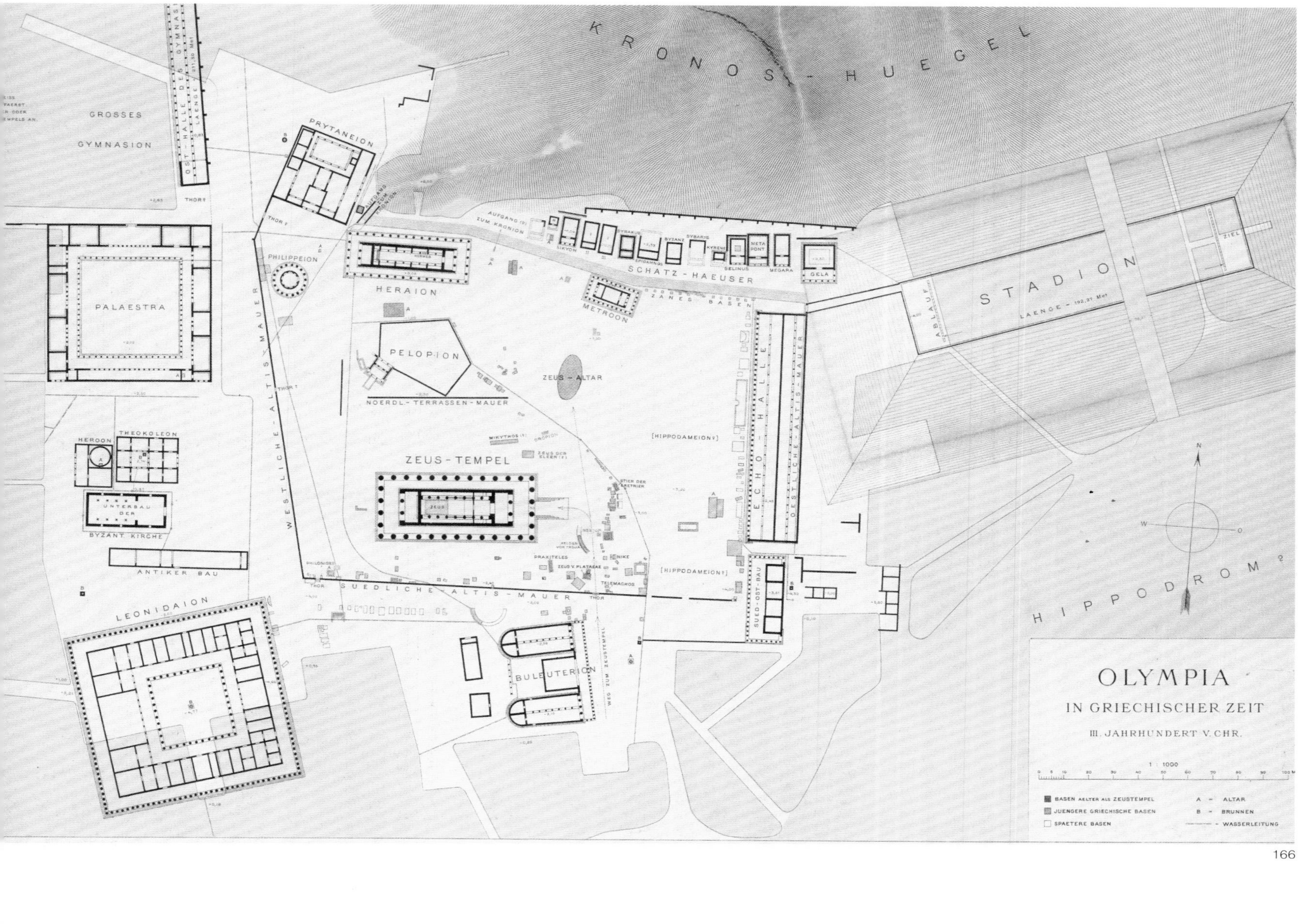

166

THE PALAESTRA

The palaestra, which was used as a training area by competitors in the heavy events, was probably dedicated by the Hellenistic king Ptolemy II. It was a square building (66.35 by 66.75 m.) with a large interior peristyle courtyard, around which were stoas and rooms. Though the brick superstructure of the walls and the timber roofs with their tiles have not survived, the plan and the elevation of the building can be deduced from 32 restored columns of the total of 72 in the peristyle and from the stone toichobate (wall base). Training took place in the courtyard, while the 19 rooms around it served as storerooms for implements, baths, changing rooms, rooms in which to oil the body, rest rooms, and so on. The largest room, in the middle of the north side, had 9 Ionic columns on the facade and benches around the sides. It was possibly the changing room, though it may also have been used as a teaching room by philosophers and men of letters during their short stay at Olympia. Athletes stayed in the palaestra at Olympia only during the games: their preparations, one month before the start, took place in the gymnasia of Elis.

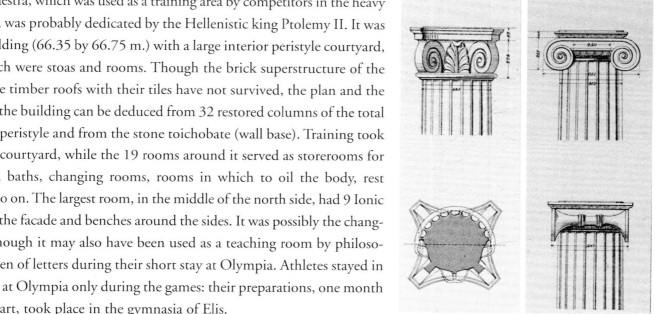

168

169

170

168, 170. Reconstruction drawings of Ionic columns from the palaestra. Athens, German Archaeological Institute.

169. The Doric colonnade of the palaestra. In the Hellenistic period the lower part of the columns was commonly left unworked to protect the delicate flutes from damage.

171. The colonnade of the stoa that encircled the courtyard of the palaestra. Behind the stoa were the rooms in which the athletes cleansed themselves, relaxed, and trained.

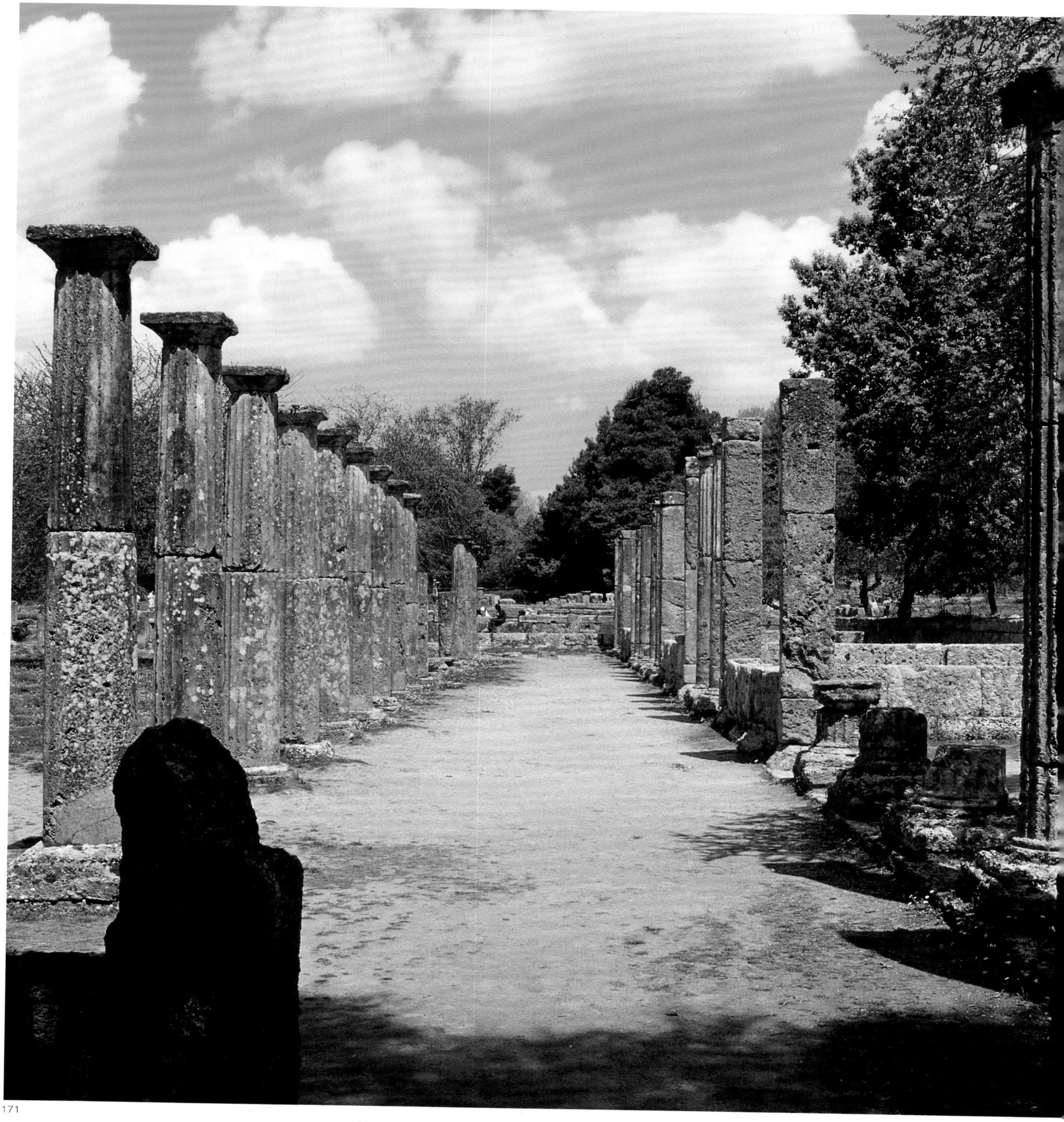

171

The most interesting feature of the courtyard of the palaestra was an area on the north side, 24.2 m. long and 5.44 m. wide. It is now beneath the earth and cannot be seen, but originally it was covered with rectangular clay slabs. It was probably the area referred to in the literary sources as the *skamma*, a special area covered with sand that was used as a training area by wrestlers, though possibly it may have served for the long jump.

172

172. Aerial view of the palaestra from the southwest, showing the peristyle courtyard and the encircling stoas. The open space at the centre was used by athletes training for the heavy events.

173. Marble relief showing athletes in the palaestra after the contest, conversing and removing the dust and sweat from their bodies with strigils (late 4th c. BC). Athens, Akropolis Museum.

173

174. Scene from the palaestra: a young athlete holding a strigil watches a javelin thrower testing his javelin. The trainer stands at the right. Attic red-figure kylix (450 BC). Athens, National Archaeological Museum.

175. The strigil and aryballos were the basic equipment used by athletes to keep themselves clean. The strigil was used to remove dust, and the aryballos contained aromatic oil. Olympia, Archaeological Museum.

176. An athlete competing in the discus, with a judge or trainer. Attic red-figure krater from Tarquinia (first half of the 5th c. BC). Tarquinia, National Museum.

177. The foundations of the porch of the gymnasium at Olympia, with one of the Corinthian capitals that adorned it. The porch was constructed in the 1st c. BC, several years after the erection of the gymnasium.

178. The krypte stoa through which the athletes entered the stadium. It allowed them to make a spectacular entrance before the spectators.

174

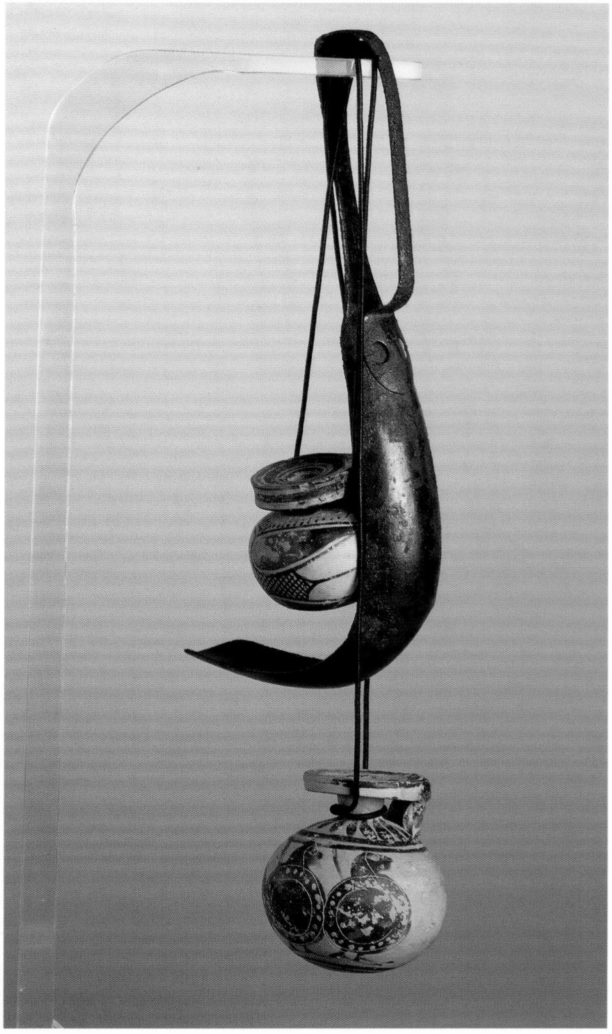
175

176

The Gymnasium

The gymnasium, which was probably built in stages in the 2nd c. BC, was contiguous with the north side of the palaestra and formed part of the same building programme. It was a huge structure measuring 220 by 120 meters, its length dictated by the distance required for the foot races. Training for the running events took place on a special track in the courtyard of the gymnasium called the *xystos* or, in bad weather, in the east stoa, known as the *paradromis*, a structure 210 by 12 meters, with 60 columns on the front and 66 inside. Practice for the throwing events – javelin and discus – also took place in the large peristyle courtyard of the gymnasium. According to Pausanias, the large two-storey stoa on its west side probably housed the lodgings of the athletes and their trainers, but nothing of this has been preserved, since it was swept away by the flooding of the Kladeos in the 4th c. AD.

177

The Krypte Stoa

Another project of the same period was the construction of the vaulted tunnel leading into the stadium, referred to in the ancient sources as the *krypte stoa*. It provided direct access to the stadium from the sanctuary; earlier, athletes, officials and spectators had to enter by ascending the embankments from the terrace of the treasuries. A monumental portal in the Corinthian order was added in front of the entrance, and statues of Nemesis, the avenging goddess, were placed to the left and right as a final reminder to the athletes as they entered not to break the rules. The krypte stoa also allowed the athletes to make a sudden, impressive entry into the stadium after their name was announced by the herald, in an age when the need was increasingly felt for this kind of 'theatrical' effect. According to more recent views, however, the krypte stoa was built in the 4th c. BC, which seems highly likely on the strength of parallels from other stadia.

178

1st c. BC - 2nd c. AD

The Roman intervention

Greece became a Roman province in 146 BC, after the defeat of the Achaian League by the Roman general Mummius. Although he razed the city of Corinth to the ground, as demanded by the Roman Senate, Mummius respected the Greek sanctuaries, as did most Romans of his period. He even followed tradition and sent 21 gilded Greek shields to the sanctuary of Olympia as the spoils of war, which were hung in the Temple of Zeus, and also four statues of Zeus. A long base at the southeast of the Altis bore the statue of Mummius and the ten Roman *legati* who assumed the administration of Greece. There was also a statue of Caecilius Metellus, the subjugator of Macedonia and Mummius's predecessor in southern Greece. In contrast, Sulla plundered the sanctuary during the Mithridatic war to fund his military operations, and transferred the 175th Olympiad of 80 BC to Rome, where he also celebrated his victory. Finally, the sanctuary, and particularly the Temple of Zeus, suffered considerable damage as a result of the earthquake of 40 BC.

179. Archaeological model by A. and E. Mallwitz of the site of Olympia as it was in Roman times. The sanctuary retained the image of the Classical and Hellenistic periods, with the addition of only a few new buildings.

180. Bronze statue of the emperor Augustus dating from 10 BC, found in the sea between Ayios Efstratios and Euboia in 1979. The sculpture is preserved from the waist up and depicts the emperor mounted on a horse, holding the reins with his left hand while raising his right hand in a gesture of blessing to his subjects. Athens, National Archaeological Museum.

179

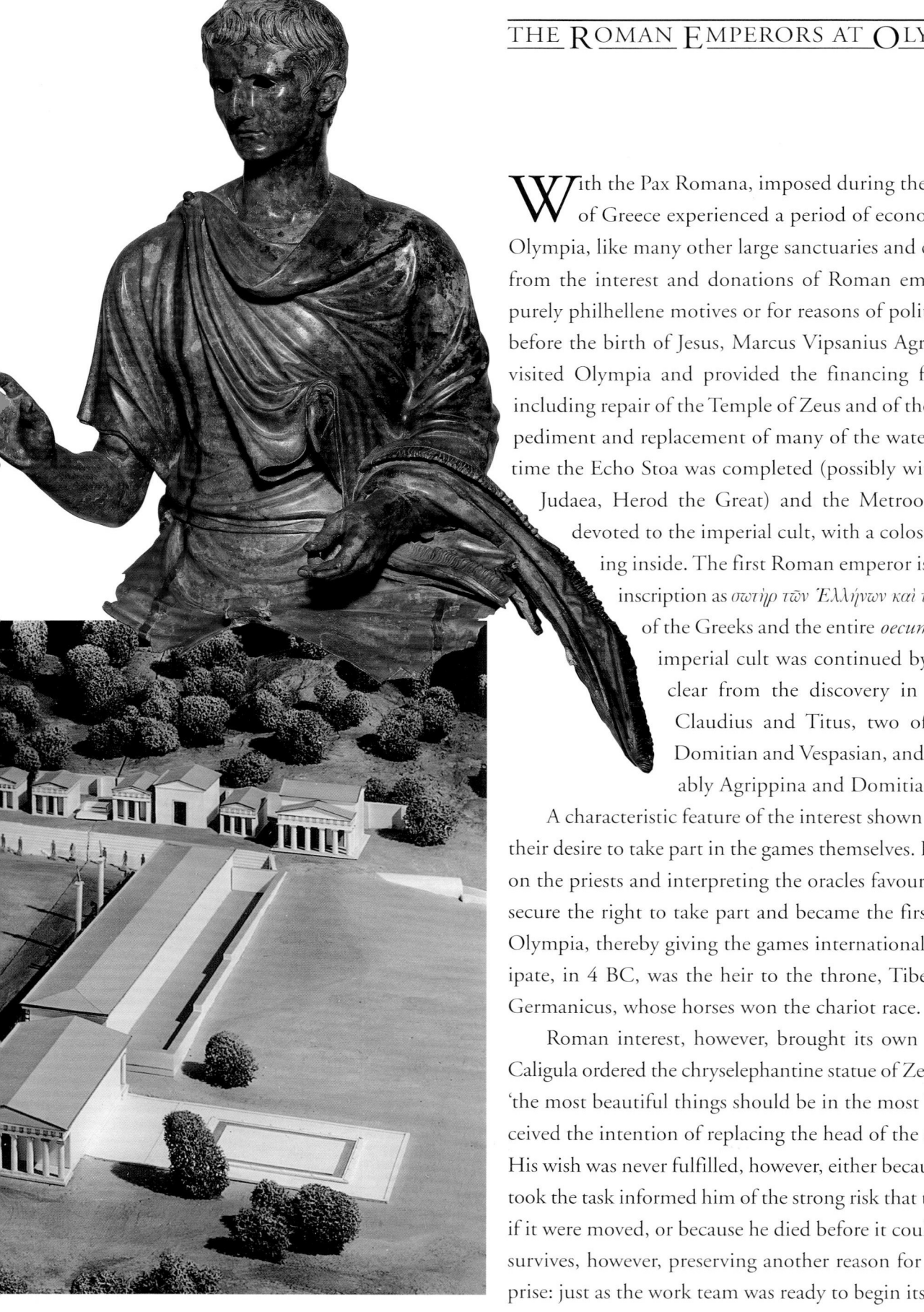

THE ROMAN EMPERORS AT OLYMPIA

With the Pax Romana, imposed during the rule of Augustus, the whole of Greece experienced a period of economic and cultural prosperity. Olympia, like many other large sanctuaries and cities, benefited significantly from the interest and donations of Roman emperors, acting either out of purely philhellene motives or for reasons of political expediency. A few years before the birth of Jesus, Marcus Vipsanius Agrippa, Augustus's son-in-law, visited Olympia and provided the financing for many building projects, including repair of the Temple of Zeus and of the extreme figures on the west pediment and replacement of many of the water spouts on the roof. At this time the Echo Stoa was completed (possibly with funding from the king of Judaea, Herod the Great) and the Metroon was renovated, the latter devoted to the imperial cult, with a colossal statue of Augustus standing inside. The first Roman emperor is greeted by the Eleians in an inscription as *σωτὴρ τῶν Ἑλλήνων καὶ τῆς οἰκουμένης πάσης* ('Saviour of the Greeks and the entire *oecumene* [inhabited world]'). The imperial cult was continued by Augustus's successors, as is clear from the discovery in the Metroon of statues of Claudius and Titus, two of other emperors, probably Domitian and Vespasian, and two of imperial wives, probably Agrippina and Domitia.

A characteristic feature of the interest shown by the Roman emperors was their desire to take part in the games themselves. By bringing influence to bear on the priests and interpreting the oracles favourably, they were easily able to secure the right to take part and became the first non-Greeks to compete at Olympia, thereby giving the games international prestige. The first to participate, in 4 BC, was the heir to the throne, Tiberius, followed in AD 17 by Germanicus, whose horses won the chariot race.

Roman interest, however, brought its own hidden dangers. In AD 40, Caligula ordered the chryselephantine statue of Zeus to be taken to Rome, since 'the most beautiful things should be in the most beautiful city.' He even conceived the intention of replacing the head of the statue with his own portrait. His wish was never fulfilled, however, either because the architects who undertook the task informed him of the strong risk that the statue would be destroyed if it were moved, or because he died before it could be transferred. A tradition survives, however, preserving another reason for the frustration of the enterprise: just as the work team was ready to begin its task, the terrible laughter of

THE NYMPHAION OF HERODES ATTICUS

The most impressive monument of the period was undoubtedly the Nymphaion of Herodes Atticus, in which practical opportunism was combined with artistic character. Through it, the problem of the water supply to the sanctuary was resolved once and for all, since drinking water was brought to it from the mountains to the east by a large system of open pipes. The pipe, over 4 km. long, ended on the south slope of the Kronios hill, where a large semicircular cistern, 30 m. in diameter, was built to receive the water after it had followed an impressive course in many basins at different levels. On the semicircular façade of the cistern was a two-storey exedra, 15 m. high, with eleven niches on each storey in which were placed statues of members of the imperial family and the family of Herodes. The majority of these statues were

184

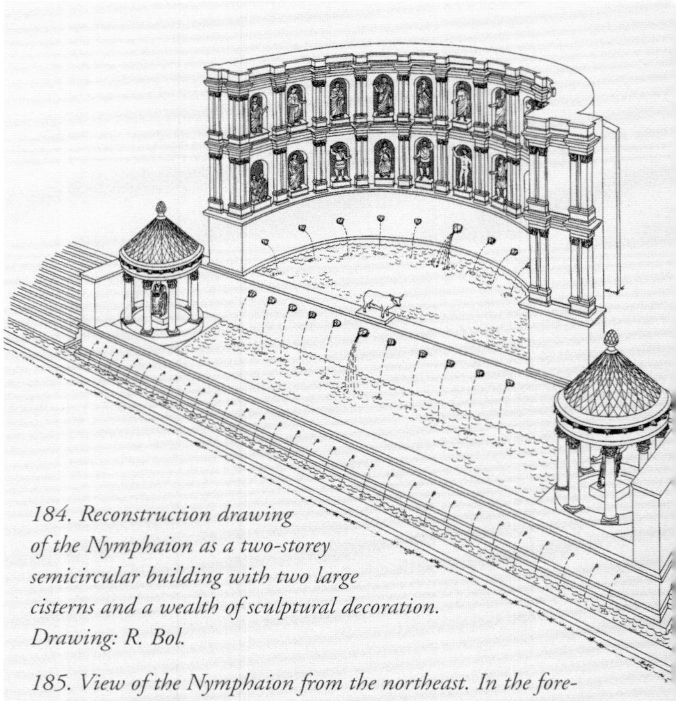

184. Reconstruction drawing of the Nymphaion as a two-storey semicircular building with two large cisterns and a wealth of sculptural decoration. Drawing: R. Bol.

185. View of the Nymphaion from the northeast. In the foreground is the semicircular apse of the cistern, coated with plaster.

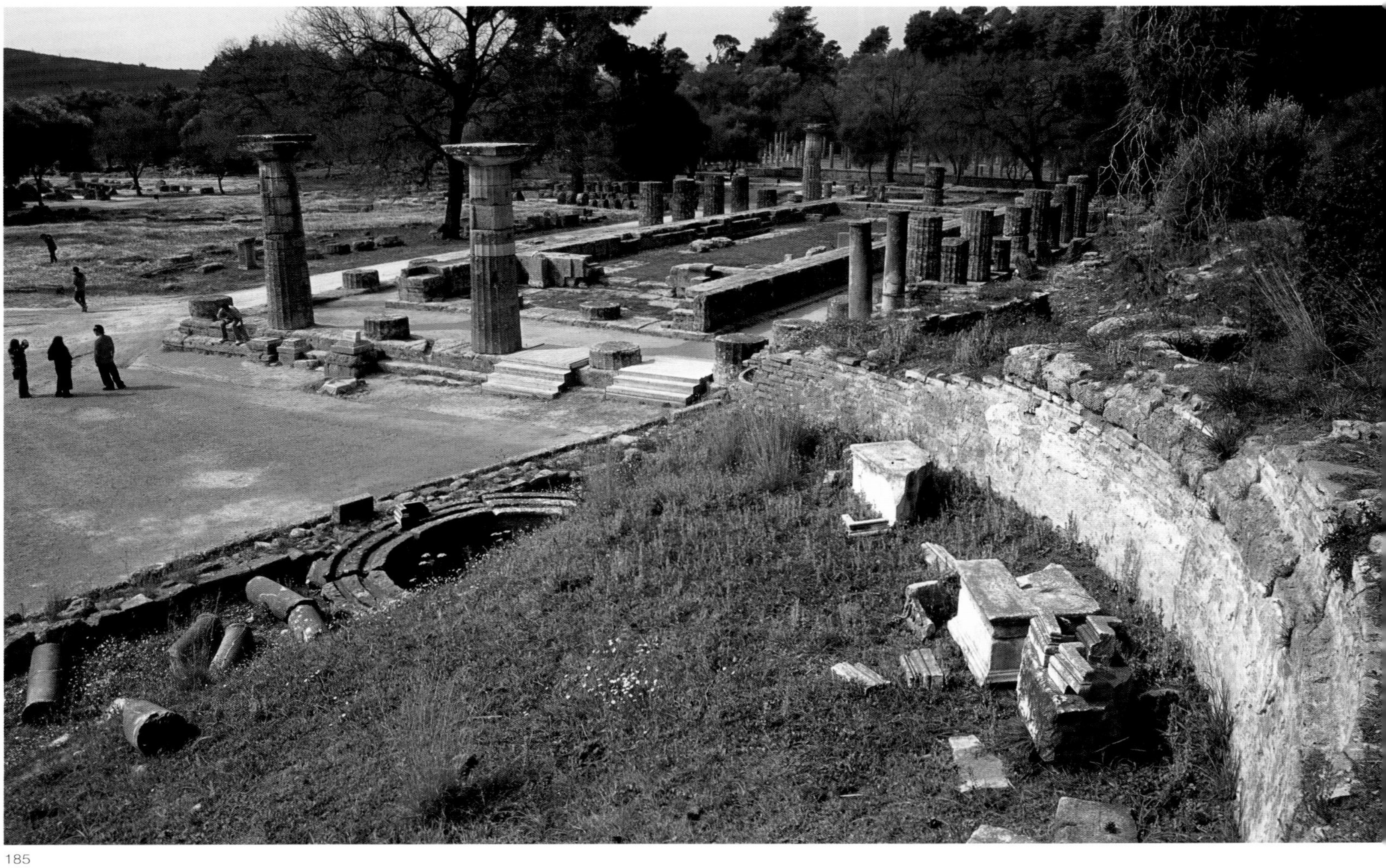

185

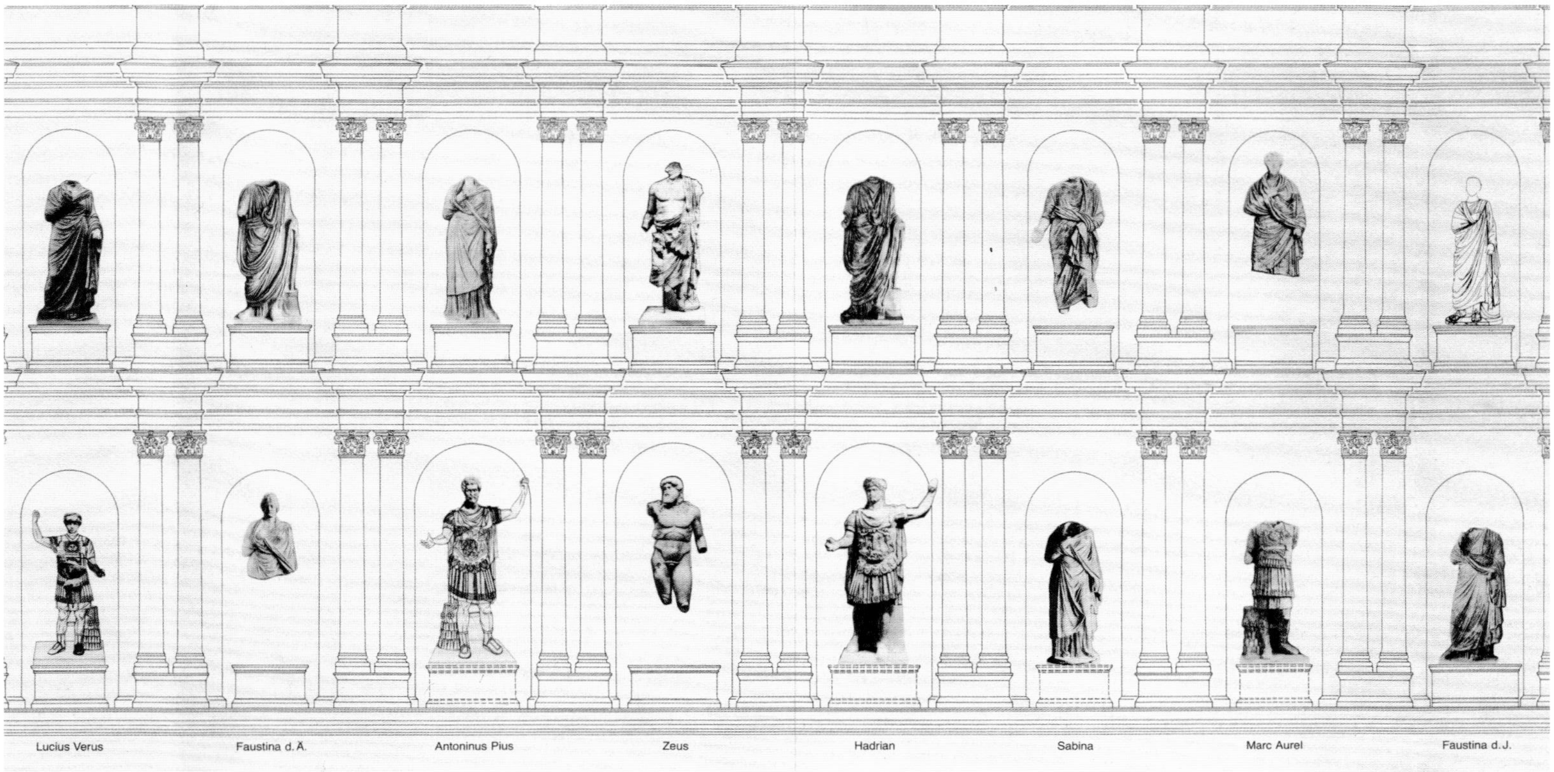
Lucius Verus
Faustina d. Ä.
Antoninus Pius
Zeus
Hadrian
Sabina
Marc Aurel
Faustina d. J.

186

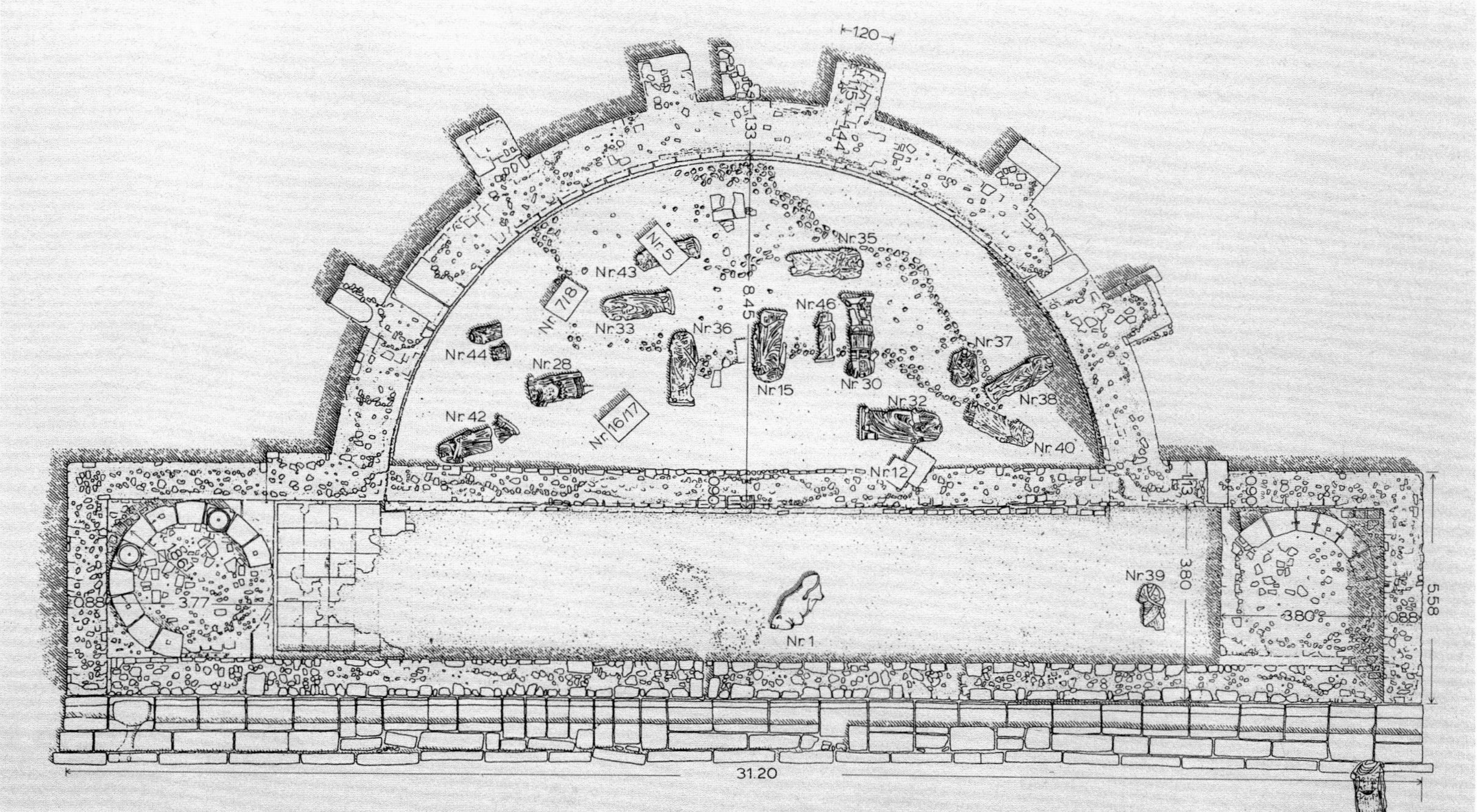
120
133
8.45
Nr. 35
Nr. 5
Nr. 43
Nr. 7/8
Nr. 46
Nr. 33
Nr. 36
Nr. 37
Nr. 44
Nr. 28
Nr. 15
Nr. 30
Nr. 38
Nr. 42
Nr. 32
Nr. 16/17
Nr. 40
Nr. 12
3.77
Nr. 1
Nr. 39
3.80
5.58
31.20
Nr. 51
0
5
10
15m

187

found during excavation, but it is not easy to assign them with complete certainty to the specific individuals whose names are recorded on the inscriptions of the statue bases on the building. Two statues were devoted to the lord of the sanctuary, Zeus, while a large marble bull, the symbolic sacrificial animal, was placed in the middle of the upper basin of the Nymphaion. On its back was carved the votive inscription: ΡΗΓΙΛΛΑ ΙΕΡΕΙΑ ΔΗΜΗΤΡΟΣ ΤΟ ΥΔΩΡ ΚΑΙ ΤΑ ΠΕΡΙ ΤΟ ΥΔΩΡ ΤΩ ΔΙΙ ('Rhegilla, the priestess of Demeter, dedicated the water and the things connected with it to Zeus').

This inscription containing the name of Herodes Atticus's wife, Rhegilla, allows us to speculate about the circumstances in which this project was carried out. Most probably, Herodes dedicated this highly expensive structure at Olympia in order to persuade the priests to allow his wife to assume the office of priestess of Demeter Chamyne for one year and thus acquire the right to watch the Olympic games, the priestess being the only woman who enjoyed this right. Herodes may also have done so in order to provide amusement for his beautiful, young wife, who came from a noble gens in Rome. No doubt stifled in the provincial environment of Greece, she also suffered from the oppressive and frequently ill-mannered behaviour of her very wealthy, but boorish, husband. At the same time, Herodes used the dedication to demonstrate his respect for the Roman imperial house by placing statues of its members in the niches on the lower storey. By way of recompense, the Eleians set statues of Herodes' family in the upper storey. All of this was in the name of the lord of the sanctuary, Zeus, to whom the dedication was addressed.

186. Reconstruction drawing of part of the two-storey facade of the Nymphaion. It had eleven niches on each level, the lower one containing statues of the emperors Hadrian, Marcus Aurelius and Antoninus Pius and their families, and the upper one statues of Herodes Atticus and his household. At the centre of each storey was a statue of Zeus. Drawing: R. Bol.

187. Plan of the Nymphaion showing the positions of the statues when they were found. Athens, German Archaeological Institute.

188. Statue of a bull from the Nymphaion engraved with an inscription dedicating it to Zeus by Rhegilla, Herodes's wife. The statue was made in AD 153, the year that the Roman lady held the office of priestess of Demeter Chamyne. Olympia, Archaeological Museum.

189. Statue of Antinoos, the favourite of the emperor Hadrian. On the emperor's orders, numerous statues of the young man were erected throughout the Roman empire (first half of the 2nd c. AD). Olympia, Archaeological Museum.

190. Plan of the sanctuary at Olympia in the Roman period. Athens, German Archaeological Institute.

188

189

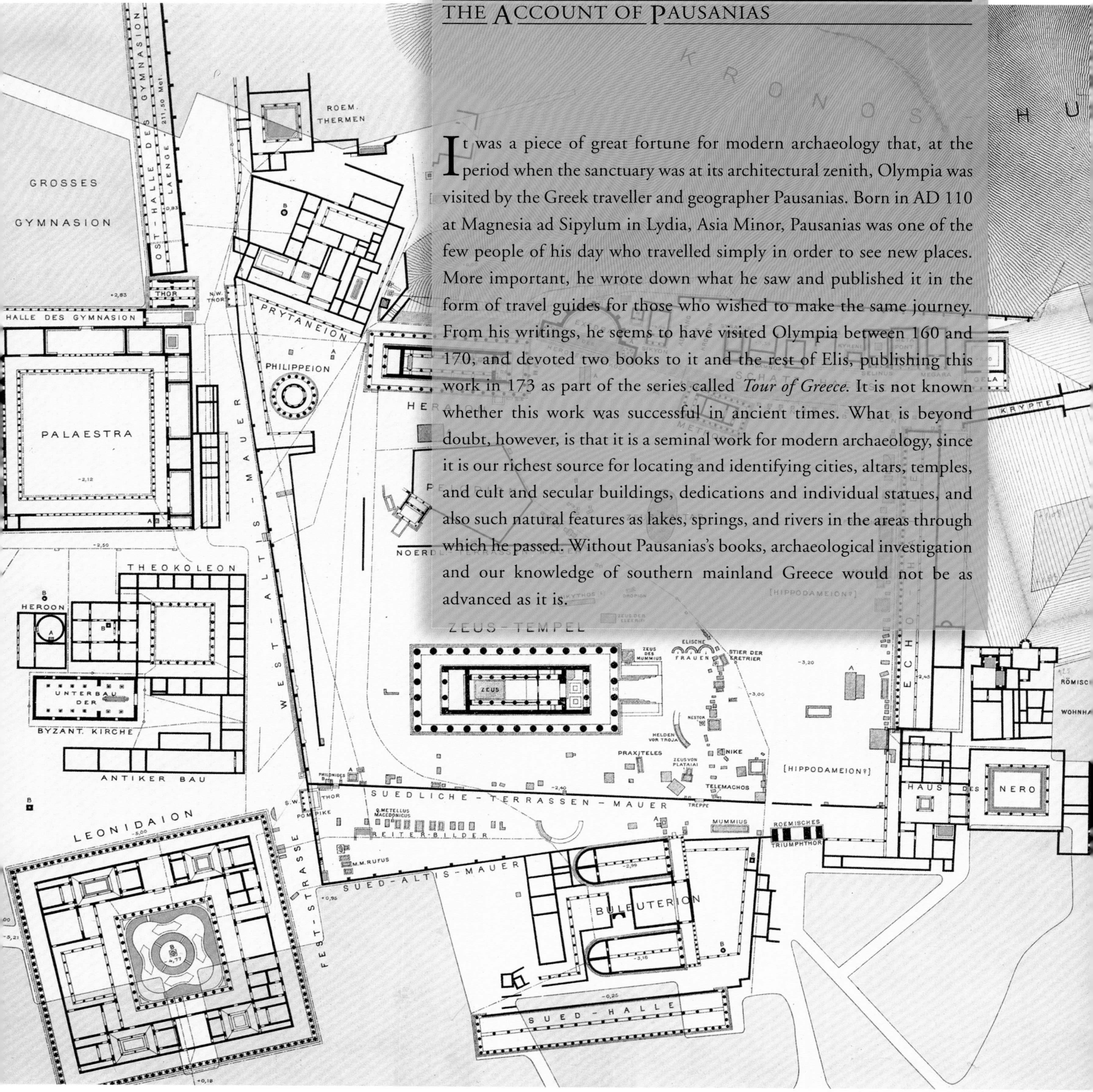

THE ACCOUNT OF PAUSANIAS

It was a piece of great fortune for modern archaeology that, at the period when the sanctuary was at its architectural zenith, Olympia was visited by the Greek traveller and geographer Pausanias. Born in AD 110 at Magnesia ad Sipylum in Lydia, Asia Minor, Pausanias was one of the few people of his day who travelled simply in order to see new places. More important, he wrote down what he saw and published it in the form of travel guides for those who wished to make the same journey. From his writings, he seems to have visited Olympia between 160 and 170, and devoted two books to it and the rest of Elis, publishing this work in 173 as part of the series called *Tour of Greece*. It is not known whether this work was successful in ancient times. What is beyond doubt, however, is that it is a seminal work for modern archaeology, since it is our richest source for locating and identifying cities, altars, temples, and cult and secular buildings, dedications and individual statues, and also such natural features as lakes, springs, and rivers in the areas through which he passed. Without Pausanias's books, archaeological investigation and our knowledge of southern mainland Greece would not be as advanced as it is.

The Games

There are many wonderful things to see and hear in Greece; but god himself cares for the mysteries at Eleusis and the games at Olympia.

Pausanias

191. Winged Victory crowns a victor. The scene is watched by another athlete and an official. Panathenaic amphora by the potter Nikodemos and the Wedding Procession Painter (363/362 BC). Los Angeles, J. Paul Getty Museum.

192. Detail from the same vase.

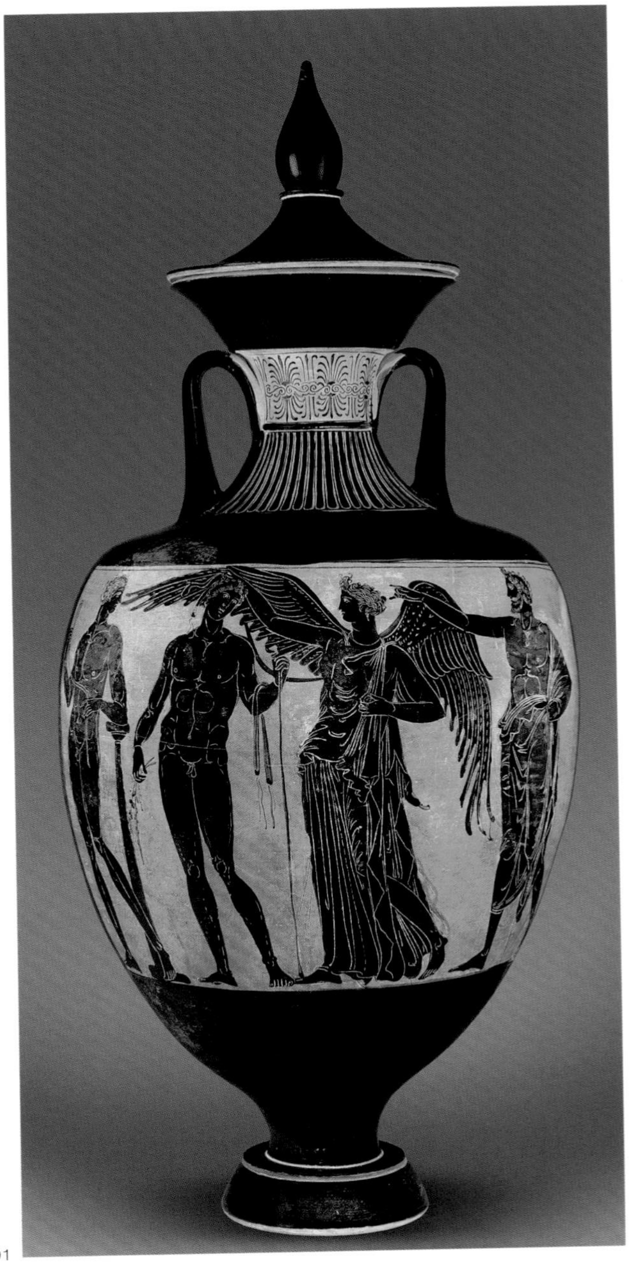

191

The Olympic games were held every four years at the second full moon after the summer solstice, falling, that is, during the first two weeks of August. The picture formed of this festival, a picture of grandeur and glory, is in keeping with the dim, glamorised picture we have of ancient Greece as a whole. Things cannot have been exactly like this, however, at least at a mundane, practical level. The confluence of about 40,000 people, judging by the capacity of the Classical stadium, the jostling together of humans with thousands of animals (some beasts of burden, some sacrificial animals), the lack of sanitation, and the warm, damp landscape next to the rivers did not form the best conditions for holding the festival and the games.

According to one ancient anecdote, a miller from Chios threatened his slave that if he didn't work well he would send him to Olympia to watch the games. And the Stoic philosopher Epictetos (1st-2nd c. AD) writes: 'And what do you do at Olympia? Don't you melt in the heat? Don't you get jostled in the crowds? Don't you encounter a thousand problems when you want to wash? Don't you get soaked when it rains? Don't you suffer from the noise, the shouting and other hassle? But it seems to me you put up with all this because what you're going to see is worth it.'

Indeed, everything that took place at Olympia was spectacular and exciting. There you could watch the greatest games of the ancient world: in the stadium you could admire the cream of youth and the greatest athletes competing in the races, the throwing events, and the heavy contests (boxing, wrestling, and pankration); in the great hippodrome were the finest breeds of horses, ridden by the finest riders, racing or pulling chariots. And all this excitement and splendor took place in a superb natural setting, full of fine temples and wonderful works of art, in an atmosphere of religious piety and devotion during the religious ceremonial, in the company of the ruling classes of all the Greek cities of motherland Greece, southern Italy, North Africa and Asia Minor.

The spectators who came to watch the games travelled on foot, by carriage, or by ship and frequently took several days to reach their destination. At a period when travel was infrequent, difficult and dangerous, it would have been a major decision to go to Olympia, and one that only the well-to-do could afford to make. It is impressive to learn that a Macedonian had attended 10 Olympic games, which means that he went from Macedonia to Olympia ten times over a period of at least 36 years.

192

193. View of the valley of Olympia today. During the games, the entire area around the sanctuary must have been full of tents and other makeshift lodgings, resembling a huge camping ground.

194. The interior courtyard of the Leonidaion, as remodelled in the Roman period, when the hotel was converted into the headquarters for the use of the Roman administration.

193

There were no permanent guest facilities for anyone other than the athletes and their trainers. Official representatives of the cities stayed in luxury tents that they brought with them and set up outside the sanctuary. The first baths complex was not erected until the 5th c. BC, and even this was probably only for the use of athletes. In the 4th c. BC, the first large hotel, the Leonidaion, was built at Olympia, only, of course, for distinguished visitors. Finally, large baths and wineshops were built in Roman times for entertaining and dining purposes, as well as fountains, which solved the problem of the supply of water to the site.

Most of the visitors lived and slept in the open, beneath the trees or in tents, ate makeshift food and, generally speaking, barely managed to meet their basic needs. None of this seriously troubled the ancient Greeks, who were accustomed to hardship and could easily endure uncomfortable conditions. What they were interested in, and took great care to achieve, was to be constantly on the move from the sanctuary to the stadium and from the temples to the hippodrome, so that they could participate in the successive cult rituals and sacrifices and watch the games in the very crowded programme.

194

195. Statue of a boy on a pedestal, probably a victor, wearing a wreath, with a bearded spectator, possibly his father or trainer, in front of him. Attic red-figure kylix by the Kiss Painter (500 BC). Baltimore, Johns Hopkins University.

196. The Leonidaion, the first large inn in the area of Olympia, built in the 4th c. BC. The Ionic capitals have been reset on their bases without the column shafts.

195

196

THE FESTIVAL PROGRAMME

The festival at Olympia usually lasted five days. On the first day, about midday, after the arrival of the priests, athletes, and trainers from Elis, where they had been preparing for a month, the organisational procedures began. All contributors to the games had to swear an oath that they would observe the rules, that they would compete fairly, and that they would not resort to cheating, bribery, or even magic. After this, the competitors enrolled, lots were drawn for the pairings in the heavy events and for the order of competition in the throwing events. In the afternoon, the entire programme for the games was written on leukomata – planks of wood painted white – and posted for all to see. The day was brought to a close with sacrifices to the gods and invocations for them to favour their own athletes and bring them victory.

On the second day, the boys' events were held in the stadium – first the heats and then the final for all the events, in turn, in which boys competed: the foot races, wrestling, boxing and pankration. The third day was devoted

197. Two athletes wearing victory wreaths and holding skewers with pieces of meat offer a sacrifice after their victories in the games. To the left of the altar with offerings is a man making a libation from a kylix; on the far right is a flute player. A winged Victory hovers above the altar. Red-figure stamnos by Polygnotos (460-440 BC). London, British Museum.

198. An athlete wearing a wreath ties his sandal. A sponge and an aryballos, used to clean the body, hang on the wall. Red-figure kylix by the Nikosthenes Painter (510-500 BC). Los Angeles, J. Paul Getty Museum.

199. An athlete prepares to throw the javelin, which he balances in his outstretched left hand. Attic red-figure lekythos in the style of the Providence Painter (470-460 BC). Athens, National Archaeological Museum.

197

200. A young athlete practices jumping. He has raised the two halteres (weights) and is leaning forward as he prepares to make a quick start. Attic red-figure lekythos by the Bowdoin Painter (475-470 BC). Athens, National Archaeological Museum.

201. A discus thrower and a judge. Panathenaic amphora (450 BC). Naples, National Archaeological Museum.

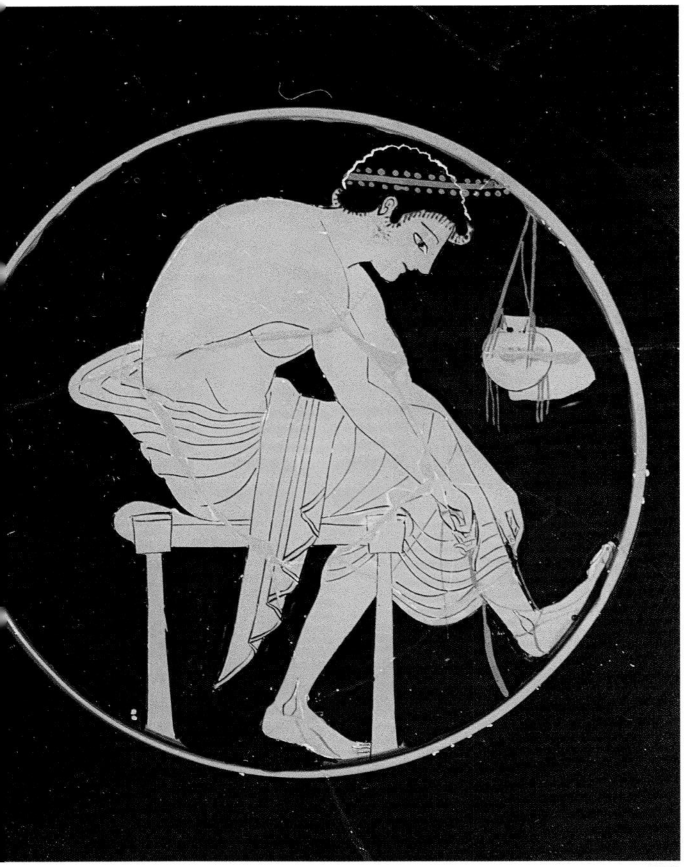

198

199

200

201

202

to equestrian events and the pentathlon. In the morning, spectators went to the hippodrome to watch the races and chariot races involving horses of various types and ages. When one reflects that about twenty chariots normally took part in the great chariot race, it is easy to understand why it was one of the most spectacular of all the events at Olympia. In the afternoon, the spectators moved to the stadium for the events in the pentathlon. The athletes competed in the jump, discus, stadion race, javelin and wrestling. In the evening, under the full August moon, religious rituals were held in honour of Pelops, the hero who founded the games.

202. Bronze relief of a jockey from the sanctuary of Zeus at Dodona. The naked rider tightly holds the reigns of the horse and urges it to gallop with his stick. This small relief served as decoration for a large bronze dedication (second half of the 6th c. BC). Athens, National Archaeological Museum.

203. Scene from a chariot race. The charioteer wearing a white chiton drives the four horses. Panathenaic amphora by the Kleophrades Painter (490-480 BC). Los Angeles, J. Paul Getty Museum.

204. The race in armour. The hoplites are shown running naked, only carrying shields and wearing helmets. Panathenaic amphora from the Nikomachos group, from Bengazi in Cyrenaica (323/322 BC). Paris, Louvre Museum.

205. Pentathlete competition, from left: jumping, javelin, discus, javelin. Panathenaic amphora by the Euphiletos Painter (530-510 BC). London, British Museum.

203

The fourth day was the most brilliant of the festival, and commenced with great religious ceremonies in honour of Zeus. A large and solemn procession, in which the priests, games officials, athletes and trainers took part, formed in the gymnasium and moved to the great altar of Zeus. This altar was the old cone of ash formed from the remains of successive sacrifices, and was ten metres in diameter and 7 high in Pausanias's day. Here a hecatomb (one hundred oxen) was offered to Zeus, after which the meat was roasted and distributed to all in attendance.

Directly afterwards, spectators rushed to the stadium for the men's events. First came the foot races: the stadion (sprint), diaulos (middle distance), and dolichos (long distance), with the heats first, followed by the final. Wrestling

204

began early in the afternoon, followed by boxing and pankration. The final athletic event of the day was the race in full hoplite armour.

The fifth and final day of the festival was given over to the announcement and crowning of the winners. This was done by the most senior Hellanodikes and took place in the pronaos of the Temple of Zeus, beneath the metopes depicting the labours of Herakles, the greatest of the heroes and the ideal model of ancient athletes. All the spectators gathered in the open area around the temple. Some stood on the stepped terrace of the treasuries and others on the embankments of the stadium so that they could watch the ceremony and cheer the victors. At midday, the Eleian organisers gave an official banquet in the Prytaneion in honour of the winners; in the evening, the whole of Olympia echoed to the parties, singing and shouting of those attending private dinners and banquets held by the relatives, friends, and even the cities of the victors.

205

These festivals were undoubtedly attended by those who had undertaken, for a high fee and after a commission from the interested parties, to immortalise the great victories: sculptors like Myron, Polykleitos and Lysippos, who carved the magnificent nude statues of the victors, and poets, such as Pindar, Bacchylides and Simonides, whose music and verses hymned the victors at the great games.

206. Two winged Victories prepare to tie ribbons around the body of a young athlete standing next to an altar. Red-figure kylix by the Briseis Painter (480 BC). Paris, Louvre Museum.

207. Scene of a victor being awarded a prize. The wreathed athlete has the ribbons symbolising his victory around his body and holds the branches offered to him by the official, who is also wearing a wreath. Red-figure kylix by Epiktetos (early 5th c.). Paris, Louvre Museum.

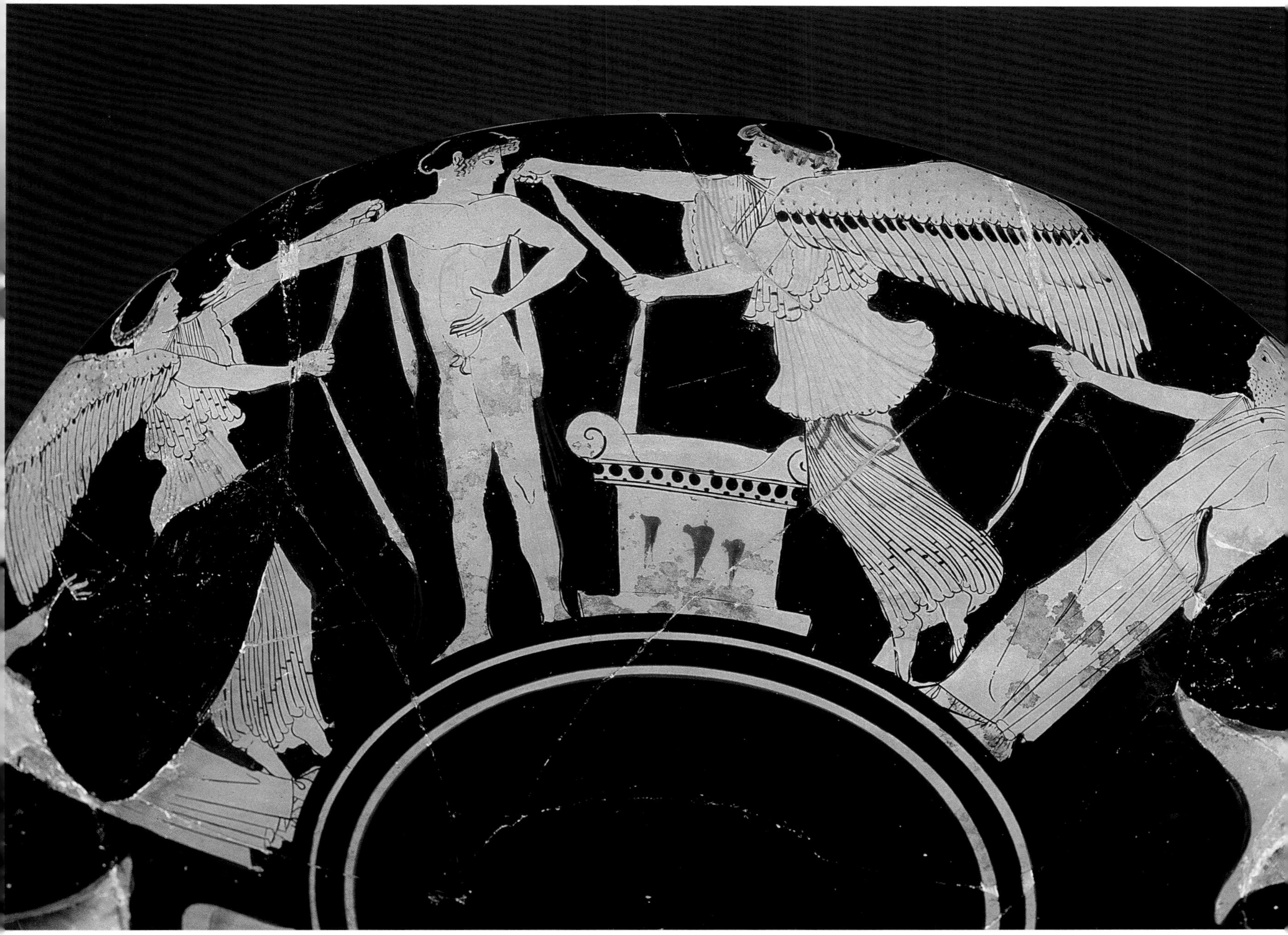

206

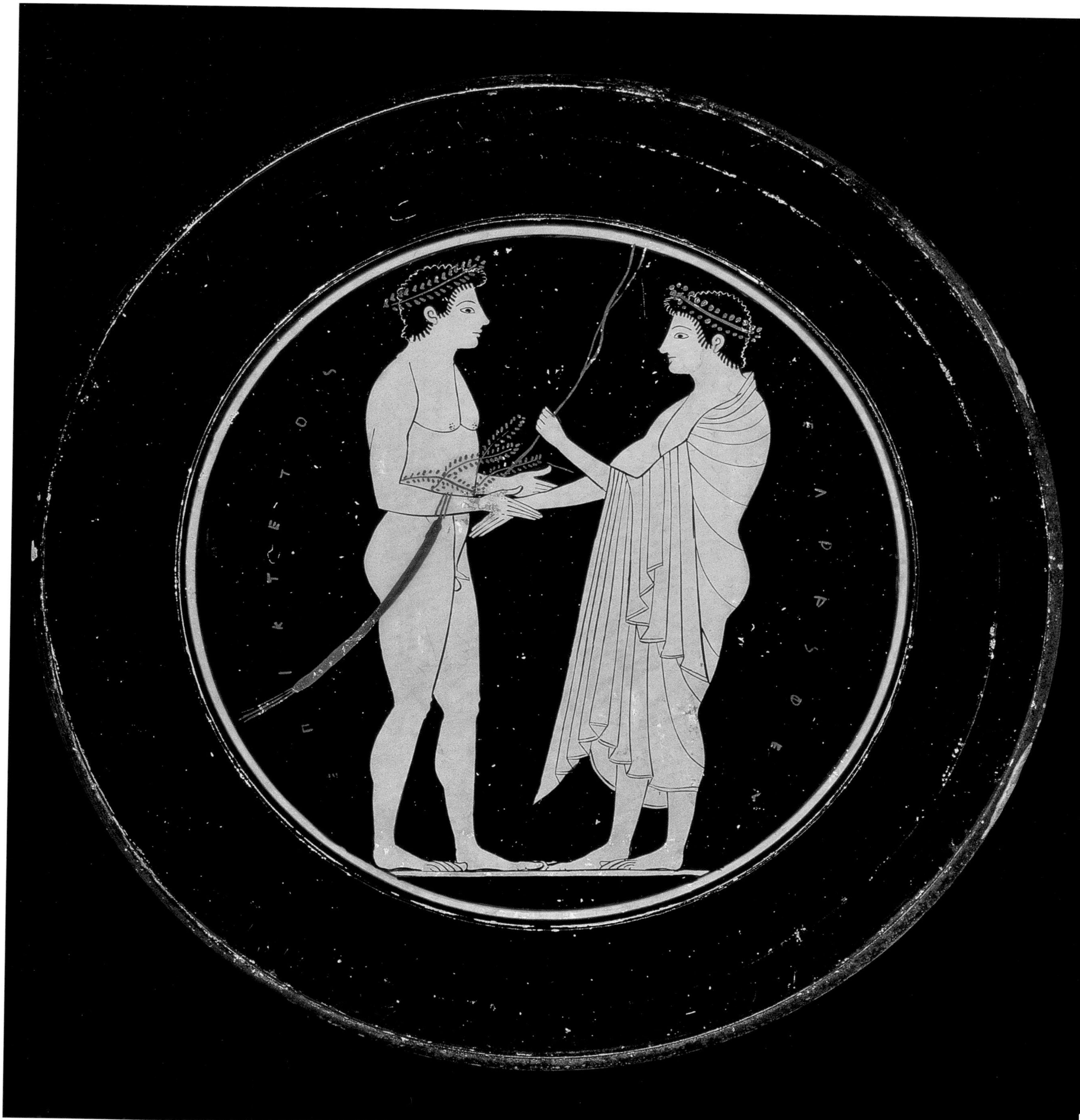

207

3rd - 4th c. AD
Olympia in Late Antiquity

The year AD 212 was an important landmark in the history of the games. It was in that year that the Roman emperor Caracalla extended the right of Roman citizenship to all free inhabitants of the empire. This right meant that any citizen of the empire, even those of barbarian origin, such as the Armenians and Galatians, had the right to compete in the Olympic games, a circumstance that gave them an ecumenical character.

In the 3rd c. AD, Olympia appears to have been struck by a series of earthquakes, resulting in the destruction of many of the old and modern buildings. Repairs have been noted to the water spouts of the Temple of Zeus, the South Stoa and the Leonidaion, while renovations and even the construction of new buildings can be seen in the baths, possibly connected with an increase in the number and the demands of visitors or with the need for facilities for athletic associations. There is no literary or archaeological evidence for the widely accepted view that Olympia was plundered in AD 267 by the barbarian tribe of Herulians, who swept over the whole of southern Greece. The fact that the chryselephantine statue of Zeus still stood in place a century later weakens this hypothesis. The priests and the inhabitants of the region seem, however, to have erected a makeshift defensive wall in the sanctuary to protect the temple and the dedications in its enclosure. This 400-meter-long wall was 3 meters thick and was constructed of material taken from many of the buildings in the sanctuary that had been reduced to ruins by the earthquakes. The Echo Stoa, Metroon, Pelopeion, Leonidaion and Bouleuterion all disappeared in this fashion. The stones of these buildings that can now be seen *in situ* came mainly from the dismemberment of the defensive wall by the first excavators of the site.

The earthquake devastation was followed by fresh flooding of the Kladeos, the waters of which broke the very ancient barrier on its left bank in the late 3rd or early 4th century and demolished and carried away the west part of the sanctuary, while covering a large part of it with mud. The excellent state of preservation of Praxiteles' Hermes and other statues found in the Heraion is owed largely to the thick layer of mud that covered them.

Given these natural disasters, we naturally form the impression that at this time Olympia was in total decline. Recent investigations and finds, however, indicate that not only was this not the case, but that the games continued to

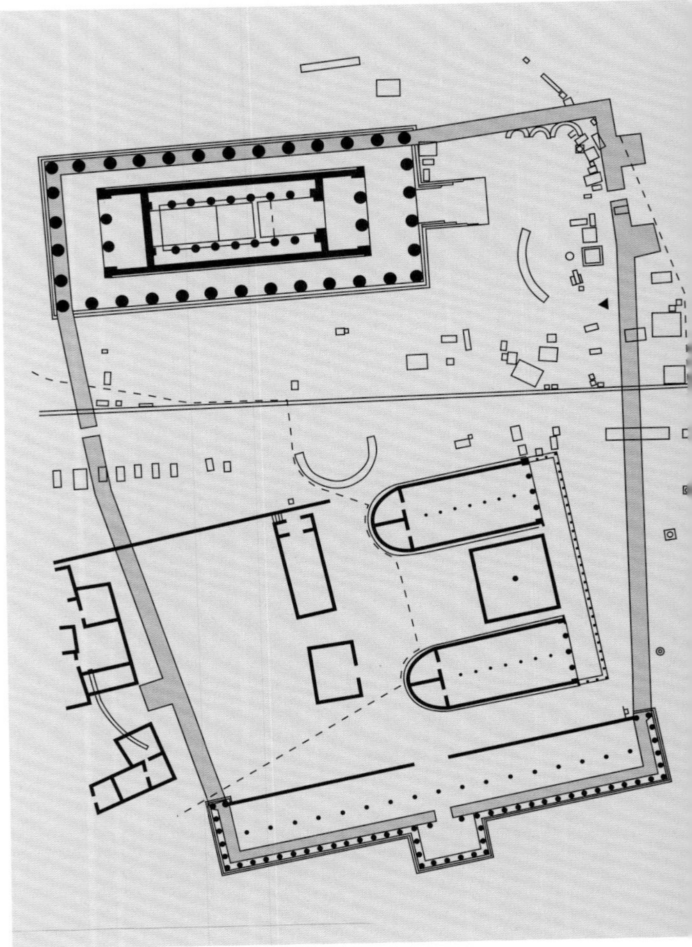

208

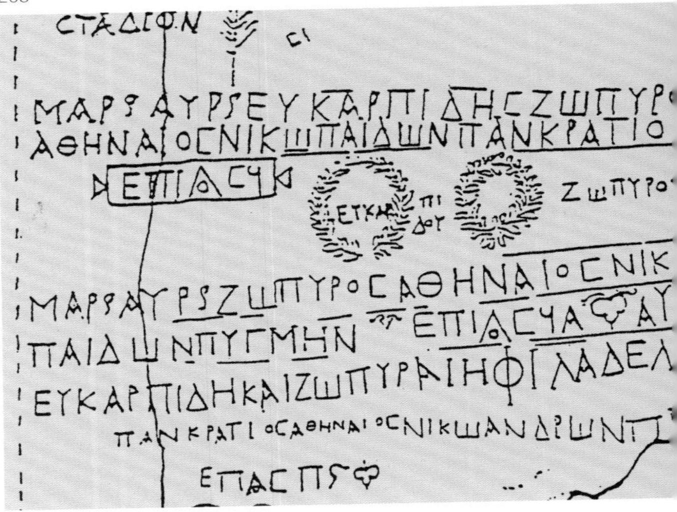

209

be held normally and the sanctuary to function fully. The find from the athletes' club mentioned above (page 139) is of very great significance: it is a bronze plaque measuring 75 by 40 cm. that bore a long inscription with the names of athletes, presumably members of the club, their birthplace, the nature of the event, and the date of their victory at Olympia. The inscription tells us that cult events and games continued to be held normally at Olympia even during the 4th c. AD, adhering faithfully to the programme established in the Classical period.

210

208. Plan showing the Late Roman wall, built around the Temple of Zeus in the 3rd c. AD, for the purpose of protecting the temple and some of the valuable dedications. It incorporated the Bouleuterion and the South Stoa.

209. Detail from a bronze inscription of the 4th c. AD referring to, among others, the Athenian Zopyros, victor in the boys' pankration.

210. Tower on the west side of the Roman wall, built of reused architectural members, most of them from the Leonidaion, which collapsed in this period as a result of an earthquake.

The view that the globalisation of the games led to the displacement of Greek athletes by others from the provinces of the Roman empire can also be shown to be erroneous. The inscription refers not only to athletes from Asia Minor but also to Greeks from Thespiai, Elis and Athens. The last Olympic victor from this particular association is said to have been an Athenian, Zopyros, who won the boys' pankration in the 291st Olympiad in AD 385.

THE END OF THE OLYMPIC GAMES

Thus, the festival at Olympia, which was held every four years, became extinct.

Kedrenos

We usually read that in AD 393, after the edict of Theodosius the Great closing the pagan sanctuaries, the Olympic games also ceased to be held. This is by no means certain, for forty years later Theodosius II the Younger was obliged to issue another edict, thereby demonstrating that the first was ineffective, as possibly was the second. The old religion, together with the strong social and economic network of professional athletes, continued to offer resistance. What can safely be said today is that the games did not disappear gradually, after a long period of decline and decay, but were abruptly terminated by an order from above, on the grounds that they were an activity associated with paganism. Whatever the case, one of the longest lasting institutions in the history of human civilisation came to an end about the beginning of the 5th century, after an impressive continuity of almost 1,170 years.

211

211. Relief scene on the pillar that supported the obelisk erected in AD 390/391 by the emperor Theodosius I in the hippodrome of Constantinople. The emperor and his family are depicted in their special box in the hippodrome, flanked by a military guard. Constantinople, Atmeidan Square.

212. View from the southwest of the Early Christian basilica built upon the walls of Pheidias's workshop.

213. Detail of an arch from the Early Christian basilica. Limestone blocks from Pheidias's workshop and parts of ancient marble architectural reliefs were used in its construction.

214. Plan of the Early Christian basilica, showing the modifications made to the original building of Pheidias's workshop to accommodate its new function. Drawing: Olympia Bericht *II, pl. 68.*

A Christian Village at Olympia

212

213

Life did not come to end on the slopes of Kronios with the dissolution of the sanctuary. The buildings that remained standing – guesthouses, baths and wineshops – were converted and began to be used as residences, since a flourishing Christian settlement involved in agricultural activities developed at Olympia in the 5th and 6th centuries. Excavations have revealed vessels and implements for farmwork in many of the houses and several facilities for processing produce, including fourteen wine presses. Pottery workshops manufacturing vases and lamps were also discovered. Study of the pottery from the settlement has shown that, in addition to local products, the inhabitants used fine-quality vases from the two large production centres of the day, North Africa and Asia Minor. Even at this period, in other words, Olympia was connected with the Mediterranean trade network, just as in its brilliant past. Much evidence was also derived from the excavation of about 200 graves found near the houses, not, as was usually the case, in an organised cemetery some distance from the settlement.

The building chosen by the inhabitants to meet the needs of their worship is also interesting. About the middle of the 5th century, the large workshop of Pheidias was selected for this purpose and converted into an Early Christian basilica. Standing opposite the ancient Temple of Zeus, the equally large Christian church clearly denoted the victory of Christianity over paganism. As he had done with the rest of his world, Zeus surrendered his largest sanctuary, Olympia, to Christianity.

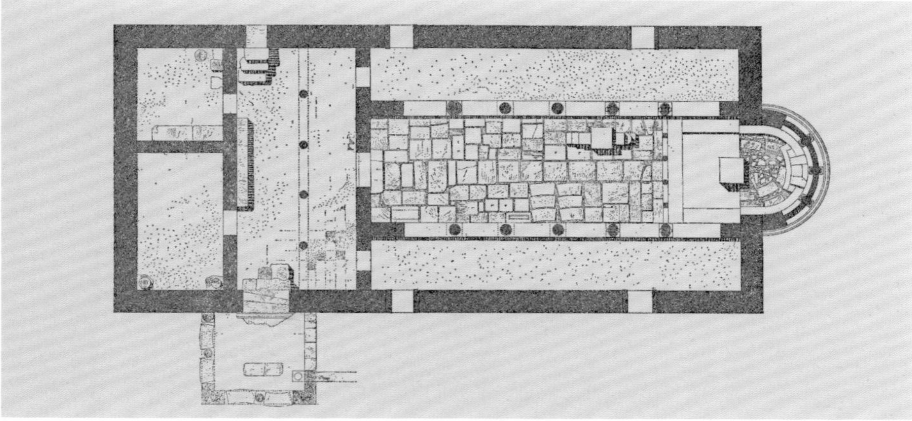
214

GYMNASION
PALAESTRA
PRYTANEION
PHILIPPEION
HERAION
PELOPION
ZEUS-TEMPEL ZEUS-TEMPEL
HEROON
BYZ. KIRCHE
LEONIDAION
DER BYZANTINISCHEN FESTUNG
BULEUTERION
BULEUTERION

215

THE ABANDONMENT OF OLYMPIA

The great earthquake that shook the Peloponnese in AD 522 or 551 appears to have reduced the settlement at Olympia to ruins. The Temple of Zeus, which had remained standing down to this time, also collapsed. After a brief resettlement of the area to the north of the Kronios hill by Slavs, which lasted until the early 7th century, the rivers covered everything that remained standing with mud.

Thus, after a millennium, an event-filled period that changed the course of history, Olympia reverted once more to a small agricultural and stockraising settlement, the form in which it had begun its rise to glory in the Early Helladic period. The Alpheios and Kladeos rivers were allowed to seal its end with mud – the same rivers that had initially supplied the incentive for the sanctuary to emerge on the stage of history and illuminate with its light not only the ancient but also the modern world.

216

215. Plan of the site of Olympia during the Early Christian period, when houses were built on the ancient ruins. Athens, German Archaeological Institute.

216. Group of vases from the Slav cemetery at Olympia, the latest evidence of habitation in the region (7th c. AD). Olympia, Archaeological Museum.

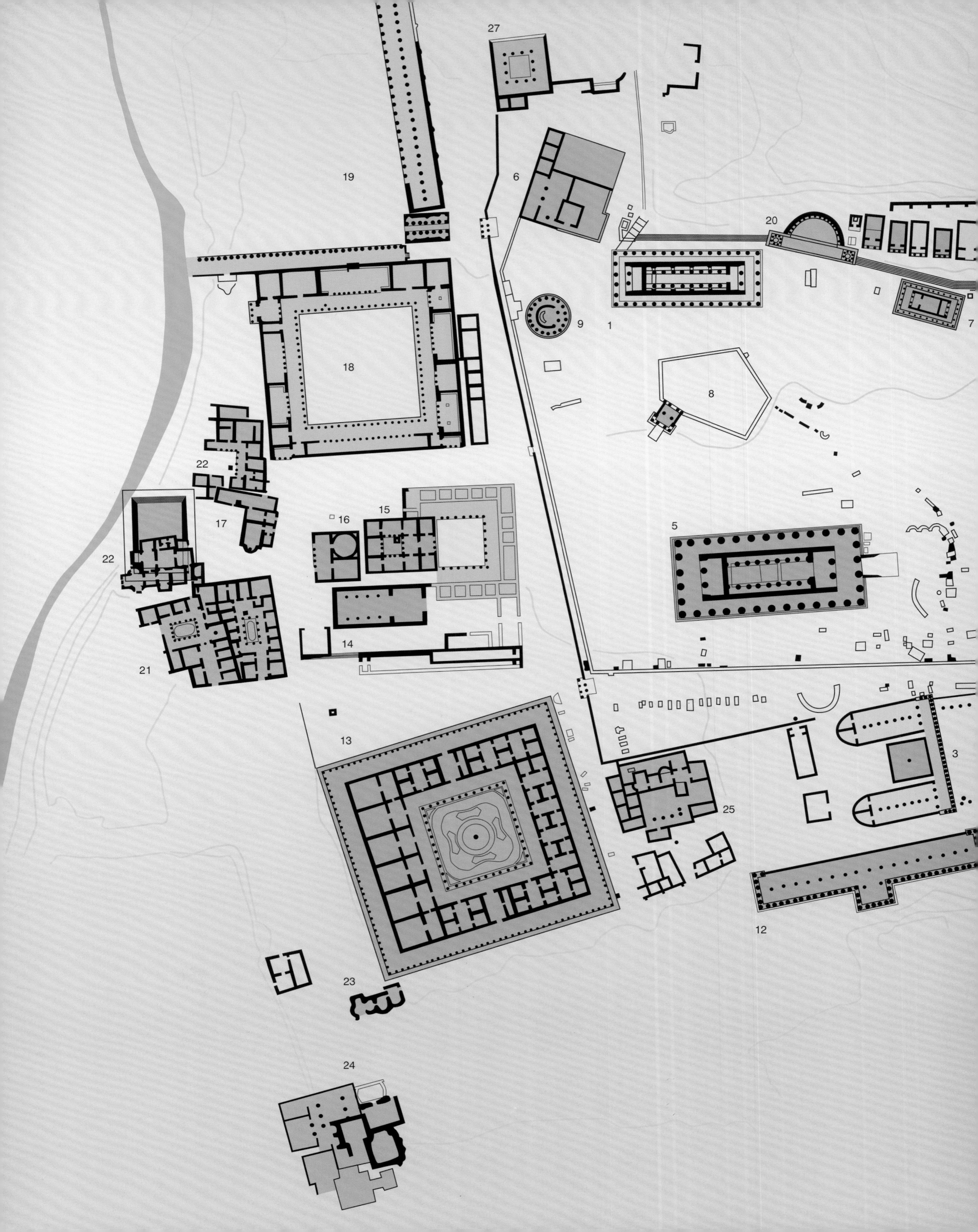
27
19
6
20
1
9
7
18
8
22
15
16
17
22
5
14
21
13
3
25
12
23
24

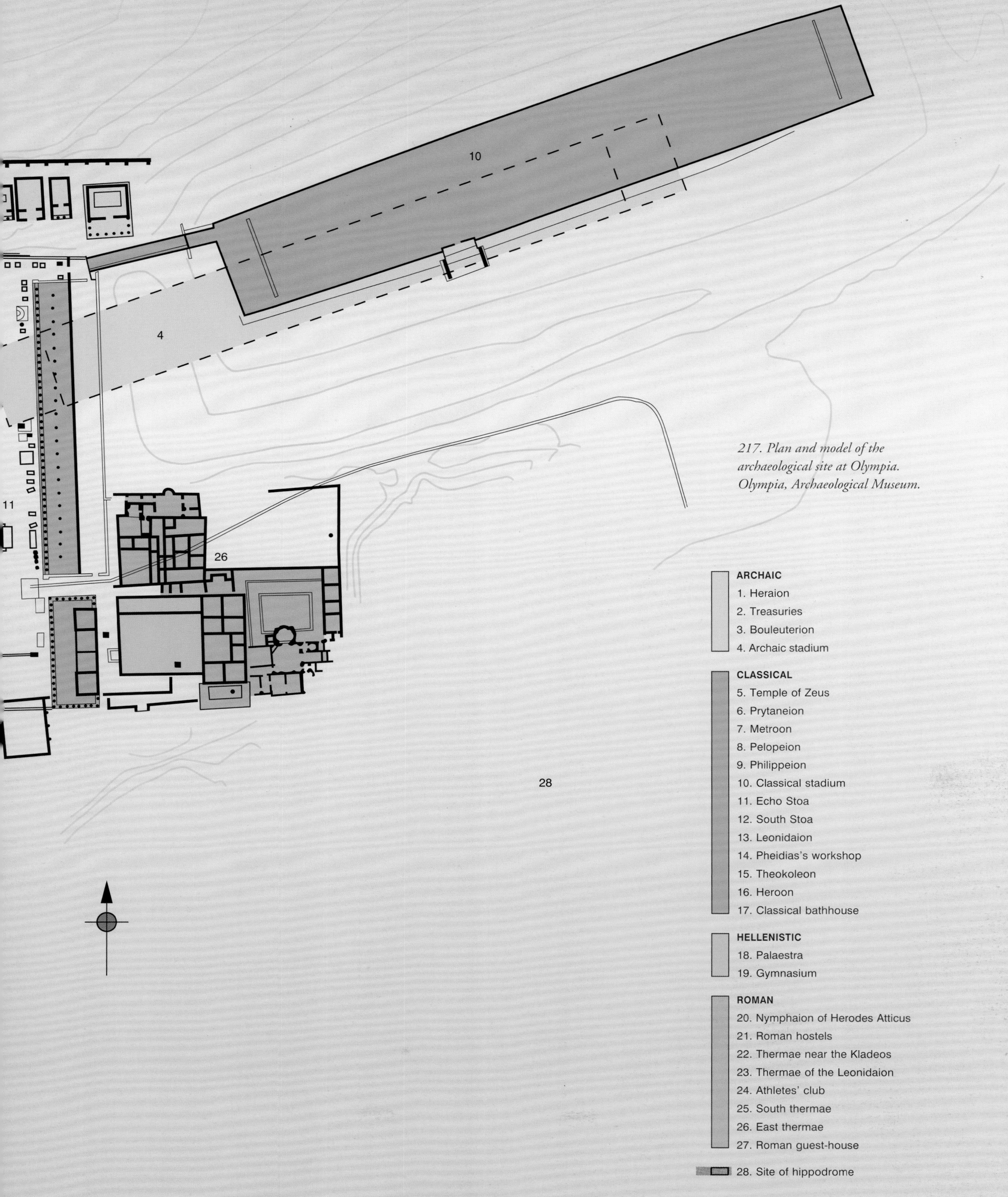

217. Plan and model of the archaeological site at Olympia. Olympia, Archaeological Museum.

DELPHI

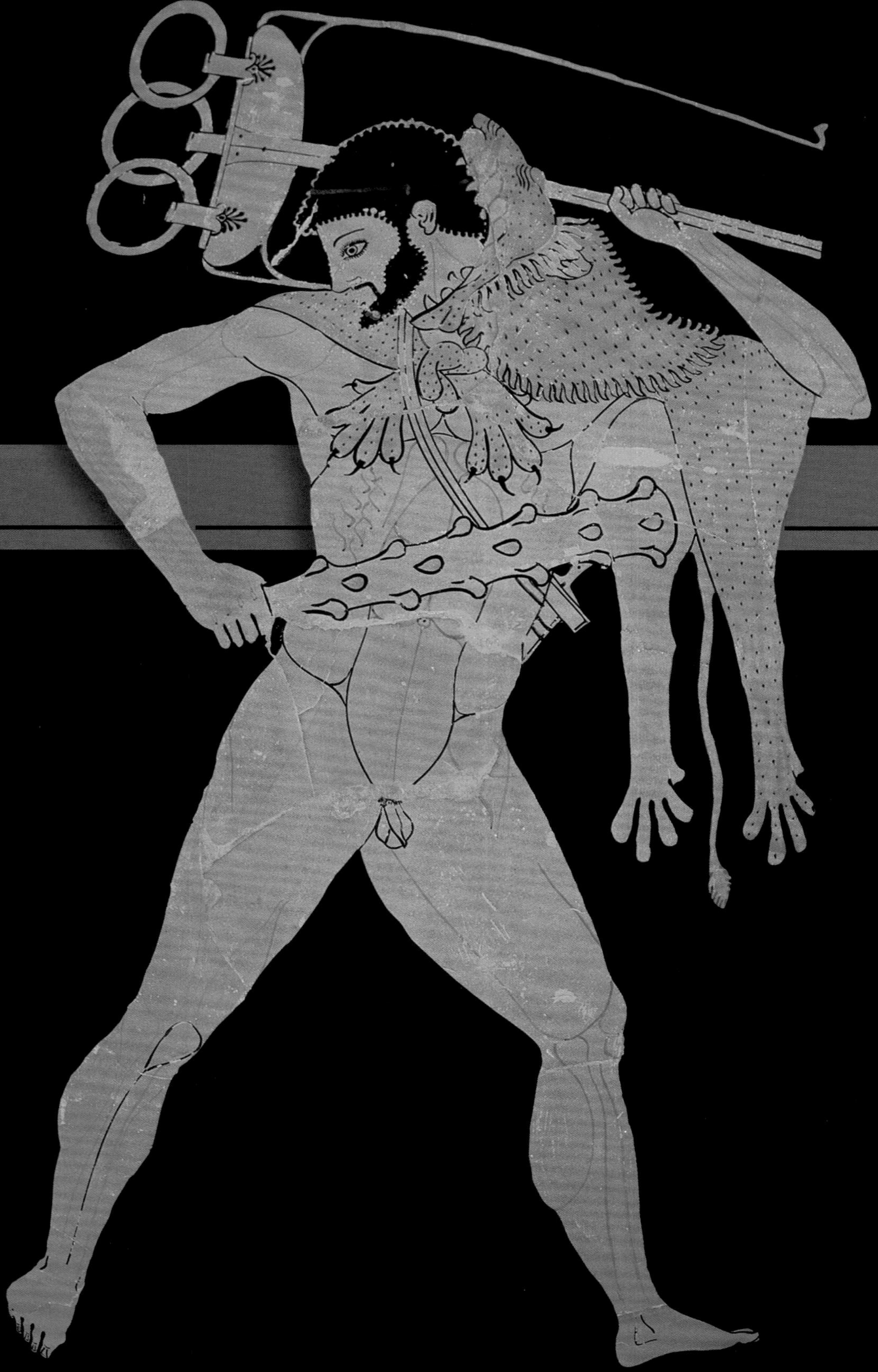

The Site

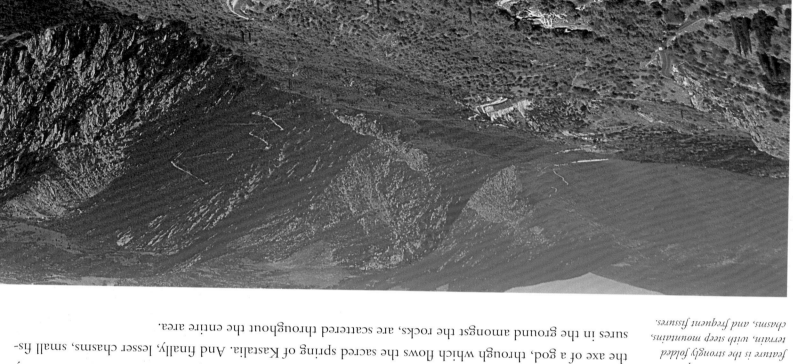

Apollo leaped swiftly to a mountain range and came to Krisa, beneath cloudy Parnassos, on a height facing west. Rocks hang over Krisa and a wild gorge passes below. There the lord Phoibos chose to build his temple.

Homeric Hymn to Apollo

218. The importance of Delphi in the ancient world has been rendered in art in a variety of ways. Here, Herakles seizes the Delphic tripod, in order to found his own oracle, according to one myth. Red-figure amphora by the Berlin Painter, early 5th c. BC. Würzburg, Martin von Wagner Museum.

219. Panoramic view of the surrounding area of Delphi to the east. The most important feature is the strongly folded terrain, with steep mountains, chasms, and frequent fissures.

Delphi is indeed a unique place, possibly the most impressive site in the Classical world. As visitors approach it, descending from Arachova along the road taken by Apollo, they sense the presence of the divine long before they see the monuments and the archaeological sites. For Delphi, built amphitheatrically on the edge of a cliff at a height of 533-600 m. above sea level, offers a sight that one rarely has the opportunity to enjoy. The sanctuary nestles in the embrace of Parnassos, dominating and offering a panoramic view over the plain of Krisa, the Gulf of Corinth, and the mountains of the northern Peloponnese. The entire area is full of unusual natural chasms. First, the deep valley of the Pleistos, between the south slope of Parnassos and Kirphys, the bare mountain that blocks our view to the south. Then the chasm between the two Phaidriades rocks, which seem to have been cleaved by the axe of a god, through which flows the sacred spring of Kastalia. And finally, lesser chasms, small fissures in the ground amongst the rocks, are scattered throughout the entire area.

219

221

222

220

221

220-222. Wishing to discover the centre of the world, Zeus released two eagles, one from the east and one from the west. The two met at Delphi, establishing the importance of the site and giving it the name of the omphalos *(navel) of the earth. This myth, certainly a fabrication of the priests of Apollo, required illustration: a conical stone with curved sides was made and called omphalos, and the two birds were placed on top of it. This stone was one of the symbols of the sanctuary at Delphi and stood in the adyton of the temple, while many copies of it were placed at different points in the sanctuary. The omphalos here, covered with the sacred woollen net, the* agrenon, *is of Roman date.*

Foundation Myths and Legends

223

The motivation behind the foundation of a cult, irrespective of the religion in question, is often provided by unaccountable natural phenomena, visions, and so on, which faith and superstition attribute to the divine presence. The ancient Greeks wove myths around such phenomena, involving gods, heroes, humans and animals.

According to an ancient myth, the foundation of the oracle at Delphi was attributed to a chasm: a shepherd noticed vapours rising from a fissure in the ground and the strange behavior of goats standing over it, and, nearing it himself, he became dizzy and began to utter inarticulate cries. His behavior soon drew the attention of many others who, gathering there, likewise became dizzy. Some fell in, and a tripod – a vessel indicating the presence of the divine – was placed above the chasm, and the oracle was founded.

Most scholars have regarded this myth as expressing an ancient popular tradition, one that provided an aetiological explanation of the main features of the oracular process: namely, the existence of a cleft in the earth below the Temple of Apollo, where the oracular responses were given, and the inspiration the priestess, the Pythia, received from breathing vapours as she sat on the oracular tripod. However, some believed that the tradition was probably not far from the truth, since, as mentioned above, many chasms did exist, and vapours arose from one of these, to the south of the Amalia Hotel, in the modern town of Delphi, until about the middle of the 20th century.

223. Aigeus, the mythical king of Athens, seeks an oracle from Themis, seated on a tripod in the sanctuary at Delphi. Themis was one of the earlier deities at Delphi who, according to tradition, occupied the site before the arrival of Apollo. Red-figure kylix by the Kodros Painter (ca. 440 BC). Berlin, Staatliche Museen zu Berlin-Preussischer Kulturbesitz, Antikensammlung.

224. Apollo welcomes Dionysos at Delphi, above the omphalos, one of the characteristic symbols of the site. Red-figure krater by the Kadmos Painter (early 4th c. BC). St. Petersburg, Hermitage Museum.

A recent investigation conducted by American geologists has provided a definitive explanation. Study of samples of the schist of Delphi from below the Temple of Apollo revealed that they contained 'frozen drops' of mild hallucinogenic gases such as ethane, methane and ethylene, which were probably carried to the surface by the waters of the springs in the area. This discovery not only confirms the truth of the foundation myth of the sanctuary, but also supports the ancient sources concerning what transpired during the issuing of an oracle (see page 262).

A different tradition regarding the foundation of the sanctuary at Delphi is to be found in the *Homeric Hymn to Apollo*, a poem in Homeric style but definitely later than Homer himself. According to this, Apollo himself came down to earth to search for a suitable place in which to found the first oracle for humans. Having wandered over several regions in central Greece, he came to Delphi, beneath cloud-covered Parnassos, and the place, which was then called Pytho, seemed a suitable one to found

225

his oracle. However, it was already occupied by other deities, such as Gaia, her daughter Themis, and Poseidon, and was guarded by a terrible female serpent called Python. According to the myth, Apollo fought and killed the Python, becoming the sole, undisputed occupant of the place. From the place-name Pytho, the god was called Pythios, his priestess Pythia, and his festival the Pythia. The god had to be purified after killing the serpent and went for this purpose to Tempe, from where he brought his sacred plant, the laurel.

This tradition seems to have been the official view of the Delphic priesthood concerning the foundation of the oracle. The style and spirit of the hymn, and the fact that it probably dates from the 7th or early 6th c. BC, indicate that the narrative was

226

created and disseminated by the Delphic priesthood at a period when the oracle was called upon to define clearly its origins and its divine descent. The presence of the old gods at Delphi points to earlier religious beliefs associated with the worship of the earth, which found expression in snake worship (the Python) and stone worship (the omphalos, Sibyl's stone). The contest between Apollo and the Python is interpreted as giving expression to the conflict between the old, pre-Greek gods of darkness and natural phenomena and the new, Olympian gods of light and order, who were brought with them by the last Greek tribes during the so-called Dorian Invasion.

Despite this change, the earlier gods did not withdraw, but remained at Delphi as minor deities, who had their altars and sanctuaries and were the object of special cults. The essence of the great pre-Greek earth goddess (Gaia) was perhaps retained in the female goddess worshipped in the sanctuary of Pronaia, who was later crystallised in the form and with the name of Athena.

225. The young Apollo, in the arms of his mother, Leto, shoots an arrow at Pytho. Expanded drawing of the representation on a black-figure lekythos dating from 470 BC.

226. Apollo sits on an elaborate throne in his temple at Delphi, amongst the omphalos and tripod cauldrons. Red-figure krater by the Kleophon Painter (440-430 BC). Ferrara, Archaeological Museum.

227. The Apollonian Triad of Delphi shown in a marble votive relief. Apollo sits on the sacred tripod with his feet resting on a high footstool. To the left is Artemis, wearing a chiton and himation, which she draws up with her left hand, while her right hand rests on her bow. At the right is their mother, Leto, wearing a peplos, with her arm tenderly touching her son's shoulder (410 BC). Athens, National Archaeological Museum.

227

Apollo, unerring archer, you who rule the vale of the Pytho and dwell in your renowned temple. I pray to you oh lord!

Pindar

Apollo

It is no coincidence that some of the most fundamental beliefs of the Greek spirit are condensed in the person of the lord of Delphi. Apollo appears originally to have been a sun god who drove the chariot of the sun, thereby not only controlling light and darkness on earth, but, by extension, also maintaining universal harmony. The most appropriate expression of such harmony was music, and the god accordingly became known later as the patron of music. At the same time, since he was responsible for maintaining balance, he was also an avenging god, killing with his arrows anyone who transcended the human measure. In these capacities, Apollo exercised control of the requirements for human happiness or unhappiness and was therefore considered the god most suitable to reveal to mortals, through his oracles, the ways in which they could pursue the former and avoid the latter.

Finally, it is no coincidence that in the god's greatest sanctuary, at Delphi, the divine teaching early acquired secular and moral dimensions, and Pythian Apollo became men's guide not only in politics, but also in their personal lives. The god's advice was condensed into the adages written on the walls of the great temple from the 6th century on, which were regarded as apophthegms of the seven sages, men of antiquity distinguished by their wisdom. The most famous of these adages were *μηδὲν ἄγαν* ('nothing in excess') and *γνῶθι σαυτὸν* ('know thyself'). Here we have, in pithy form, two of the basic beliefs of ancient Greek ethics – moderation and self-knowledge – which have also been two of the most essential principles guiding mortals throughout the history of the human race.

228. The Belvedere Apollo. One of the finest statues of Apollo, strongly emphasising the essence of his divine nature. Roman marble copy of a bronze original dating from the second half of the 4th c. BC., attributed to the sculptor Leochares. Rome, Vatican Museum.

229. Many of the features of Apollo's divine substance are combined in this scene: the god plays music (musician) while seated on the prophetic tripod (prophet). The tripod has wings and flies above the sea, alluding to Apollo's original role as a sun god. Attic red-figure hydria by the Berlin Painter (5th c. BC). Rome, Vatican Museum.

229

Delphi Through the Ages

16th - 11th c. BC

The prehistoric settlement

The archaeological record suggests that Delphi was inhabited from as early as the 16th c. BC. The selection of this site for settlement was probably based on its strongly defensible position and the existence of a large number of copious springs. The earliest certain architectural remains, dating from the Late Mycenaean period (14th-12th c. BC), are house foundations in the east part of the sanctuary of Apollo and chamber tombs in the area near the present archaeological museum. An excavation beneath the temple revealed part of a fortification or retaining wall from this settlement that is 2 m. thick. About 1100 BC,

231. Map showing the springs at Delphi and the prehistoric remains excavated beneath the visible ruins of historical times. Drawing: S. Müller.

232. Five Late Mycenaean female figurines from the sanctuary of Athena Pronaia, stylised clay grave offerings from chamber tombs in the sanctuary (13th-12th c. BC). Delphi, Archaeological Museum.

233. Mycenaean vases from the chamber tombs in the area of the Museum (13th-12th c. BC). Delphi, Archaeological Museum.

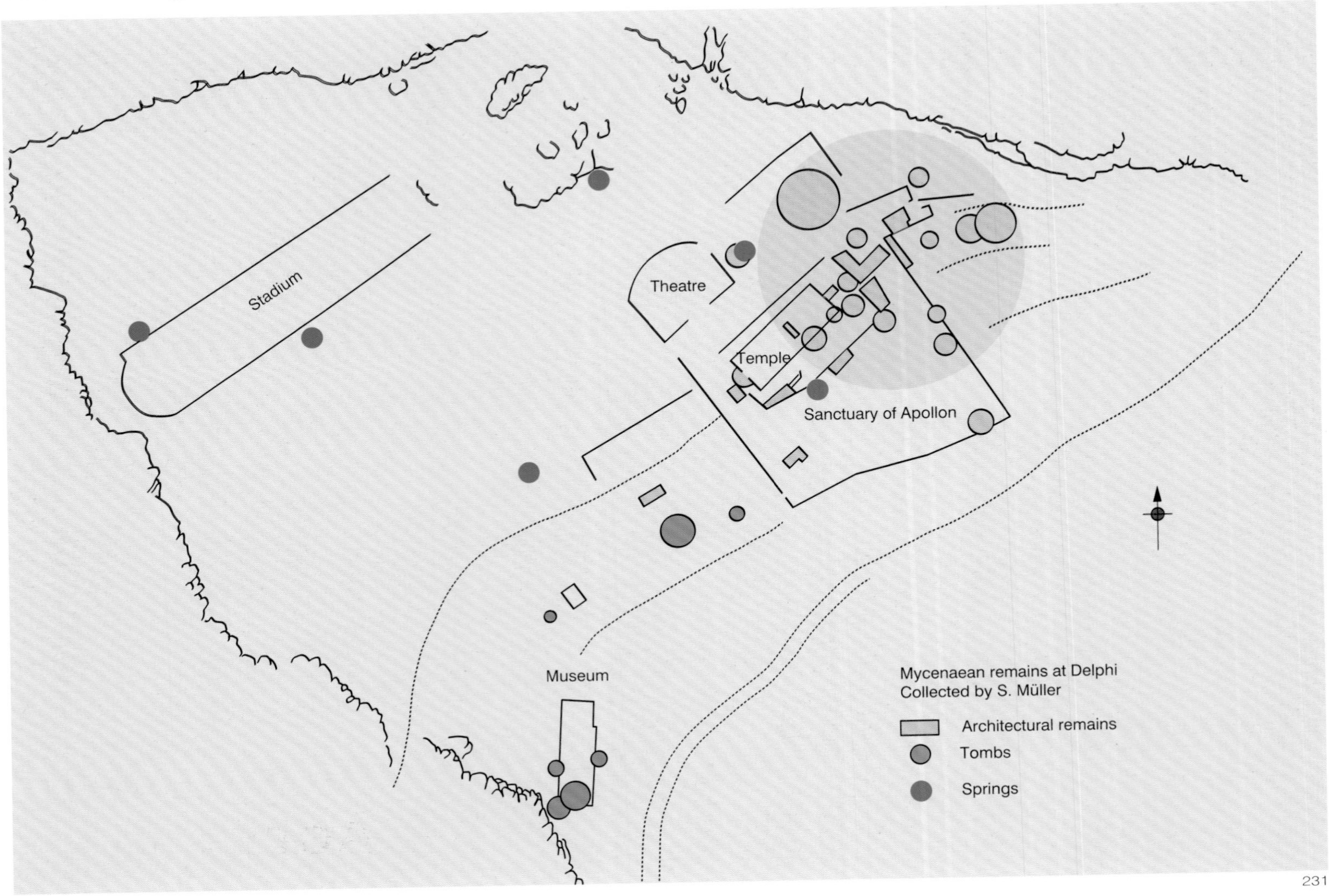

231

232

major landslides of mud and rock from the Phaidriades destroyed most of the houses and led to the abandonment of the larger part of the settlement.

The most important finds from the prehistoric settlement consist of fragments of clay and stone rhyta and of stylised terracotta figurines of women and bulls. These point to the existence of a cult, which probably formed the core of the later sanctuary of Apollo, though it cannot be assigned to a specific area.

A large group of 175 Mycenaean terracotta female figurines was found, together with many vases and small finds, beneath the altar of Athena in the sanctuary of the Pronaia. For many years, this find provided support for the view that the cult of a female deity existed on this site in Mycenaean times already and that this cult crystallised in historical times around Athena. More recent study of the find, however, has demonstrated that the figurines and other objects were grave offerings from Mycenaean tombs, which the ancient Greeks may have found nearby and buried when they established the first temple of Athena in the 7th c. BC. In this way they reinforced the sacred character of the site of the new temple. The view that there was a prehistoric cult dedicated to the Pronaia should, therefore, be ruled out.

233

10th - 8th c. BC

The arrival of Apollo

234

235

During the following period (10th-9th c. BC), the finds are far fewer, but without interruption. From the 8th century onwards, the settlement expanded once more, the number of finds increases impressively, and, by about 800 BC, dedications characteristic of the cult of Apollo – tripods and bronze male figurines – make their appearance, thus attesting to the god's arrival and establishment at Delphi.

Though we cannot follow these early processes as clearly as we would like, the sanctuary and oracle were developing within the settlement already in the 8th century, while a second cult made its appearance shortly afterwards in the sanctuary of the Pronaia. The dedications show that, from the same time, many pilgrims from nearby regions (mainly Attica, Boeotia, Thessaly, Euboea, Achaia, the Argolid and Corinth) and also from further afield (e.g., Crete and Cyprus) came to Delphi to worship and seek the advice of the god. From the very beginning, the oracle formed the core of the cult of Apollo, and there can be no doubt that a significant contribution was made to the consolidation and dissemination of the sanctuary's fame by the priestesses, who may have been true mediums and whose guidance helped people in their decision-making. At this early period, the oracular cult was practised in the open air, had a popular character, and was not yet under the control of any state authority.

In the Homeric poems, which date from the second half of the 8th century, Delphi, then called Pytho, was already famous for its wealth and dedications (*Iliad* IX, 401-5). In the *Odyssey* (VIII, 79-81), Agamemnon sought the advice of the oracle before setting out for Troy, an incident that undoubtedly reflects the important role played by the oracle in the Greek colonisation movement. From the middle of the 8th century, the acquisition of sea routes, trade, and above all the great social and political difficulties that arose in the Greek cities between rival aristocratic clans led to the founding of colonies on the coasts of the entire Mediterranean. In this colonisation movement, the oracle was invariably consulted about the regions to which the colonies were sent, the leadership of the individual missions, and the likely success of the enterprise. Its responses were of decisive importance.

234. Bronze male figurines of the Geometric period. These are the earliest dedications in the sanctuary and provide the first evidence for the cult of Apollo at Delphi (8th c. BC). Delphi, Archaeological Museum.

235. Group of three Sirens that were attached to the rims of bronze cauldrons. The motif of the Siren came from the eastern Mediterranean and was quickly hellenised (late 8th c. BC). Delphi, Archaeological Museum.

236. Group of four ring-handles from bronze tripod cauldrons. These were the most commonly dedicated objects in early sanctuaries, especially the one at Delphi, where the tripod was also used as a vessel in the oracular process (first half of the 8th c. BC). Delphi, Archaeological Museum.

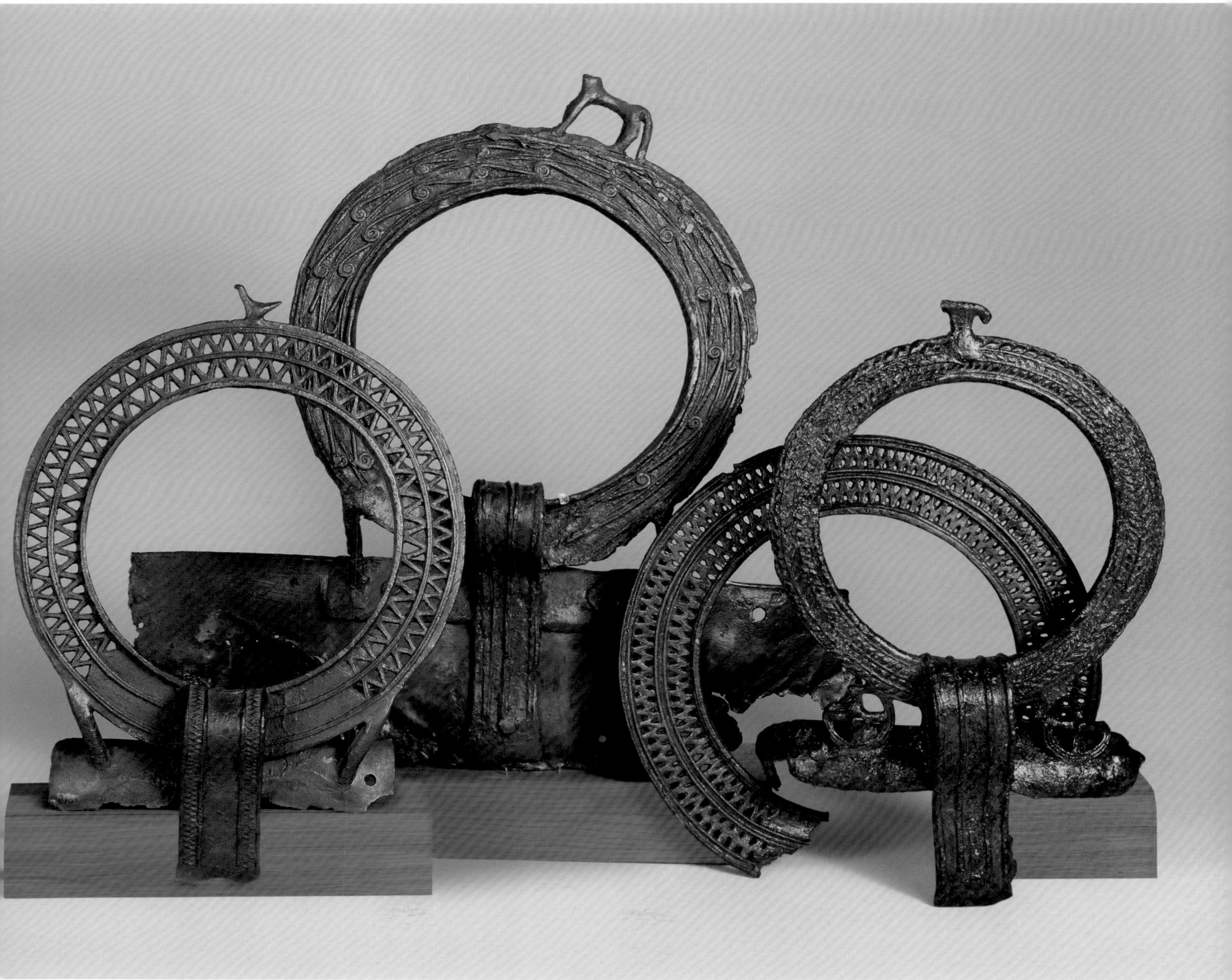

236

No visible architectural remains are preserved in the sanctuary from this period, but a general picture can be formed from small finds. Common dedications included bronze figurines, weapons, vessels and, most characteristic of all, tripod cauldrons, which played a special role in the oracular process. We learn from ancient authors that at this period the entire sanctuary was adorned not with statues, but with bronze tripod cauldrons.

237-238. Group of four griffin's heads and three lions, which were attached to the rims of bronze votive cauldrons or other vessels. Such cauldrons, adorned with motifs drawn from the eastern Mediterranean, replaced Geometric tripods in the 7th c. BC. Delphi, Archaeological Museum.

239. A cauldron set on a tripod. The two objects do not belong together but are composed in this way to give an idea of how these vessels originally appeared. The hammered cauldron stands on the cast 'fluted' legs, which are connected by crossed reinforcing pieces (8th c. BC). Delphi, Archaeological Museum.

237

238

239

240

240. Reconstruction drawing of a Cretan shield decorated with a row of sphinxes and a row of grazing deer. It belongs to a Cretan shield type. The existence of dedications from such remote places indicates the wide prestige enjoyed by Delphi already in the 8th c. BC. Athens, French Archaeological School.

241. Bronze jewellery-dedications dating from the 8th and 7th c. BC. They consist of pins and fibulae, which were used to fasten clothing and are commonly found as dedications or grave offerings in female tombs. Delphi, Archaeological Museum.

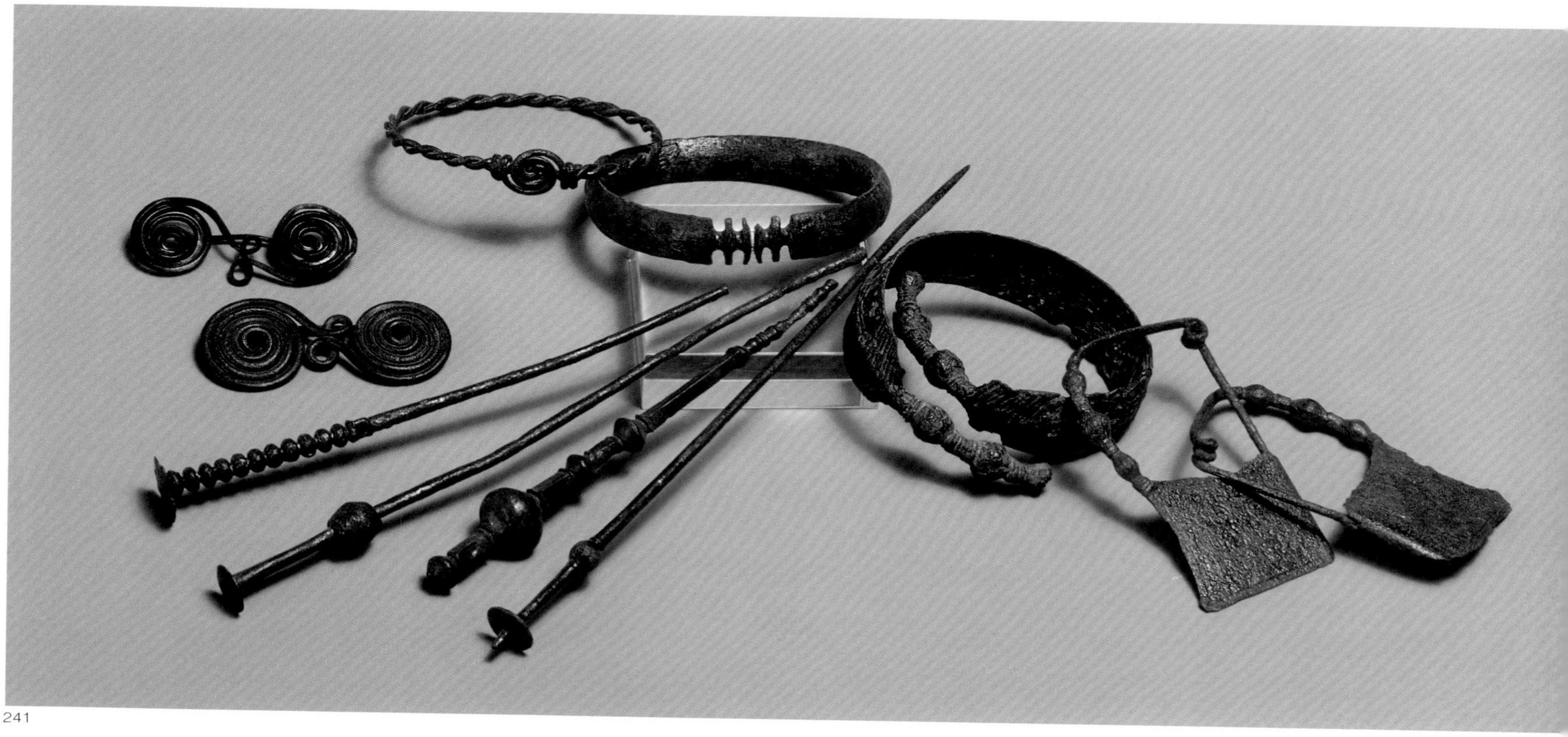

241

7th - 6th c. BC

The great development of the sanctuary and the Amphictyony

242

The 7th and 6th centuries were a period of major economic, social and political development for all the Greek city-states, and the even greater role in the Greek world that Delphi and its oracle began to play was reflected in the evolution of the cult itself. An indication of its importance is the steady expansion of the enclosure walls bounding the sanctuary, leading to the gradual elimination of the settlement to the east and west of it.

It was probably in the 7th century B.C. that a very important event took place, which set its seal on the life of the sanctuary and the role played by it in Greek history. At this period, the sanctuary was associated with the Amphictyonic League of the cities of Thessaly and central Greece, a union of neighbouring cities centred on the sanctuary of Demeter at Anthele near Thermopylae. At some point during the 7th century, the autumn meeting of the members was transferred to Delphi, which gradually became the religious and political centre of the league. As a result, the Amphictyonic League exercised direct control over the sanctuary and protected it from the envious designs of its neighbours. At the same time, given the prestige of the sanctuary and oracle, the league rapidly outgrew its local character and emerged as a panhellenic political force. It frequently intervened as arbitrator in disputes between city-states, and for many centuries it played a significant general role on the political stage of ancient Greece. As Christos Karouzos, one of the most important Greek archaeologists, has written: 'In these years the Delphic sanctuary was not merely a passive mirror of Greek history, but an active factor in it. That is to say, it was not simply enriched by dedications made by the powerful of the day, nor did it wait for the vicissitudes of history to determine its fate, but intervened actively in historical events and influenced their course to a significant degree, either directly through its oracles or indirectly through the power of the Amphictyonic League.'

243

242. Silver stater issued by the Delphic Amphictyony, bearing the inscription ΑΜΦΙΚΤΙΟΝΩΝ ('of the Amphictyons'). Apollo Kitharodos is depicted seated on the omphalos, and a small tripod cauldron can be seen in front of him (336-334 BC). Athens, Numismatic Museum.

243. The small (19 cm. high) bronze kouros of Delphi, an outstanding example of Daidalic art. The figure wears the belt found in figurines of warriors, and the general rendering of his body, in which the left foot and right arm are slightly advanced, pays great attention to proportion. His imposing stance foreshadows the monumental kouroi of the Archaic period (second half of the 7th c. BC). Delphi, Archaeological Museum.

244. Ivory cutout with five figures, rendering a scene from the myth of Phineus, which served as the decoration for a wooden casket dedicated at Delphi by Greeks from Ionia (second half of the 6th c. BC). Delphi, Archaeological Museum.

245. Ivory statuette that probably depicts an early figure of Apollo of Oriental origin, as 'Lord of the Animals'. Early dedication from Asia Minor (ca. 680 BC). Delphi, Archaeological Museum.

Valuable Dedications

Incontestable proof of the fame, prestige and international authority acquired throughout the world by the sanctuary is provided by the fabulous dedications made at Delphi by all the great powers of the period and reported by Herodotos: a gold throne offered by Midas; six gold kraters and many silver dedications by Gyges of Lydia; and enormous silver pithoi and perirrhanteria, along with 117 gold bricks that formed a pedestal 1.5 m. high to support a gold lion, by Kroisos. Valuable dedications were also made by Amasis, the king of Egypt. For a long period, from the early 7th to the middle of the 6th century, all these rulers sought, through their exotic gifts, to win the favour of the god and to elicit propitious oracles that would help them to consolidate and extend their power.

An idea of the wealth of the dedications at this period is given by exhibits in the archaeological museum in Delphi: fragments of a silver bull, remains of gold and ivory statues and smaller dedications of bronze and ivory. These were found in 1939 buried in pits beneath the paving slabs of the Sacred Way, in front of the Stoa of the Athenians. They were partly burned and appear to have been kept in one of the treasuries in the sanctuary that was destroyed by fire in the middle of the 5th c. BC. Since most of the dedications were the work of artists from Asia Minor, the view has been advanced that they were dedicated by one of the wealthy Greek cities of Ionia.

244

245

246-247. Two heads of chryselephantine statues, probably depicting Apollo and his sister Artemis. The faces were of ivory and the hair and jewellery of hammered gold sheet. The eyes were made of glass paste and inlaid. They are rare examples of chryselephantine statues that have survived, and provide a good idea of the form, as well as an indication of the wealth of the dedications in the great sanctuaries (ca. 560 BC). Delphi, Archaeological Museum.

248-249. Hammered gold sheeting from the clothing of the chryselephantine statues. Nailed to the wooden core of the statue, these panels contained superbly rendered real or imaginary animals (about 560 BC). Delphi, Archaeological Museum.

250. Drawings of a column capital and a reconstructed column from the first temple of Athena Pronaia (about 650 BC). This is one of the earliest preserved capitals in ancient Greek architecture. Athens, French Archaeological School.

247

246

248

THE FIRST STONE TEMPLE

According to Delphic tradition, six temples were built one after the other in the same part of the sanctuary of Apollo. The first was of laurel branches, the second of wax and bees' wings, and the third of bronze. The fourth, which is the first that can be documented archaeologically, was built about 650 BC and was of poros, local limestone; architectural members of this temple have been found built into later structures in the sanctuary. According to the *Homeric Hymn to Apollo*, its foundations were laid by the god himself, while the building was the work of two mythical architects, Trophonios and Agamedes. Of the first temple of Athena Pronaia, which was contemporary with it, a few column drums and twelve Doric basket capitals have been preserved: these are the earliest such members of monumental Greek architecture. They have survived because they were reused as building material in the foundations of the succeeding Temple of Athena, a practice very common in the ancient world that has preserved much valuable material, particularly of the early periods.

Another important building of the period, contemporary with the two temples and probably the first in a long series of structures characteristic of the sanctuary at Delphi, is the treasury of the Corinthians. This was built by the tyrant of Corinth, Kypselos, the father of Periandros, to house the valuable dedications made by Corinth, which was one of the strongest powers of the day.

249

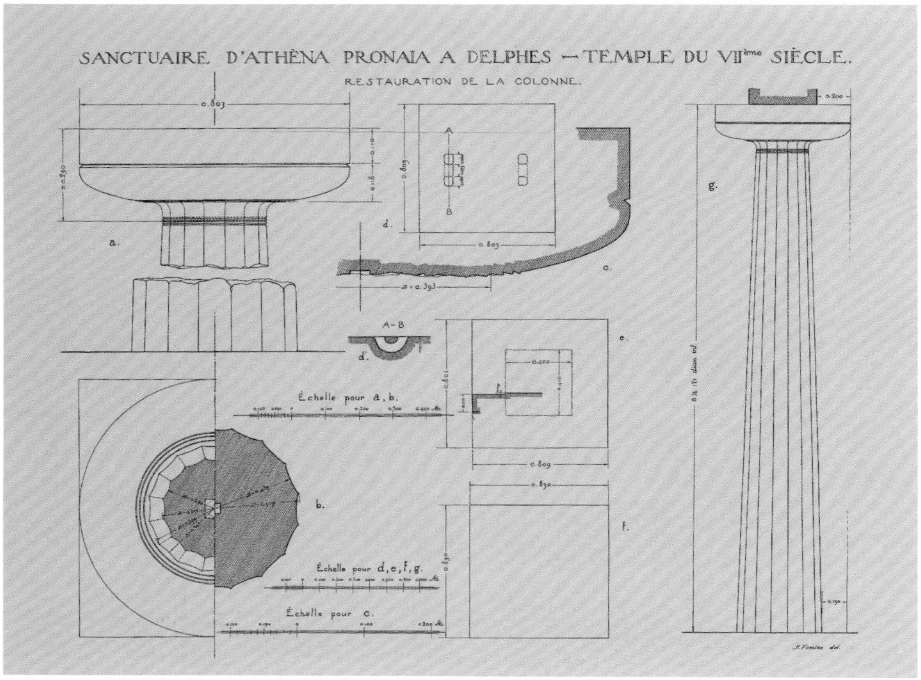

250

THE SACRED WARS

251

251. Bronze votive shield of a rare type, possibly a dedication from Cyprus or Crete. The chevrons at the centre are an artistic allusion to a spearhead (late 8th-early 7th c. BC). Delphi, Archaeological Museum.

The 6th century found Delphi at the centre of a major dispute, which was perhaps to be expected. The fame of the sanctuary, the large number of pilgrims that converged on it from all over the world, the wealth of the dedications, and the influence exercised by the oracle naturally led to strife and warfare aimed at winning control of it, while its riches also aroused envious designs. The main contenders were the Lokrians of Amphissa and their neighbours the Phokians, who sought to benefit either from cultivating the 'sacred land' of the plain of Krisa (now the vineyards of Khrisos) or from exacting tolls on pilgrims disembarking in the port of Kirrha (near modern Itea), the gateway to Delphi from the sea. The guardians of the autonomy and rights of the sanctuary, however, the Amphictyonic League, ensured, usually by recourse to arms, that the profaners were punished and order restored.

Over the course of ancient history, four wars, known as Sacred Wars, were declared by the Amphictyonic League. The first, against the Phokians, began in 600 BC and lasted ten years. Interestingly, all the great powers of the period sided with the sanctuary: the Aleuadai of Thessaly, the Athenians, Solon and the Alkmeonidai, and the powerful tyrant of Sikyon, Kleisthenes. They were led by Eurylochos of Thessaly, a circumstance that reveals the influence of the Thessalians on the sanctuary at this early period. After the war, the Phokians were contained and two of their cities, Kirrha and Krisa, were destroyed and their land given to the sanctuary, with orders that it should remain uncultivated. The following wars were fought in the 5th and 4th centuries.

252. Scene on a kalyx krater found at Pharsala in Thessaly. It depicts a battle between Greeks and Trojans over the body of Patroklos. Although the figures depicted are Homeric heroes, their armour is that of the 6th c. BC, the date at which the First Sacred War was fought (third quarter of the 6th c. BC). Athens, National Archaeological Museum.

253. Group of weapons dedicated in the sanctuary of Apollo. They include helmets, spearheads and arrows, sword-sheaths and shield grips (6th-4th c. BC). Delphi, Archaeological Museum.

254. Panoramic view of the plain of Krissa, which was a bone of contention and one of the reasons that led to the Sacred Wars. Kirrha, the port of Delphi on the Corinthian gulf, was in the left background, to the east of Itea.

252

253

The Pythian games

The most glorious ornament in the Games of Greece

Sophocles, *Elektra*

255

256

Delphi emerged stronger from the First Sacred War, and there is every indication that the immediately following period, from 590 to 575 BC, was decisive for the future of the sanctuary. The victory was marked by splendid celebrations, and it appears to have been at this time that the decision was made to radically reorganise the Pythia. This was an ancient festival that was originally celebrated every eight years to commemorate the slaying of the Python by Apollo. In addition to religious ceremonies it included only music contests, mainly in kitharodia – that is, singing to the accompaniment of the kithara – marking the special relationship of the Delphic god with music. In the new festival, which was to be held every four years, athletic and equestrian events were added to the music contests, in imitation of Olympia. The prizes awarded at the first games in 586 BC were the spoils of war, and 582 BC, the year in which the laurel wreath became established as the prize, was regarded by the ancient Greeks as the true beginning of the panhellenic festival of the Pythia.

Like all the major panhellenic festivals, the Pythia was a panegyris: that is, it included religious ceremonies (sacrifices, processions, prayers and feasting), competitions (musical, athletic and equestrian contests), and a variety of social events (dinners and commercial activity) among the participants, who included members of the ruling class (kings, princes, rulers and officials) from all the Greek cities of motherland Greece and the colonies. One can easily imagine, therefore, the importance of the Delphic and other panhellenic festivals in the development of a common national consciousness and the role these festivals played in political, social, athletic, artistic and scientific affairs throughout the whole of the Mediterranean. Delphi was indeed the omphalos, the navel, the political, social and cultural centre of the entire civilised world.

255-256. Coin of Chalcis bearing the inscription 'of the Chalcidians'. On one side is the head of Apollo crowned with a laurel wreath and on the other the god's most characteristic musical instrument, the kithara (4th c. BC). Athens, Numismatic Museum.

257. Apollo stands before Zeus holding the lyre in his left hand and a branch in his right. Behind him can be seen his sister Artemis and her sacred animal, the deer. Attic black-figure oinochoe by the Amasis painter (550-540 BC). Rome, Vatican Museum.

PREPARATIONS FOR THE FESTIVAL

The Pythia took place in the third year of the Olympic cycle and was held in the month of Boukation at the end of summer (mid-August to mid-September), coinciding with the autumn meeting of the Amphictyonic League, which was responsible for holding the festival. The preparations began six months earlier, when nine citizens, the *theoroi*, left Delphi in different directions to proclaim the date of the commencement of the festival to all Greek cities, from the Crimea to Marseilles and from Cyrenaica to Asia Minor, asking them to send athletes. This method was essential in ancient Greece, since there was no common calendar and there was general anarchy with regard to dates. The routes of the theoroi are known from inscriptions relating to them found at Delphi and from others in the receiving cities, in which the names are cited of *theorodokoi* – that is, the citizens of the receiving cities who entertained the emissaries and helped them to carry out their mission.

At the same time, the Pythian *hieromenia* began. This was the sacred truce, which lasted one year. Its objective was not to secure the protection of the sanctuary, which was always sheltered by Apollo, but mainly to protect the theoroi and the pilgrims, who had to be able to move around freely and in safety. Any city that did not observe the truce, but became involved in conflict or robbery, was excluded from the sanctuary and none of its citizens was allowed to take part in the contests or seek advice from the oracle.

Another obligation incumbent on the Amphictyony was to maintain and prepare the facilities for the celebrations and athletic events by repairing and embellishing all structures, from temples and fountains to roads and public squares. The facilities were of course not neglected in the period intervening between festivals. There were always visitors to Delphi, since the oracle functioned all year round apart from the three winter months, and, generally speaking, public property was constantly maintained in ancient times. Nevertheless, a complete renovation was required for the festival and games so that the sanctuary presented its best aspect. Particular care was given to the maintenance and preparation of the athletic facilities, especially the stadium and the gymnasium. We learn from an inscription (247/6 BC) containing the terms of a work contract that 23 businessmen and craftsmen undertook to complete about 40 projects: the contractors had to clear growth from the gymnasium

258

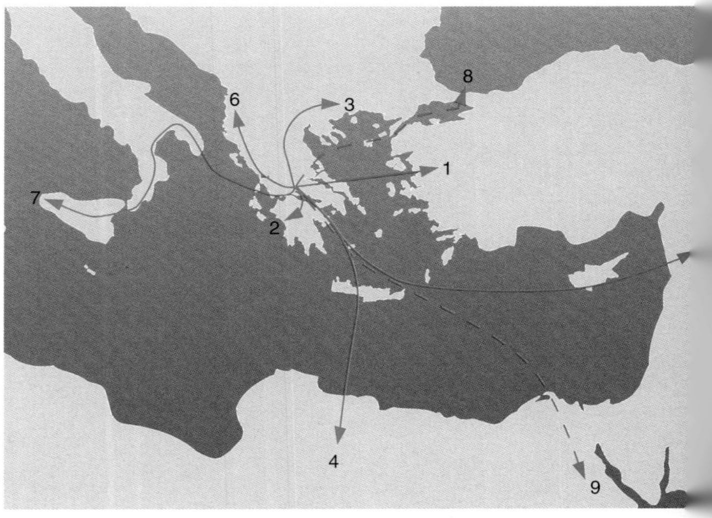

258. Map of the Mediterranean showing the routes followed by the theoroi, *who travelled from Delphi to all the Greek cities to announce the beginning of the Pythian Games and the sacred truce: 1. Asia Minor, 2. Mainland Greece, 3. Macedonia - Thrace, 4. North Africa, 5. Cyprus-Syropalaistian coast, 6. Western Greece - Adriatic colonies, 7. Southern Italy - Sicily - Western Mediterranean, 8. Black Sea - Crimea, 9. Egypt. Drawing: W. Decker.*

259. Modern copy of the Kyreneia II, *a ship of the 4th c. BC, during its experimental voyage in the Aegean. The theoroi travelled on ships like these for weeks and months, until they had completed their mission.*

and stadium, plough and level them, and spread a layer of fine, soft earth, 8 cm. thick, on the ground to protect the bare feet of the runners and the competitors in the heavy events. They also had to put in place the special pegs that defined the positions of the runners at the start and finishing posts, and the wooden parts of the starting apparatus.

The cities participating in the festival made similar preparations. They organised an official mission, the *theoria*, consisting of the athletes, officials and elite citizens, who often supported the mission by personal donations. The offerings and dedications to the gods, and the animals for the sacrifices, formed an essential feature of the theoria. The theoria had a predominantly religious character, though the political aspect was never absent. Every city sought by its presence to create an impression not only on the gods and priests, but also on the rest of the Greeks, thus creating a suitable ideological climate for favourable treatment in its international relations.

262

262. This precious dedication of an Archaic bull, rendered at almost life size (2.61 × 1.46 m.), has been admirably reassembled from hundreds of fragments of silver sheet that were forged on a wooden matrix and riveted to an internal bronze skeleton. The horns, ears, forehead and hooves are gilded (middle of the 6th c. BC). Delphi, Archaeological Museum.

A good idea of the wealth and form of a theoria is given by the mission to Delphi organised by Jason, the tyrant of Ferrhai in Thessaly, at the beginning of the 4th century: 'And since the festival of the Pythia was drawing near, he sent a message to the cities in his realm to prepare oxen, sheep, goats and pigs for the sacrifice. And they say that, although the order was not a strict one, more than one thousand oxen were assembled, while the other animals surpassed ten thousand in number. He also declared that he would award a gold wreath to the city that reared for the god the most splendid ox, which would walk at the head of the other sacrificial animals' (Xenophon, *Hellenika* 6.4.29-30).

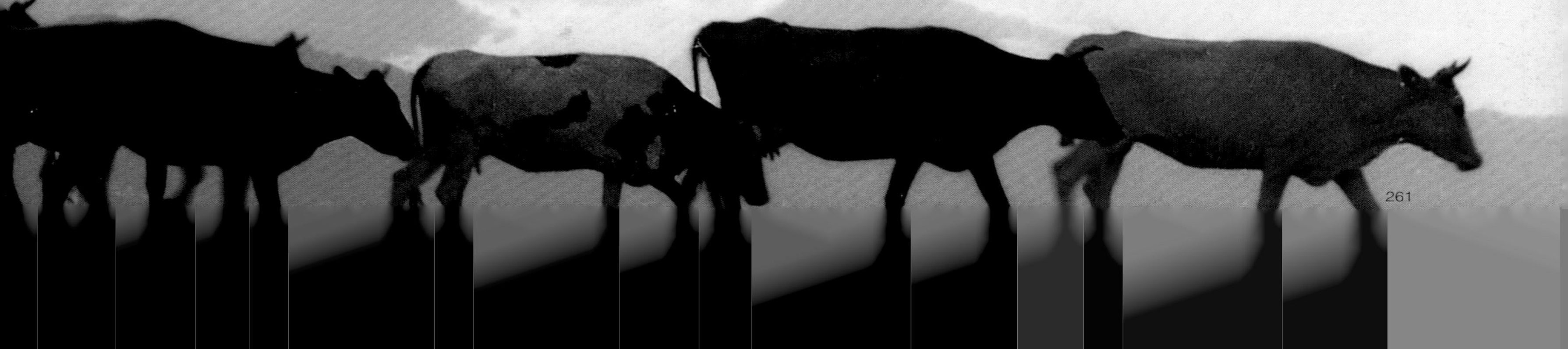

261

264 265 266

264. A central section of the seating of the theatre of Delphi.

265. Bronze figurine of a flute player from the early 5th c. BC. Flute contests were established in 582 BC. The winner of the first competition was the Argive Sakadas, who invented the 'Pythian mode', a piece of music with a constant form and specific parts, hymning Apollo's struggle against the Pytho. In the 3rd century, the music competitions were held in the stadium, and were moved to the theatre in the 2nd c. BC. Delphi, Archaeological Museum.

266. Graeco-Roman figurine of a comic actor giving a pantomime performance (ca. Early 4th c.). Athens, National Archaeological Museum.

267. Two mounted riders galloping swiftly. The equestrian games at the Pythia were amongst the most important in ancient Greece. Black-figure amphora, dating from 500-480 BC. London, British Museum.

268-269. On one side of the vase the kitharodos plays his instrument and sings. The treatment of the swirling drapery intensifies the sense of movement. On the other side, the judge listens carefully, holding a staff as symbol of his office. Red-figure amphora by the Berlin Painter (490 BC). New York, The Metropolitan Museum of Art.

The significance of horse races at the Pythia, which were the most important events after the music contests, is demonstrated by the seven of twelve Pythian odes Pindar devoted to victors in equestrian events. Some of these victors were famous Greek rulers of the time, like the Athenian Alkmeonid Megakles, Hieron of Syracuse, and Arkesilas, the king of Cyrene. In his description of the victory won by the last-named at the Pythia of 466 BC, Pindar states that 40 chariots competed, though we cannot say whether this was the actual number or the product of poetic licence. According to Pindar, after his victory Arkesilas dedicated his chariot to the sanctuary, placing it in a wooden building. Sophocles gives a superb description of a chariot race at the Pythia in a famous scene of *Elektra* (lines 709-717) in which he presents the fake death of Orestes:

'After they had all lined up in the positions determined by lot by the judges, and had set their chariots in line, they set off to the sound of the brazen trumpet. They at once gave the command to their horses and pulled on the reins with both hands. And the track was full of the noise of the thunderous chariots. And the place was filled with dust, and, all entangled together, they whipped their horses to run as fast as their breath and the axles of the chariots could bear.'

267

268

269

6th c. BC
The Archaic period

270. View of the steep natural incline of the sanctuary at Delphi. To construct the buildings and erect the dedications, seven terraces were constructed with a series of retaining walls.

271. Photograph of Delphi just after the beginning of excavations in 1892. The first houses have been demolished, revealing the large polygonal retaining wall and part of the Stoa of the Athenians.

272. Artist's drawing of the archaeological site at Delphi, made by A. Tournaire during the great excavation (1893). The houses of the village of Kastri can be seen, which covered the entire site of the Temple of Apollo.

As the fame of the sanctuary spread, its architecture evolved with the addition of new buildings. Given the steeply sloping site, it had to be organised into a series of terraces, resulting in the construction of hundreds of retaining walls. Indeed, the walls of Delphi offer a panorama of ancient building, the variety and beauty of which still fascinate visitors.

One event that stamped the evolution of architecture at Delphi was the fire that broke out in 548 BC, which completely consumed the earlier temple of Apollo and other buildings. Efforts began at once to erect a more resplendent temple, the budget for which was as high as 300 talents. Of this sum, the Amphictyony provided 225 talents, while the other 75 had to be given by Delphi. Since this proved impossible, fundraising was undertaken not only in Greece but also in neighbouring states. According to Herodotos (2.180), 'The Delphians travelled from city to city collecting contributions.' It was on this occasion that the depth of respect enjoyed by the oracle throughout the entire world became evident, with even Kroisos of Lydia and Amasis of Egypt offering substantial sums for the project.

271

272

THE TEMPLE OF APOLLO

Take care of my temple and welcome the men who will gather here at my orders.

Homeric Hymn to Apollo

The contract for a new temple of Apollo was undertaken by the Athenian noble family of the Alkmeonidai, who lived far from Athens, exiled by their political opponent Peisistratos. The temple was completed just before 510 BC and was a truly impressive structure, since the Alkmeonidai made it more luxurious than was required by the contract, out of a desire to win the favour of the god and the priesthood. Though the material quoted in the contract was poros, the facade was constructed of Parian marble. The god apparently always honoured his generous believers for, displeased with the policy of Peisistratos, he continually urged the Spartans, both secretly and openly through his oracles, to overthrow the Peisistratid tyranny. This was achieved in 510 BC and led to a period of conflict, after which the reins of power in

273

274

275

276

273. The preserved lower part of a figure, possibly of Athena, from the west pediment of the old temple of Apollo, on which was depicted a Gigantomachy (515-510 BC). Delphi, Archaeological Museum.

274. Reconstruction drawing of the facade of the old temple of Apollo. On the pediment is depicted the arrival of the Apollonian triad (Apollo, Leto, Artemis) at Delphi in a chariot. They are welcomed by young men and women of the city. In the corners lions pull down a bull and a deer. The sculptures were by Athenian artists.

275. The central akroterion of the east side of the old temple was a flying winged Victory, rendered in the Archaic manner (515-510 BC). Delphi, Archaeological Museum.

276. The torso of one of the korai from the east pediment of the old temple of Apollo (515-510 BC). Delphi, Archaeological Museum.

Athens were seized by the Alkmeonid Kleisthenes, who established the Athenian democracy.

The Apollo temple was a Doric peripteral structure with 6 columns on the narrow sides and 15 on the long. Of the sculptural decoration, several figures from the pedimental compositions have survived and are on display in the archaeological museum. Apollo's arrival at Delphi was depicted on the east pediment, and a Gigantomachy on the west. Since this temple was much larger than its predecessor, the terrace on which it stood had to be extended. To hold back the earth deposits of the terrace, an enormous retaining wall was built with Lesbian masonry (stones with curved joints), which is more commonly known as polygonal masonry. Since this wall was the first large flat surface to meet the eye in the sanctuary, it was later used as an archive. About 800 inscriptions were carved on the surfaces of its stones. Most of these decisions were acts of manumission of slaves, who placed their liberty under the guarantee of Apollo.

277. View of the polygonal retaining wall built about 530 BC to support the infrastructure of the Temple of Apollo. The stones in it are bound together in the system known as 'Lesbian masonry', with curved joints. In the Hellenistic period the wall became an open-air archive of inscriptions manumitting slaves who in this way placed their liberty under the protection of the god. The inscription also gave wide publicity to the act, to counter any likely dispute.

277

278. Some of the hundreds of manumission inscriptions carved on blocks of the polygonal wall. The act of manumission normally took the form of the sale of a slave to the god, on condition that he be set free. The affair was conducted by Apollo through one of his priests. The amount of money that was deposited with the temple is stated, as is the place it was to be left (e.g., on the threshold of the temple). As in all commercial transactions, the names of the guarantor of the sale and the witnesses are recorded at the end. The original document was deposited in the temple archives.

278

THE BUILDINGS OF THE SIKYONIANS

Two buildings of the 6th century, dating from about 560 BC, were connected with Sikyon, since architectural members from them were reused in the foundations of the later treasury of the Sikyonians (after 545 BC). The first is a monopteral building, a small rectangular structure of 4 by 5 columns in the peristyle which, since it had no walls, probably housed a dedication open for all to view. According to one suggestion, it may have contained the chariot of Kleisthenes, the tyrant of Sikyon and winner of the first chariot-race, who dedicated it to the sanctuary. Of this monopteral building, five of the fourteen metopes are preserved, adorned with subjects drawn from mythology. The other Sikyonian building of this period was a circular structure, one of the earliest *tholoi* of ancient Greek architecture, surrounded by thirteen perimetric Doric columns.

279

279. Reconstruction drawing of the tholos of the Sikyonians, after H. Pomtow. The building, which was bold for its time, was a centralised structure with 13 Doric columns and a diameter of 6.32 m. Poros remains from it were used, along with the remains of the slightly later monopteral building, in the foundations of the treasury the Sikyonians erected about 500 BC.

280. The Kalydonian boar, one of the surviving poros metopes of the monopteral building erected by the Sikyonians (ca. 560 BC). Delphi, Archaeological Museum.

280

281

281. The foundations of the treasury of the Sikyonians, dating from about 500 BC. Material from the two earlier Sikyonian buildings was used in its construction, after they apparently collapsed as the result of an earthquake. Inside it can be seen the curved members of the Archaic tholos.

282. Another of the metopes of the monopteral building of the Sikyonians carved with a mythical subject. The Dioskouroi and the sons of Aphareus return from an attack, bringing with them their booty of stolen oxen (ca. 560 BC). Delphi, Archaeological Museum.

282

THE TREASURY OF THE SIPHNIANS

283, 284. Painting of two parts of the frieze on the treasury of the Siphnians. East side: scene from the Trojan War with pairs of Greeks and Trojans fighting for the dead body of a warrior lying between them; on either side are the horses of the chariot that brought the warriors to the battlefield. Athens, French Archaeological Institute.

285. Artist's reconstruction of the facade of the treasury of the Siphnians. There are many mistakes in this drawing, particularly regarding the form of the pediment, which belongs to the other side of the treasury, and the frieze, but it gives a general picture of the building and its wealth. Paris, École Supérieure des Beaux-Arts.

About 530 BC, one of the finest treasuries was built in the sanctuary of Athena Pronaia, probably by Massilia in southern France, while in 525 BC, the treasury of the Siphnians was erected at the first bend in the Sacred Way. This is a small, though elaborate, building of great importance, since it is preserved in very good condition and enables us to enjoy a virtually intact Archaic building in the Ionic order. It is completely covered with mouldings, relief representations, and many decorative motifs, which stress even further the sculptural value of the monument at the expense of the architectural. The two columns on the facade are caryatids – figures of girls – while the

283

284

pediment and the relief frieze, 30 m. long, that encircles the entire building, amongst the finest examples of Cycladic art, are preserved in excellent condition. The pediment has a depiction of a Delphic tradition – the dispute between Apollo and Herakles for the Delphic tripod. According to the myth, the Pythia refused to give an oracular response to Herakles because he had not received purification after a murder, whereupon the hero carried off the tripod in a rage, to found his own oracle. The quarrel was ended by the intervention of Zeus, who is depicted in the centre of the pediment attempting to reconcile the two protagonists. Various subjects from ancient Greek mythology are depicted on the four sides of the frieze: a battle between Greeks and Trojans, a Gigantomachy, the judgement of Paris, and a mythical abduction of women. Finally, about 500 BC, a new temple of Athena was built in the sanctuary of Pronaia after the first temple had been destroyed. Since there was not enough space available for a longer building on the narrow terrace, this, too, was a Doric peripteral temple with 6 columns on the narrow sides and 12 on the long.

286. Part of the east frieze of the treasury of the Siphnians, with a depiction of five gods. From the left: part of the shield of Ares, Eos (the mother of Memnon), Aphrodite, Apollo, and part of Zeus's body (530-525 BC). Delphi, Archaeological Museum.

287. Detail from the door frame of the treasury of the Siphnians with bead-and-reel ornaments and a zone of palmettes-lotuses. The 4th-century inscription renews the privilege of promanteia of the oracle, secured by the Siphnians through dedicating this luxurious building (530-525 BC). Delphi, Archaeological Museum.

288. Part of the north frieze of the treasury of the Siphnians depicting the Gigantomachy. Themis, riding on a chariot drawn by lions, attacks the Giants. Behind her can be seen Dionysos wearing the lion's pelt. In front of her are the barely discernible figures of Apollo and Artemis (530-525 BC). Delphi, Archaeological Museum.

289. Part of the north frieze, depicting the Gigantomachy. At left, Hera stoops to deliver the coup de grâce to a fallen Giant. Next to her, Athena has smitten two Giants. Nearby, Ares fights two more Giants, one of whom raises a stone to strike the god (530-525 BC). Delphi, Archaeological Museum.

286

287

288

289

DEDICATIONS

In addition to the buildings, the sanctuary of Apollo was also adorned with many dedications in the 6th century. The earliest, from about 600 BC, are the two kouroi that possibly depict the Dioskouroi, Kastor and Polydeukes, or the Argives Kleobis and Biton. According to Solon, these two were happier than the fabulously wealthy Kroisos because, having pulled their mother, the priestess of Hera, to the sanctuary in her cart, they died there the same evening, happy that they had done their duty.

290. The two kouros figures by the Argive sculptor Polymedes were originally identified with Kleobis and Biton, known from Herodotus, but are now believed to represent the Dioskouroi (ca. 600 BC). Delphi, Archaeological Museum.

291. Photograph of the excavation, after the discovery of the two kouroi in the area behind the treasury of the Athenians on May 28, 1894.

292, 293. The sphinx of the Naxians, 2.32 m. high, and a reconstruction drawing (by A. Tournaire) of it on the Ionic column, about 10 m. high. This imposing dedication stood to the south of the large temple of Apollo and faced east (ca. 560 BC). Delphi, Archaeological Museum.

290

291

Another important monument of Archaic art was the sphinx of the Naxians, dedicated to the sanctuary about 560 BC, when Naxos enjoyed great prosperity. The sphinx, a monster of ancient mythology and art, with the body of a lion, the face of a woman, and the wings of a bird, was originally adopted from neighbouring civilisations in the eastern Mediterranean. Its daemonic nature soon made it a symbolic adornment of tombs and a common dedication in sanctuaries. The sphinx of the Naxians stood atop a tall column 10 m. high, between the treasury and Stoa of the Athenians, where the most ancient and most sacred monuments of Delphi were erected. It is not known precisely why the Naxians dedicated the sphinx at Delphi, but in return for their donation, they received *promanteia* – right of prior consultation of the oracle – as we learn from an inscription carved in the 4th century on one of the drums of the column.

292

293

5th - 4th c. BC
Classical period

294. Model of the sanctuary of Apollo. The reconstruction is based on ruins and the evidence of literary sources. The entry to the precinct is at the bottom right. On either side of the Sacred Way are the imposing multifigural dedications made by Greek city-states, followed by their treasuries. The temple was the main building, as centre of the cult and oracle. Above it is the theatre, in which the music contests were held. Gift of the French Archaeological School of Athens to the mayoralty of Delphi.

295. The laurel, the sacred plant of Apollo and Delphi.

THE FIRST PHASE AFTER THE PERSIAN WARS

At the end of the Archaic period, about 480 BC, the sanctuary and oracle, like the rest of Greece, found itself facing the Persian threat.

At this crucial juncture, the oracle maintained an ambivalent position. It had long maintained its neutrality with regards to the rich power of the East. When the Persian armies invaded Greece, defeatist responses were offered to all the Greek cities that hastened to consult the oracle: they should not attempt to resist, but should abandon their cities. This position was perhaps due to the pro-Persian policy pursued by many members of the Amphictyonic League, especially the Thessalians and Boeotians, to the impossibility of offering resistance to so great an army, and to the fear that the treasures of the sanctuary would be looted by the invaders.

294

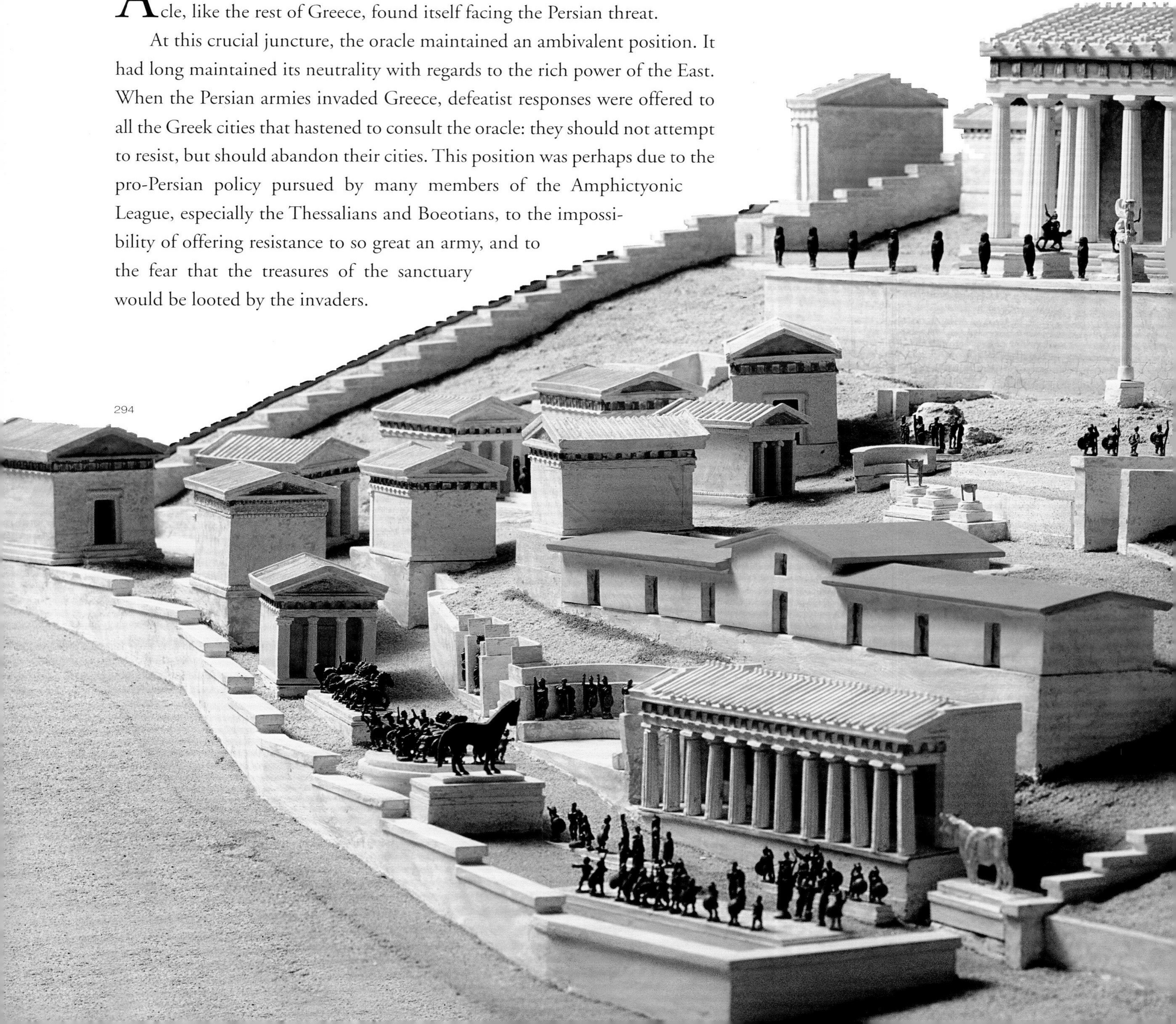

296. Artist's reconstruction of the sanctuary of Apollo from the south. The buildings and dedications were crowded into a rectangular enclosure 135 by 190 m. The huge statue (15-16 m.) in front of the temple (top right) is of Apollo Sitalkas and was dedicated by the Amphictyony in 346 BC, after the end of the Third Sacred War. Paris, École Nationale Supérieure des Beaux-Arts.

RESTAVRATION DV TEMENOS D'APOLLON

ECHELLE

THE TREASURY OF THE ATHENIANS

The hostile stance of the oracle to the Greeks was forgotten after the favourable outcome of the struggle against the Persians, and the moral authority of the oracle was not damaged. After the victory, the gratitude of the Greeks resulted in the embellishment of the sanctuary at Delphi with wealthy gifts, most of them unique works of art. The Athenians used their tithe of the spoils taken after the Battle of Marathon (490 BC) to build a treasury entirely of marble, in the Doric order. Restored about a century ago (1903-1906) at the expense of the Municipality of Athens, it gives a very good idea of a type of building that abounded at Delphi. On the metopes of the north and west sides were depicted the labours of Herakles, with the feats of Theseus on the more conspicuous south

297-298. Reconstruction drawings of the east and south sides of the treasury of the Athenians, by A. Tournaire. The architectural form of the building is rendered correctly, but the dedications around it are entirely imaginary. Recent research has assigned to the pediments of the treasury some fragments of sculptures that permit the hypothesis that one pediment had a representation of a battle and the other a scene with two four-horse chariots. The Athenians displayed the spoils taken from the Persians on the south side, exploiting one of the most important points of the Sacred Way for political purposes. Paris, École Supérieure des Beaux-Arts.

297

and east sides. This rendering of mythical scenes, particularly in sanctuaries, was a main method of political instruction in ancient times. The historical present was promoted through the mythical past, and the victories or achievements of early heroes depicted on the buildings reflected present Greek strength.

According to an inscription on a triangular pedestal to the south of their treasury, the Athenians displayed spoils taken from the Persians at the Battle of Marathon: ΑΘΕΝΑΙΟΙ ΤΩ ΑΠΟΛΛΩΝΙ ΑΠΟ ΜΕΔΟΝ ΤΑΚΡΟΘΙΝΙΑ ΛΑΒΟΝΤΕΣ ΜΑΡΑΘΩΝΙ ΜΑΧΕΣ ('the Athenians dedicated to Apollo the spoils, having taken them from the Medes at Marathon').

From the 3rd c. BC onwards the walls of the treasury were carved with a large number of inscriptions relating to the Athenian presence at Delphi, i.e. such as decrees and records of the victories of Athenian athletes at the Pythian games. The most important inscriptions are two hymns in honour of Apollo, sung by the Athenian embassies at the Pythian festivals of 138 and 128 BC. These shed light on ancient Greek music, since the notation for the musical accompaniment was carved above the verses.

298

299

299. From the 3rd c. BC the stone blocks of the treasury of the Athenians were used as an open-air public archive on which inscriptions were carved relating to various aspects of the Athenian presence at Delphi.

300. One of the best-preserved metopes on the north side of the treasury of the Athenians, which depict the labours of Herakles. The hero rushes to seize the Kerynian hind by the head. The anatomical details are rendered with admirable accuracy (500-480 BC). Delphi, Archaeological Museum.

301. The facade of the treasury of the Athenians as reconstituted after the restoration of the building in 1903-1906.

302. The Ionic columns and the stylobate of the Stoa of the Athenians. The spoils taken from the Persians at the Battle of Salamis were displayed at the stoa. The existence of so many Athenian works of art in important monuments on the Sacred Way is an indication of the strength of Athens after the Persian Wars.

300

301

THE STOA OF THE ATHENIANS

Another Athenian building erected on the occasion of the victories won during the Persian Wars was an Ionic stoa (30 by 40 m.) in front of the polygonal wall. It had seven monolithic columns of Pentelic marble and bore an inscription in capitals on its stylobate: ΑΘΕΝΑΙΟΙ ΑΝΕΘΕΣΑΝ ΤΕΝ ΣΤΟΑΝ ΚΑΙ ΤΑ ΗΟΠΛΑ ΚΑΙ ΤΑΚΡΟΤΕΡΙΑ ΗΕΛΟΝΤΕΣ ΤΩΝ ΠΟΛΕΜΙΩΝ ('The Athenians dedicated the stoa and the weapons and the prows, having taken them from the enemy'). The reference is to the weapons, ropes and prows of

302

Persian ships, presumably from the Battle of Salamis (480 BC), which were displayed inside the stoa. To celebrate the same victory, the Athenians dedicated a colossal statue of Apollo in the sanctuary. After the victory at Marathon, another Athenian dedication was erected at the beginning of the Sacred Way, at the instigation of Kimon, son of Miltiades, the victorious general in the battle. It consisted of sixteen bronze statues placed next to each other, all fashioned by Pheidias, depicting Athena, Apollo, Miltiades and mythical Attic heroes. Some archaeologists believe that the two statues recovered from Riace, off the coast of Italy, may come from this group.

Finally, a dedication from the Persian Wars that stood in front of the Temple of Apollo was a bronze palm tree with a gilded statue of Athena atop it. This was dedicated by the Athenians after their victory over the Persians at the mouth of the Eurymedon river in 469 BC, under the command of Kimon.

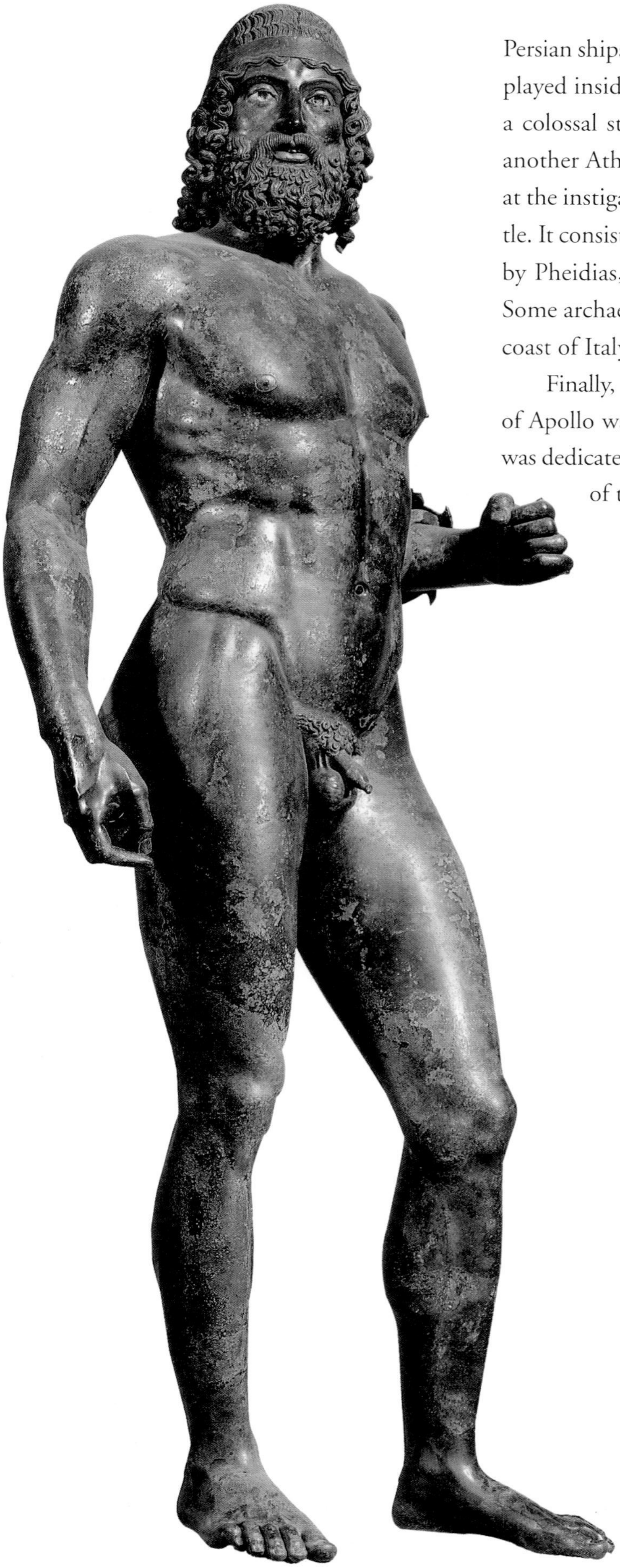

303

303. One of the two bronze Riace warriors, found at the bottom of the sea off southern Italy in 1972. They were part of the cargo of a Roman ship that sank. According to some scholars, these statues belong to the multifigural Athenian dedication made at Delphi about 460 BC after the Battle of Marathon. These original bronzes give us an idea of the actual appearance of Classical art. Calabria, Reggio Museum.

304

304. One of the two bases of the gold tripods dedicated by the Deinomenid tyrants of Sicily in 479 BC after the victory of the Greek Sicilians over the Carthagenians at Himera. In front stands a later dedication in the form of a bull.

305
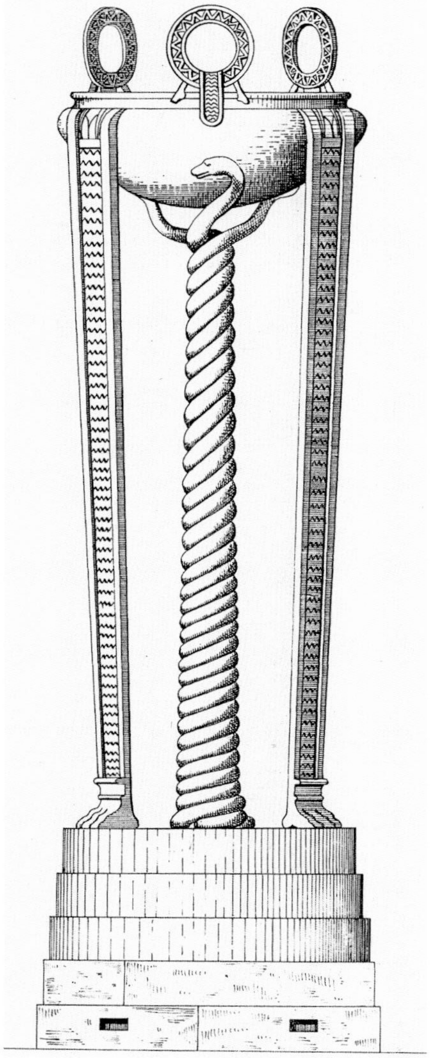
306

307

Other 5th-Century Dedications

The gold of the richly-wrought tripods standing by the temple flashes and sparkles.

Bacchylides

TRIPODS DEDICATED BY MILITARY VICTORS

Delphi reflected the entire spectrum of Greek history vividly. In no other sanctuary was the historical memory of Hellenism condensed in so few square metres of land, particularly the great victories over the barbarians that secured Greece's smooth historical continuity and led it to the great achievements of the Classical period. For instance, after the Battle at Plataia (479 BC), the Spartans dedicated an enormous bronze tripod supported on the bodies of three snakes coiling upwards. The epigram on the base originally glorified only the victor Pausanias, but it was erased and the names of the Greek cities that had taken part in the battle were carved on the snakes. The tripod cauldron was erected to the right of the Sacred Way, just before the temple, but Constantine the Great carried it off to Constantinople in AD 330, where the snake column is preserved to this day in the Hippodrome. Also on the Sacred Way, in the clearing in front of the Temple of Apollo, are preserved two monuments associated with Greek victories over the Carthaginians at Himera in Sicily in 479 BC. These are the bell-shaped pedestals of two tripods, dedicated by Hieron and Gelon, the tyrants of Syracuse and the brothers of Polyzalos, who dedicated the Charioteer. An inscription on the base states: '[I, Gelon], son of Deinomenes, of Syracuse, dedicate to Apollo the victory and the tripod, the work of Bion of Miletos, son of Diodoros.' There was also a dedication by the people of Taras, a colony in southern Italy, after a victory by the city over its barbarian neighbours, the Messapians.

305-306. Bronze snake column, as preserved today in the Hippodrome of Constantinople, that supported the tripod of the Plataians, and a reconstruction drawing of the entire dedication.

307. Only the bases survive in front of the temple of the dedications made after the Persian Wars. At left is the pestal for the tripod of the Plataians as reconstructed a few years ago.

308-310. The Charioteer and the uncovering of its lower portion together with the pedestal on April, 28, 1896 (ca. 470 BC). Delphi, Archaeological Museum.

309

THE CHARIOTEER

The creation of one of the most important sculptures in ancient Greek art is assigned to the years directly after the Persian Wars. The Charioteer, the most famous sculpture at Delphi, owes its construction to a victory in the chariot race about 474 BC by Polyzalos, brother of Gelon and Hieron, the tyrants of Syracuse. To immortalise his victory, Polyzalos dedicated to the sanctuary a large-scale sculpture group of a four-horse chariot, to which the statue belonged.

The Charioteer, 1.80 m high, gives an idea of the orignal bronze works of ancient Greek sculpture that made their mark on the history of art. He stood in his chariot wearing the long chiton associated with charioteers, which was tied under the arms and at the back by straps, to prevent it from billowing in the wind and impeding the course of the chariot. He is not depicted during the contest, for he would otherwise be shown in a more intense posture, but after his victory, as, calm and happy, he makes a lap of triumph in the Hippodrome. His eyes, made of semi-precious stones, have a magnetic quality and convey what the Greeks referred to as ethos and balance. His movement is at once immediate and eternal. Despite his great victory, there is no arrogance, only confidence. The Charioteer beyond doubt expresses the spirit of the Classical period as few other works have done.

310

5TH-CENTURY CONFLICTS BETWEEN THE CITIES

311

The first important event after the Persian Wars was the outbreak of the Second Sacred War, in which the two great powers of the day, Athens and Sparta, became embroiled. The Phokians, with the support of the Athenians, seized the sanctuary and its wealth, but a Spartan army expelled them in 449 BC. As soon as the Spartans departed, however, an Athenian expeditionary force under Perikles restored Delphi to the Phokians. The sanctuary did not become independent again until 421 BC. During the Peloponnesian War (421-404 BC), the oracle openly sided with the Spartans, though this did not deter the Athenians, who continued to seek the advice of the god, from taking part in the Pythian festivals by sending splendid theorias, or from dedicating valuable gifts.

The disputes between the Greek cities in the 5th century are reflected in the dedications erected on both sides of the Sacred Way, mostly in the first section, which were financed from the tithe of spoils taken by the victors from the vanquished. Delphi was fertile ground for this kind of competition, and through their dedications the cities could also project their achievements and humiliate their foes. Nothing has survived of these fine works of art. Information about their position and form can be derived from the descriptions in ancient authors and from a few inscriptions preserved on their bases. A characteristic display was two groups of seven statues erected along the Sacred Way – the Seven against Thebes and the Epigonoi – dedicated by the Argives after a victory over the Lakedaimonians at Oinoe in the Argolid (456 BC). Something like a response can be seen in the arrogant dedication by the latter, after their victory over the Athenians in the Peloponnesian War in 404 BC. This was a group of thirty-seven statues in which Lysander, the Spartan naval commander who defeated the Athenians and brought the war to an end, is crowned by the gods. Several centuries later, all this confrontation expressed through rival dedications evoked the anger of Plutarch, who felt ashamed of his fellow-Greeks when he saw them.

312

313

311. *Excavations in 1894 on the monument of the Argives.*

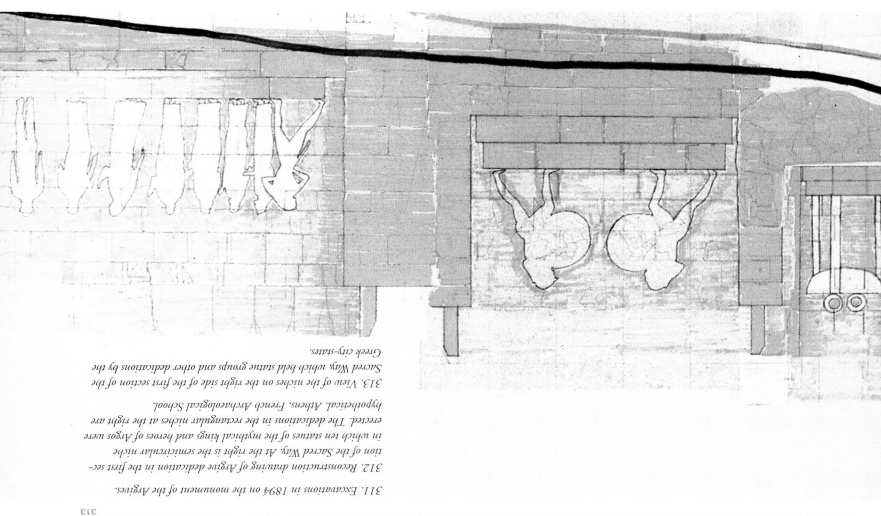

312. *Reconstruction drawing of Argive dedication in the first section of the Sacred Way. At the right is the semicircular niche in which ten statues of the mythical kings and heroes of Argos were erected. The dedications in the rectangular niches at the right are hypothetical. Athens, French Archaeological School.*

313. *View of the niches on the right side of the first section of the Sacred Way, which held statue groups and other dedications by the Greek city-states.*

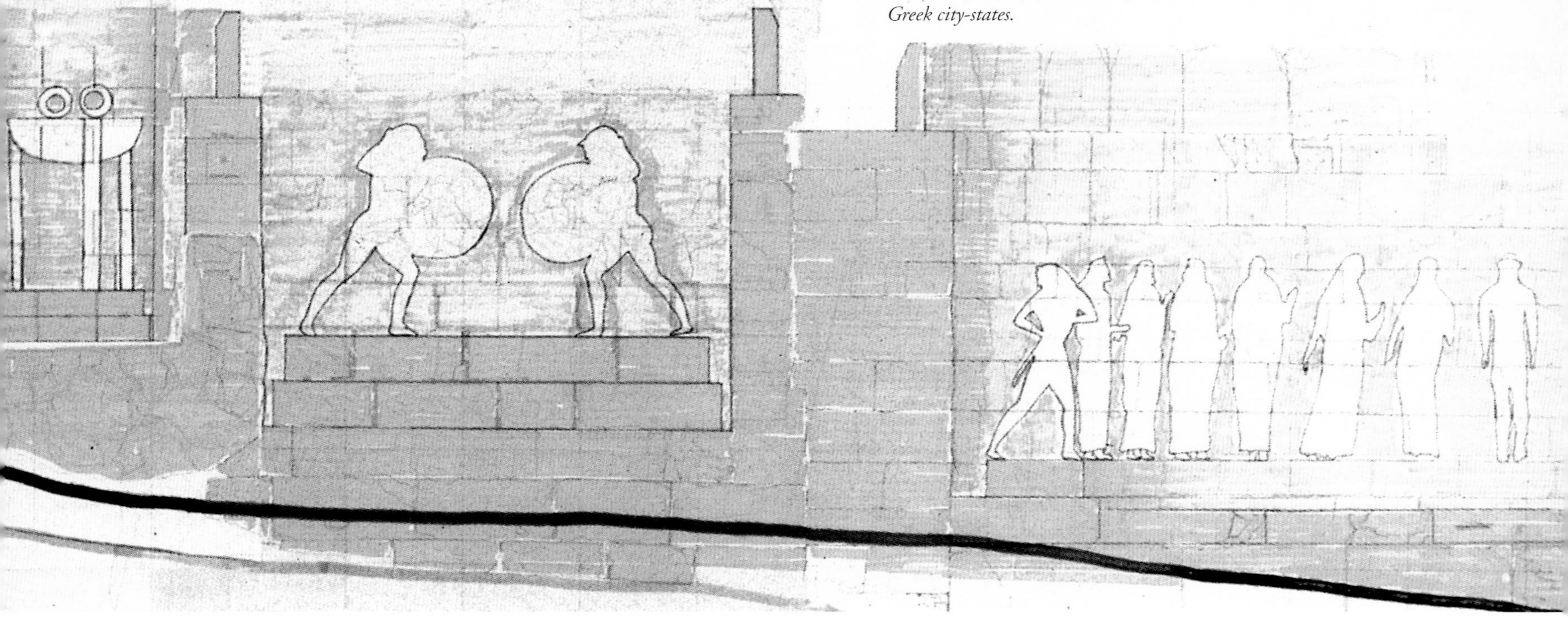

315

316

314

317

314-319. Since few of the dedications that were erected at Delphi have left any traces, some of the small votive bronzes convey the wealth of offerings at the sanctuary.

314. Odysseus escaping from the cave of Polyphemos, tied beneath a ram (early Archaic period).

315-316. Herakles bringing the Erymanthian boar to Eurystheus, who hides in a pithos (late 6th c. BC).

317. A group of bronze figurines depicting Apollo and athletes (6th-4th c. BC).

318. A bronze censer supported on a peplophoros kore with raised arms. Outstanding work of the decade 460-450 BC.

319. Bronze dedications of Roman times.

318

319

4TH-CENTURY ARCHITECTURAL DEVELOPMENT

THE THOLOS

In the first quarter of the 4th century, one of the most interesting monuments of ancient Greek architecture was erected in the sanctuary of Athena Pronaia: the tholos by the architect Theodoros from Phokaia in Asia Minor. This circular building, 13.50 m. in diameter, was surrounded by 20 Doric columns on the outside and had 10 Corinthian columns on the inside. The superstructure is of Pentelic marble, but the walls are set on a layer of dark Eleusinian stone, giving the building a fine two-colour appearance. Despite being in the Doric order, the tholos was lavishly adorned with superb mouldings and relief metopes in the diorama of the peristyle and the wall. With its light proportions, clear sculpted lines and high-quality workmanship, it is one of the finest works of architecture of antiquity. Its function is not completely clear. It was thought to have been connected with a chthonic cult of a god or local hero, like the tholos at Epidauros, but the most recent theory sees it as simply a circular treasury in which statues were kept, like the Philippeion at Olympia.

In 373 BC, a major natural disaster struck the sanctuary: the same earthquakes that caused damage throughout the Corinthian gulf and led to the

320

321

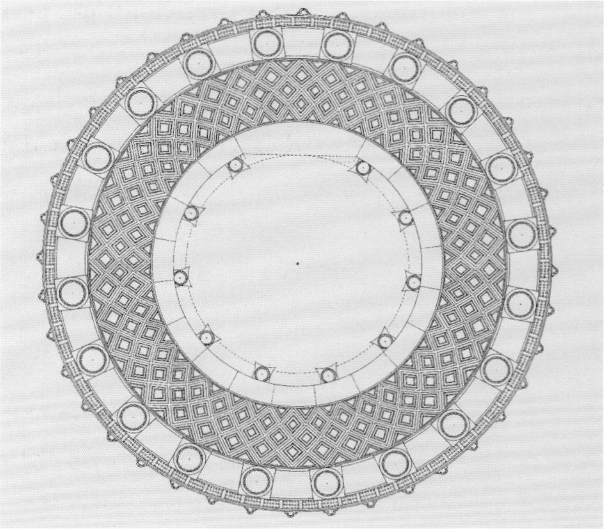
322

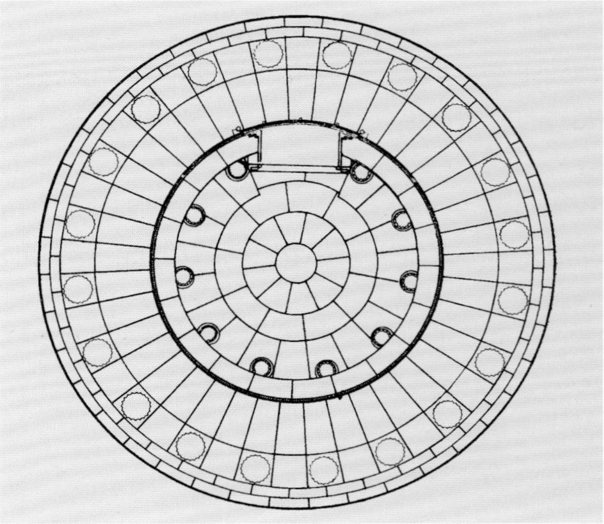
323

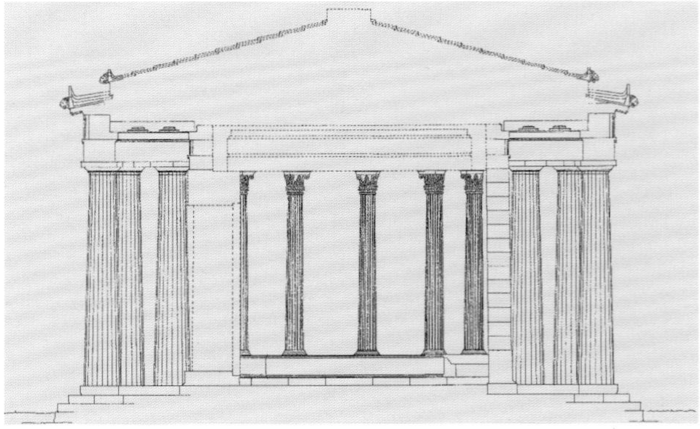
324

325

320-321. Aerial view from the northwest of the ruins of the sanctuary of Athena Pronaia, with a three-dimensional reconstruction of the most important building, the tholos. The sculpted akroteria at the edge of the roof are particularly impressive. Athens, French Archaeological School.

322-324. Three drawings of, from top to bottom, the ceiling, the plan, and the lateral section of the circular building, known as the tholos at Delphi. Athens, French Archaeological School.

disappearance of Helike caused a fall of stones from the Phaidriades rocks that destroyed the temples of Apollo and Athena, as well as many dedications, including the Charioteer, which had remained standing for 100 years on the terrace above the temple. Once again, Delphi was obliged to seek contributions from Greek cities of the Mediterranean to cover the sum needed to build the new temple. The contributions were recorded on stone slabs erected in the sanctuary. It is interesting to note that the smallest sum was noted, even though the cost of inscribing the name of the donor was greater than the donation itself. In the eyes of the god, all contributions were of equal value.

The construction of the new temple of Apollo began in 370 BC, under the supervision of special officials called *naopoioi.* Work did not proceed without obstacles, however, since at this period, two more sacred wars were declared that created turmoil throughout the whole of central Greece. During the Third Sacred War, the Phokians once more cultivated the sacred land of Apollo. They were severely punished by the Amphictyonic League, in reaction to which the Phokians seized the sanctuary and defended it for ten years (356-346 BC). To meet the costs of the war, they not only seized the sanctuary's funds but also melted down many of the dedications, one of which was the bronze tripod of the Plataians, to strike coins. Despite the fact that these actions called forth the wrath of the Greeks, both the Athenians and the Spartans sided with the Phokians for political reasons, mainly to obstruct the intervention of Philip of Macedon, who was waiting in the wings. In the end, Philip did intervene and obliged the profaners to surrender unconditionally. The Phokians were expelled from the Amphictyonic League, and their two votes were appropriated by Philip, who then assumed the status of official protector of Delphi. The Phokians were also obliged to deposit huge sums of money with the sanctuary as compensation, which made a significant contribution to the resumption of building work on the temple. To commemorate this victory, the Amphictyony dedicated a huge statue of Apollo, 15-16 m. high, in front of the temple, with the epithet 'Sitalkas,' that is, patron of grain and the harvest in general.

The Fourth Sacred War broke out a few years later, in 339 BC. The cause on this occasion was the encroachment of the Lokrians on the plain of Krisa and their erection of a fortification wall around the port of Kirrha. The Amphictyonic League declared war, and, at the urging of the Athenian delegate at Delphi, the orator Aischines, Philip assumed responsibility for its conduct. Having destroyed Amphissa and restored order, Philip returned to central Greece and comprehensively defeated an alliance of Athens and Thebes at Chaironeia in 338 BC, thereby removing the final obstacle to his expansion southwards.

325. A view of the three restored columns and part of the entablature.

326. Axonometric reconstruction of the later temple of Athena Pronaia. The temple, which was built in the decade 370-360 BC, was hexastyle prostyle, with only six columns on the facade. Athens, French Archaeological School.

327. Three-dimensional reconstruction of the buildings in the sanctuary of Athena Pronaia. From the left: the new, prostyle temple of Athena, made of grey stone; the tholos, a masterpiece of the 4th c. BC; and two treasuries. The earlier treasury, dating to about 530 BC, is attributed to the Massiliotes; the Doric treasury dates from just after the Persian Wars. In the right foreground is the Doric poros temple of the 6th c. BC. Athens, French Archaeological School.

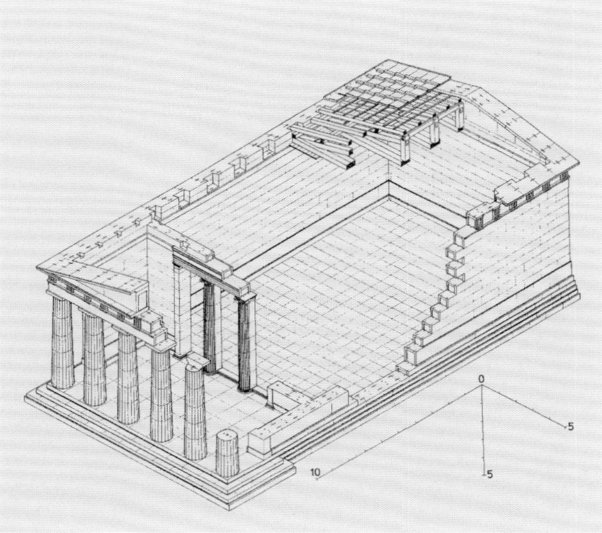

326

327

THE NEW TEMPLE OF APOLLO

328. General view of the new temple of Apollo from the southeast. The ruins are dominated by the columns of the temple, vying with the tall cypress trees.

329. Apollo is depicted seated on a folding stool in the interior of a white-ground kylix. He wears a laurel wreath in his finely coiffed hair. His dress – peplos and himation – is unusual in a male figure. He holds the lyre in his left hand and a libation bowl in his right, which he holds out before him in a ritual gesture. Opposite him, on a ground-line, stands a crow, which was regarded as a bird with powers of prophecy. (About 470 BC). Delphi, Archaeological Museum.

330. View of the new temple of Apollo. Before it can be seen the altar of the Chians, the ramp leading up to the pronaos, and some of the dedications in front of the temple. The columns, made of Corinthian poros, were restored in 1938-1941.

331. General view from the northwest of the temple of Apollo. Note the contrast between the sculpted parts of the temple and the rough natural Phaedriades rocks in the background.

Finally, in 330 BC, a large new temple of Apollo was inaugurated in the presence of delegates from all the Greek cities. The Athenian mission led by the orators Lykourgos and Demades amongst others, offered a bronze tripod 1.75 m. high to Apollo. The temple, the remains of which can still be seen, was the most important building in the sanctuary and the centre of the cult and the oracle: in it stood the cult statue of Apollo, and the oracular process took place in its innermost sanctuary. It was an elongated Doric building with columns and an entablature of Corinthian poros, while the foundation, pavement and walls were of hard light blue limestone from Parnassos. The pedimental compositions were carved by Athenian sculptors: the east pediment depicted the epiphany of the god between Leto, Artemis and the Muses, while the west showed Dionysos amongst his Delphic attendants, the Thyiades. Persian shields taken at the Battle of Marathon were nailed to the undecorated metopes of the temple.

Very little is known of the interior layout of the temple. The dicta 'know thyself' and 'nothing in excess', attributed to the seven sages, were carved on the walls of the pronaos, as was the enigmatic letter E, originally in wood and later in bronze, finally being made gold by Livia, the wife of Augustus. In the pronaos, there was also a bronze bust of Homer on a stele, on which was inscribed the famous oracle for the many cities who claimed the poet as their own. According to the ancient literary sources, the cella of the temple was divided into two parts. In the first was an altar of Poseidon, statues of Zeus, Apollo and the Fates, the altar of Hestia with the 'undying fire,' and the throne of Pindar, on which the poet sat and sang 'all the songs to Apollo.'

Recent research into the architecture of the temple has shown that the cella had two side doors at the east end. Of the interior colonnade, only the four columns to the east were erected. The rest was designed at three or four different levels leading to the adyton at the back of the cella, the place in which the prophesies were made.

The presence of Dionysos at Delphi is noteworthy. The coexistence of this god with Apollo is at first sight incomprehensible: how can the god of moderation and rationality exist in the same place with the god of intoxication and

328

329

the irrational? This paradox, however, is another example of the breadth and receptivity of the Greek spirit to expressions of different character. Indeed, the god of Delphi and his oracle officially supported the cult of the new god, which, as we know from Euripides' *Bacchai*, initially met with great hostility. This support went so far that Apollo ceded to Dionysos not only a place in his temple but also time: during the three winter months that he was absent from Delphi, the sanctuary was given over to Dionysiac celebrations, with the Bacchai ascending Mount Parnassos and the companions of Dionysos, the Thyiades, whirling orgiastically. To quote Christos Karouzos once again, 'It was the period when the paeans for Apollo ceased, and the dithyrambs of Dionysos echoed.' Thus, Delphi integrated the mystic peace and harmony of the Apollonian spirit and the inspired madness of the Dionysiac in a unique balance. The strong presence of Dionysos at Delphi has led modern scholars to suggest that this god is the crystallisation of earlier, prehistoric cults of nature and fertility at Delphi, which never ceased to be practised alongside the great cult of the god of light.

330

THE GYMNASIUM

This same period was one of great prosperity and produced many works of architecture. From about 330 BC, it dates the construction of the facilities of the gymnasium of Delphi, one of the earliest examples of such a structure. They were built on two long terraces in the steeply sloping mountainside between Kastalia and the sanctuary of Athena Pronaia. On the upper of these terraces are two parallel tracks about 180 m. long, which were used for practice for the running events. One, sheltered by a stoa for practice in bad weather, was called the *xystos* level, since it had to be scraped (*xyno*). The paradromis in front of and parallel with it was used for practice in good weather.

On the lower terrace was the palaestra, a rectangular building with an interior peristyle courtyard surrounded by rooms for various purposes connected with athletes' training. To the west of the palaestra are preserved the open-air baths, which had 11 fountain heads and basins fed by water from the Kastalian Spring, and a large circular cistern 10 m. in diameter and 1.80 m. deep, in which the athletes finished off their bath and could also swim to relax from the tension of training and competition.

At the same period, as part of a general reorganisation, the Delphians assigned to Aristotle and his nephew Kallisthenes the task of compiling a new list of victors at the Pythian games, since the archives, which were kept in the old temple, had been destroyed. The Delphians passed a decree honouring the two sages for this important work, though, unfortunately, it has not survived – unlike the corresponding list of Olympic victors.

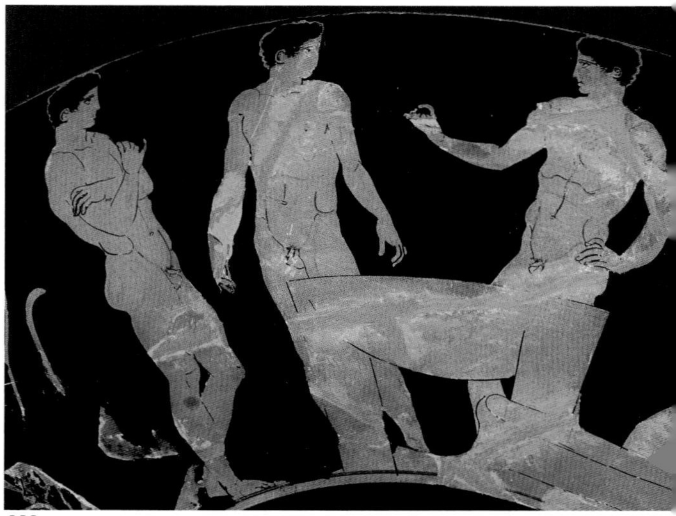
333

334

332

332. Model of the gymnasium at Delphi. In the background is the dominating long stoa of the xystos, with the palaestra, the circular pool and their annexes lower down the slope. Gift of the French Archaeological School of Athens to the mayoralty of Delphi.

333. Gymnasia contained facilities for bathing, in which the athletes could wash after training. Here youths wash at basins. Attic red-figure kylix (420 BC). London, British Museum.

334. Athletes cared for their physical well-being in the gymnasium. Here an athlete massages the back of a fellow-competitor. Attic red-figure kylix (ca. 460 BC). Rome, Museo di Villa Giulia.

335. General view of the ruins and of the gymnasium and palaestra at Delphi from the northwest. The buildings were constructed on terraces that followed the features of the terrain.

335

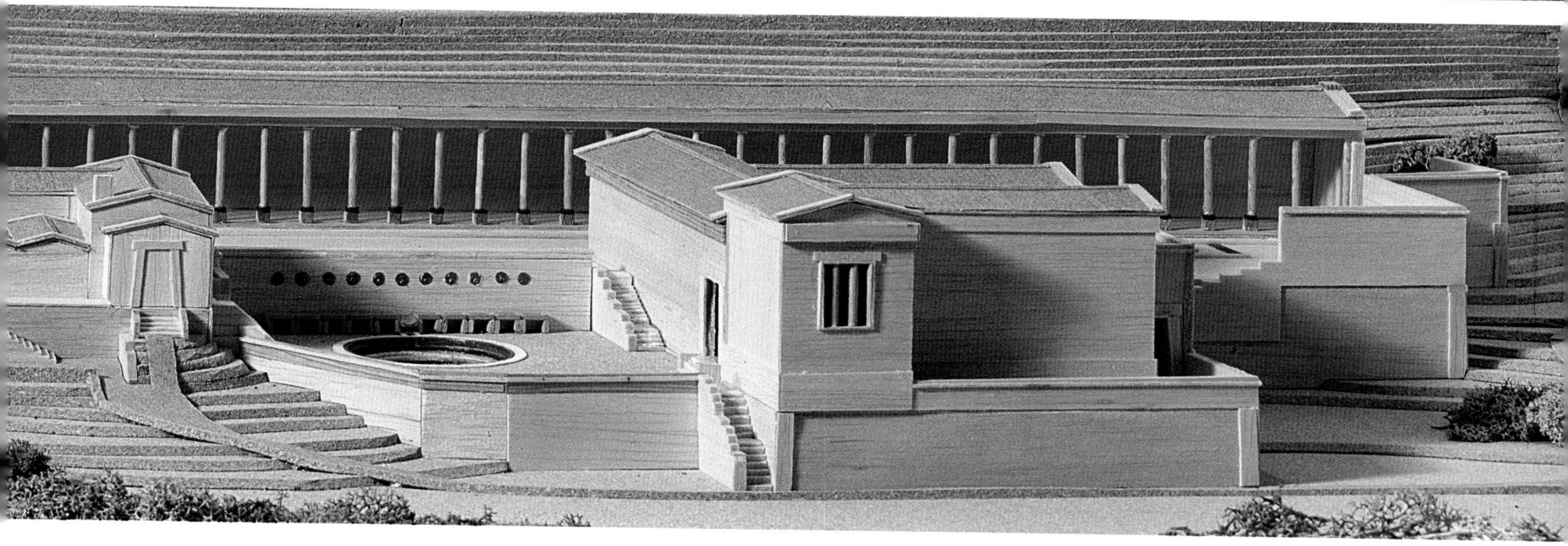

336-337. Athletes prepared for the contests in the gymnasia and palaestras. The preparation included exercises and training and medicinal baths. The athletes depicted here are named by inscriptions. On one side, a young slave massages the sole of his master's foot. Another athlete pours oil from his aryballos on his hand and prepares to rub it on his body before exercising. A third, on the right, carefully takes off his himation, watched by his young slave. On the other side of the vase, a young athlete binds his penis, while in the centre a discus-thrower practices under the guidance of a trainer wearing a himation. To the right, an athlete preparing to train hands over the garment he has just taken off. Kalyx krater by Euphronios (510-500 BC). Berlin, Staatliche Museen zu Berlin-Preussischer Kulturbesitz, Antikensammlung.

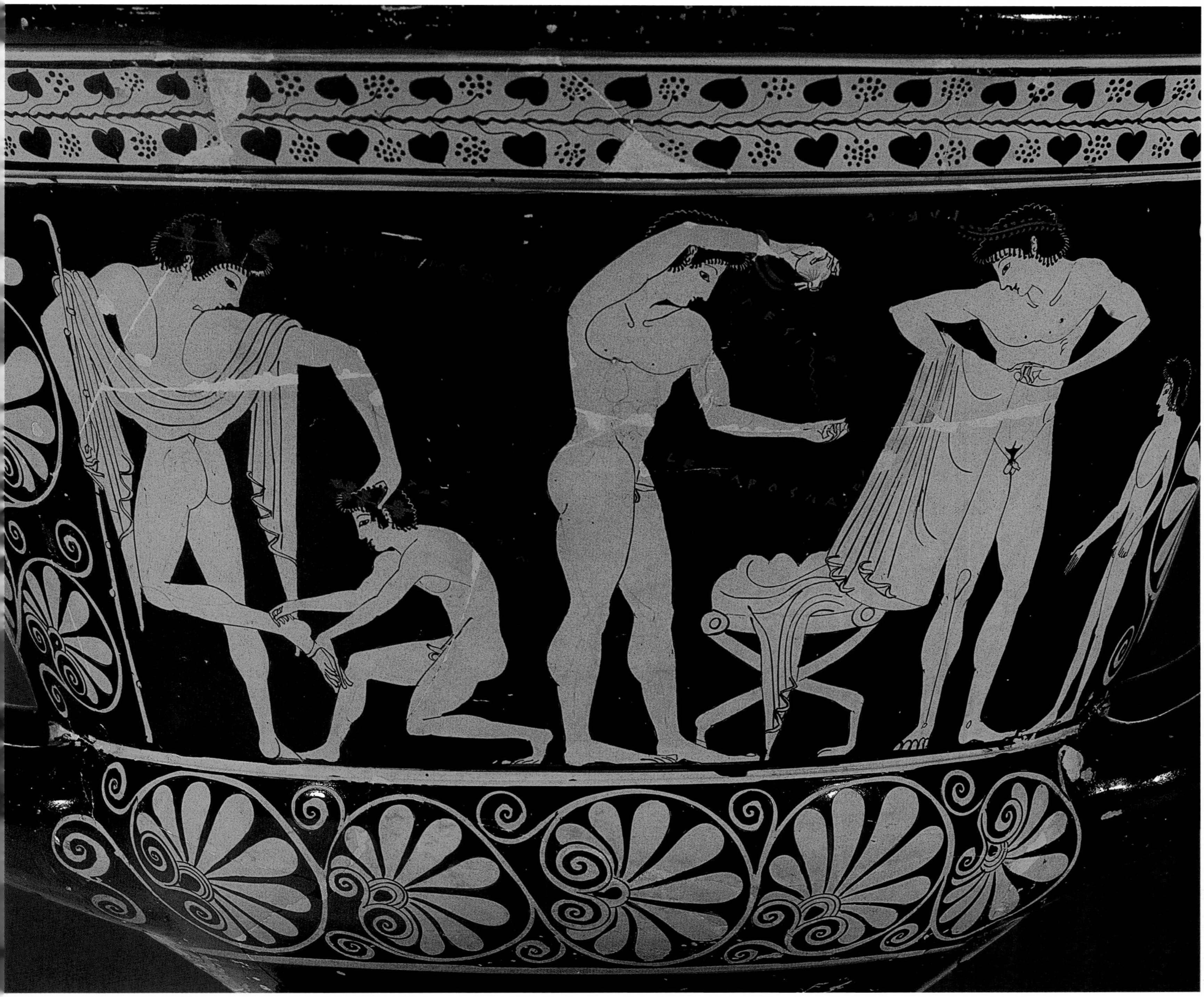

336

337

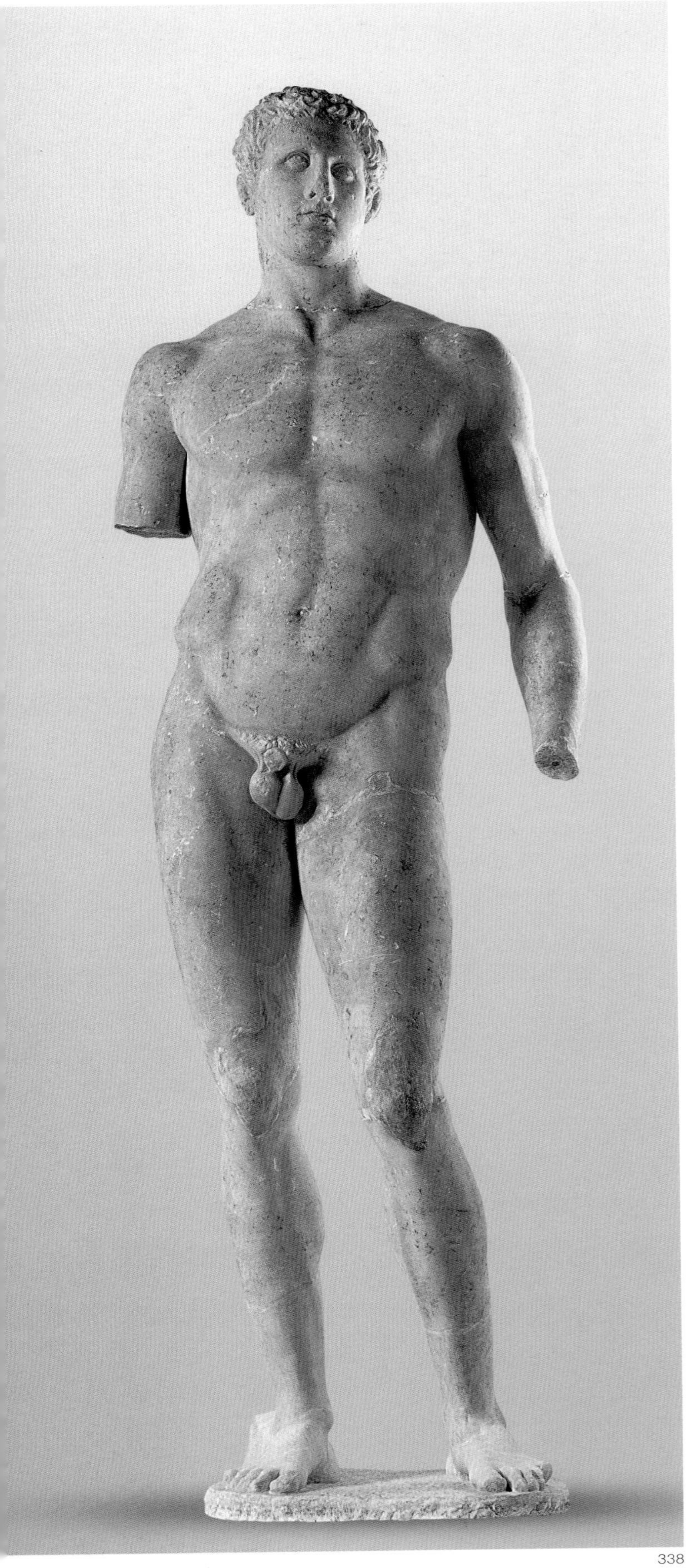

338

DEDICATIONS

Of the many dedications offered in the sanctuary in the 4th century, we may note three of a political character. They were dedicated by Peloponnesians in the decade 370-360 BC after victories won against the Lakedaimonians during the campaign in the Peloponnese by Epaminondas of Thebes. One was by the Arkadians, one by the Tegeans and one by the Argives. Only the pedestals survive, together with inscriptions referring to the dedicators and the people depicted.

Two dedications of this period survive in a very good state of preservation. One is the group of nine statues offered in 336-332 BC by Daochos II of Pharsala, tetrarch of Thessaly, when he was the Thessalian delegate to the Amphictyonic League. Apart from the seated Apollo, all the other standing figures were ancestors and members of Daochos's family. Three of those depicted, who were famous athletes of the 5th century, had won great victories in athletic contests at the Pythia. The pankratiast Agias, one of the greatest athletes of his day, had secured victories at all four great panhellenic games and had won five times at the Pythia. Indeed, in one of the Pythian games Agias and his two brothers, Telemachos and Agelaos, had achieved a feat unique in the history of sport, by winning victories in three different events on the same day: Agias in the pankration, Telemachos in wrestling, and Agelaos in the boys' stadion.

A few years after Daochos's dedication, possibly in the decade 332-322 BC, the Athenians erected an impressive monument: the Acanthus Column. It was 11 m. high and was topped by three dancing women, each 2 m. high, balancing a tripod on their heads with their hands. According to one view, they depict Herse, Pandrosos and Aglauros, the three daughters of Kekrops, the mythical founding father of the Athenians, supporting the famous Delphic tripod and thereby demonstrating the good relations between Athens and Delphi.

Finally, an example of the symbolic presence of Alexander the Great at Delphi is provided by the dedication offered after the king's death by Krateros, son of the Macedonian general of the same name, commemorating an incident in which he had saved Alexander's life. The monument is a rectangular niche to the west of the temple, in which was placed a group of bronze statues by Lysippos and Leochares, depicting Alexander and his general, Krateros, fighting a lion with the aid of hunting dogs.

At the end of the 4th century, the Rhodians erected a gold four-horse chariot behind the tripod of the Plataians. All that now survives of this chariot is the votive inscription: 'The people of Rhodes to Pythian Apollo.'

338. The pankratiast Agias. The best-preserved of the nine statues of the dedication made by Daochos at Delphi, in which the Thessalian tetrarch had depicted the distinguished male members of his family (336-332 BC). Delphi, Archaeological Museum.

339-341. An artistic reconstruction of the top of the acanthus column with the three dancing girls and the head of one of them. On the baskets they carried on their heads stood a bronze tripod cauldron in which, according to a recent suggestion, the omphalos depicted in fig. 222 was placed. According to the inscription on the base, the three figures were dedicated by the Athenians during the period 332-322 BC, and probably depict the three daughters of the mythical founding father of the Athenians, Kekrops. Delphi, Archaeological Museum.

339

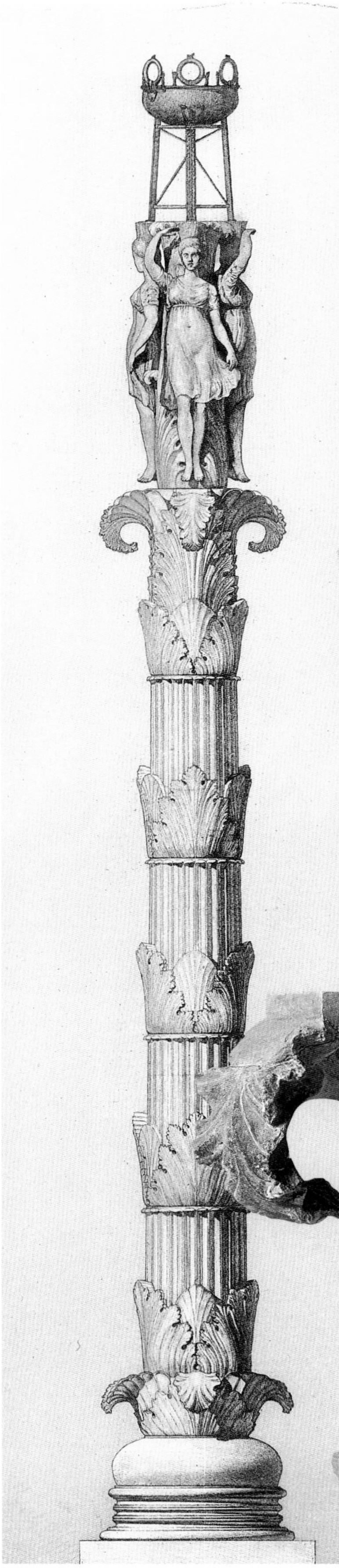

340

341

3rd - 2nd c. BC
The Hellenistic period

342. Marble statue of a philosopher or priest in the Delphic sanctuary. Characteristic work of the Hellenistic period (ca. 280 BC). Delphi, Archaeological Museum.

343. Entrance to the stadium at Delphi, where a monumental propylon with three niches for honorific statues was constructed in the 2nd c. AD. To the right can be seen the balbis *– the starting line for races – at the east of the stadium.*

After the dissolution of the city-state, there were two predominant forms of political organisation amongst the Greek states: either they had a democratic character, like the various confederacies, or they were absolutist, like the Hellenistic kingdoms founded by the Diadochi and Epigoni. In this international climate, Delphi could no longer sustain the role and power it had enjoyed in the Archaic and Classical periods. As Christos Karouzos states, 'The sanctuary at Delphi now played an entirely passive role, and was simply a mirror reflecting what was happening around it. It was still revered, but the powerful tended to ask it to confirm their wishes, and did not allow it any initiative. Their dedications were less a demon-

343

stration of piety or gratitude to the god and more an ostentatious proclamation of their personal success.'

The most important event in the history of the sanctuary in the 3rd century was the attack by the Gauls in 279 BC, occasioned by the fame of the treasures. Thanks to the resistance offered by the Aitolians, protectors of Delphi as the most important Greek power in this period, the Gauls were repulsed with great losses and the sanctuary was saved. To commemorate this event, another festival was founded at Delphi – the Soteria, which henceforth took place annually and included several of the events also held at the Pythia.

342

THE STADIUM

344. View of the stadium at Delphi from the west. The north side has twelve tiers and the south six.

It was probably at this period that the stadium at Delphi, some distance above the sanctuary, acquired monumental form, for it seems that hitherto the games had been held in the plain. The stadium was 600 feet (about 180 m.), the distance of the main event, the stadion race, and had 20 lanes for the runners. The form of the stadium today is the result of the renovation funded by the wealthy patron and scholar Herodes Atticus about the middle of the 2nd c. AD. Stone benches were constructed, 12 rows on the north side and 6 on the south, creating seating for about 6,500 spectators. A monumental propylon was built at the entrance to the stadium, with three arches and places for honorific statues, and part of the rock above was formed into a stepped balcony, giving a privileged view.

344

345

346

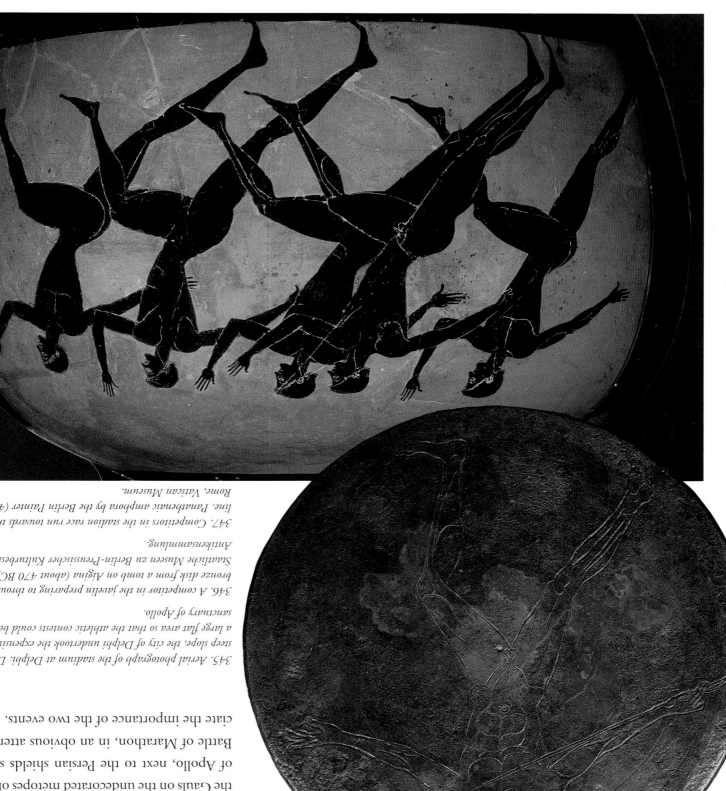

On the occasion of the victory over the Gauls, the Aitolians also built a large stoa outside the enclosure wall of the sanctuary, since there was no available space inside; in this stoa they displayed the spoils taken from the Gauls. They also hung the shields of the Gauls on the undecorated metopes of the Temple of Apollo, next to the Persian shields seized at the Battle of Marathon, in an obvious attempt to associate the importance of the two events.

345. Aerial photograph of the stadium at Delphi. Despite the steep slope, the city of Delphi undertook the expensive creation of a large flat area so that the athletic contests could be held near the sanctuary of Apollo.

346. A competitor in the javelin preparing to throw. Engraved bronze disk from a tomb on Aigina (about 470 BC). Berlin, Staatliche Museen zu Berlin-Preussischer Kulturbesitz, Antikensammlung.

347. Competitors in the stadion race run towards the finishing line. Panathenaic amphora by the Berlin Painter (480-460 BC). Rome, Vatican Museum.

347

THE THEATRE

The Hellenistic rulers of the East, who sought to emphasise their connection with motherland Greece through lavish benefactions to all the panhellenic sanctuaries, also contributed greatly to the architectural development of Delphi. Attalos I, king of Pergamon, erected a large Doric stoa, and his son, Eumenes II, either built or repaired the theatre, solely to house the musical and dramatic contests. The theatre at Delphi had 35 rows of seats and could hold about 5,000 spectators. Attalos II sent a team of painters from Pergamon to conserve the paintings in the stoa erected by his father, and also those in the Knidian Club that had been executed 300 years earlier by the famous painter Polygnotos. In the same period, Prousias, king of Bithynia, dedicated an equestrian statue of himself, standing on a very high pillar-shaped pedestal, in the open area in front of the temple. Finally, when the Delphians needed slaves for their flocks and for the temple, they addressed themselves to another king of Bithynia, Nikomedes, who possessed the finest, and he responded immediately.

348. The theatre of Delphi from above. The orchestra and the foundations of the stage can be seen, as well as the view enjoyed by the audience.

349. Scene from the performance of Euripides' Suppliants *staged in the ancient theatre at Delphi in 1930 by Angelos and Eva Sikelianos, as part of the Delphic Festival.*

349

1st c. BC - 4th c. AD
Roman times

Apart from the threat from the Gauls, the 3rd century passed by peacefully enough. At the beginning of the 2nd century, however, the rising power of Rome reached the sanctuary: in 191 BC, the Romans conquered the Aitolians and obliged them to abandon the territories under their control, including Delphi. In 168 BC, the consul Aemilius Paulus defeated the last king of Macedonia, Perseus, at the Battle of Pydna. This victory was sealed by a corresponding gesture to the sanctuary: a very high pedestal in front of the temple, which had been prepared for a statue of Perseus, received instead an equestrian statue of the Roman conqueror. The oracle naturally continued to function as usual, issuing responses even on public affairs. The words of the Pythia did not have the same force as before, however, since it was well known that major decisions were now taken by Rome, the ruler of the world.

The behaviour of the Romans in this period is reflected in the actions of the general Sulla. In 86 BC, Sulla was besieging Athens as part of his war against Mithridates, the king of Pontos, and was badly in need of money. He therefore asked the sanctuary to send him its valuable dedications, saying that it would be safer for him to protect them, and that if he used them, he would return them with interest. The priests did, in fact, send him many dedications, including the last of the silver pithoi dedicated by Kroisos, which were broken into pieces for easier transport.

Three years later, the damage was completed by attacks by Thracian tribes, who ravaged the sanctuary and torched the temple. These events and an increasing indifference to the oracle on the part of all the Greeks, as a result of its loss of prestige and splendour, resulted in Delphi falling into a state of abandonment that barely recalled earlier periods. This situation is described in stark terms by authors of the period, such as Cicero and Strabo, who visited the sanctuary.

350

THE ROMAN EMPERORS

350. The pedestal of the dedication of the Aitolians in honour of the Hellenistic ruler of Bithynia, Prousias, next to the southeast corner of the temple. It bore a bronze equestrian statue of the king.

351. Impost block from a dedication dating from the Roman period. The inscription refers to honours accorded by the city of Delphi to a Roman emperor. The stone at the bottom had a Greek inscription, over which the Latin inscription was carved.

352-353. Two of the six slabs of the frieze from the stage building of the theatre at Delphi, depicting the labours of Herakles. The hero struggles against the Lernaian hydra and wrestles with the giant Antaios (top) and the triple-bodied Geryones and the horses of Diomedes (bottom). The frieze was created to celebrate Nero's visit to Delphi in AD 67.

The visit by the emperor Nero in AD 67 proved devastating to Delphi, both materially and morally. He changed the year in which the Pythian games were held so that he himself could take part, winning, of course, the chariot race. He then distributed the plain of Krisa, which belonged to the sanctuary, to his soldiers. Finally, when he left, he carried off about 500 statues to Rome. In his honour, the Delphians carved the twelve labours of Herakles on a marble frieze that covered the proscenium of the theatre, since they knew that the emperor identified himself with the hero.

Other Roman emperors, however, showed their concern for Delphi, as well as for many other ancient sanctuaries, which experienced their last glimmering during the imperial period. Domitian visited Delphi in AD 84 and repaired

351

352

353

the Temple of Apollo, as is attested by a large Latin inscription. Hadrian, philhellene and classicist, showed great interest and paid two visits, in AD 125 and 129, on each of which he was named *eponymous archon* and honoured with statues and inscriptions. On the second occasion he was accompanied by his handsome favourite Antinoos, who, after drowning in the Nile, was honoured as a god throughout the empire on the emperor's orders. One of the finest statues of him has been preserved at Delphi.

During this period Delphi, like many other regions of Greece, was the recipient of benefactions by the fabulously wealthy Athenian Herodes Atticus who, inter alia, made the donation mentioned above and provided the financing for the construction of the stone benches of the stadium. At the same time, the courtyard with shops was laid out in front of the sanctuary of Apollo, and hot baths were built in the gymnasium.

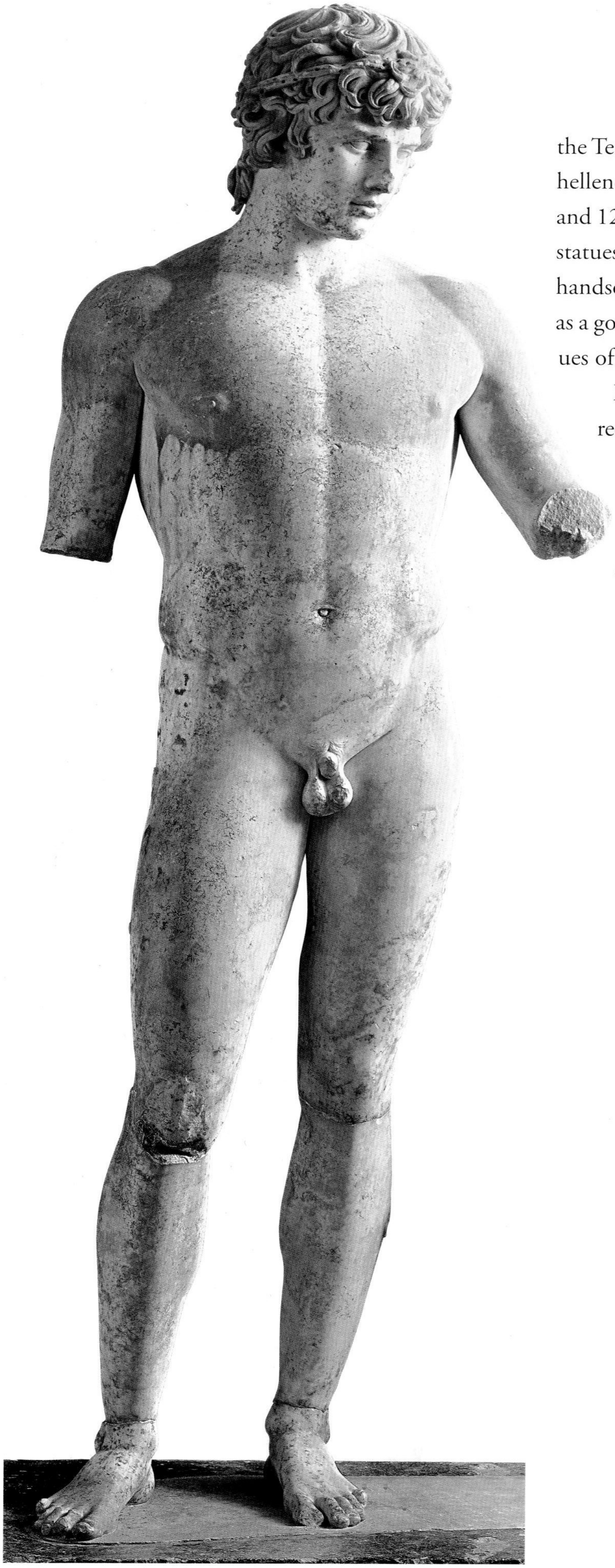

354

354, 356. The statue of Antinoos, the favourite of the emperor Hadrian (AD 130-138). Delphi, Archaeological Museum.

355. The statue at its discovery on July 13, 1894. It was discovered next to a brick wall behind the Temple of Apollo.

355

PLUTARCH AND PAUSANIAS

Two writers contributed important literary works relating to Delphi during the Roman period. The philosopher Plutarch, from Chaironeia in Boeotia, became priest of Apollo about AD 95 and held the office until his death in AD 125. In three works he has preserved a considerable quantity of evidence concerning the form of the sanctuary and the dedications in it, which he described as he walked and talked with his friends on the Sacred Way. Much information can also be derived from these writings on the cult and financial procedures of the sanctuary, of which he had personal experience. An idea of the respect for Plutarch entertained by the Delphians is provided by the inscription carved beneath his bust, a distant echo of the epigram of Thermopylae: 'Delphi and the Chaironeians together erected this bust of Plutarch, obedient to the decisions of the Amphictyons.'

357

357. View of the Roman forum at Delphi; in the background are the shops created in the 2nd c. AD.

358

358. The inscription carved by the inhabitants of Delphi on the pedestal of the bust of the philosopher Plutarch, who was priest at Delphi for about 30 years. Delphi, Archaeological Museum.

Another important literary document is the detailed description of the sanctuary by the traveller Pausanias, who visited Delphi about the middle of the 2nd c. AD. Since he mentions the monuments in the order in which he saw them, one after the other, this work was of the greatest assistance to the French excavators in identifying the monuments as they uncovered them in the 19th c. Without these two valuable literary sources, much of what we know of Delphi would never have become known.

In the 3rd c. AD, the so-called eastern baths were built outside the precinct for use by wealthy visitors, and the stoa erected by Attalos during the Hellenistic period was converted into a water cistern. Later, at the beginning of the 4th century, Constantine the Great, despite the honour that Delphi had accorded him with the erection of two statues, did not hesitate to remove other statues and the snakes from the tripod of the Plataians, which had survived to this date, and to carry them off to Constantinople to adorn his new capital city.

359

360

359. Portrait, probably of Titus Quintus Flamininus, the Roman consul who defeated Philip V at the battle of Cynoscephalai in 197 BC, thereby preparing the ground for the final subjection of Greece to the Romans (2nd c. BC). Delphi, Archaeological Museum.

360. Bust rendering the portrait of an unknown philosopher of the imperial period (2nd c. AD). Delphi, Archaeological Museum.

361. The last section of the Sacred Way after it was paved in Roman times. Plutarch and Pausanias walked over these slabs in the 2nd c. AD as they ascended to the Temple of Apollo.

361

The end of the sanctuary

Despite sporadic endeavours on the part of emperors and ordinary citizens in the 3rd and 4th c. AD, the sanctuary's life was now at an end. Indifference and the lack of pilgrims proved a bigger threat than plundering and destruction. The once glorious cities of Greece, now in decline and subjugation, no longer saw any point in seeking oracles or embellishing the sanctuary with dedications. Moreover, the rapid spread of the new religion led to the marginalisation of all regions in which the old religion had flourished. By now, Delphi was no more than a meeting place for a few pagan sages.

The Christian sages, in their unremitting struggle againts the idols, reviled the condition of the oracle in their writings: 'The oak no longer shines, no oracles are pronounced on the tripod. The office of Pythia is not filled. Kastalia is silent and the water is no longer prophetic, but ridiculous. Apollo is once again an unspeaking statue. The laurel is once more a plant mourned in myth,' wrote Gregory Nazianzenos.

The oracle itself accepted this situation. Although the authorship is disputed of the legendary oracle given by the Pythia to the last pagan emperor, Julian (360-363), the words still express graphically the true situation of the

363

362

362. Clay lamps from the Early Christian settlement that evolved at Delphi after the decline of ancient religion (5th c. AD). Delphi, Archaeological Museum.

363. The personification of Summer, one of the figurative compositions of the mosaic floor in the Early Christian basilica west of the sanctuary of Delphi.

364-365. Two closure slabs from an Early Christian basilica at Delphi.

366. Two representative clay vessels, a disk and a flask with red slip, from the Early Christian settlement at Delphi (5th c. AD). Delphi, Archaeological Museum.

364

365

366

sanctuary and the entire Greek world at that time. In response to Julian's attempts to revive the ancient religion during his brief reign, the oracle is said to have responded: 'Tell the king the decorated courts have been destroyed, Phoibos no longer has a home, nor prophetic laurel, nor a spring to talk, and the speaking water is silent.'

The end of Delphi was sealed, purely as a formality, by the edict of Theodosius the Great in 393/394, forbidding the practice of ancient religion and the conducting of the panhellenic games. Life at Delphi went on, however. In the 5th c. AD, a dynamic Christian community lived here, with a bishop's residence. Many of the ancient buildings in the sanctuary were converted into houses, and others into cisterns and bathhouses. To drive the ancient spirits far away it often sufficed to carve crosses and other Christian symbols, as on the altar of the Chians. Much has been written about the fate of the Temple of Apollo, but recent investigations have shown that it probably gradually fell into abandonment, and was not burned and destroyed by Christians. The impression given by the first excavations, however, which speak of the total destruction of its interior, is confirmed.

After the firm establishment of Christianity, three Early Christian basilicas were built in the area. In one, to the west of the sanctuary, near the modern village, are preserved mosaic floors with fine figurative compositions depicting the personifications of the seasons. Several luxury villas with hot baths, which have not yet been excavated, were also built in the surrounding area as far as Kastalia, and there were also pottery workshops that continued production until AD 620, when the village seems to have been abandoned, probably as a result of Slav invasions.

Delphi was reoccupied during the Byzantine period, when it was called Kastri. It continued to exist under this name until 1892, when the village was moved to a location about 1 km. west of the sanctuary, at a cost of 750,000 gold French francs of the day. Thereafter began the great excavation of the ancient site by the French Archaeological School of Athens, and the restoration of the sanctuary to the use of believers in the Greek past and to the study of those who slake their thirst at the springs of ancient wisdom.

Epilogue

The first oracle for mankind.

Homeric Hymn to Apollo

ORACLES AND THE ORACULAR PROCESS

The ancient evidence for the rituals at Delphi is not very extensive, though this lack does not imply that the priesthood forbade reporting of them, as in the case of other mystery cults, such as that at Eleusis. Most of our information is drawn from the relevant works of Plutarch, while Pausanias, in contrast, is quite sparing, possibly out of his excessive respect and religious zeal. Much is also known from the writings of the Church Fathers, though these are dominated by an outspoken prejudice against ancient religion.

The issuing of an oracle took place in the adyton of Apollo's temple, where the god himself was present in the form of his statue, and in which everything needed to engage in communication with him had been assembled. The adyton was divided into two rooms. The first, which was called the *oikos*, was a long rectangular room, in which waited the priests and the *theopropoi*, the people seeking the oracle. The second room, the *antron* (cave), was entered only by the Pythia. In it were all the sacred signs and objects connected with the oracle, such as the chasm in the earth from which vapour arose; the tripod on which the Pythia sat above or next to it; the omphalos; the sacred laurel; the water from Kassotis, a sacred spring to the east of the sanctuary; a gold statue of Apollo; and the grave of the Python or Dionysos.

As is revealed by the name of the room ('cave') and by its design, an effort was made to re-create, in the man-made adyton of the temple, the natural setting in which the oracular process was carried out in the first period of the ancient cult, before the erection of the temple. The essential elements are either natural (cave, chasm, tree, water), symbolic objects (tripod, omphalos), or artefacts suggesting the divine presence (statue, grave of the Python or Dionysos). Light is shed on this subject by the findings of recent investigations inside the temple, which indicate that efforts were made to keep the area as natural as possible.

367-368. Plan and reconstruction of the adyton of the Temple of Apollo, where the oracular process took place. These are based on the scattered evidence of the sources, since the site had been completely destroyed when it was excavated.

369. The facade of the Kastalia Spring in the Hellenistic period, as cut into the vertical face of the Phaidriades rocks. Actual or symbolic washing in the water of Kastalia was necessary for all those connected with the oracular process.

370. The oracular tripod on which the Pythia sat was a sacred vessel which, in the view of the ancients, helped her to make contact with the god. Modern copy of a Geometric tripod dating from the 8th c. BC. Olympia, Archaeological Museum.

367

The most truthful of all oracles.
Strabo

Interpretation of the Delphic Oracle

It is not easy to provide a clear answer to the question of precisely what went on at Delphi. The views of scholars range between two extremes. Pragmatists believe that the entire process was a well-conceived charade aimed at exploiting the ignorance, faith and superstition of the ancient Greeks. Adherents of mysticism believe that the Pythian priestesses were actually mediums, who had the power to communicate with the 'other side' and could somehow foresee the future. A series of facts should be taken into account by anyone wishing to investigate the phenomenon in greater depth.

Ancient Greeks lived in an atmosphere of superstition and, regardless of their level of education, had a great thirst for specific guidance, both in their daily problems and in great historical decisions. Oracles were natural recipients of the anxiety of both individuals and city-states seeking help.

The Pythia, who acted as the intermediary between the god and the faithful, was not selected at random. She had to be a highly sensitive woman who was able to fall into a trance, not only believing that she communicated with the god, but also convincing others of this ability. It is probable that the first priestesses or some specific woman from Delphi possessed this gift, which led to the oracle's becoming famous. The Pythia was probably chosen by the priesthood on the basis of her faith and devotion to the cult of Apollo, and was therefore selected only from the surrounding area, where the population must have lived in an atmosphere of extreme reverence for the god. The certainty that Apollo regarded the future Pythia as his chosen one would undoubtedly have affected the psychology of some women, cultivating in them a predisposition to fill the office. It is not impossible that, in the selection of a new Pythia, the procedure followed was similar to the one observed today in the choice of a new Dalai Lama in Tibet. That is, a young girl on whom the choice fell would be brought up with the necessary theoretical and practical teaching to make her worthy of serving in the temple when a successor to a priestess was required.

The priesthood at Delphi, which ultimately recorded and composed the oracles, consisted of intelligent, educated and experienced men. Plutarch, whose intellect emerges clearly from his writings, was a priest at Delphi in the 2nd c. AD. He was not an isolated instance. The priests had to be truly wise, and to have an understanding of psychology, in order to deal with personal questions. For oracles relating to distant regions (e.g., questions relating to colonisation) and for responses on international affairs, they had to be familiar with the mythology and history of every land, as well as its geography, politics and social conditions. On all these matters, they may have received information from representatives, or 'agents', in these regions.

An important role in the oracular process was also played by *proxenoi*. These were inhabitants of Delphi who acted as representatives of specific cities and had a duty to act as guides to pilgrims and assist them at every phase of the oracular process. There can be no doubt that, during their dealings at Delphi, interested parties would be discreetly questioned by the proxenoi, who were thus able to learn about their condition, the problems concerning them, and so on. All of this would be channelled to the priests, who would certainly take it into account in composing the final oracle.

The oracles, normally very general and ambivalent, left the interested parties wide scope for interpretation. The priests had great experience in the art of formulating the words of the Pythia in a response that was ambiguous or contradictory, cast in the form of a riddle, or even had several different meanings. These oracles usually needed further interpretation, and, once the petitioners had returned home, they would have recourse to local seers and interpreters.

Many ancient historians report complaints made by believers that the god had deceived them with his 'dark', obscure words. In the end, however, the god was always shown to be right, because an interpretation could be provided that differed from the one originally accepted by the believer. The error was therefore never ascribed to the god, but to the humans who had misinterpreted his words. The seeker may not have been satisfied, but the god's words were no doubt widely believed.

In the end, even if the oracles could be proved to be erroneous, the priesthood itself or local seers would circulate false oracles or mythical stories through which they sought to provide a convincing explanation of the oracular response

372

373

374

given by the Pythia. Such false oracles, known as prophecies after the event, were a common phenomenon, judging by the large number found in ancient literature.

375

376

372-374. The altar of the Chians (372), with inscriptions that provide a vivid picture of the relations between the priesthood, the god and the dedicators. In the founder's inscription (374), the Chians dedicated the altar to Apollo and in return, the city of Delphi granted the Chians the right of priority of consultation of the oracle (373).

375. Shard of an Attic red-figure krater with the figure of Apollo. Next to him can be seen the tip of the laurel branch he was holding (middle of the 5th c. BC). Athens, National Archaeological Museum.

376. Measured drawing of the remains of ancient buildings in the sanctuary of Apollo just before the start of the major excavation in 1892. Athens, French Archaeological School.

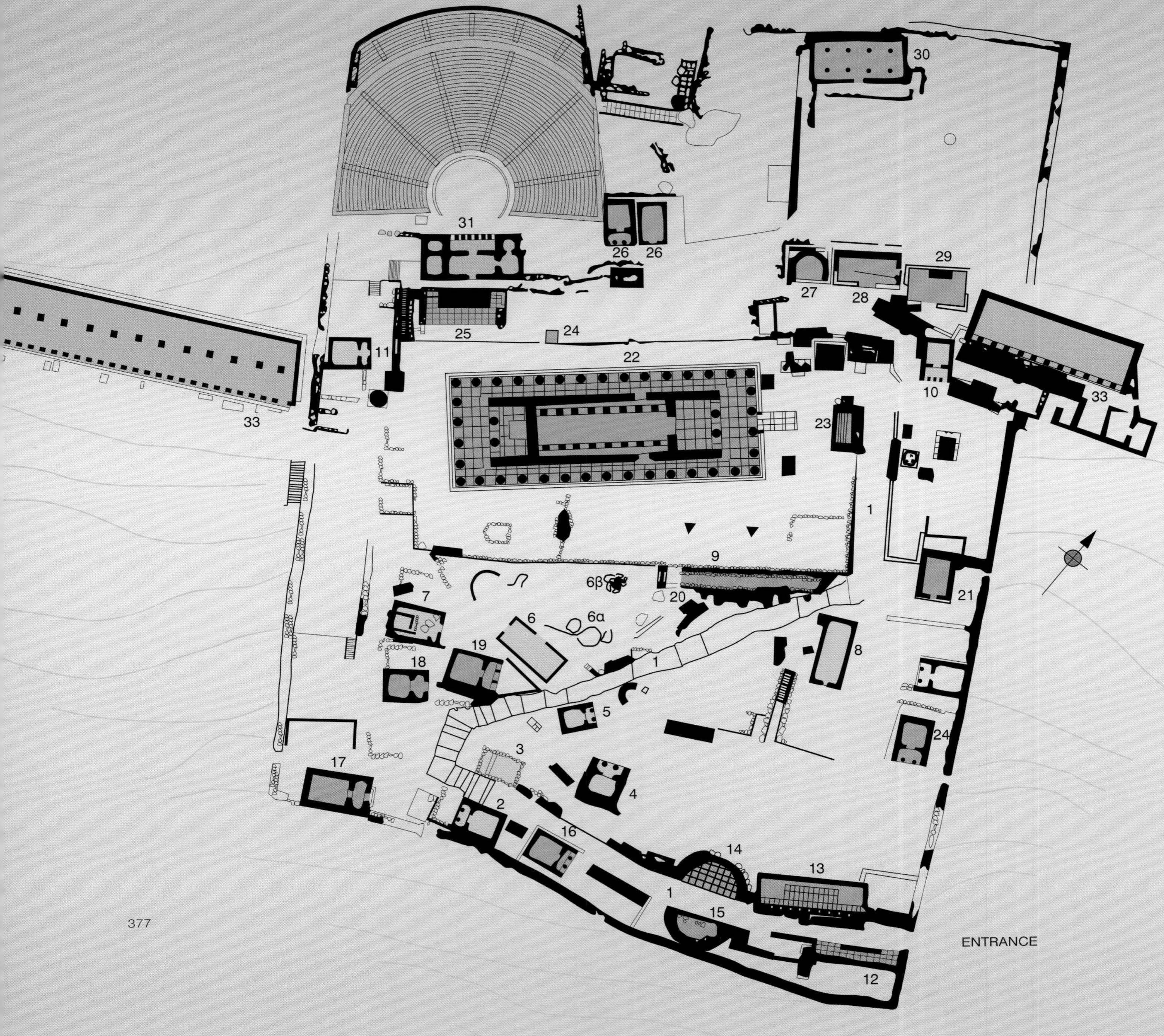

377

1. Sacred Way

ARCHAIC PERIOD

2. Treasury of the Siphnians
3. Treasury of the Megarians
4. Aiolian treasury
5. Treasuries of the Knidians
6. Bouleuterion
6α. Rock of the Sibyl
6β. Site of the Sphinx of the Naxians
7. Archaic treasury
8. Treasury of the Corinthians
9. Polygonal retaining wall
10, 11. Treasuries of the Archaic period

CLASSICAL PERIOD

12. Dedication of the Lakedaimonians
13. Dedication of the Tegeans
14, 15. Argive dedications
16. Treasury of the Sikyonians
17. Treasury of the Thebans
18. Treasury of the Potideans
19. Treasury of the Athenians
20. Stoa of the Athenians
21. Classical treasury
22. Temple of Apollo
23. Altar of the Chians
24. Site of the discovery of the Charioteer
25. Dedication of Krateros
26. Treasuries
27. Niche for a dedication
28. Dedication of Daochos
29. Precinct of Neoptolemos
30. Lesche of the Knidians

HELLENISTIC PERIOD

31. Theatre
32. Stoa of the Aitolians
33. Stoa of Attalos

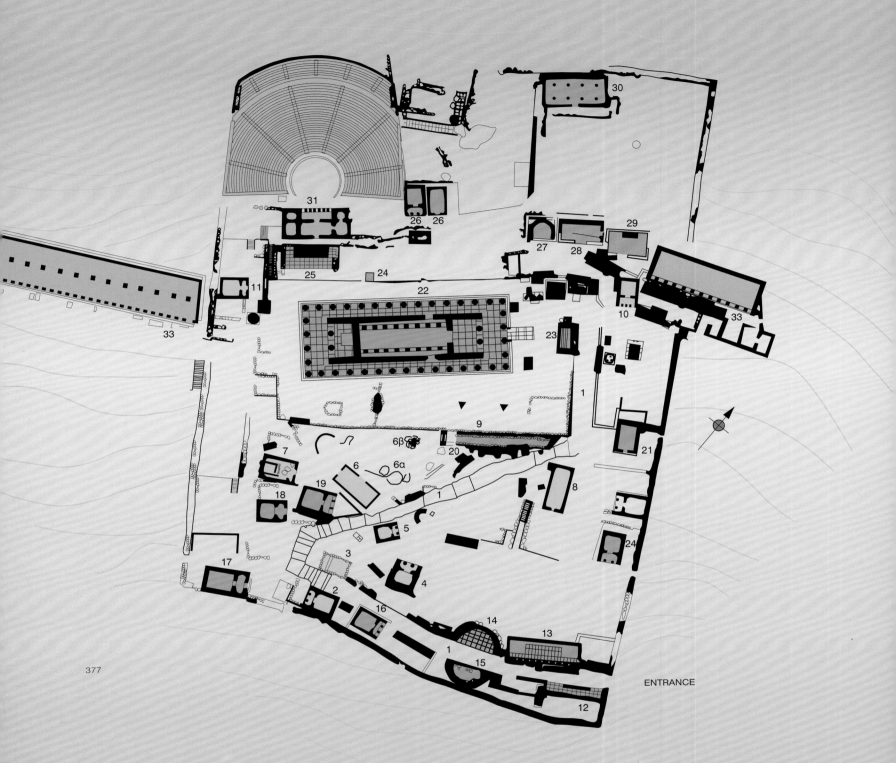

377. Modern drawing of the excavated area, with the buildings and dedications set according to eras. Paris, École Nationale Supérieure des Beaux-Arts.

378. Measured drawing of the excavated area and buildings of the sanctuary of Apollo just after the end of the major excavation.

Where the most splendid of oracles is to be found.

Origen

THE ORACULAR PROCESS

The formal procedure for issuing an oracle was roughly as follows. The Pythia, the priests and the theopropoi, who were to enter the adyton, first had to purify themselves by washing in the water of Kastalia. The theopropoi also had to pay a sum of money, offer a barley cake kneaded with honey, somewhat like the Christian offering of bread, and sacrifice an animal on the altar. After they entered the adyton, the priests and theopropoi stayed in the oikos while the Pythia descended into the cave, which was probably at a slightly lower level. There she listened to the question, drank the water of Kassotis, sat on the tripod, chewed laurel leaves and inhaled the vapours from the chasm. In combination with religious ecstasy and the belief that she was in communication with the god, the priestess abandoned her human substance and fell into the inspired state of a medium. She then began to express the god's will through inarticulate cries and incomprehensible syllables. The priests interpreted these in their own way, on the basis of fixed rules, and gave the answer in verse or prose. This is the version of the procedure agreed upon by most scholars, though some believe that the Pythia was not in an ecstatic state, and that she, not the priests, gave the answer directly. Whatever the precise procedure, the most important feature was that it could only take place in a specific place, the residence of the god, and that he sent his messages to humans only through the vehicle of specific persons, who were inspired.

The answer received by those who consulted the oracle was usually ambiguous and unclear. Famous is the oracle given to the king of Lydia, Kroisos, when he asked whether he should declare war on Cyrus, the king of Persia: 'If Kroisos crosses the river Halys [the border between the two countries], he will destroy a mighty empire.' The empire he destroyed, however, was not that of Cyrus, as

369

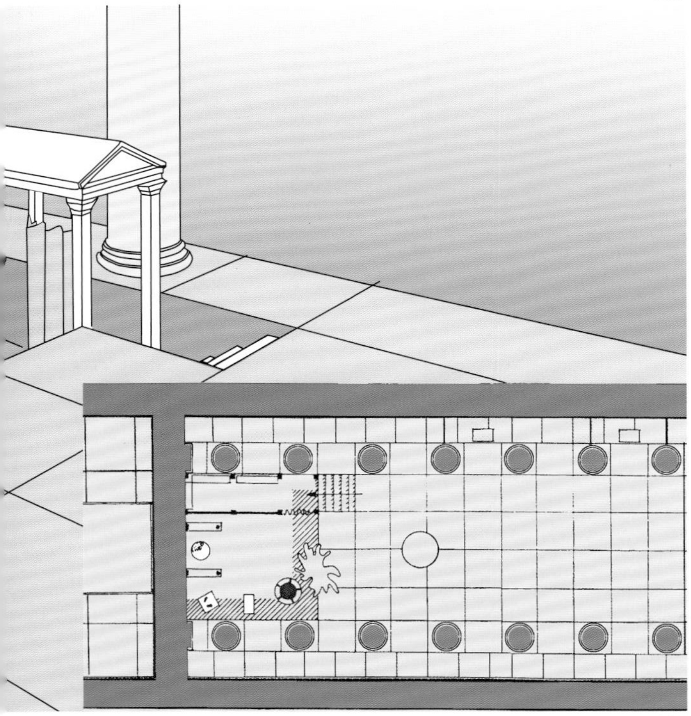

368

370

Kroisos expected, but his own. Another proverbial response was given by the Pythia to a man who asked if he would return alive from the war: 'You will go and come not in war to die.' Here the word 'not' can refer forwards or backwards, giving two contradictory meanings to the expression. Because of such ambiguous oracles, Apollo received the epithet *Loxias* ('Crooked', i.e., oblique, disingenuous). As the philosopher Herakleitos wrote: 'The king who has his oracle at Delphi neither reveals nor conceals, but gives signs.'

In the beginning, oracular responses were given once a year by a single Pythia. Later, however, in keeping up with demand, the number of priestesses was increased to three and the days on which oracles were given to nine – that is, one day a month, apart from the three winter months when the god was absent from Delphi. The first to be allowed to consult the god were the inhabitants of Delphi and those who enjoyed *promanteia* (right of prior consultation) thanks to their special relations with the sanctuary. This right was secured mainly by major dedications, by the Chians, for example, after they built the great altar, the Siphnians, after dedicating their treasury, and the Naxians for their offering of the Sphinx. The next to consult the oracle were the cities of the Amphictyonic League, followed by the rest of the Greeks, and finally the barbarians.

The questions addressed to the oracle were either of a personal nature or involved large groups (clans, cities, states, and so on). People believed that Apollo was wise when it came to the best interests of individuals or states, and were convinced of the rightness of the god's response. Private individuals wanted to now whether they should undertake a journey, whether they should embark upon an enterprise, or whether they should marry. The questions asked by cities related to declarations of war or the conclusion of peace, the adoption of a cult, the place to which a colony should be sent out, and so on. Of the 615 surviving oracular responses issued at Delphi, 73 relate to the foundation of colonies, while 130 have a political content. Of the total, 388 responses were connected with matters that directly or indirectly influenced the course of Greek history, whereas 185 dealt with questions of public religion. These numbers alone are enough to reveal the great importance of the oracle at Delphi.

371

371. Another view of the Kastalia Spring. The conduit that channelled the water into the ravine can be seen in front of the niches and at bottom left.

DELPHES
PLAN DV TEMENOS D'APOLLON
DIAZOMA
THEATRE
LESCHÉ DE CNIDE
Angle NE de l'enceinte
BARRAGE DE PROTECTION DES
Fontaine Kassotis
Scène
Offrande des Thessaliens
La Chasse d'Alexandre
Citerne romaine
Offrande de Gelon
Thermes
sacrée
CRAND TEMPLE D'APOLLON
Grand Autel de Chio
Char des Rhodiens
Trépied de Platée
Paul Emile
l'enceinte
Thermes romains
TERRASSE DE SOVBASSEMENT
Portique des Athéniens
Colonne des Naxiens
VOIE SACRÉE
Bouleutérion
Trésor des Athéniens
DE L'ECOLE
ANCAISE
Mur
Trésor des Béotiens
Trésor des Corinthiens
Trésor des Thébains
Trésor Siphniens
Trésor des Cnidiens
VOIE
Trésor des Sicyoniens
SACRÉE
Rois d'Argos
Ex-voto d'Ægos-Potamos
PORTIQVE
Epigones
l'enceinte
Entrée principale du Sanctuaire
ACTVELLE
D'ITÉA
Thermes
AT ACTVEL DES FOVILLES

ISTHMIA

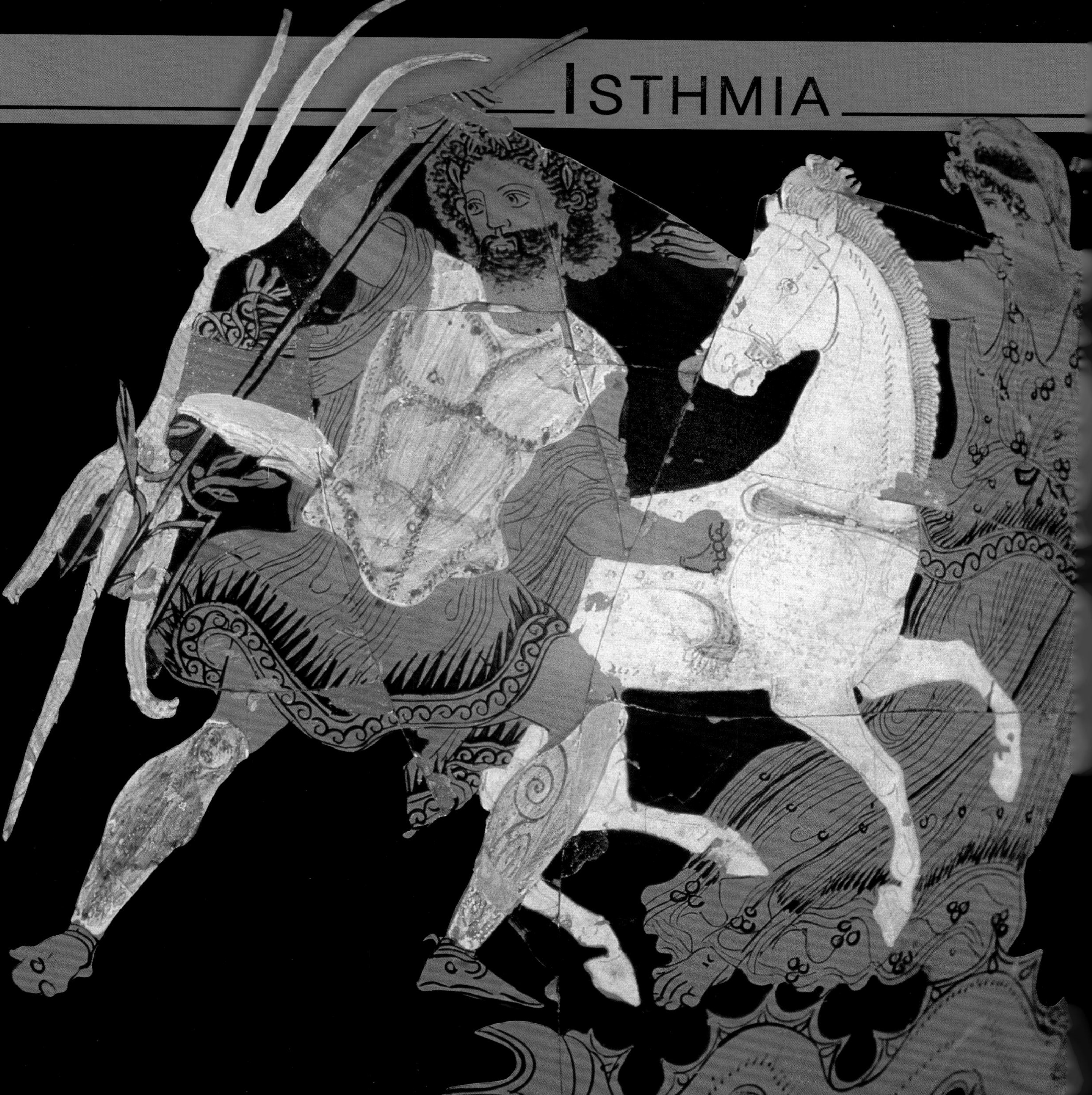

The Site

And at the Isthmus, that divides the restless sea like a bridge, we come to the festival where dwellers nearby come together amidst bull sacrifices at the altar of Poseidon…

Pindar

The importance of Isthmia and its emergence as a panhellenic sanctuary are owed to its location at the eastern edge of the Isthmus of Corinth, directly on the ancient road from Attica and northern Greece to the Peloponnese. The sanctuary is about 700 m. from the modern Corinthian canal and less than 1,500 m. from the coast of the Saronic Gulf. Furthermore, the beginning of the slipway, along which goods and possibly also the ships carrying them were transferred by merchants between the Saronic and Corinthian gulfs, was also near Isthmia. Isthmia, in short, was the gateway to the Peloponnese, and none of the ancient Greeks failed to break his journey at the sanctuary.

This role as gateway to the Peloponnese is attested in ancient times by an inscribed pillar, erected, according to Plutarch, by the Athenian hero Theseus. On the east side, this was inscribed: *This is not the Peloponnese, but Ionia*, and on the west: *This is the Peloponnese, not Ionia.*

379. Poseidon, the patron god of Isthmia, is represented as both sea and horse god in a contest with Athena. He is accompanied by his consort, Amphitrite. Fragment of an Attic red-figure hydria (late 5th c. BC). Pella, Archaeological Museum.

380

380. Part of the slipway over which the ancient Corinthians transported goods (and entire ships, according to some scholars) from the Saronic port Kenchreai to the port of Lechaion on the Corinthian Gulf, in order to avoid sailing round the Peloponnese. The important geographical position of Corinth was the main reason for the development of trade and the great fame acquired by the city.

381. Part of the slipway showing the two parallel tracks upon which carriages travelled to make the crossing swifter and safer.

382. Aerial photograph of the archaeological site of Isthmia from the west. At the right can be seen the few remains of the temple of Poseidon, with the theatre in the centre, and part of the bathhouse at the bottom left. The Saronic Gulf can be seen in the background.

381

382

Foundation Myths and Legends

Three myths were prevalent in ancient times regarding the foundation of the festival and games at Isthmia. According to the first of them, Athamas, the king of Thessaly, enraged at his wife, Ino, and their son Palaimon, pursued them, causing them to jump into the sea from the Skironian rocks and drown. However, a dolphin carried the child's body to the coast at Isthmia, where it was found by the mythical king of Corinth, Sisyphos (famous for the torment he suffered in Hades). Sisyphos called the child Melikertes, buried him, and founded the Isthmian festival in his honour. This legend suggests that there was originally an early cult of the dead (a hero cult) here, which was later supplanted by the cult of one of the Olympian gods. In this case the god was Poseidon, as we learn from the second of the three myths. According to this, the festival was founded by Poseidon after his victory over the sun god Helios, with whom he contended for control of the area. Finally, in contrast with these two traditions, which express the Corinthian version, the third myth is an Athenian creation. The games were founded by Theseus, on analogy with Herakles the founder of the Olympic festival, either because he cleared the sea of pirates, or in order to attain purification for the murder of the robber Sinis the Pine-bender, whom he encountered in the area of Isthmia on his way from Troizen to Athens.

383. According to Athenian mythical tradition, the Isthmian festival was founded by Theseus after he had exterminated the robber Sinis the Pine-bender in this area. Sinis killed passers-by by tying their legs to the branches of pine trees that he had bent over, and then releasing the branches. On this red-figure kylix, Theseus is shown killing Sinis in the same way (440-430 BC). London, British Museum.

383

384. Pedestal with the inscription 'Sisyphos', on which stood the statue of the mythical king of Corinth. According to the myth, it was Sisyphos who discovered the body of Melik-Palaimon, whom he called Melikertes, and buried it at Isthmia, therewith founding the sanctuary and games in his honour.

385. After their flight and leap into the sea, Ino and Palaimon were transformed into sea deities, with the names Leukothea and Melikertes. On this silver plate from Egypt they are shown in the sea, riding on a sea centaur (first half of the 7th c. AD). Athens, Benaki Museum.

384

385

Poseidon

386. The majesty exuded by the bronze statue found in a shipwreck in the sea off Artemision certainly renders the figure of a god, Zeus or Poseidon (about 460 BC). Athens, National Archaeological Museum.

387. The fortunes of the sanctuary at Isthmia over the centuries were connected directly with those of Corinth, the city that controlled the sanctuary. Aerial photograph of the archaeological site of ancient Corinth, next to the modern village of the same name, with the Corinthian Gulf in the background.

The god to whom the sanctuary at Isthmia was dedicated and in whose honour the Isthmian festival was celebrated was Poseidon, the ancient Greek god of the sea. He is mentioned in this capacity in the Homeric poems, which relate that when Kronos distributed power to his three male children, Zeus received heaven, Hades the Underworld, and Poseidon the sea. There is a superb description in book XII of the *Iliad*, where the god goes from Mount Olympos to his gold palace in the depths of the Aegean sea in three strides that make the mountains tremble. There he harnesses his two horses, climbs into his gold chariot, and drives it over the waves, without the axles getting wet. The waters joyfully open for him, and the sea creatures and monsters of the depths frolic in recognition of their lord.

A picture of the dangerous and fearful aspect of both the sea and the god emerges from another Homeric passage, in the *Odyssey*. From a mountaintop, Poseidon espies Odysseus on his raft; in a fury he seizes his trident and stirs up the sea, rouses the winds, covers everything with clouds and, finally, smashes the Ithacan's raft with an enormous wave, before returning, muttering to himself, to his palace in the sea.

In the figure of Poseidon, then, the ancient Greeks personified both the beneficial and the destructive aspects of the sea. It was natural, therefore, that his cult be found in areas that engaged in considerable maritime activity, such as Cape Mykale in Asia Minor and Capes Sounion and Tainaron in mainland Greece, as well as on Poros (ancient Kalaureia). Poseidon, however, appears to have been an older and originally more important god than Zeus, since his name is recorded on the Linear B tablets. The bull sacrifices held in his honour link him with Minoan Crete, and the Homeric epithets *enosichthon* and *ennosigaios* ('earth-shaker') also associate him with the earth, since they hold him responsible for earthquakes and other natural disasters.

The god was also looked upon as the ancestral father of tribes and the founder of many cities, such as Potidaia in Chalkidiki and Poseidonia in Southern Italy, and he also laid claim to other areas such as Athens, where he was the rival of Athena. In a similar riralry, his paternity of the sanctuary at Isthmia is attributed by myth to a contest with the sun god Helios similar to the contest with Athena. The choice of Poseidon as the deity worshipped in the sanctuary at Isthmia should certainly be associated with the site occupied by Corinth, mistress of the seas, the city whose mercantile ships dominated the Mediterranean during the Geometric and Archaic periods (ca. 1050-480 BC).

Isthmia Over the Centuries

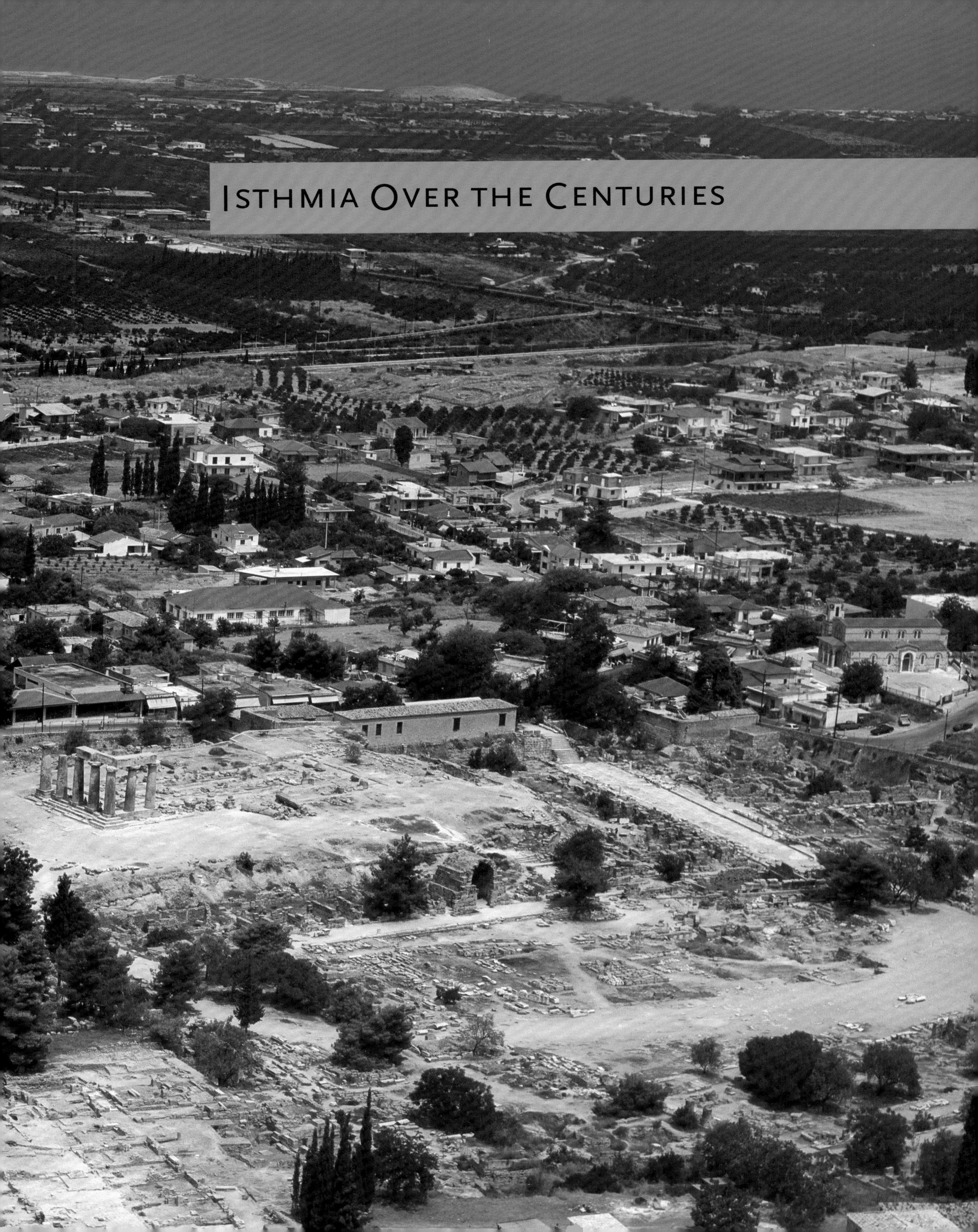

11th - 6th c. BC

Early history of the sanctuary

For the early history of Isthmia we rely exclusively on the evidence yielded by archaeological excavations in the area. The earliest indication of a cult is afforded by ashes from sacrifices carried out on the flat rock on which the altar was later erected. These ashes contained burnt bones of sheep, goats, pigs and birds, as well as broken unpainted clay vases dating from the Protogeometric period, about the middle of the 11th century. These finds indicate common feasts after sacrifices, with participants leaving behind the vessels they had used for food and drink. The sacrifices continued into the Geometric period, when the first dedications make their appearance in the sanctuary, in the form of bronze pins, terracotta animal figurines, and a few weapons and tripods.

388-390. Early dedications from the sanctuary at Isthmia, mainly bronze and terracotta figurines, most of them the products of Corinthian workshops. Particular interest attaches to the models of ships, which are associated with Poseidon's capacity as god of the sea. The small gold figure of a bull is connected with sacrificial animals.

391. The three darics (gold coins issued by the Persian king) are valuable dedications at a period when very few owned items of such great value (7th-6th c. BC). Isthmia, Archaeological Museum.

392. Reconstruction drawing showing the ground plan of the first temple of Poseidon. A long, rectangular building with 187 columns, it is one of the earliest temples of ancient Greek architecture (first half of the 7th c. BC). Drawing: F.P. Hemans.

388

389

390

THE FIRST TEMPLE OF POSEIDON

The first temple of Poseidon was built by the Corinthians in the first half of the 7th c. BC. This temple and another in Corinth itself are the earliest examples of monumental temple architecture and attest to the major contribution made by Corinth to the creation of the Doric order in Greece. The remains, though scanty, of the first temple at Isthmia enable scholars to reconstruct its form: it was a peripteral temple with 7 columns on the narrow sides and 18 on the long sides. On its longitudinal axis it had an interior colonnade with 7 columns, two of which were in the pronaos and 5 in the cella, which had two entrances, one for each aisle. The major innovations of the temple lie a) in the walls of the cella, which were built completely of stone and had painted decorations on the outside, and b) in the use of large double terracotta tiles, manufactured for the first time on this occasion, to cover the roof.

A bronze tripod of Geometric date was erected inside the cella, with a large marble *perirrhanterion* – a ritual bowl supported on four female statuettes standing on lions – next to it. Perirrhanteria seem to have been popular dedications in the sanctuary, since 75 others, made of terracotta, were set around

391

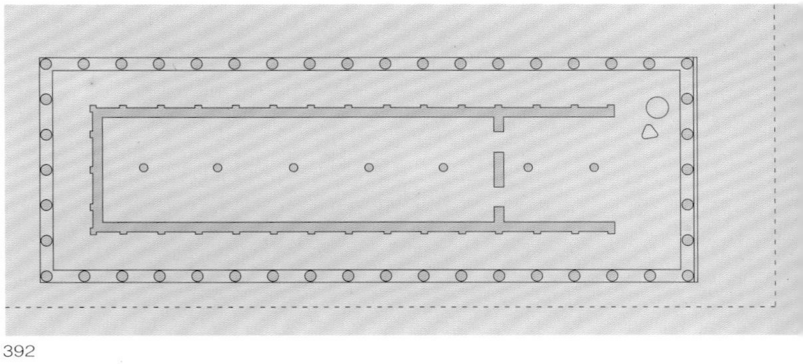

392

the temple in the 7th and 6th c. BC. In this period the number of votives – tripods, weapons, harnesses, jewellery and figurines as well as many terracotta utensils and vessels – increases, pointing to the growing reputation of the sanctuary. The first altar was probably erected at the same time as the first temple, in front of its facade.

393-395. Perirrhanteria, which were amongst the most common early dedications in the sanctuary of Isthmia, were connected with ritual purifications. Shown here are a marble perirrhanterion supported by four small korai, a restored clay one, and the base of a third on which the paint is very well preserved (7th-6th c. BC). Isthmia, Archaeological Museum.

393

394

Let us sing praises worthy of his victory at the Isthmian games.

Pindar

The games

THE HISTORY OF THE GAMES

In 582 BC, the Kypselid tyrants of Corinth who controlled the sanctuary decided to reorganise the old festival and, in this context, introduced contests on the model of the games at Olympia. Henceforth the festival was held every two years in spring, and its programme included, besides athletic and equestrian contests, *amilla neon*, a form of rowing, which was not held at any of the other panhellenic festivals. In addition to the three foot races known at Olympia, a fourth was added at Isthmia – the *hippeios*, a horse race run over a distance of four stades, possibly in honour of Poseidon, the protector of horses. The Isthmian festival also included music, poetry-recitation and painting. The prize was a wreath taken from the pine tree under which, according to the legend, Sisyphos found the body of Melikertes, though in fact, the pine was the most common tree in the region. The prize changed in the early 5th century, when a wreath of celery was awarded, in imitation of the Nemean

395

396. Head from a marble statue of a victor in wrestling at the Isthmian games. On his head, the youth wears a pine wreath, the prize for winners, which was cut from the sacred pine tree (1st-2nd c. AD). Isthmia, Archaeological Museum.

396

games. Both plants were used in Roman times. Throughout the entire period that the festival was held, it was supervised by Corinth, which also organised the games. The geographical position and rich, cosmopolitan character of the city were factors contributing to the development of the sanctuary into a major religious centre and to the fame acquired by the games throughout Greece.

The importance of Isthmia as a panhellenic centre is also evident from the fact that it was selected as the venue for some of the most important political gatherings of the leaders of the Greek city-states. It was here, in 481 BC, that the congress of 31 Greek cities was held at the initiative of Athens and Sparta to deal with the second Persian invasion under Xerxes. Here, too, were held two panhellenic congresses to decide on the Greek campaign against the Persians in 338 BC, led by Philip and, after his death in 336 BC, by Alexander the Great. Isthmia was also later chosen by the Roman general Flamininus to proclaim the 'freedom' of the Greeks after his victory over the Macedonian king Philip V at Kynoskephalai in 196/195 BC. This proclamation was repeated by the Roman emperor Nero in AD 67, when he visited the sanc-

397

398

397-400. When the Isthmian festival was reorganised in 582 BC, the events held at the Olympic games were introduced into the celebrations.

397. Scene from a jumping contest, showing the athlete raising his right leg and improving his performance by using halteres *(jumping weights). Interior of a black-figure kylix (510 BC). Paris, Louvre Museum.*

398. Intensive practice was required for the javelin event. Here, the athlete is learning the technique under the strict supervision of the trainer. Red-figure krater by the Kleophrades Painter (500 BC). Tarquinia, Etruscan Museum.

399. Four young riders in an equestrian event. Nude, they urge on their horses to gallop faster, using only movements of the reins. The equestrian contests at the Isthmian games are connected with Poseidon's capacity as patron god of horses. Attic black-figure column krater (550-450 BC). Athens, National Archaeological Museum.

400. Scene of a four-horse chariot and charioteer, nude and with a ribbon in his hair. He is depicted just as he gets on the chariot. He holds the reins in his left hand and a stick with which to spur on the horses in his right. Attic black-figure kylix (about 510-500 BC.). Thebes, Archaeological Museum.

399

400

tuary to take part in the games. We may note that the Romans acquired the right to take part in the Isthmian games much earlier than at Olympia, where they first participated in 4 BC. They were allowed to compete at Isthmia as early as the end of the 3rd c. BC, as an expression of gratitude for their clearing the seas of piracy in 229 BC.

401. Alongside the athletic events at the Isthmian games there were also music contests. On the left, a victorious kitharode on a stepped podium between a hovering Victory and a seated judge. Attic red-figure pelike (440-430 BC). Athens, National Archaeological Museum.

402. A victorious athlete places the wreath on his head, or perhaps simply touches it. Attic white-ground alabastron (about 480 BC). Berlin, Staatliche Museen zu Berlin-Preussischer Kulturbesitz, Antikensammlung.

403-404. Two marble victory stelai of Roman date, erected in the sanctuary at Isthmia. On the left, a stele with the portrait of the flute-player Cornelius of Corinth, victor at many panhellenic games, including the Isthmian, Pythian, Nemean, Actian, and Panathenaic games. The stele on the right is decorated with relief wreaths of various plants, in which are inscribed the names of the games for which they were awarded as prizes: the Olympic, Capitolian, Actian and other games (2nd c. AD). Isthmia, Archaeological Museum.

401

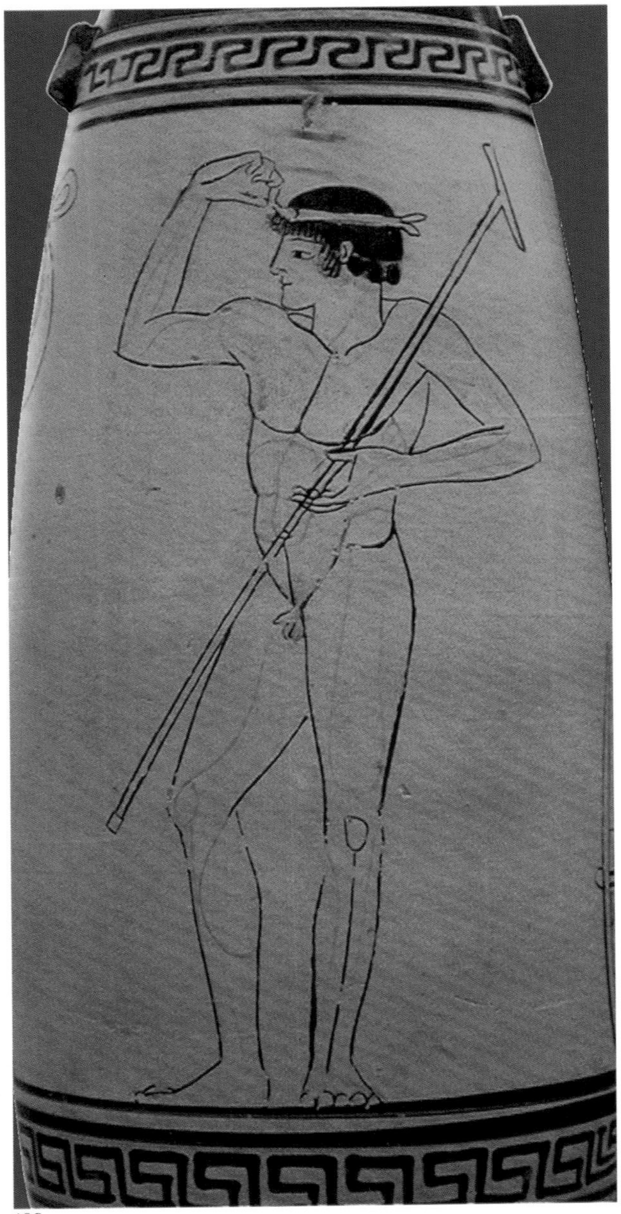

402

403

404

THE 6TH-CENTURY STADIUM

After the games were instituted, the need arose for buildings and facilities, especially for the new contests and activities. The first stadium was built with its starting gate near the temple of Poseidon. Several remains have been found of this temple, enabling us to restore a large part of the track, which measured 600 ancient Greek feet (192 m.). In order to construct the track on the uneven, steeply sloping site, over 5,000 cubic metres of earth were deposited at its east end. This project, which required enormous effort and expense, reveals the great importance attached by the Corinthians to the holding of games during the Isthmian festival. Remains have also been discovered of the embankment seats for the spectators, which are the earliest surviving facilities of this kind of any stadium in the ancient world.

Just before the middle of the 5th century, new retaining walls were added to the stadium, increasing its capacity, while a pioneering starting apparatus was created: this was called *hysplex* by the ancient Greeks, and it prevented runners from 'jumping the gun.' The starting-machine consisted of a triangular stone threshold with wooden posts fixed in the long side, defining the positions of 16 runners. At the top of each post was a wooden horizontal arm that prevented each runner from starting. The runners could only start when the starter, who sat in a pit 1 m. deep at the apex of the triangle, released the ropes he was holding, the other ends of which held the wooden arms in the horizontal position. This triangular mechanism and the hysplex were abandoned a few decades later and replaced with a simple rectangular stone starting post, though this was moved 11 metres further forward, thereby reducing the length of the track.

The earliest dedications at Isthmia associated with the games are eight *halteres* (jumping weights), one of them inscribed, dating from the middle of the 6th century, dedicated by the pentathlete Kratippos, who had won the jumping event three times. The remains of a chariot wheel and the metal parts of a harness have also been found, suggesting a dedication after a victory in the chariot race. The victors of the chariot races, that is, appear to have dedicated their victory chariot to the sanctuary, along with the harnesses of their horses.

405

406

405-406. Two sides of a Panathenaic amphora dedicated by a Corinthian victor at the Panathenaic games. The name of the winner is painted in white letters on the black part of the vase: ΔΑΜΩΝ ('Damon'). The event in which he won was probably the dolichos race, as is clear from the depiction of the event on the other side (about 530 BC). Isthmia, Archaeological Museum.

407. Reconstruction drawing of the stadia at Isthmia. The 6th-century stadium had a starting line next to the temple of Poseidon, unlike the later one, which was built 250 m. away from it. Drawing: O. Broneer.

408. The most interesting part of the first stadium was the starting mechanism (hysplex)*, which prevented false starts during the track events. Preserved parts of the mechanism are shown here.*

409-410. Plan and reconstruction drawing of the starting mechanism. Drawings: O. Broneer.

408

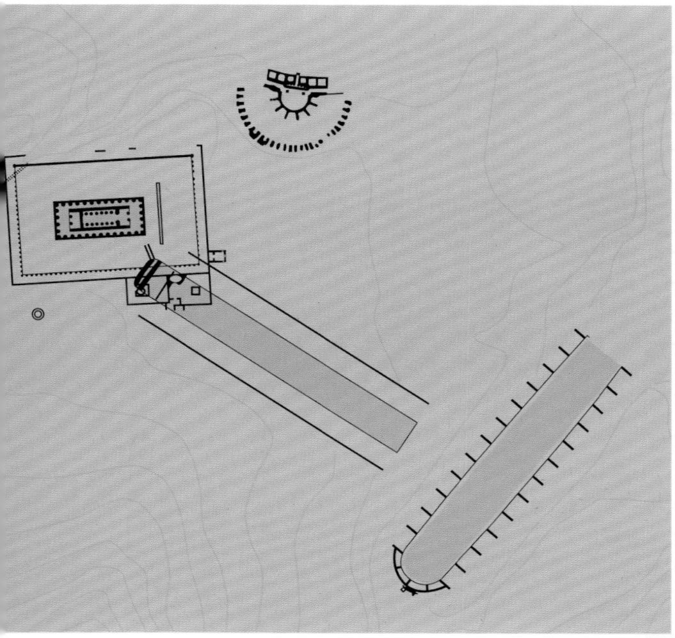

407

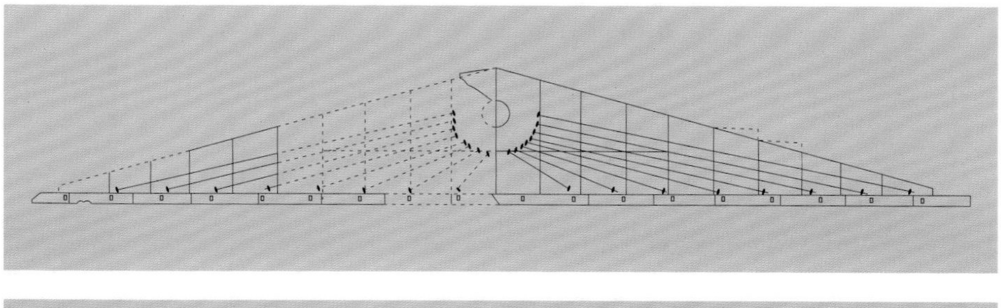

409

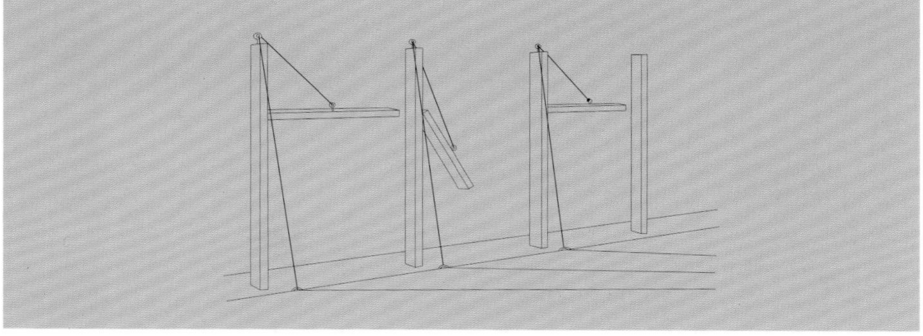

410

411 412

5th - 4th c. BC
The Classical period

THE NEW TEMPLE OF POSEIDON

411. Bronze statuette of Poseidon, 0.45 m. high, which probably renders the original statue by Lysippos in his temple at Isthmia. Athens, National Archaeological Museum.

412. Aerial photograph of the temple of Poseidon at Isthmia from the west. The form of the temple is known principally from the foundation trenches for the colonnades and walls, since all the architectural members from it have been looted, from as early as the 5th c. AD. The remains of its rectangular altar can be seen in front of the temple.

413. Part of the marble sima of the Classical temple of Poseidon at Isthmia, decorated with a running spiral, palmettes and lions' heads. This temple was the second largest in the Peloponnese, after the Temple of Zeus at Olympia (about 460 BC). Isthmia, Archaeological Museum.

At the beginning of the 5th century, we find in Pindar the first unequivocal evidence relating to the cult of Melikertes-Palaimon at Isthmia, and a cult precinct was created for the hero between the temple and the stadium in the middle of this century. There is nothing to rule out the possibility – indeed, it is quite likely – that this hero was the object of the cult from the very foundation of the sanctuary, as indicated both by the myth and by the archaeological evidence.

During the decade 470-460 BC, a great fire entirely destroyed the sanctuary, an event that dictated the renovation of the temple at a rapid pace. The new temple of Poseidon was quickly constructed on the same site as its predecessor, though considerably larger, being the second largest temple in the Peloponnese after that of Zeus at Olympia. The altar was also made longer, in keeping with the dimensions of the new temple. The temple itself had a peristyle of 6 by 13 columns and was made of local limestone, with marble used for the sima and roof tiles. Inside it, the rationale of a longitudinal colonnade with 6 columns was retained, as well as the two entrances to the cella, leading

413

into the two aisles; this feature was probably due to the existence of two statues, of Poseidon and Amphitrite.

The Classical temple was destroyed by fire in 390 BC during the Corinthian War, in the course of hostilities between the Spartan king Agesilaos and the Corinthians, Argives and Athenians under Iphikrates (Xenophon, *Hellenika* 4.5.4). Its restoration was delayed by the further consequences of this war, and the modifications seem ultimately to have been confined to the internal colonnade, which was made a double (2 by 6 columns), possibly two-storey, structure.

414. Aerial photograph of the temple of Poseidon at Isthmia from the northwest. The necessary theatre for the musical events dominates. At the top, the remains of the temple with its rectangular enclosure; at bottom right, sections of the bathhouse.

415. Recontstruction drawing of the third phase of the theatre of the middle of the third century. The building had this form until the time of Nero. Drawing: E. Gephard.

416. View of the inside of one of the cult caves at Isthmia.

414

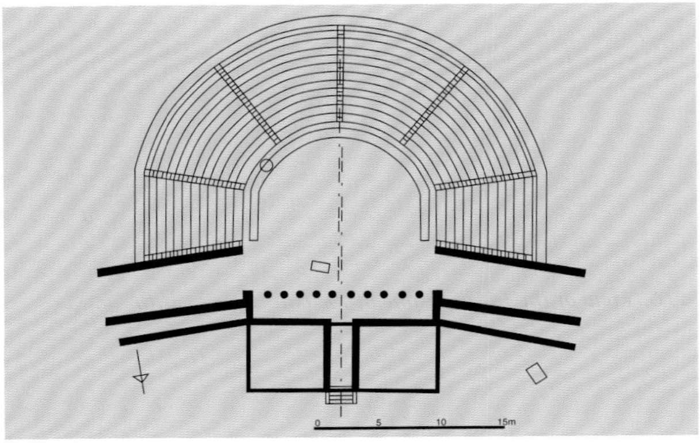

415

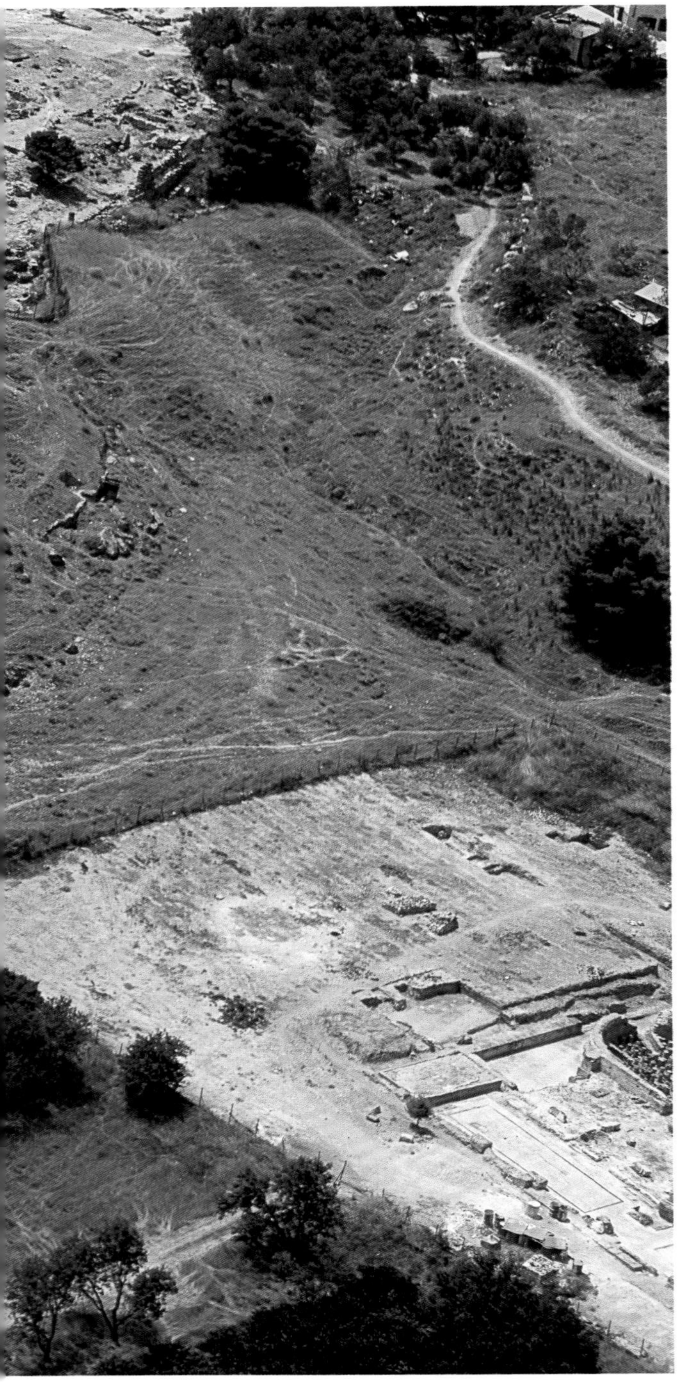

THE THEATRE AND CULT CAVES

About 400 BC, a theatre was built in a natural cavity about 50 m. north-east of the temple to house the music and poetry contests at the Isthmia. The theatre had a rectangular orchestra and a three-sided cavea with seats for about 500 spectators. This building underwent several modifications in the 4th century, the most interesting being the installation of a proscenium with wooden supports, with painted panels set between them, forming a kind of proscenium.

416

Two cult caves hewn from the soft rock of the area also date from the Classical period. They consist of a courtyard and two rooms, in which there was a total of eleven couches cut in the walls and other cuttings that served as altars or hearths. This layout and the discovery of the remains of banquet vessels have suggested that the caves were the sites of a cult of a local hero of chthonic character, probably Melikertes-Palaimon, which involved common meals shared by a group of worshippers who were members of a religious association. These banquets are thought to be a survival of the immemorial common meals shared by all the adherents around the altar, from the very beginning of the cult.

3rd - 2nd c. BC
The Hellenistic period

THE NEW STADIUM

The most important architectural change in this period was the abandonment of the stadium inside the sanctuary and the creation of a new one in a natural depression about 250 m. southeast of the temple of Poseidon. This new stadium required banking up, and earth was brought to it from the embankments of the old stadium. This freed and levelled near the temple a fairly large space, which was used for other cult activities that had to be carried out nearby. In any case, the links between games and cult had become looser at this period, making it possible to remove the stadium from the cult centres of sanctuaries. The construction of the new stadium should be considered part of the building programme of Philip II and Alexander the Great, though there are signs that the old stadium was still in use in 300 BC, possibly while the new one was being built.

The new stadium was oriented NE-SW, in the opposite direction from the old. It has not yet been excavated and lies beneath modern farmland. However,

417. General view of the position of the later stadium at Isthmia. The site has not been excavated completely, but the natural depression in which it was built can be made out.

418. Pentathletes participating in the games or training under the guidance of a trainer or the supervision of a judge to the accompaniment of a flute. Two of the events of the pentathlon are represented (jump and stadion). The discus beneath the feet of the runners is an allusion to this event. Black-figure amphora (about 510 BC). Würzburg, Martin von Wagner Museum.

417

a number of trial trenches have made it possible to study all its features. The track is 181 m. long, and along its sides is a water pipe on the surface, with basins, to provide water for the athletes and spectators. At either end are the elongated stone slabs of the starting gate, which could cater for 16 runners. The bases of the hysplex mechanisms have been preserved at the ends of the starting gate, indicating that the new stadium had a new starting system, more advanced than the old. Now, there were no individual barriers for each athlete; instead, a single rope was stretched in front of the runners, at waist and breast height. The ends of this rope were fastened to two vertical posts fixed into a mechanism that was operated by the starter behind the runners. The athletes could start only after the rope had fallen in front of them, allowing them to run.

The embankment seats of the stadium were cut into the bedrock and had staircases at intervals; at some points, such as on the curve or near the finishing line, there were stone benches, possibly providing seating for the judges.

An isolated find in the countryside 2 km. to the west of the sanctuary has been considered evidence for the site of the hippodrome. It consists of a pit in which were found ashes, a gold olive wreath, strigils, weapons and vases. Next to it were discovered the remains of wheels of a carriage or chariot, together with three perirrhanteria. The whole ensemble was covered by a mound of earth, on three sides of which an enclosure wall was built at a later date. This heroon – a hero shrine – to an unknown athlete and the natural formation of the site where it was created are an indication that the hippodrome of Isthmia, known from the literary sources, was located here.

The sanctuary was abandoned in the Late Hellenistic period, probably as a result of the pillaging it suffered in 146 BC at the hands of the Romans under Mummius, who, after their final victory over the Greeks at the Battle of Corinth, razed the city to the ground. The abandonment is attested graphically by the ruts of the chariot wheels that pass above the altar, indicating that, at this period, the road ran over it.

This evidence does not mean that the Isthmian games were abandoned, since Pausanias states that they continued to be held regularly under the supervision of the Sikyonians, though he does not tell us where they were held.

418

1st c. B.C. - 3rd c. AD
Roman times

Although Corinth was resettled on the instructions of Julius Caesar, one century after its destruction (44 BC), activity in the great Corinthian sanctuary did not recover its regular rhythm until much later, about the middle of the 1st c. AD. The first evidence for the resuscitation of the cult is the creation of a pit in which the sacrificial animals, which were small black bulls, were burned whole (*holokautoma*). The faithful stood around it and watched the fire, holding lamps in their hands – evidence that the ritual took place at night. The restoration of the cult is attributable to the new Roman inhabitants of Corinth, who identified the sea hero Palaimon, the patron god of sailors, with the Roman god of harbours, Portunus.

The games did not return to the sanctuary until AD 67, the occasion being Nero's wish to participate in them. The stadium was used once more for ath-

419. View of the large pit in which dead bulls were burned at Isthmia in the Roman period. The small pit with ditches in the foreground is part of the water-supply system of the earlier stadium, as, too, are the two stones with small cavities.

420. Various types of lamps held by participants during nocturnal rituals involving burnt offerings in the sanctuary at Isthmia in the Roman period. One has a sense of intensity and initiation on the part of those who gathered around the pits to follow the sacrifice. Isthmia, Archaeological Museum.

419

420

421

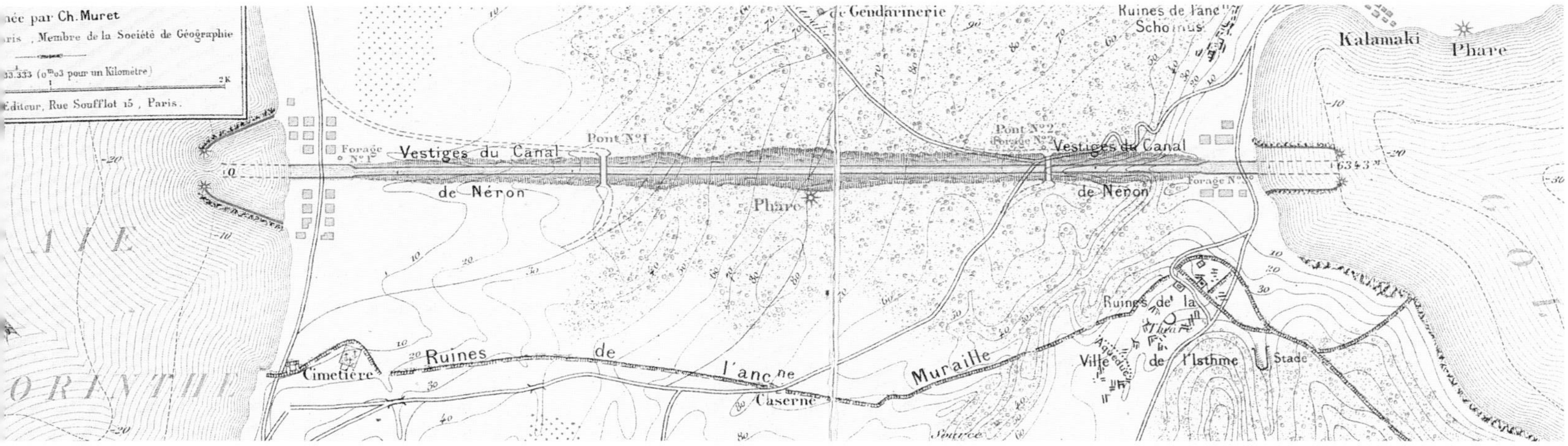

422

letic contests, and there was a radical renovation of the theatre, so that the emperor could appear in it as a great musician and actor. The stage-building was enlarged, the orchestra made semicircular, and the cavea acquired new seats. During his stay in Corinth, the emperor also set in train his plan to dig a canal through the isthmus. His engineers drew up the designs, and the project was ceremoniously inaugurated by the emperor himself, using a gold pickaxe. After his death a year later, however, the project was abandoned. Remarkably, when the modern canal was dug in the 19th century, at the initiative of Charilaos Trikoupis, Nero's ditches still survived and were followed by the modern engineers.

421-422. The digging of the Corinthian canal in the 19th century, during the premiership of Charilaos Trikoupis, and the map showing the project. The modern engineers followed exactly the plans made by Nero's engineers.

THE RENOVATION OF THE SANCTUARY

Extensive renovation of the sanctuary was undertaken in the 2nd c. AD. The temple was enclosed by a rectangular wall with an Ionic colonnade and a propylon on the northeast side. Inside it was placed a marble statue group consisting of a standing Poseidon and a seated Amphitrite, the sea god's wife. The torso of the latter has been preserved, as have slabs from the relief decoration of its base, depicting the hunt for the Kalydonian boar and the killing of the children of Niobe. The group was probably replaced by another one like it, but made of gold and ivory, which was dedicated by Herodes Atticus according to the description by Pausanias. It depicted Poseidon and Amphitrite on a four-horsed chariot accompanied by Tritons, and Palaimon on a dolphin. The personification of the sea was shown at the centre of the base, holding the young Aphrodite surrounded by Nereids.

423

424

425

426

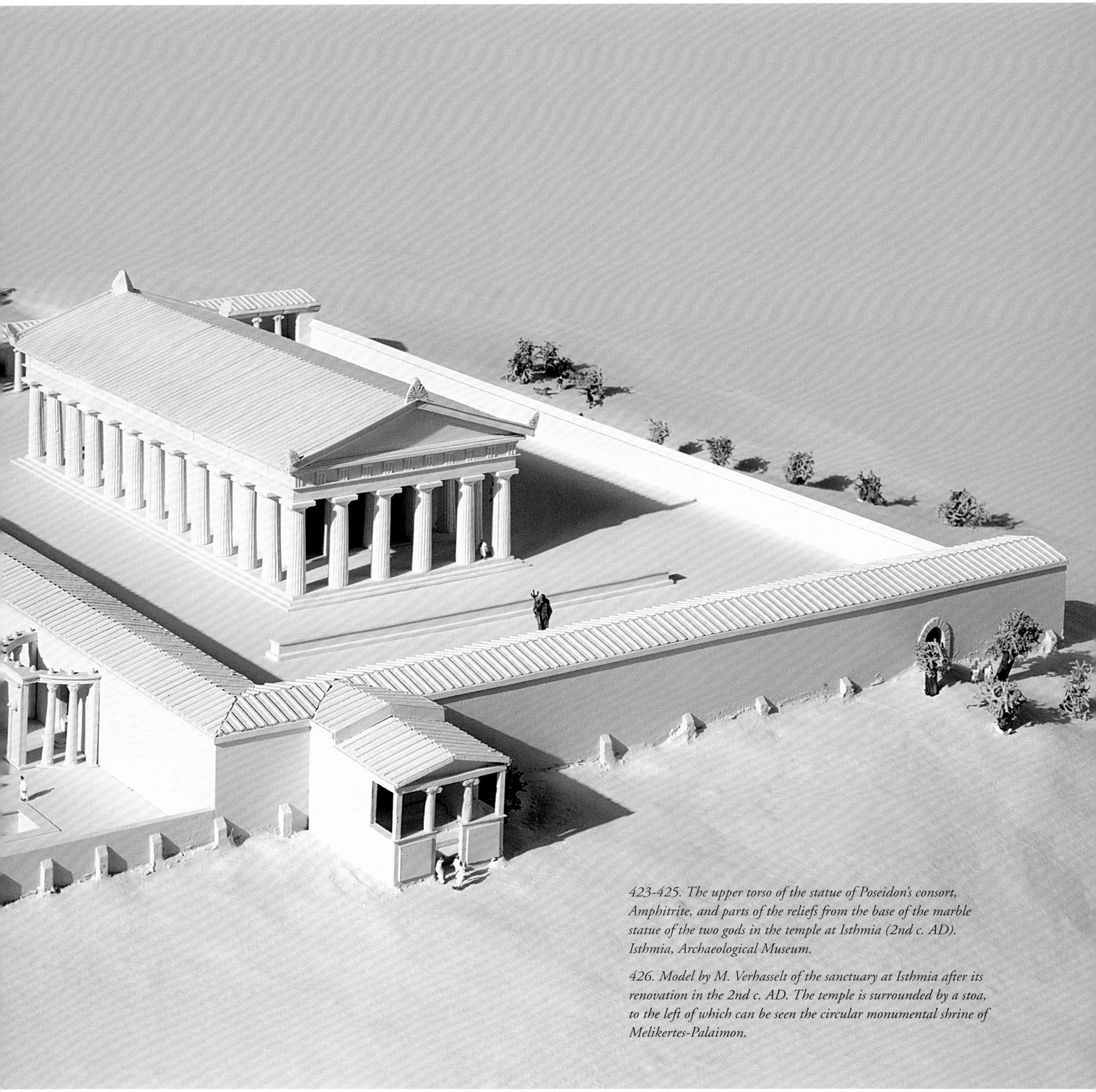

423-425. The upper torso of the statue of Poseidon's consort, Amphitrite, and parts of the reliefs from the base of the marble statue of the two gods in the temple at Isthmia (2nd c. AD). Isthmia, Archaeological Museum.

426. Model by M. Verhasselt of the sanctuary at Isthmia after its renovation in the 2nd c. AD. The temple is surrounded by a stoa, to the left of which can be seen the circular monumental shrine of Melikertes-Palaimon.

THE TEMPLE OF MELIKERTES-PALAIMON

427

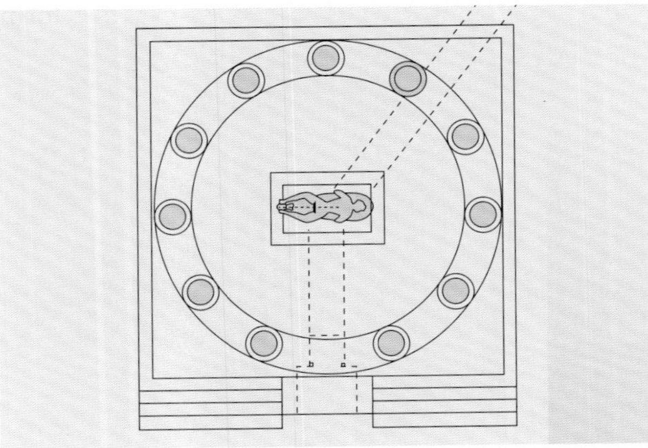
428

In the 2nd c. AD, the cult of Melikertes-Palaimon was also given monumental form. A monopteral circular building was erected to the southeast of the temple, near the pits in which the sacrificial animals were burned, precisely on the start of the old stadium. Inside this small temple, which had no walls but eleven Corinthian columns, was placed a group with a dolphin carrying the dead body of the child on its back. There was an adyton, possibly intended for a mystery cult, inside the bulky podium of the temple. This may have been the place 'where they say Palaimon was buried' mentioned by Pausanias (2.2.1-2). It is, in fact, an earlier water conduit that served the Classical stadium, which was mistakenly interpreted by later worshippers as the hero's tomb. Next to the temple grew the sacred *pitys* – the pine tree from which the wreaths were cut for the victors at the Isthmia. The entire area of the Palaimonion was provided with an enclosure wall, in which there was a propylon. It is evident, then, that in the Roman period there was a revival of the old cult, accompanied by the monumental display of the features associated with the founding legend of the sanctuary and games.

429

THE BATHS COMPLEX

An impressive baths complex was erected to the north of the temple, above a similar building of Classical date. The complex consisted of 14 rooms, 4 of which were heated by hypocausts. The main part of the baths was a large rectangular room at the centre, measuring 24.40 by 11.70 m., with a niche and pedestals for statues. The floor of this room was decorated with an impressive mosaic, still in an excellent state of preservation – a bicolour mosaic of Italian type, consisting of black and white tesserae forming a variety of geometric motifs (chessboard pattern, lozenges, guilloches, etc.). The two central panels are adorned by a figurative depiction of a Triton carrying a Nereid on his back; the two are surrounded by dolphins, fish, octopuses and other sea creatures. This superb composition is perfectly in keeping with the character of the building and of the sanctuary as a whole, which was dedicated to sea deities (Poseidon, Amphitrite and Palaimon).

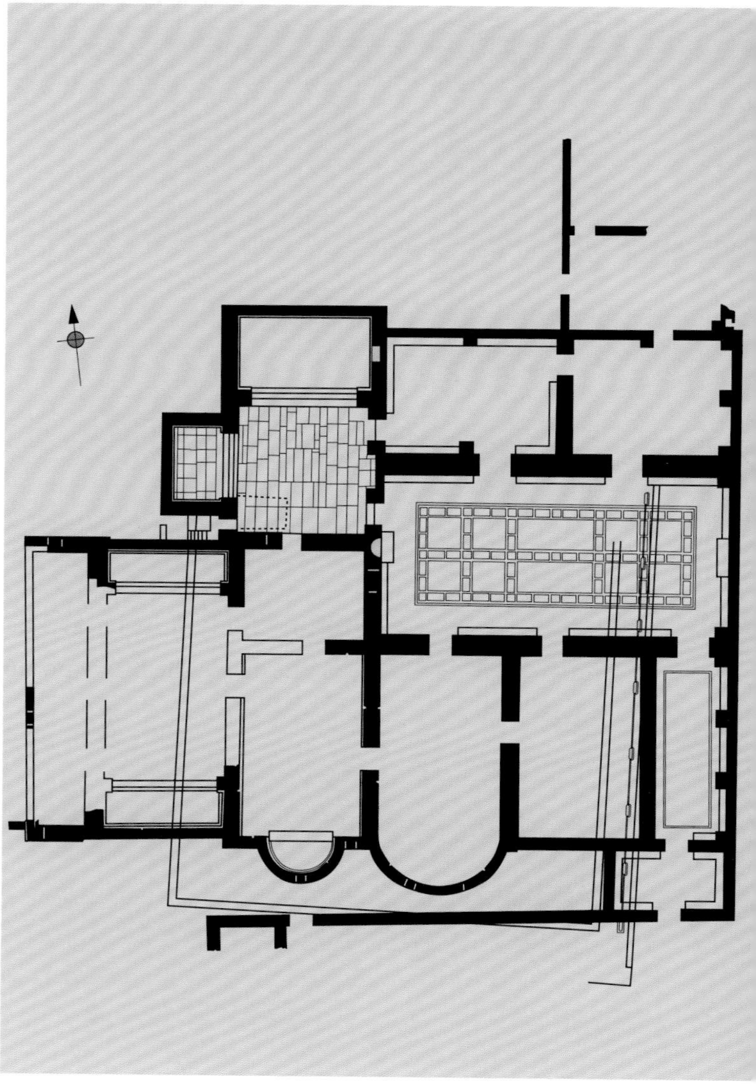

431

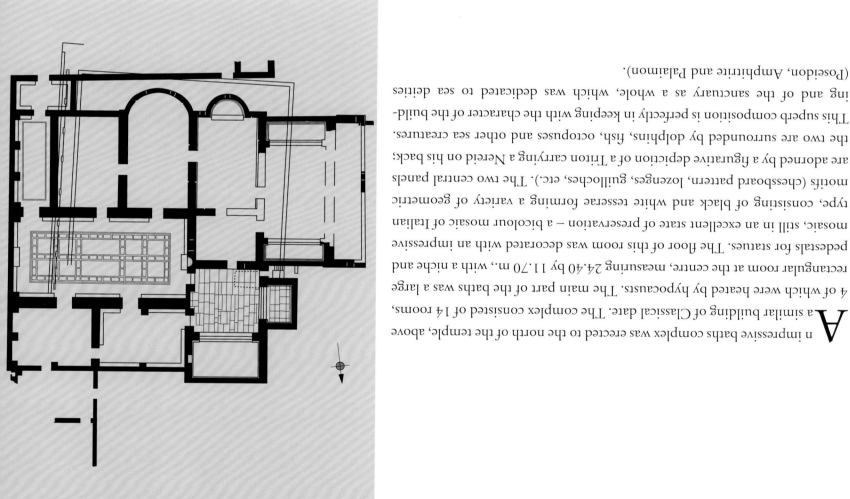

427-429. Reconstruction drawings by O. Broneer of the ground plan and east elevation of the stone podium of the temple of Melikertes-Palaimon, and a contemporary view of the excavation.

430-431. Ground plan of the baths complex in the sanctuary at Isthmia, and a view of part of its floor with a variety of mosaics.

430

432

432, 434-435. Reconstruction and views of the mosaic floor of the rectangular main room of the bathhouse with a variety of geometric designs and scenes from the mythology of the sea. Nereids and Tritons are depicted surrounded by fish, octopuses and other sea creatures.

433. View of one of the rooms with hypocausts, in which the water was heated for the bathhouse. Hypocausts were usually subterranean rooms, whose floor was supported by clay colonnettes. They served as furnaces which heated cisterns containing water, which then circulated as hot water or steam throughout the rooms of the bathhouse. The opening in the wall at the bottom right served to admit fuel for the furnaces.

433

434

435

The end of Isthmia and of the festival

436. Reconstruction drawing of the arched entrance to the sanctuary in Roman times, which survived as a gate in the Hexamilion wall. Drawing: W. B. Dinsmoor, Jr.

437. View of the main fort of the Hexamilion and one of its 153 towers.

438. Drawing of the course of the Hexamilion wall. The entire wall, from the Saronic to the Corinthian Gulf, was constructed of material plundered from the buildings of the nearby sanctuary at Isthmia.

The sanctuary continued to function and the Isthmian games were held regularly until at least the end of the 3rd c. AD, and may even have survived into the 4th century. After this, the site was gradually abandoned and the majority of its buildings fell into ruins.

Thus, when the Peloponnese was threatened by the barbarian raids of Alarich's Goths in 411-420, the inhabitants were obliged to build a long fortification wall to protect the isthmus. This wall ran from Corinth to the Saronic Gulf and, since it covered a distance of six miles, was called the Hexamilion. There were 153 towers distributed throughout its length, and the main fort was built on a natural hill near the sanctuary. All the material available in the sanctuary was used in the construction of the Hexamilion, resulting in the disappearance of all the structures above ground and the creation of the sorry picture the sanctuary presents today. It is indicative of the important position occupied by the sanctuary that the monumental arched entrance of Roman times was incorporated into the Isthmus fortification wall and became the main gate of the fort. In this way, Isthmia continued to form the monumental entrance to the Peloponnese, even after its famous sanctuary had disappeared.

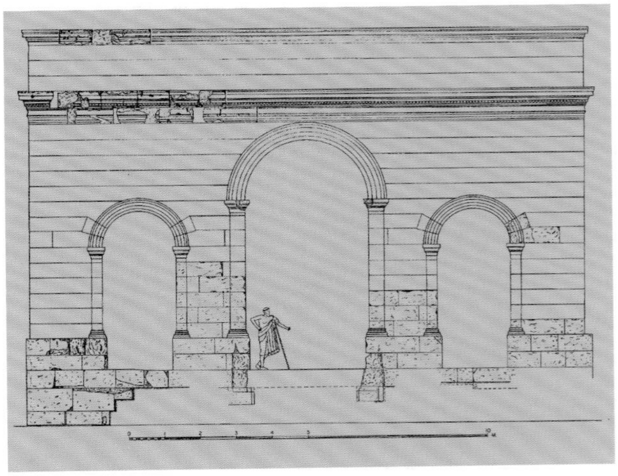

436

437

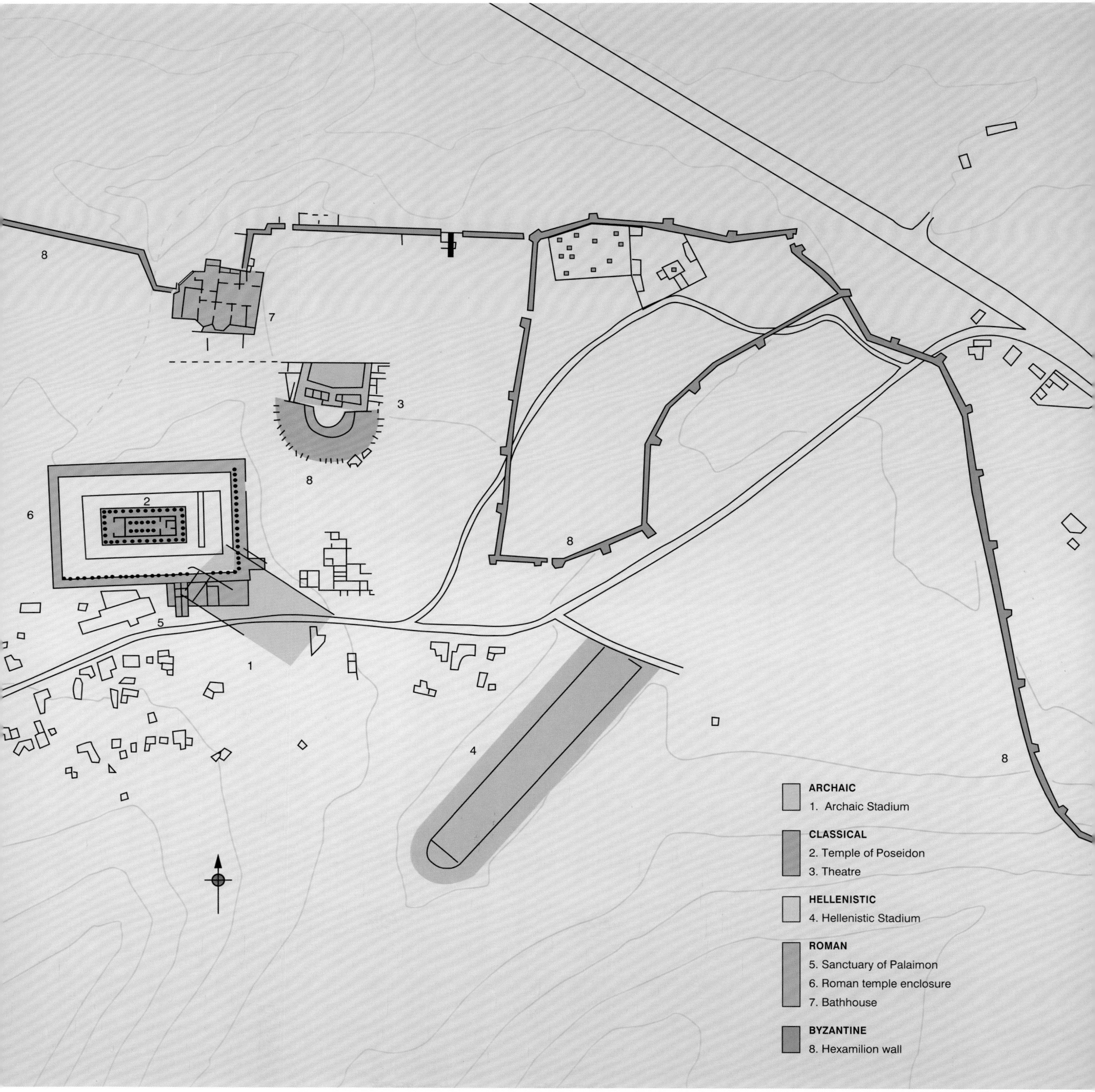
8
7
3
8
2
6
8
5
1
4
8
ARCHAIC
1. Archaic Stadium
CLASSICAL
2. Temple of Poseidon
3. Theatre
HELLENISTIC
4. Hellenistic Stadium
ROMAN
5. Sanctuary of Palaimon
6. Roman temple enclosure
7. Bathhouse
BYZANTINE
8. Hexamilion wall

Nemea

The Site

Nemea recalls Zeus. It inspires an outstanding song to Zeus. Here we should hymn the king of the gods.

Pindar

439. Herakles' labour involving the lion of Nemea is one of the foundation myths of the festival. Herakles captures the lion in the presence of Athena and Iolaos. Attic black-figure krater (late 6th c. BC). Athens, National Archaeological Museum.

440. General view of the valley of Nemea, set between high mountains at the borders of four Peloponnesian city-states.

The name of the site derives from the word *nemos*, meaning glade or wooded pasture, which accordingly refers to the natural environment. Nemea is a fertile plateau set amidst wooded mountains near the borders of Corinthia, the Argolid, Achaia and Arkadia. This location, between different tribal and political groups, together with its great distance from the large urban centres, gave Nemea the status of neutral territory. As such, it was suitable for the creation of an 'international' religious centre, which emerged as the headquarters of the Nemean games, the fourth such festival of panhellenic repute.

The plateau is crossed by the River Nemeas, and the surrounding mountains are full of caves, which accounts for the setting here of the myth of Herakles and the lion, from which the hero took the lion-skin that he carried with him all his life. According to a later version, which is not found in the written sources before the Roman period, this labour was one of the foundation myths of the games: the hero founded the games in honour of his father, Zeus, who helped him to overcome the lion.

440

Foundation Myths

442

The earliest mythical tradition relating to the foundation of the Nemean games, however, dates from at least the 5th century, since it is mentioned in the poems of Pindar and Bacchylides and also in Euripides' tragedy *Hypsipyle*. According to this version, Lykourgos, the king of Nemea and priest of Zeus, and his wife, Eurydike, had a son, Opheltes, after much difficulty. They at once consulted the Delphic oracle to learn how to make their child strong and healthy. The Pythia replied that they should not put the boy on the ground until he could walk. The child was at once placed in the care of Hypsipyle, a slave from Lemnos, with instructions never to set Opheltes on the ground. One day, however, the nurse was walking in the countryside outside Nemea with the baby in her arms, when she met the seven kings of Argos, who were marching against Thebes. They asked her for water and, in order to show them the spring, the woman set the child down on fresh wild celery. At once, a snake bit the baby, killing him. One of the kings, the seer Amphiaraos, realised that this was an ill omen for their own expedition, and named the child Archemoros (*arche*, beginning; *moira*, destiny). The Argives promptly killed the snake, buried the infant, and founded the Nemean festival in its honour. In these first, mythical games, each of the Seven won an event: Adrastos the horse race, Eteokles the foot race, Tydeus the boxing, Amphiaraos the jump and discus, Laodokos the javelin, Polyneikes the wrestling and Parthenopaios the archery contest.

This myth has many levels of meaning. It provides an interpretation for some of the actual features of the games at Nemea, such as the use of a wreath of wild celery to crown the victors, the black clothes worn by the Hellanodikai, and the sacred grove of cypresses – a tree that still symbolises grieving – in the middle of the sanctuary. It also suggests that, as at the other panhellenic sanctuaries, the starting point for the worship was a cult of chthonic character, which was later displaced by the cult of an Olympian god, in this case Zeus. The myth also reveals clearly, if not the role of Argos in the foundation of the games, then at least the city's claims to organise them and the festival: for the protagonists in both foundation myths – Herakles and the Seven – were Argives.

441

441. The earlier of the foundation myths associated with the sanctuary at Nemea is linked with the death of the young Archemoros-Opheltes. This small, bronze figurine of the boy was discovered in his sanctuary at Nemea (Hellenistic period). Nemea, Archaeological Museum.

442. Marble group from a fountain, depicting the later foundation myth associated with the sanctuary, Herakles and the Nemean lion (2nd c. AD). Isthmia, Archaeological Museum.

443. Herakles wrestles down the Nemean lion, flanked by Athena and Iolaos. Attic red-figure amphora by the Andoides Painter (529 BC). London, British Museum.

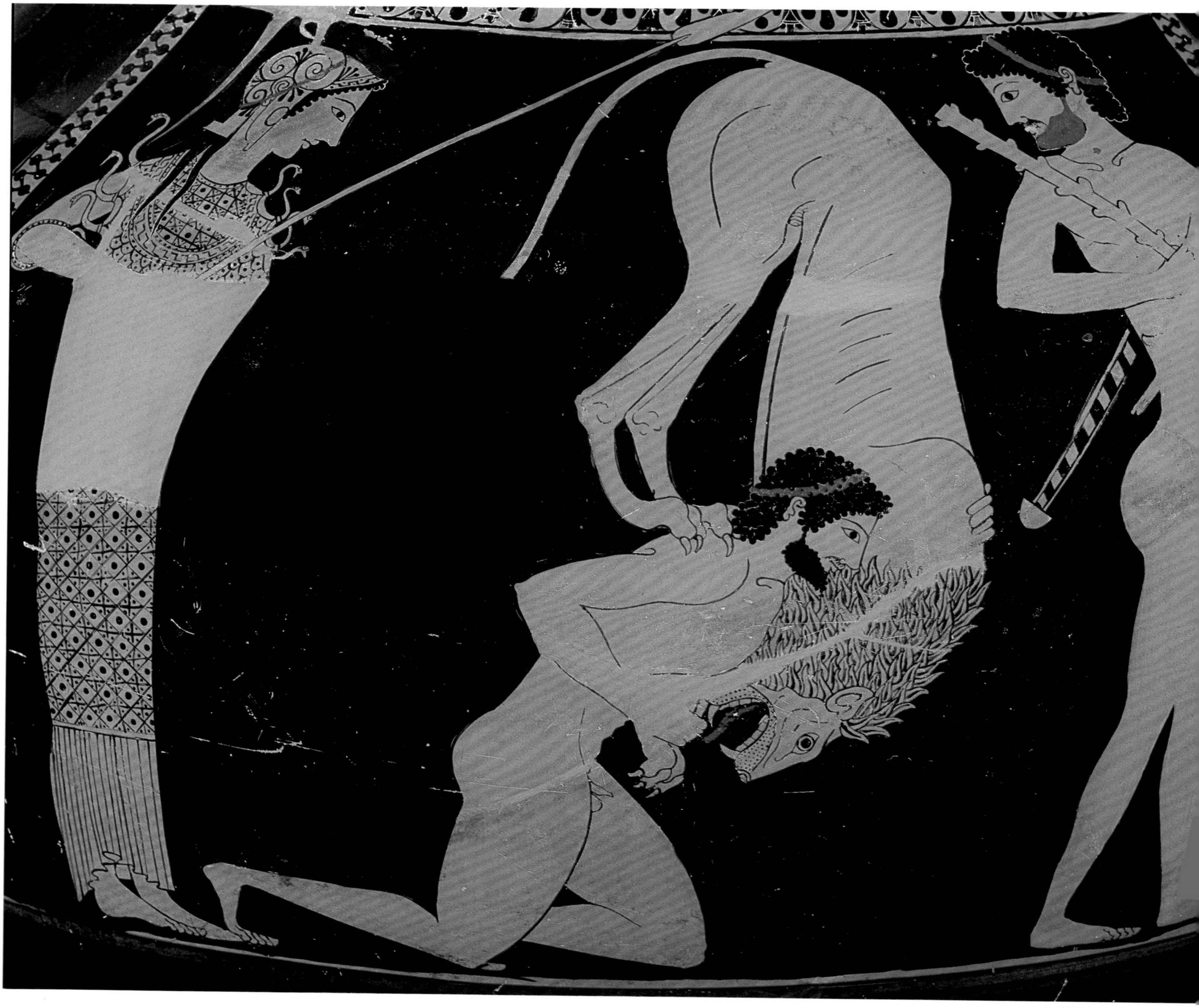

443

The games

THE HISTORY OF THE GAMES

Blessed are those mortals who will, at Nemea, crown their blond hair with the [three-year] wreath.

Bacchylides

In the context of the disputes between the city-states of the Peloponnese in the Archaic period, control of the major panhellenic sanctuaries and their games was invariably an objective of the great powers of the day. After their unsuccessful attempt to win control of the Olympic games at the time of the tyrant Pheidon, the Argives apparently decided to found their own games, or at least to contest paternity of the nearest existing contests. They selected a region on the margins of their own state, which was then under the control of the neighbouring city of Kleonai, and in 583 or 573 BC founded or revived the games, endeavouring to disseminate the appropriate mythical tradition to confirm their ancient relationship with Nemea. In the first period, Kleonai appears to have been responsible for the games, formally at least, down to the end of the 5th century, when they were finally taken over by the Argives, who transferred them to Argos. It is indicative of the strength of the Argive desire to control the Nemean games that, over the one thousand years of their history, the games were held in the place after which they were named only one quarter of the time, and were held at Argos for the remainder.

After their original removal to Argos, the games returned to their birthplace in 340-330 BC, as part of the policy of Philip II and Alexander the Great, who sought to rally the Greeks by strengthening all panhellenic ties and common activities. They only remained at Nemea for 70-80 years, however, since the Argives transferred them to Argos once more before the middle of the 3rd century. Shortly thereafter in 235 BC, Aratos of Sikyon, the leader of the Achaean League and a fierce foe of Argos, decided to hold the Nemean games at Nemea, in order to humiliate the Argives. Accordingly, he requested the athletes to participate in his games and not the ones held at Argos. The athletes found themselves in a dilemma, for they were aware that the official games were those at Argos and that a victory at Nemea would not be recognised. In the end, Aratos issued an order to arrest all those who tried to compete at Argos and sell them as slaves. This episode, described by Plutarch (*Aratos*, 28), was regarded by the ancient Greeks as one of the worst cases of violation of the sacred truce. The final period during which the Nemean games were held at Nemea began in 146 BC, on the instructions of Mummius, the conqueror of Corinth, but they reverted to Argos once more within fifty years.

444

444. A runner in the stadion race. The vigorous movements of his arms and legs suggest his speed, and the backward turn of his head the anxiety of the leader. Black-figure kylix from Corinth (about 570-560 BC). Athens, National Archaeological Museum.

445. Bronze strigil with the handle in the form of a girl who herself holds a strigil. In addition to the men's events at Nemea, there were also contests for girls (about 300 BC). London, British Museum.

446. Women's involvement in athletics might go back to the mythical model of Atalanta, the heroine who competed with men on equal terms. Here, she wrestles with the hero Peleus, at the games in honour of Peleus. Attic black-figure amphora (about 500 BC). Munich, Staatliche Antikensammlung.

445

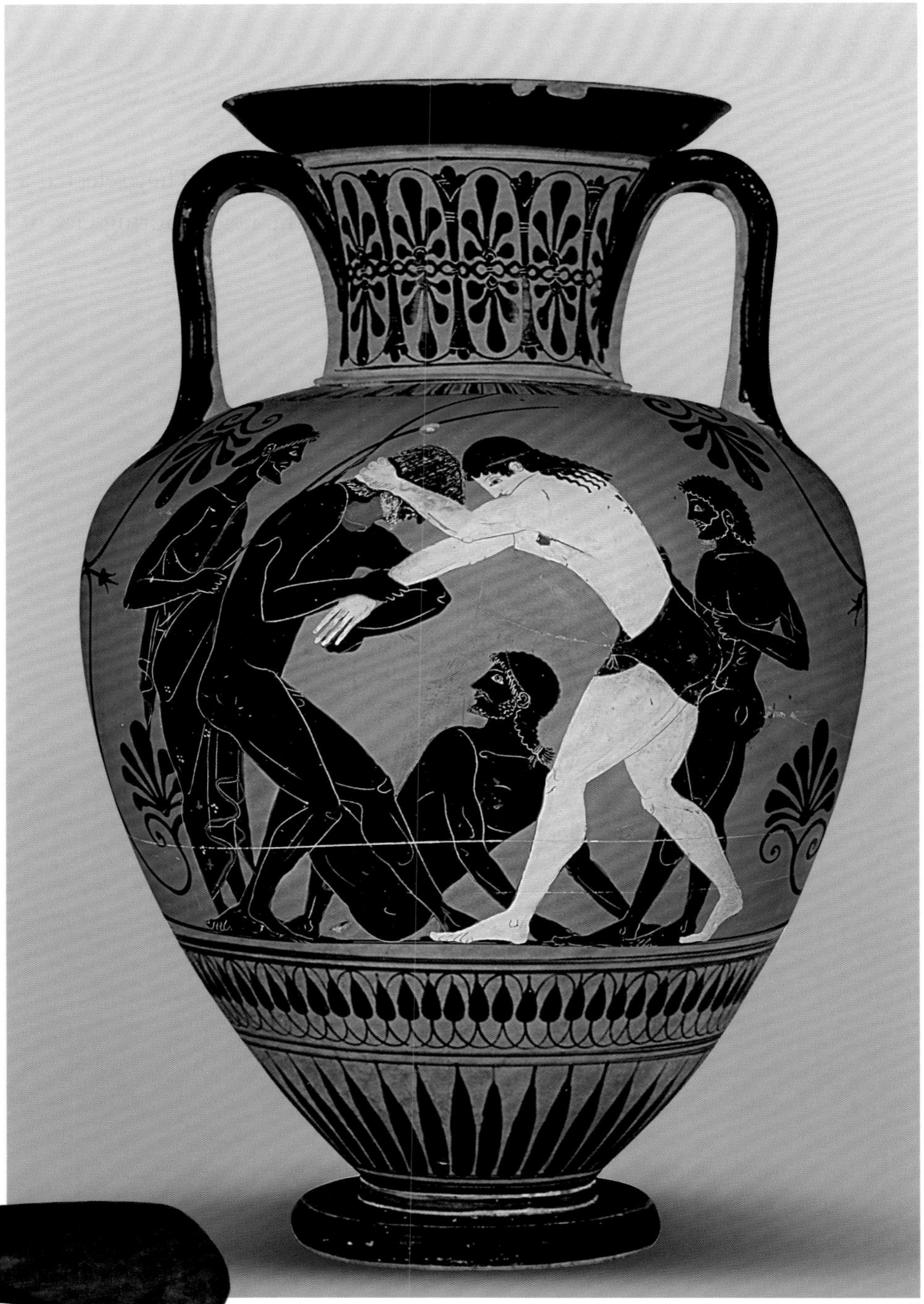

446

THE INTERVAL OF THE GAMES AND THE KINDS OF CONTESTS

The Nemean games were held every two years, in the second and fourth year of the Olympiad, at the second full moon after the summer solstice, that is, in the months of July or August. The programme included almost all the athletic contests held at Olympia (stadion, diaulos, dolichos, race in full armour, boxing, pankration and pentathlon, though the only equestrian events seem to have been the race for four-horse chariots and just one horse race. To these should be added the contests for trumpeters and heralds, which, as at Olympia, took place before the other events. Music competitions, involving kitharodia and flute-playing, seem also to have been added to the Nemean games in the Hellenistic and Roman periods. One difference from the other panhellenic games was that here the athletes were divided into three age groups: children (12-16 years) 'beardless youths' (16-20) and men (above 20 years). Interestingly, in the later period women had the right to compete in the athletic games at Nemea. We learn from a decree at Delphi dating from AD 47 that Hedea, one of the daughters of Hermesianax, from Tralles in Asia Minor, came in first at Nemea in the girls' stadion.

We have no evidence for the programme or duration of the games. On analogy with the other festivals, it may be supposed that they lasted several days, during which a truce was imposed. After the formal religious ceremony, with sacrifices to Nemean Zeus, the contests would have taken place one after the other, based on the model of Olympia. Our evidence for the festival, generally speaking, is sparse. Although it belonged to the 'circuit' of panhellenic games, the ancient Greeks do not seem to have held it in great esteem, judging by the caustic comment made by the Cynic philosopher Diogenes, who, seeing an Olympic champion tending sheep, said 'My good man, you've soon come down from the Olympic to the Nemean games!'

447

447. Bronze figurine of a girl taking part in a women's race, from a Lakonian workshop dedicated in the sanctuary of Zeus at Dodona. She wears a short chiton, which she raises with one hand (middle of the 6th c. BC). Athens, National Archaeological Museum. Karapanos Collection.

448. Characteristic view of the architectural remains of the temple of Zeus at Nemea. The three standing columns of the temple have stood like this since ancient times, serving as a visual symbol of the temple.

Nemea Over the Centuries

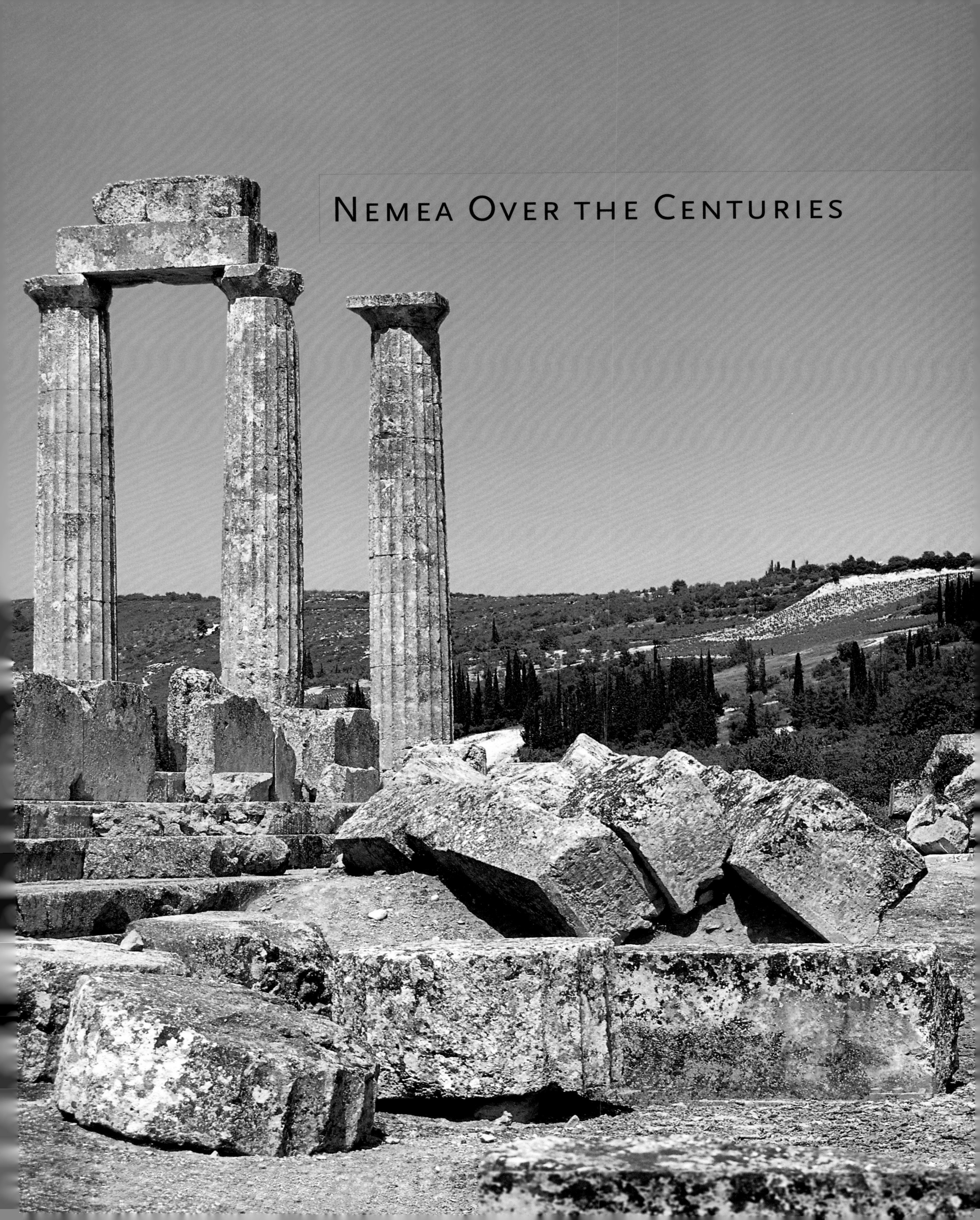

6th c. BC

The early history of the sanctuary

At Nemea, the evidence for an earlier cult before the foundation of the games is very scant, and the few Mycenaean and Geometric shards do not attest to continuity from earlier periods. The earliest building activity in the sanctuary makes its appearance at the same period as the foundation of the games (second quarter of the 6th century). The site was levelled and covered with a layer of white clay, which can be detected in various places. The earliest structures were the temple of Zeus and the heroon of Opheltes. The temple of Zeus was built on the same site as its Late Classical successor, had the same orientation, but was considerably smaller, measuring only 10 by 36 m. Part of its foundations can still be seen today in the adyton of the later temple. It probably lacked a colonnade, and there was a pediment only on the facade, which had painted, not sculpted, decoration. At the same time as the temple in which the cult of the god of heaven was practised, a heroon was created to Opheltes, which housed the cult of the chthonic deity. This structure lay to the southwest of the temple, on the left bank of the river. In its original form it was probably a mound of earth with a tomb and altars for the cult. It was surrounded by a sacred grove and perhaps also by an enclosure wall. In the second half of the 6th century, the heroon was renovated, as, too, was the great temple.

There are no architectural remains connected with the sporting facilities of the early period, but in recent years the excavation record has suggested to excavators that the tumulus of Opheltes had a slightly elongated shape and that on either side of it were the simple structures of the stadium and hippodrome. According to this hypothesis, the athletic contests might have been held on one side of the mound, and the equestrian on the other, in the dry riverbed. In other words, a very close relationship is postulated between the chthonic cult and the games, which could be watched by spectators either standing on the slope of the tumulus or from the banks of the river. Whatever the case, three slabs with a groove for the runner's feet has been assigned to this early stadium.

One of the earliest athletic dedications in the sanctuary appears to be the inscribed base of Kleonaios Aristis, who won the pankration four times in succession about the middle of the 6th century BC. Also of interest are an iron discus, a lead jumping weight and two javelin tips, found in a pit near the temple of Zeus, together with spits and vases, possibly from a victory banquet held by a pentathlete.

449. Base of a dedication by Aristis of Kleonai. According to the inscription, Aristis made the dedication because he had won the pankration four times at Nemea (about 550 BC). Nemea, Archaeological Museum.

450. A group of objects and vases associated with athletics, found in a pit to the east of the temple of Zeus. They were probably dedicated by a pentathlete after a victory in the games as indicated by the discus and weights (about 500 BC). Nemea, Archaeological Museum.

451. Large and miniature vases, dedications in the sanctuary of Zeus. The dedicator was obviously more interested in the number of vases than in their size (6th c. BC). Nemea, Archaeological Museum.

449

450

451

5th c. BC
The Classical period

The growth of the games in the first half of the 5th c. BC led to the dedication of at least three bronze votive sculptures, of which only the bases are preserved, in the open area to the south of the temple. This area was planted with tall cypresses which gave the sanctuary the appearance of a grove, as we learn from references by the poets of the period. The pits for these trees were discovered during excavations, and in 1978 new trees were planted in exactly the same places as the old ones, in an attempt to approximate the original appearance of the sanctuary.

452-453. Parts of a painted terracotta sima with a lion's-head waterspout. Found in a well along with other rubbish, they are the remains of a Classical building, the precise location of which in the sanctuary is unknown. They attest to a destruction in the last quarter of the 5th c. BC, for which there is otherwise no historical evidence. Nemea, Archaeological Museum.

452

453

454. Bronze figurine of a discus thrower (middle of the 5th c. BC). Athens, National Archaeological Museum.

455. Rim of a bronze hydria found in a well. It is decorated with a female head, and the inscription attests that it was a dedication in the sanctuary of Zeus (late 6th c. BC). Nemea, Archaeological Museum.

THE OIKOI

In this period a row of nine buildings, to which the conventional name *oikoi* has been given, was erected in about the middle of the sanctuary, facing the open area and the temple. Two inscriptions found in two of these buildings (of the Rhodians and the Epidaurians) suggest that they were dedications by city-states. Although they resemble the treasuries at Olympia in that they were built in a row, they are larger and have a different design. They could, therefore, have been treasuries, storerooms or, most probably, club rooms that served as meeting places for pilgrims from these cities, since rooms given over to the preparation of food have been found in some of them.

In the last quarter of the 5th century, there was probably a major battle on the site of the sanctuary that resulted in the destruction of the temple of Zeus and other early buildings, since burnt architectural members, together with ash, charcoal and tiles were found in a level dating from this period. The battle is also attested archaeologically by spearheads and bronze arrows found in the same level. No literary source mentions any such battle at Nemea, but we can be certain that this episode led to the abandonment of the sanctuary and the transfer of the games to Argos.

No evidence of life is found at Nemea from 410 to 340 BC. It is characteristic that of the 4,000 coins that have been found, only three date from this period.

454

455

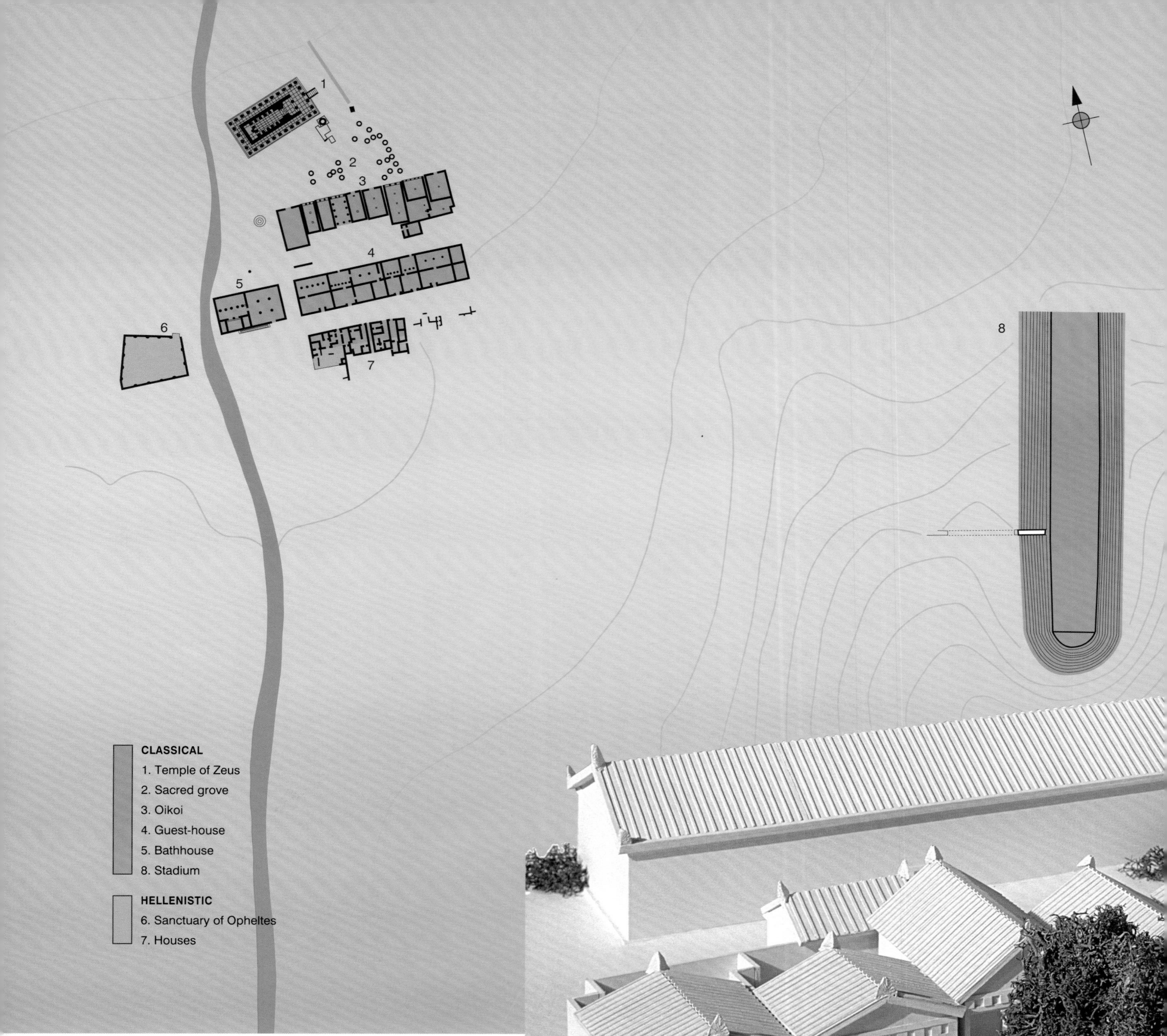

456

456. Plan of the surrounding area of the sanctuary of Zeus, showing clearly the bed of the river and the spatial relationship between the sanctuary and the stadium.

457. Reconstruction model of the buildings in the sanctuary of Zeus, from the northwest. To the right is the dominating volume of the temple, with the row of oikoi *behind the sacred grove and the rectangular hostel and baths complex in the background. At the top right, on the other bank of the river, is the enclosure of the heroon of Opheltes.*

458. Marble head of a colossal statue of Zeus, the god in whose honour the Nemean games were held. From Aigeira in Achaia (second half of the 4th c. BC). Athens, National Archaeological Museum.

457

340/30 - 270/60 BC

The return of the games to their cradle

The return of the games to Nemea is attested by the flurry of building activity noted in the sanctuary at the end of the 4th c. BC, which has been linked with the building programme of the Macedonian kings. To it belong the construction of a new temple of Zeus and many functional buildings, such as a guesthouse and baths and, above all, the athletic facilities, with a stadium and changing rooms.

458

THE NEW TEMPLE OF ZEUS

The new temple of Zeus, measuring 22 by 45 m., was larger than its predecessor, and was built of local grey poros extracted from a quarry near Kleonai, found directly on the modern national highway from Corinth to Tripoli. The temple had an exterior colonnade of 6 by 12 columns, with two more columns in the pronaos, and also an interior two-storey U-shaped colonnade with 6 by 4 columns. The exterior colonnade was Doric, and the interior is Corinthian in the lower storey and Ionic in the upper. The temple of Zeus at Nemea is thus one of the earliest examples in ancient Greek architecture employing all three orders. A

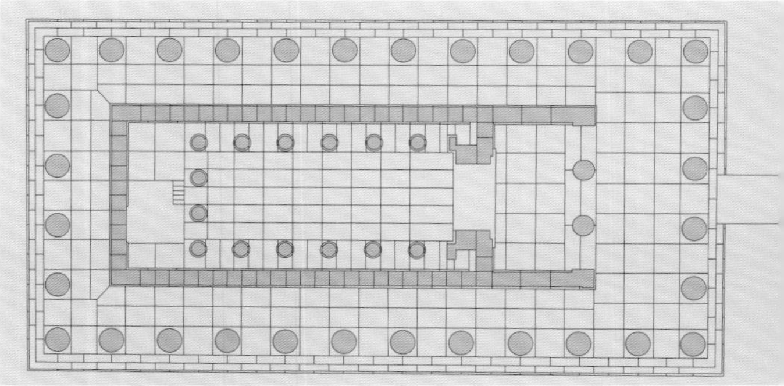

459

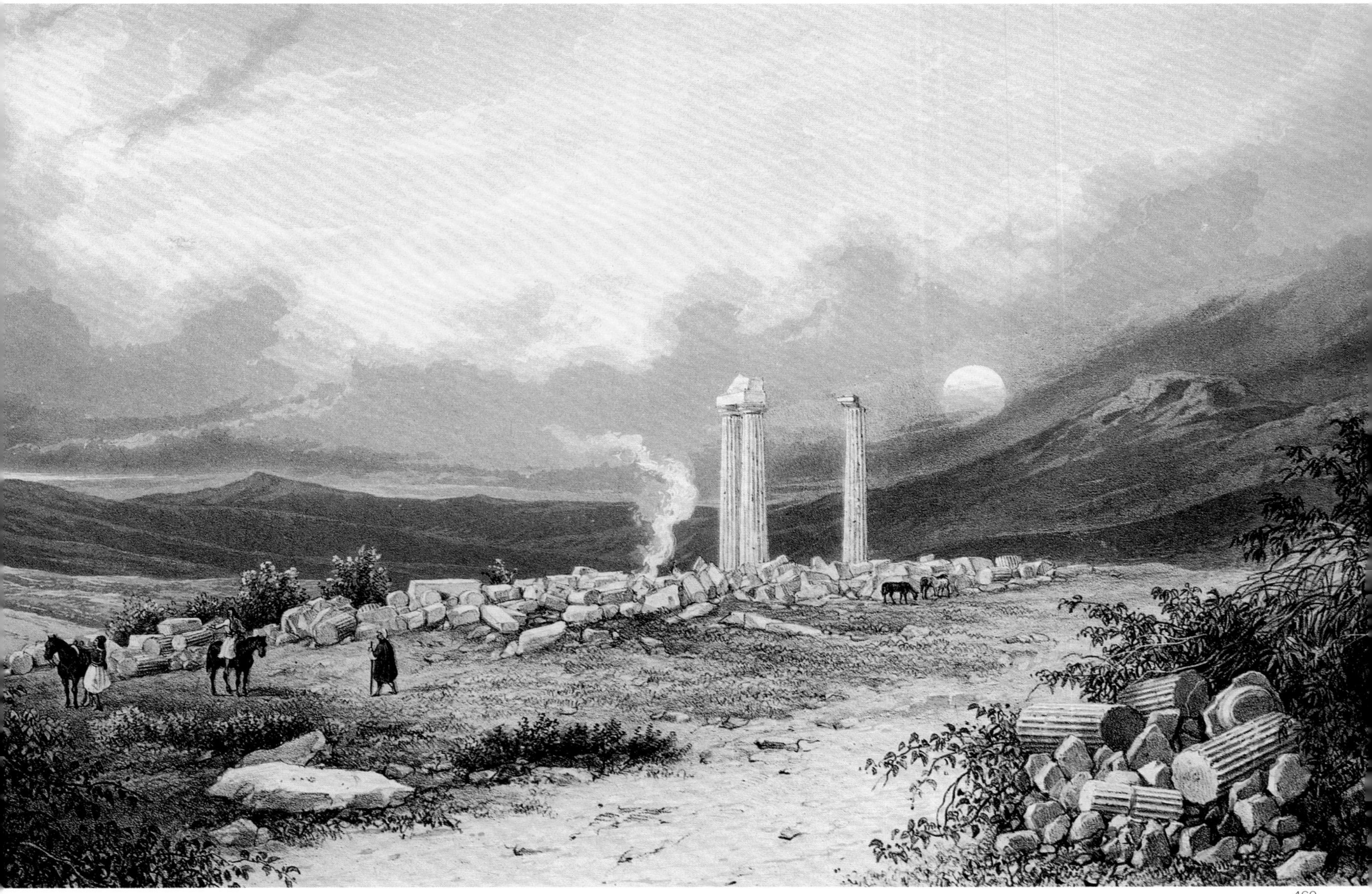

460

461

462

notable feature of the columns is their very slender proportions, which foreshadow Hellenistic forms. Of the 48 columns of the temple, only three have remained standing since antiquity, though a major restoration programme, currently in progress, will raise a further five, radically altering the appearance of the temple.

There were no sculptures on the pediments or metopes, and the only decorative feature of the entablature was the fine relief marble sima, with alternating lions' heads and palmettes, like the one in the temple of Athena Alea at Tegea. This resemblance, together with other common architectural features, initially suggested that the temple at Nemea was by the great Tegean sculptor and architect Skopas, though this hypothesis cannot be proven.

Another notable feature of the temple is the existence of an underground crypt at the back of the cella, forming a kind of adyton with 6 steps leading down to it. Structures of this kind are normally found in temples at which oracular responses are issued, which suggests that there was an oracle at Nemea, for which, however, there is no other evidence. In front of the temple is preserved its altar, which was over 41 m. long. As at Isthmia, this great length may have been due to the need to sacrifice a large number of animals simultaneously.

460. Engraving by V. Davidov of the temple of Zeus at Nemea. (1835-1839).

459, 461. Plan and reconstruction drawing of the façade of the new temple of Zeus at Nemea, built about 330 BC. All its features presage forms of architecture that were to become predominant in the Hellenistic period. From B.H. Bill, The Temple of Zeus at Nemea *(1966), pl. 4,6.*

462. View of the underground crypt at the back of the cella of the temple of Zeus. The access staircase can be seen, with the foundation of the earlier temple next to it.

463. Characteristic view of the poros quarry near Kleonai, which was discovered during the laying of the new national highway from Corinth to Tripoli. It produced all the construction material for the buildings in the sanctuary of Zeus at Nemea.

463

464. Part of a column from the internal colonnade of the temple of Zeus, with its Corinthian capital. The temple at Nemea is one of the earliest in Greek architecture in which all three architectural orders were employed. About 330 BC. Nemea, Archaeological Museum.

465. Aerial photograph of the temple of Zeus, in 1977. The characteristic position of the column drums points to the gradual collapse of the temple, as a result initially of earthquakes in the 4th c. AD and, thereafter, of gradual abandonment. Athens, American School of Classical Studies.

464

465

466

466. Aerial photograph of the sanctuary of Zeus at Nemea, from the north, with the temple in the foreground and the altar to its left. The architectural members from the temple are laid out for study and probable restoration in the clearing of the sacred cypress grove. On a second level can be seen the foundations of the row of oikoi, and behind them the hostel, with the early Christian basilica built to its west side.

467. The southeast corner column of the peristyle of the temple of Zeus. The manner in which it collapsed and the fact that the drums were preserved in a row are of great assistance in its restoration.

468. View of the temple of Zeus at Nemea after the completion of the first phase of the restoration programme in 2002. After the raising of two columns of the north pteron, there are now five standing columns.

467

468

THE HEROON OF OPHELTES

Towards the end of the 4th century, the heroon of Opheltes was redesigned. It was enclosed by an irregular pentagonal enclosure wall, which copied the similar wall of the Pelopeion at Olympia, representing another attempt to associate the Nemean with the Olympic games.

THE GUESTHOUSE

The largest of the secular buildings was the guesthouse, which was 85 m. long and had 14 large rooms, probably for the use of athletes and their trainers during the games. All the apartments on the north side have a colonnade to support an upper storey, and are therefore considered to have been bedrooms and sitting rooms; those on the south, in which hearths and vessels associated with eating and drinking have been found, have been interpreted as kitchens and dining rooms. A large part of the guesthouse is covered by the large Early Christian basilica of the 5th-6th c. AD.

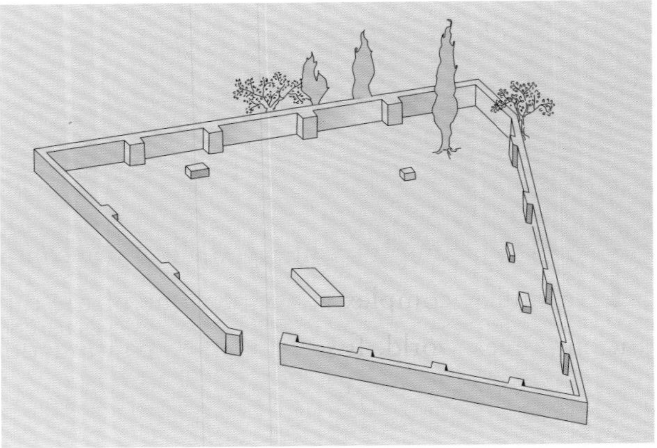

469

469. Reconstruction drawing of the sanctuary of Opheltes. Inside were probably trees and a number of altars, one of which was interpreted by Pausanias as the tomb of Opheltes. Drawing: S. G. Miller.

470. View of the easternmost room of the hostel. Despite its unusual form, this building has yielded enough excavation evidence to make its identification certain.

471. View of the interior of the south part of the bathhouse, showing the main cistern and the bathtubs in the back.

472. View of the south part of the bathhouse at Nemea with the drainage pipe that led off the water to the river.

473. View of the row of basins in the south part of the bathhouse at Nemea.

470

471

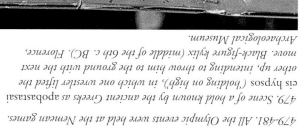

479-481. All the Olympic events were held at the Nemean games.

479. Scene of a hold known by the ancient Greeks as apobastasai eis hypsos *('holding on high'), in which one wrestler lifted the other up, intending to throw him to the ground with the next move. Black-figure kylix (middle of the 6th c. BC). Florence, Archaeological Museum.*

480. Depiction of a boxing match between two youths under the eye of the trainer or judge. Attic red-figure kylix (480 BC). Athens, N.P. Goulandris Museum of Cycladic Art.

479

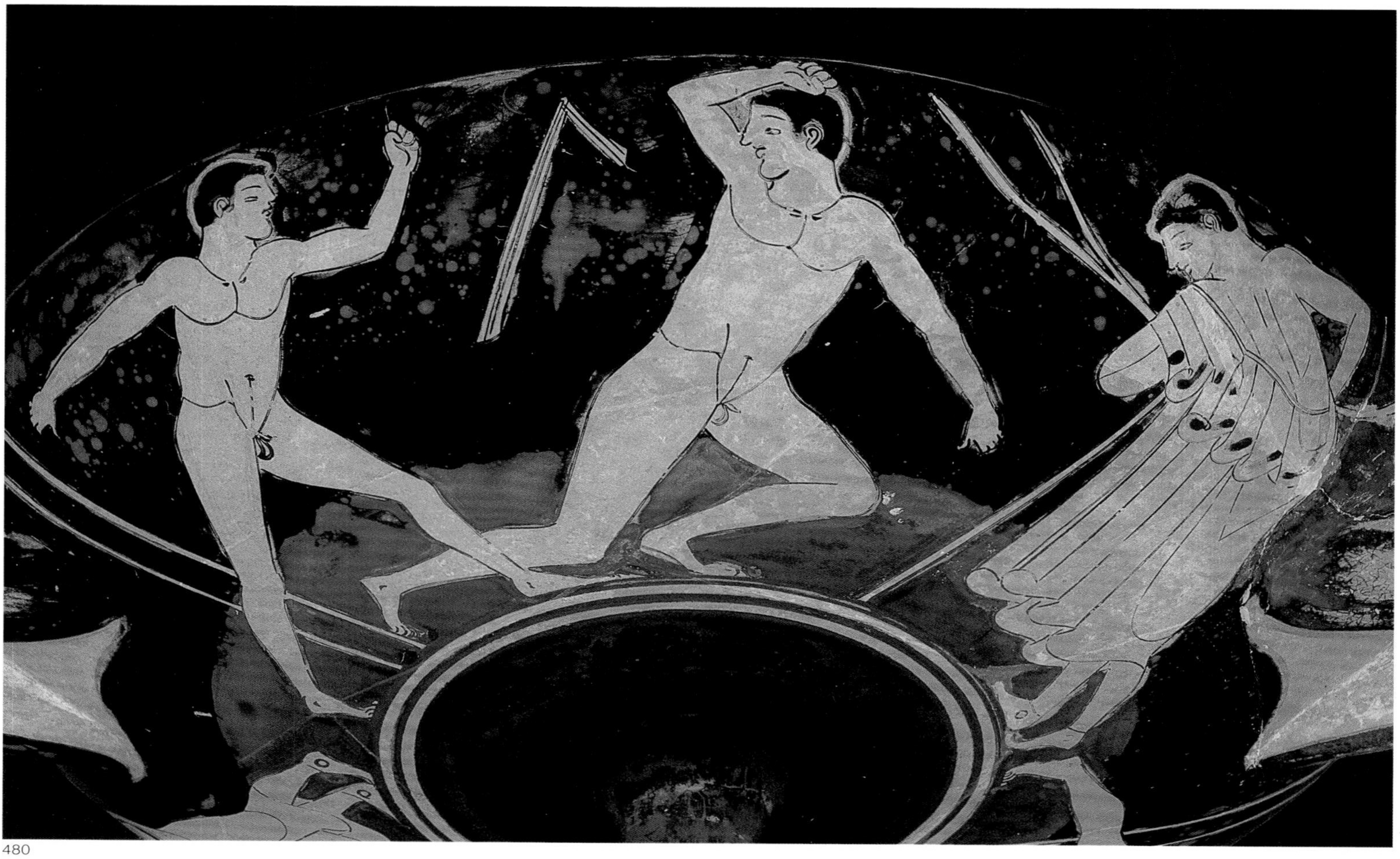

480

THE STADIUM

The stadium at Nemea is about 400 m. to the southeast of the sanctuary, with which it was connected by a sacred way. This was followed by the faithful who, after sacrifices to Nemean Zeus and the other rituals, proceeded to the stadium to watch the athletic events. The same route was also followed by the sacred procession of priests, officials in charge of the games, and athletes. These last, however, stopped at the changing room, a rectangular building that had an interior courtyard with stoas on three sides, with a total of nine columns. The stoas probably had wooden benches on which they could leave their clothes in order to prepare for the contest by anointing themselves with oil and so forth. The entrance to the building was in the middle of the north wall, while the exit, at the rear, in the southeast corner, led to a tunnel 36.35 m. long and about 2.5 m. high, roofed with a barrel vault, through which athletes emerged directly into the stadium. Several inscriptions are roughly carved on the walls near the exit, probably by the hands of the athletes themselves, while they were waiting for the herald to call their names. One of them carved the word *niko* ('I win'), and others their names. A certain Telestas is probably to be identified with the boxer known from Olympia, who was victorious in the games of 340 BC, while Akrotatos, whose name is accompanied by the adjective *kalos* ('beautiful'), is probably a member of the royal house of Sparta of this name.

The stadium was built in a natural valley, and the earth removed during its modelling was used to build up its north end. It is one of the best-preserved stadia of the Late Classical period, and received no modifications in later centuries. It presented roughly the picture we see today, that of a long horseshoe, and held about 30,000 spectators. It is one of the oldest surviving stadia with

474

474. Aerial photograph of the stadium at Nemea, from the southeast. The north part had already disappeared in the Byzantine period. At the top can be seen part of the sanctuary of Zeus. Every two years, when the games were held, the entire valley was converted into a huge camping ground for the athletes, ordinary spectators, and the official missions sent by the Greek city-states.

THE BATHS COMPLEX

The baths complex, which contained two contiguous rooms, is, along with a similar complex at Delphi, one of the earliest such buildings in the ancient Greek world. It seems to be a continuation of the guesthouse to the west. The function of the first room, which has four columns in the middle, remains unknown, because its entire floor was dug over in the Early Christian period, obliterating all ancient traces. Some scholars assert that it may have been a palaestra. The second room is divided into two parts: the north part may have been a changing room, in which the bathers left their clothes; the south part contained basins for washing and cleansing. In the middle is a large cistern with four steps leading into it, which might have been a swimming pool. On either side of it are rooms containing four stone bathtubs each, in which the patrons could wash in water carried by an aqueduct on the south side. The waste water was led off into the river.

To the south of the guesthouse and baths is a row of houses of the same period, which were probably used for residential purposes by the priesthood and the Hellanodikai, since no permanent facilities were created at Nemea in ancient times.

472

473

481. Another scene of two wrestlers locked together. They are watched by a judge and a third athlete. Panathenaic amphora from Eretria (360-359 BC). Athens, National Archaeological Museum.

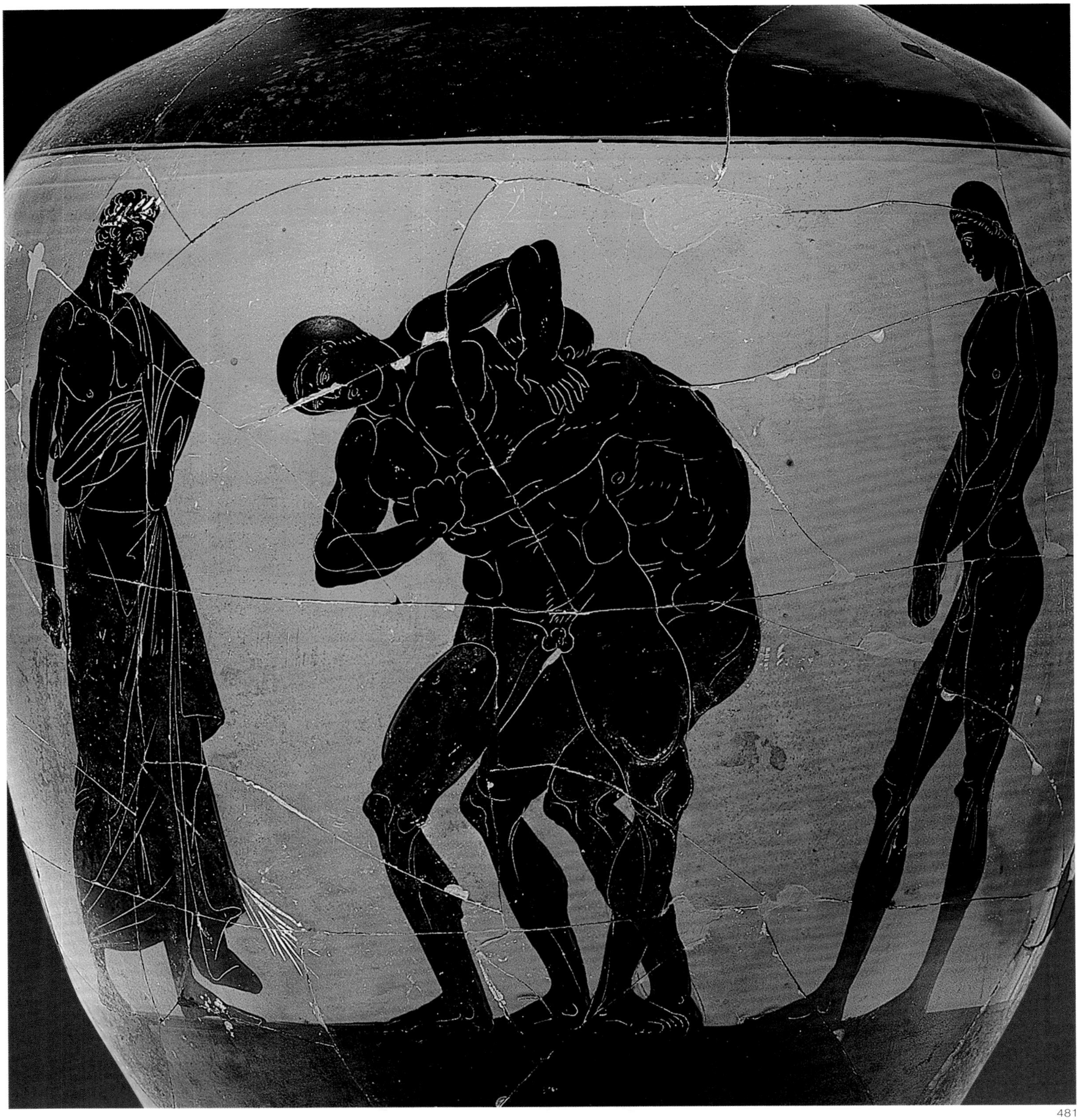

481

The Starting Mechanism

The most interesting remains of the stadium track concern the start for the foot races. At the south end, the starting gate is preserved intact. This was a row of slabs carved with two parallel grooves (*balbis*), in which the runners put their toes. Holes are preserved about 1.60 m. apart, in which wooden poles were inserted, defining starting places for 13 runners. It is probable that the track was marked with lines, possibly in white paint, starting from the posts and designating individual lanes. There are stepped bases at each end of the starting gate, which probably bore statues of Victory, as we learn from ancient victory epigrams.

A few years after the construction of the starting gate, stone bases were added in front of each end for the starting mechanism (*hysplex*), which prevented false starts in the foot races. The hysplex system is the same as the one we saw in the later stadium at Isthmia, though in the present case the bases are in a better state of preservation and enable us to make a detailed reconstruction of the entire mechanism in detail. It has, in fact, been reconstructed at life size and set in its original position, and it operated flawlessly during a revival of the Nemean games. (These revivals take place every four years, one month before the Olympic games.)

The hysplex consisted of two moveable posts fixed in the mechanism, which was supported by the base at either end. These posts held two horizontal ropes tight, at knee height and waist height to the runners. The bottom end of each post was stuck into a system of twisted animal sinews, which created the necessary tension to allow the posts and horizontal ropes to fall suddenly in front of the runners, at the start of the race. The hysplex was operated by a starter, who stood behind the runners holding the two ropes in his hands.

482

483

The only surviving turning post is also preserved at Nemea. This was the wooden post around which long-distance runners turned. Its stone base is preserved off centre, a few metres in front of the starting post.

482. Bronze figurine of a runner in the starting position. From ancient Olympia (480 BC). Olympia, Archaeological Museum.

483. Reconstruction drawing of runners preparing to start a race in the stadium at Nemea. The stance adopted by the runners is based on relevant ancient works of art, such as the bronze figurine in the previous illustration. The starter, who stands behind the athletes, holds the two ropes with which he will actvate the hysplex mechanism. Olympia, Archaeological Museum. Drawing: S.G. Miller.

484. View from the south of the curve of the stadium at Nemea, showing the row of stone slabs in the balbis, the starting line for races.

485. Depiction of the dolichos race with three runners. Attic pseudo-Panathenaic amphora from Rhodes (500 BC). Rhodes, Archaeological Museum.

484

485

The end of Nemea and the games

Despite the erection of so many fine and costly facilities, the games did not last many years at Nemea. As has been mentioned, reasons of political expediency apparently induced the Argives, about 270/260 BC, to transfer the games to their capital, where they continued to be held down to Roman times. Pausanias tells us that winter Nemean games were held at the time of Hadrian. This has been interpreted as an attempt by the emperor to revitalise Nemea, which was in decline, by organising games in the winter, without influencing the 'regular' Nemean games held at Argos. The last evidence for the holding of games at Argos is a coin from the time of the Roman emperor Gordian (AD 225-244) in the 3rd c. AD, on the reverse of which is a wreath of wild celery.

At Nemea itself, no major building projects were carried out after the removal of the games in 270 BC, though there were some minor interventions during those brief periods when the games returned. The sanctuary fell into complete decline. When Pausanias made a visit about the middle of the 2nd c. AD, the roof of the temple of Zeus had collapsed, and all the buildings were reduced to ruins. The traveller refers only to the cypress grove, a spring, and the heroon of Opheltes.

Early Christian Nemea

Many years before games were officially banned, particular local circumstances led to the gradual decline of an important sanctuary at which great games were held. Life returned to Nemea in the 5th c. AD, when a fairly large Early Christian settlement of farmers and stockbreeders emerged. They used material from the ancient monuments to build their houses, and situated their cemetery close by. For their house of worship, they erected a fine three-aisled basilica. The aisles were separated by two colonnades, in which the Corinthian columns from the cella of the temple of Zeus were used. The floor was paved with ceramic tiles. In the 6th century, a baptistery was added to the north side, which probably had windows with coloured panes.

The area was finally abandoned about the end of the 6th century, because of the continuous raiding and pillaging of central Greece and the Peloponnese by Slav tribes.

486

486. Model of the sanctuary of Zeus at Nemea in the Early Christian period. Part of the ancient temple was demolished and a large basilica constructed with an elevated central aisle and a baptistery to the south. The rest of the sanctuary was used for growing crops, and the cemetery was located next to the basilica.

THE PANATHENAIA

To see contests not only of swiftness and strength, but also of word and opinion, and all the other arts, and the prizes for these are great.

Isocrates, *Paneg.*, 45

The Panathenaia was the most splendid festival of Athens and the greatest of the non-panhellenic, 'local' festivals. It was as great as the city that organised it, and in some periods, such as the 5th century, its brilliance was equal, if not superior, to that of the panhellenic festivals. The Panathenaia had not only a religious, but also a 'national,' character: the participation of the entire Athenian people, the formal guests of the city, officials and embassies, as well as athletes from all over the Greek world, emphasised the political and intellectual superiority of Athens at that period. The festival also had something of the character of a popular celebration, since it provided the ancient Greeks with one of the greatest opportunities to entertain themselves by listening to music and songs, watching plays and attending major athletic contests.

The festival of the Great Panathenaia was founded in 566/565 BC, a few years after the institution of the last of the four panhellenic festivals, and was held in honour of the great goddess of the city, Athena. The initiative in this was taken by the tyrant Peisistratos, who realised the political importance of the games on the international stage and the role they might play as a means of realising the Athenian ambition to become a great power. The foundation of the new, grand games was based on the reorganisation of an old, annual, ancestral Athenian festival that was enhanced by the addition of many new religious celebrations and competitive events.

490. A relief of the contemplative Athena. The goddess leans on her spear in contemplation, possibly in front of a stele carved with the names of the fallen in a battle. Her posture is completely in accord with her role as patron goddess of the city (about 460 BC). Athens, Akropolis Museum.

491. Athena Promachos as depicted on the front of the characteristic vases of the Panathenaic games, the Panathenaic amphoras. She turns to the left, brandishes her spear, and holds forth her shield as defender of the city. She is depicted here on a vase produced in the archonship of Charikleides (363/362 BC), found at Eretria. Athens, National Archaeological Museum.

491

Foundation Myths and Traditions

494

In the eyes of the ancient Athenians, the historical founder of the Panathenaia was less important than the mythical founders. According to Athenian myths, the Panathenaic festival was instituted by King Erichthonios, who was half-man and half-snake, to celebrate Athena's role in the victory over the Giants. A different myth attributes their inception to Erechtheus, a sacred child, after whom was named the Erechtheion, one of the most important temples on the Acropolis. It is no coincidence that it was the statue of Athena in the Erechtheion, not in the Parthenon, that was the object of the main event of the Panathenaia, the Panathenaic procession, as we shall see below.

494. Theseus, the great Attic hero, was inevitably involved in the foundation myth of the Panathenaic games. Attic red-figure kylix by the Kodros Painter depicting the feats of Theseus (440-430 BC). London, British Museum.

495. Excellent depiction of Athena Promachos facing right on a Panathenaic amphora produced in the archonship of Charikleides (363/362 BC). It has two inscriptions: ΤΟΝ ΑΘΕΝΕΘΕΝ ΑΘΛΟΝ *('From the prizes at Athens') and* ΝΙΚΟΔΗΜΟΣ ΕΠΟΙΕΣΕΝ *('Made by Nikodemos'), the signature of the potter. Los Angeles, J. Paul Getty Museum.*

Finally, according to a third myth, which undoubtedly has a historical basis, the founder was the hero and king of Athens, Theseus, who united all the inhabitants of Attica into a single state, through a synoecism, or union, of the demes, or local governments. To reinforce this unification by giving it a religious content, he obliged all the demes to participate in a joint festival and sacrifice, which formed the starting point for the Panathenaia. Homer probably refers to some such occasion in the *Iliad* (II, 549-551), where he describes ram and bull sacrifices on the Akropolis in honour of Athena.

495

496

496-498. The Erechtheion, the temple in which two of the mythical heroes of Athens associated with the foundation of the Panathenaic festival, Erichthonios and Erechtheus, were worshipped.

496, 497. Reconstructions of the east and west sides of the Erechtheion, by J. Tetaz (1847-1848). These reconstructions point out the difference in soil level and the superb manner by which the architect succeeded in unifying the building. Paris, École Nationale Supérieure des Beaux-Arts.

498. The Caryatid porch from the south side.

497

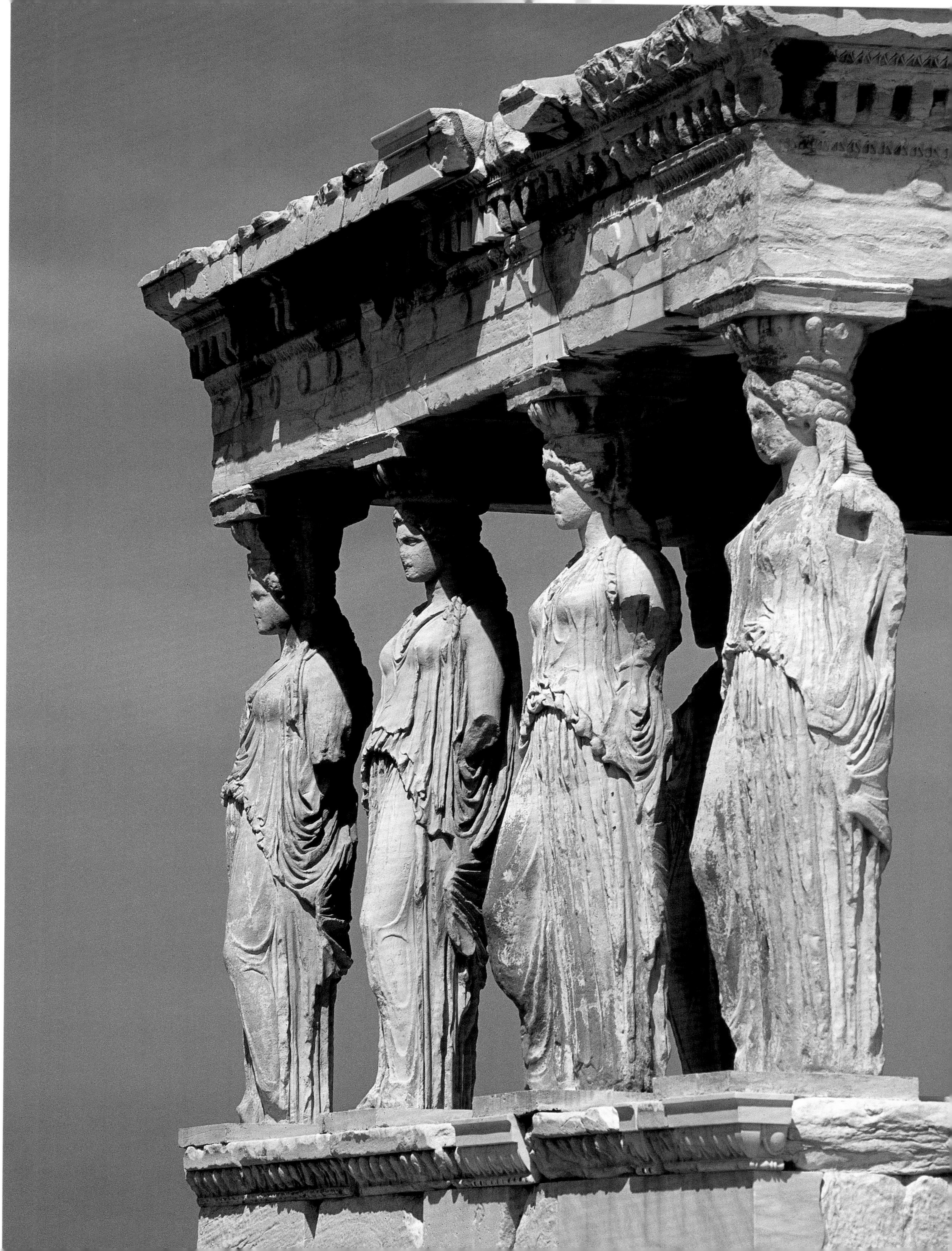

501

THE ORGANISATION AND CONDUCT OF THE FESTIVAL

The Great Panathenaia was held every four years, clearly in imitation of the Olympic festival, with which the Athenians sought by all means possible to associate their own. The festival was held in the third year of every Olympiad, at the end of the month Hekatombaion, that is, around the 15th of August, the same·time of year as the Olympic games. Its duration varied over its history, though there is strong evidence that in the Classical period it might have lasted as long as eight days. The length of the festival is accounted for by the wealth and variety of events, since the Athenians not only introduced the new Olympic events but also retained many of the ancestral ones and the celebrations connected with their old festival.

502

501. Imaginary reconstruction drawing of the east side of the Parthenon made by the French architect A. Paccard in 1845. Paris, École Nationale Supérieure des Beaux-Arts.

502. Group of the three goddesses (Hestia, Dione and Aphrodite) from the east pediment, now in the British Museum. The Parthenon was directly connected with the Panathenaic festival, and both were very important to Athenian political propaganda in ancient times. London, British Museum.

The preparation of the festival. The officials

For the Panathenaia, as for the panhellenic festivals, special embassies, called *spondophoroi*, were dispatched to all the cities of the Mediterranean, announcing the date of the festival and inviting cities, allies and monarchs to participate in the games.

Responsibility for the preparation and conduct of the Panathenaia lay with special officials chosen every four years. In the 6th century there were eight *hieropoioi*, but from the late 5th century on the task fell to ten *athlothetai*, one from each tribe. We learn of their duties from Aristotle (*Ath. Pol.*, 60): 'They organise the Panathenaic procession and the music contest and the athletics contest and the horse race, and they make the peplos and they make the amphoras with the council and they distribute the oil to the athletes.' Given that almost all the offices under the Athenian democracy were held for a single year, the period of office of the athlothetai is therefore striking, the implication being that preparations for the following festival began as soon as the previous one had ended. In addition to organising the procession and the contests, their most important concerns were the preparation of the Panathenaic peplos, and the making of the Panathenaic oil from the sacred olive trees of Athena. The responsibility for this process was assumed by each of the annual eponymous archons of the city during the years between two festivals. This period of time was necessary to collect the required amounts of oil, for 60-70 tons of oil were awarded by the city to victors at each Panathenaic festival.

The public expenditure on all the events of the festival was very great: Demosthenes compared it to the costs of an entire military campaign.

503

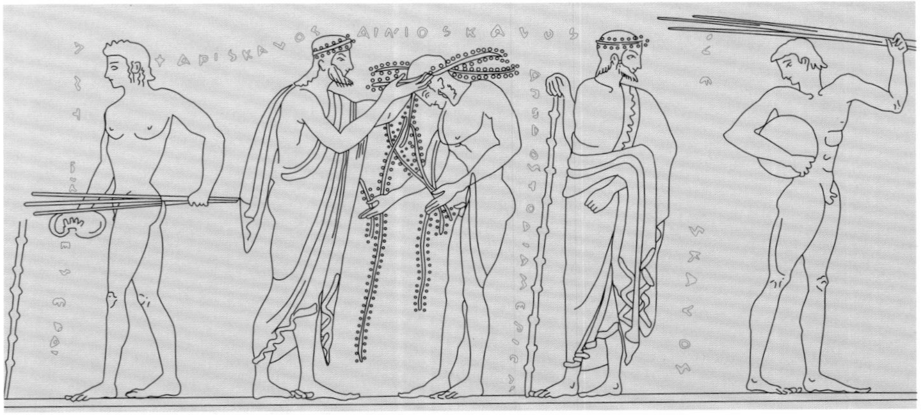

504

503, 505. Scene of the declaration of a Panathenaic winner and the awarding of the prize by the festival officials. Panathenaic amphora produced in the archonship of Theophrastos (340/339 BC), whose name is inscribed on the main side of the same vase. Paris, Louvre Museum.

504. Drawing of a now lost lekythos dating from the late 6th c. BC. depicting the declaration of a winner and the awarding of the prize in the pentathlon. The officials wear the himation and wreaths, while the athletes are nude.

506. In the iconography of the Panathenaic games, the role of the official who awarded the prize to the winner was often played by the personification of Victory. Here, Victory hovers above a chariot and offers a Panathenaic amphora to the charioteer. Attic red-figure amphora dating from 440 BC. Athens, Ancient Agora Museum.

507. Part of the base of a dedication made by the winners in a pyrrichios contest. The inscriptions on the base refer to the victories won by the choregos, *the man who funded the event, who received a large measure of the honour (about 375 BC). Athens, National Archaeological Museum.*

Accordingly, in conformity with a practice known in similar cases in the Athenian democracy, a portion of the costs was met from donations made by wealthy citizens or foreign rulers, who, as *agonothetai*, undertook to fund either the entire festival or individual events, such as the torch race.

505

506

507

The Panathenaic procession

508. Model of Athens in the 2nd c. AD from the west. The Panathenaic way can clearly be seen. It begins at the Pompeion, the building between the two gates in the fortification wall and proceeds in a straight line between stoas to the open area of the Agora, which it crosses diagonally before ascending to the Akropolis. Plan by J. Travlos and D. Giraud (1985), construction by N. Gerassimoff.

509. View of the Panathenaic way through the Agora to the Akropolis.

The central religious ceremony of the Panathenaia was the procession held on the goddess's birthday, the 28th Hekatombaion. The preparations for it were carried out in and around the Pompeion, the large public building in the Kerameikos in which the sacred items for the procession (*pompeia*) were kept. The most important object, not only of the procession, but of the entire festival, was the Panathenaic peplos, a large, rectangular piece of material woven over a period of 9 months by women and girls from distinguished families of the city, who were called *ergastinai* and *arrephoroi*. The peplos was adorned with representations depicting the goddess's feats in the Gigantomachy and extolling her contribution to the subjugation of the powers of darkness. It was carried

509

as a sail hanging from the mast of the Panathenaic ship, which moved on wheels; this was associated with the belief that Athena made the first ship. The symbolism also afforded an opportunity to demonstrate the strength of the Athenian fleet. The earliest evidence of the use of a ship in the Panathenaic procession goes back only to the beginning of the 3rd century, but some scholars assert that the custom was instituted as early as the first Panathenaia, and others after the naval battle of Salamis, for obvious reasons.

The procession moved slowly at a solemn rate, the rhythm being kept by musicians, and checks were made of its progress at intervals by special officials. In it walked the entire Athenian people, the theorias of allied cities, embassies and formal guests invited from other city-states and, of course, the victors in the games, who occupied a prominent position. Particular groups of Athenian citizens and metics (foreign residents), sturdy old men, young girls, and handsome youths held olive branches (*thallophoroi*) or items containing offerings for the goddess, such as bowls (*skaphephoroi*), vases (*hydriaphoroi*) and trays or baskets (*kanephoroi*). Squadrons of the Athenian cavalry also participated in the procession, as did the sacrificial animals, especially the hundred oxen that were to be sacrificed to the goddess (*hecatomb*).

Starting from the Kerameikos and following the Panathenaic way, the procession came to the Agora, which it crossed obliquely before ascending the Akropolis. After completing a journey of over one kilometre, the ship came to a halt on a small plateau beneath the Propylaia, from where the peplos was taken by hand and offered to the ancient xoanon of Athena kept in the Erechtheion. According to recent research, there were not one but two peploi: a small one wound around the xoanon like a garment, and a large one that was transported by the ship and then folded, before being offered in thanks to the goddess or, according to a different view, spread out as a backcloth behind Pheidias's chryselephantine statue in the Parthenon.

The procession was followed by the great sacrifice, the hecatomb, carried out on the goddess's large altar on the sacred rock, the fire of which was lit by the winner of a torch race. The sacrifice of the one hundred oxen took place on the Akropolis, but the meat was apparently roasted and distributed to the participants in the area of the Kerameikos. The official guests were received by the city in the seven *andrones* – seven specially designed rooms with couches in the Pompeion – while everyone else ate and celebrated in the surrounding area, both inside and outside the city wall, in the shade of tents, awnings and trees. There will have been an abundance of meat, judging by an ironical comment by Socrates in Aristophanes' *Clouds* (ll. 386-87), in which the philosopher associates the Panathenaia with indigestion.

510. Imaginary drawing by J. Travlos of the Panathenaic procession crossing the Agora in front of the temple of Ares and the Odeion of Agrippa. It is led by the Panathenaic ship with the peplos hanging from its mast.

511. The Propylaia from the west as it was in 1864. Drawing: L.-F. Boitte. Paris, École Nationale Supérieure des Beaux-Arts.

512. Drawing by the French architect L.-F. Boitte of the Propylaia concealed behind the Late Roman wall built in the 3rd c. AD. Paris, École Nationale Supérieure des Beaux-Arts.

510

511

512

THE PARTHENON FRIEZE

513. Slab from the east frieze of the Parthenon with three of the Olympian gods: Poseidon, Apollo and Artemis. The east frieze depicted the culmination of the Panathenaic festival, with the gods watching the delivery of the peplos. Athens, Akropolis Museum.

The most splendid representation of the Panathenaic procession is that on the Parthenon frieze. This is the first time in the history of architecture that so characteristically Ionic an element is used in a temple of the Doric order. And this is not fortuitous. When Iktinos and Pheidias designed the building, they wanted a part of the temple in which it would be possible to depict the long, continuous procession. Since no such space was available in the Doric order, they borrowed it from the Ionic, setting it above the walls of the temple and creating what has been called the Attic style of ancient Greek architecture. This solution was dictated by the need to render the Panathenaic procession in an impressive fashion on the goddess's great temple, since the procession was the most characteristic element of the festival and could be used to give prominence to the splendour both of itself and of the entire city. This is the first time in history that mortals were depicted in a sacred building, next to gods and heroes – a position connected with the political implications and ideological messages transmitted by the entire sculptural decoration of the temple. In this way highly artistic expression was given to the values and beliefs of the Athenian democracy regarding the position and purposes of men in a well-ordered society – values and beliefs

513

514
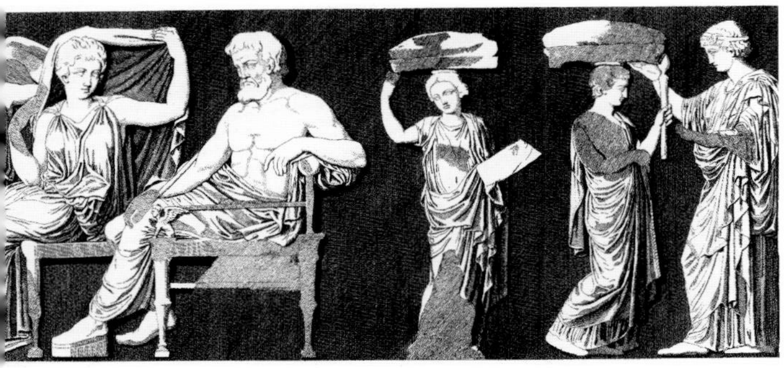
515

516

517
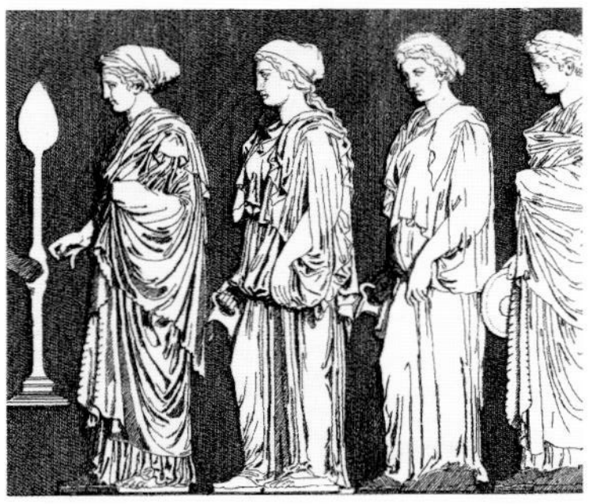

514-517. Reconstruction drawing of parts of the Parthenon frieze made by J. Stuart and N. Revett in 1751-1753.

514. Part of the east frieze depicting the handover of the peplos of Athena (right) and Iris, Hera and Zeus (left).

515. A slab from the south frieze with youths leading the sacrificial cows.

516. Part of the rhythmical decoration of the north frieze. Youths lead the way carrying bowls, containing offerings for the goddess, on their shoulders.

517. Part of the procession of women on the east frieze. The first woman carries a censer and the others vases for the rituals held on the sacred rock.

described by Thucydides in the funeral oration of Perikles in 431 BC for those who had died during the first year of the Peloponnesian War.

The procession is developed over a surface 160 m. long, in an admirable composition consisting of over 360 figures of humans and 250 animals, mainly horses. All three stages of the procession are depicted: on the west side the preparations and formations; on the two long sides the procession itself; and on the east side the most important ceremony of the festival. The larger part of the frieze is occupied by horsemen, who were organised in rhythmically ranked groups that made it possible not only to create an outstanding artistic composition but also to depict the organisation of the Athenian state and by extension of the Athenian democracy. The horsemen are divided on the basis of their dress into 10 groups, alluding to the ten tribes into which the population of Attica had been divided since the foundation of the democracy at the time of Kleisthenes (506 BC).

The cavalry procession is followed by a depiction of the *apobates* contest, possibly symbolising the competitive aspect of the festival. Twelve chariots are rendered, and the event was possibly selected as a very ancient Athenian contest that had been established, according to tradition, by Erichthonios, the mythical Attic hero. Next comes the sacrificial procession, with oxen and rams accompanied by musicians and people bringing offerings to the goddess. The most important part of the procession is featured on the east side, above the main entrance to the temple. At both ends of this side are female figures holding sacred vessels and censers; they are followed by two groups with a total of ten mature men, who have been interpreted as the mythical eponymous heroes of the ten Athenian tribes, or perhaps the ten athlothetai, the officials responsible for organising the festival. Finally, in the centre of the east frieze, is depicted the most sacred moment of the procession, and indeed of the entire festival – the handing over of the peplos. Here, the priest or the archon basileus receives the peplos from a child, while the priestess of Athena Polias welcomes two young girls carrying on their heads sacred stools or, according to another view, folded pieces of cloth. The scene takes place before the twelve Olympian gods, who are depicted seated and therefore on a larger scale, in two groups. The very bold (in ancient terms) scene, depicting gods and mortals on the same level, owes its artistic conception to Pheidias himself, though it also gives full expression to the Athenian belief in the preeminence of the city of Athens in Greece during its Golden Age, namely, the middle of the 5th c. BC.

518. The west frieze of the Parthenon had a depiction of the preparations for the Panathenaic procession. These two pictures give a good idea of the difficulties facing the ancient Greeks themselves when they wanted to see the frieze. They had to view it from a particular spot outside the building, trying to make out the parts hidden behind the columns and the peristyle.

519-520. Two slabs from the north frieze of the Parthenon. A large part of the Panathenaic procession consisted of young horsemen mounted on noble steeds. The procession presented an opportunity for the city to show off its splendour, and the effort to do so is strongly depicted in the frieze.
519. Athens, Akropolis Museum.
520. London, British Museum.

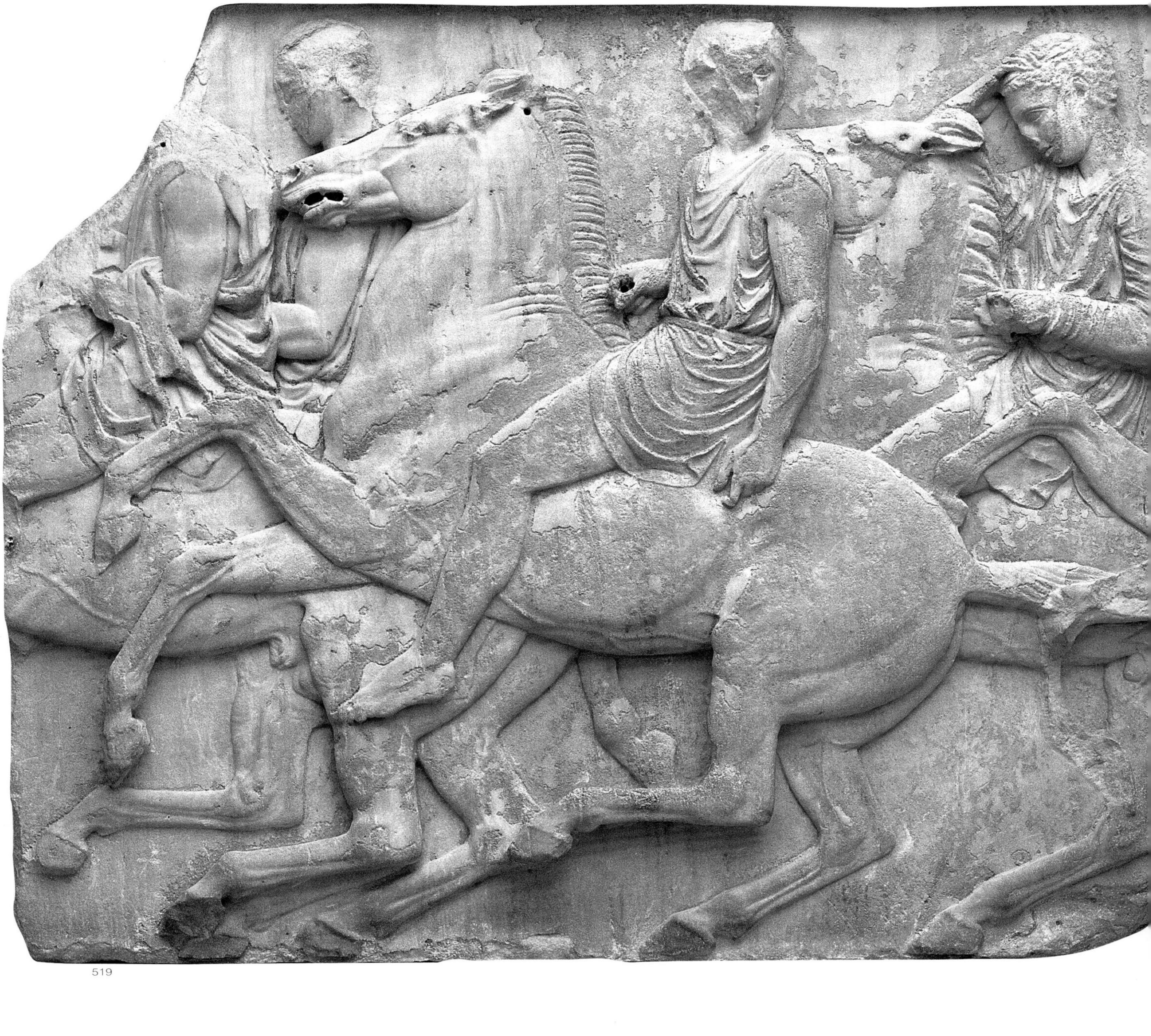

519

520

The contests

The festival included athletic, equestrian, musical and rhapsodical (recitation of Homer) contests. Much of our information on these contests is derived from ancient writers and from the thousands of Attic black- and red-figure vases showing athletic scenes. These, we can confidently assert, were inspired by the contests in the Panathenaia and by youths training in Athenian gymnasia. None of these vases was connected with the Olympic or other pan-

521

hellenic games in ancient times. They are all the work of Athenian artists and were commissioned and manufactured in Athens. This, of course, does not detract from their importance as evidence for ancient athletics in general, or for the rules and details of events instituted in imitation of the contests at Olympia. The athletic events at the Panathenaia were divided into two categories: the first consisted of the contests of the Olympic programme, in which all Greeks were allowed to compete, as in the panhellenic games. These were foot races (stadion, diaulos, dolichos and the race in full armour), heavy events (wrestling, boxing and pankration) and the pentathlon. As at Nemea, the competitors were divided into three age groups: boys, "beardless youths" and men.

The second category included contests associated with Athenian traditions, which might more properly be called religious, military or popular events. Only Athenians were allowed to take part in these, and they normally competed by tribe. The most characteristic religious-athletic event was the torch race (a relay

521-524. The pyrrichios, apobates race and boat race were old Athenian contests that survived in new form in the Panathenaic games.

521. Above, the base of a victorious dedication made by the choregos Atarbos, with a representation of two groups of four nude dancers in a pyrrichios contest (330-320 BC). Athens, Akropolis Museum.

522. An apobates race is depicted on part of the relief from Oropos, with the hoplite ready to leap from the moving chariot (400 BC). Athens, National Archaeological Museum.

523. Relief of a boat with a crew of eight comes from the bottom part of an honorific stele connected with the awarding of prizes to the victors in a boat race (2nd c. AD). Athens, National Archaeological Museum.

524. The relief at the bottom right is believed to depict a man dancing the pyrrichios or running in the race in armour (ca. 500 BC). Athens, National Archaeological Museum.

522

race with a burning torch for the baton), which calls to mind the starting point of the athletic festivals. This race began at the altar of Prometheus in the gymnasium of the Academy (the modern Akadimia Platonos) and, after a course of about 2.5 kilometres, ended at the Akropolis, where the winner lit the sacrificial fire on the great altar of Athena. Other events were the *pyrrichios*, a group dance in armour, and the *euandria*, a kind of beauty contest to display the physical and personality attributes of the Athenian male population. The athletic contests were originally held in the Agora, and after 330 BC in the Panathenaic stadium. Rowing events (*amilla neon*), which included exercises of speed and manoeuvrability involving boats or triremes, were held at Phaliron or Piraeus.

The equestrian events included the Olympic contests, with a variety of horse and chariot races in different categories and, additionally, some local events of a military character. These were the *apobates* contest, or *apobates* race,

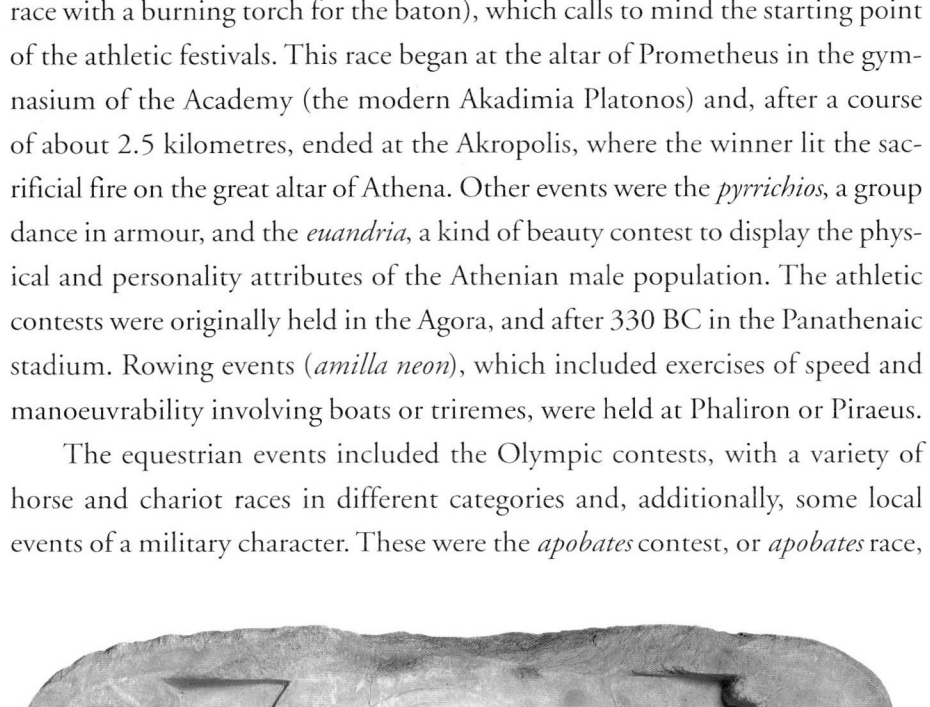

523

524

525. Anthipassia—*mock cavalry battles—was another purely Athenian event. On this relief, five youthful horsemen from the tribe Leontis gallop rhythmically, led by the bearded leader of the tribe (left) (early 4th c. BC). Athens, Ancient Agora Museum.*

526. A victor in a torch race stands, nude, next to an altar holding a lighted torch in his left hand. On his head he wears a diadem with two lance-shaped decorations. He is approached from the right by a Victory who offers him a long ribbon. At the sides, two officials wearing wreaths (the one on the left beardless and the one on the right bearded) look on. Bell krater (410-400 BC). Florence, Museo Nazionale, Soprintendenza Archeologica per la Toscana.

in which a hoplite had to mount and then dismount from a moving chariot driven by a charioteer; *anthippasia*, a mock cavalry battle in which two teams of horsemen repeatedly charged each other; and the *aphippou akontismos*, javelin from horseback, in which the rider had to throw a javelin at a shield placed on a post, while riding his horse. Inscriptions dating from the 2nd c. BC and associated with a renewal of the festival state that at that time the Panathenaia included 18 equestrian events. Some of these were held in the Agora, on the Panathenaic way, on the section that led up the north slope of the Akropolis to the Eleusinion. The mock cavalry battle probably took place on the 'dromos' of the gymnasium in the Lyceum. The equestrian events of the Olympic programme were held in the hippodrome, which, according to the ancient literary sources, was in the deme of Echelidai near modern Phaliro, where there was a large flat area. No remains of this monument have survived.

The music contests included competitions for the kithara and the aulos, as well as singing accompanied by these two instruments (*kitharodia* and *aulodia*). The poetry-recitation contests (*rhapsodia*) involved the reciting of the Homeric poems by professional rhapsodes. They were held only at this festival and were one of its main events from the 6th century on. This was probably connected with the fact that the Homeric poems were first written down in Athens at this period, by the poet Onomakritos, on the initiative of the Peisistratid tyrants. Hitherto, the epics had been transmitted only orally.

The recording of the Homeric poems in Athens and the rhapsodia contests contributed to the wide dissemination of the epics and to Athenian familiarity with them. This had two further consequences. First, the epic poems became an important source of inspiration and material for black-figure vase-painting in the 6th century, when thousands of scenes from Homer were depicted on these vases. Second, since children learned reading and writing from the texts of Homer, the use of the Ionian dialect of the Asia Minor coast became

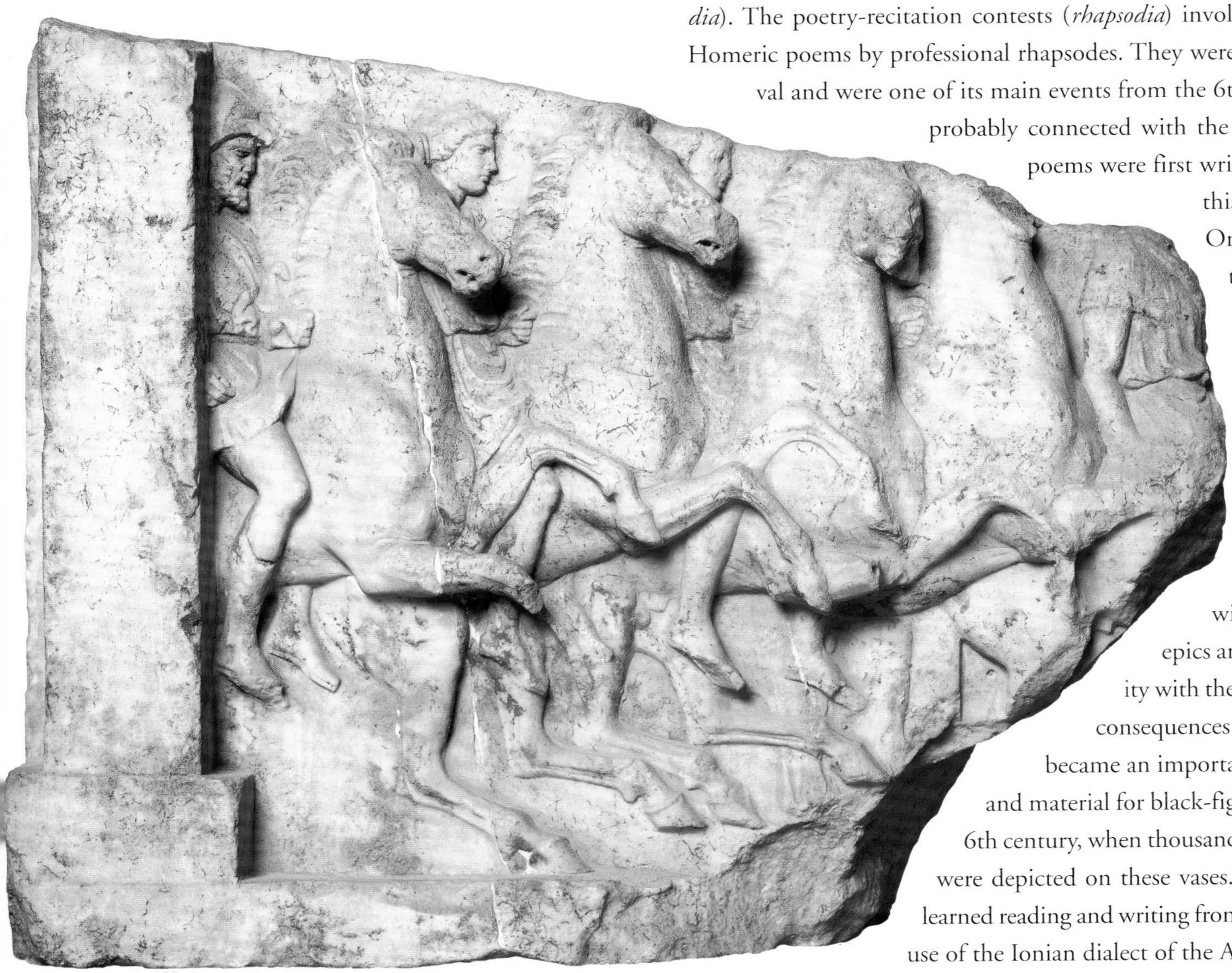

525

526

widespread in Athens, and at the end of the 5th century, the Athenian state abandoned the Attic alphabet and adopted the Ionian.

The rhapsodia contests, like the music competitions, were originally held in the open air, probably in the building known as the orchestra in the Athenian Agora. In the middle of the 5th century, however, they were transferred to the Odeion built for the purpose by Perikles on the south slope of the Akropolis. In 162 BC, dramatic contests were also introduced into the Panathenaia, on the model of the Great Dionysia, and were naturally held in the theatre of Dionysos.

527

528

527. Depiction of a wrestling match at the Panathenaic games, at the stage at which the opponents fell to the ground, which was called alindesis *or* kylisis *by the ancient Greeks. The artist has rendered it as though seen from on high, under the gaze of another wrestler and two Victories, one standing and one hovering. Panathenaic amphora produced in the archonship of Kallimedes (360/359 BC). Athens, National Archaeological Museum.*

528. A fight in armour watched by two judges. This event was a relic of military exercises. Black-figure amphora dating from the middle of the 6th c. BC. Ghent University, Archaeological Collection.

529. The music contests were held on the first day of the Panathenaic festival. Here the young kitharode stands on a podium and plays to a splendidly dressed audience. Attic red-figure amphora by the Andokides Painter (530 BC). Paris, Louvre Museum.

530. Clay aryballos (oil container) in the shape of a kneeling young victor. In his raised hands he held the victory ribbon, which he was tying around his head. The work was presumably a fine gift for a young athlete, who trained in the gymnasium and used this vase to carry his oil (540-530 BC). Athens, Ancient Agora Museum.

529

THE PROGRAMME

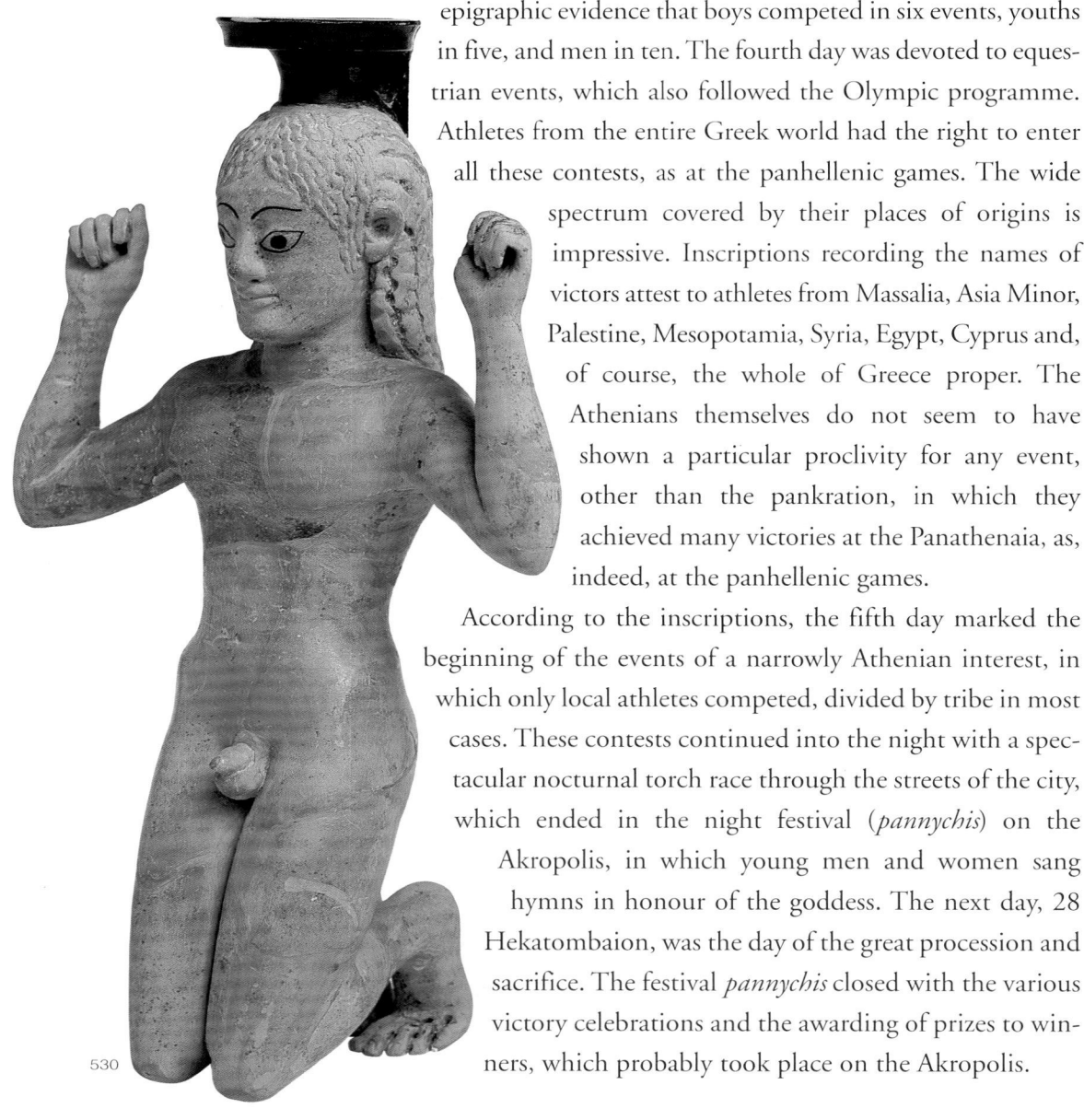

The programme of the festival, which at its height might last for up to eight days, may be reconstructed on the basis of the sequence of the contests recorded in an inscription of the early 4th c. BC. The festival began with the music contests, of which there were two categories, one for men and one for boys, and also the rhapsodia contests. The second day was given over to the athletic events for boys and youths, and the third to the corresponding contests for men. If we regard the pentathlon as a single event, is may be deduced from the epigraphic evidence that boys competed in six events, youths in five, and men in ten. The fourth day was devoted to equestrian events, which also followed the Olympic programme. Athletes from the entire Greek world had the right to enter all these contests, as at the panhellenic games. The wide spectrum covered by their places of origins is impressive. Inscriptions recording the names of victors attest to athletes from Massalia, Asia Minor, Palestine, Mesopotamia, Syria, Egypt, Cyprus and, of course, the whole of Greece proper. The Athenians themselves do not seem to have shown a particular proclivity for any event, other than the pankration, in which they achieved many victories at the Panathenaia, as, indeed, at the panhellenic games.

According to the inscriptions, the fifth day marked the beginning of the events of a narrowly Athenian interest, in which only local athletes competed, divided by tribe in most cases. These contests continued into the night with a spectacular nocturnal torch race through the streets of the city, which ended in the night festival (*pannychis*) on the Akropolis, in which young men and women sang hymns in honour of the goddess. The next day, 28 Hekatombaion, was the day of the great procession and sacrifice. The festival *pannychis* closed with the various victory celebrations and the awarding of prizes to winners, which probably took place on the Akropolis.

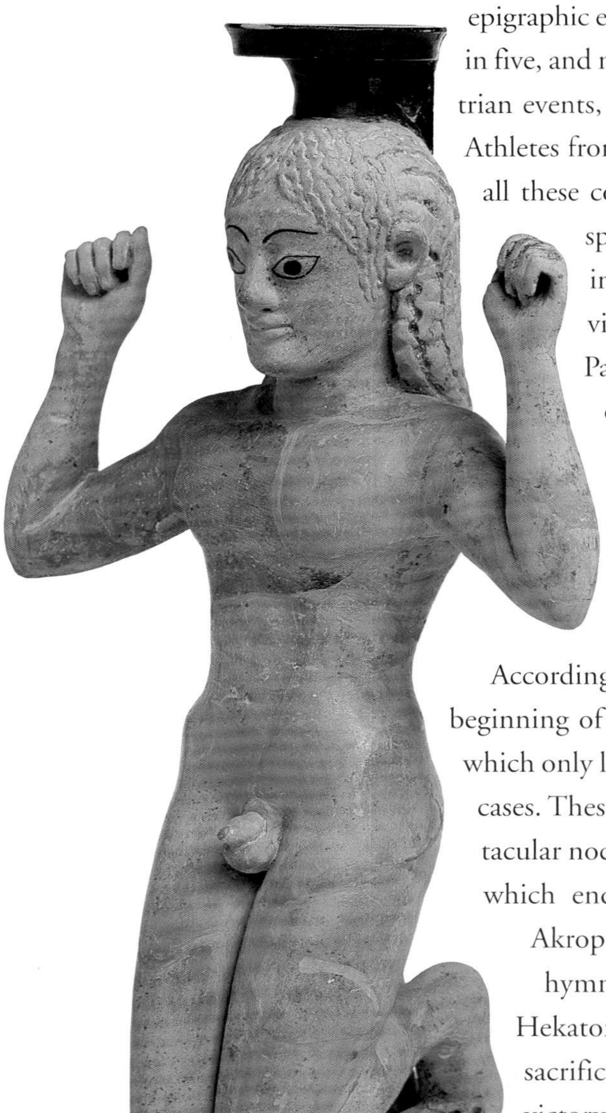

530

531. All three prizes won by the victors in the Panathenaic games depicted on the top part of an honorific stele: a wreath, a Panathenaic amphora, and a palm branch (AD 126/127). Athens, Epigraphic Museum.

532-533. The prizes awarded at all the games were usually wreaths. At some they were the only prize, at others they were symbolic and were accompanied by more valuable prizes. Here are two depictions of wreaths, one of gold, dating from the Hellenistic period and found in a tomb at Amphipolis (Kavala Museum), and a rendering of it in a Classical relief from Brauron (Brauron Museum).

534. The statue of the Diadoumenos from Delos depicts a victor tying a ribbon around his head. Marble copy made in 100 BC of a bronze original statue by Polykleitos dating from the third quarter of the 5th c. BC. Athens, National Archaeological Museum.

531

THE PRIZES

The prizes awarded at the Panathenaia were not simply wreaths, but also items with considerable financial value, which was one way to tempt fine, famous athletes to the festival, who would lend it greater prestige and reputation. 'For the prizes awarded were of silver and gold for those who were victorious in music, shields for those who won the *euandria*, and oil for the athletic and equestrian contests,' writes Aristotle. In addition to the material prizes, of course, the athletes were also crowned with an olive wreath, selected because of the importance of this tree to the economy of Attica, its relation to Athena, and the role played by oil in the games. Some connection with Olympia, where the wreath was also taken from an olive tree, cannot be ruled out. In Olympia, however, the olive wreath was from a wild olive, whereas in Athens from a cultivated fruit-bearing tree.

The inscription from the early 4th c. BC, besides containing the programme of the games, also records the prizes awarded not only to the winners but also to those who came in second in each event. In the kitharodia contest, indeed, the first five received a prize. The awarding of prizes to competitors other than the winner is an innovation of the Panathenaic games and is unknown elsewhere; its objective was to stimulate as much interest in them as possible and to sharpen the competitive spirit of the participants.

The first prizes recorded are those for the music competitions, which were gold and silver wreaths. The winner of the kitharodia received a gold wreath worth 1000 drachmas, and 500 silver drachmas in cash. The competitor who came in second was awarded 1200 drachmas, the third 600, the fourth 400 and the fifth 300. The victor in the aulodia was awarded a wreath worth 300 drachmas and the second 100 drachmas. These great differences in the value of the prizes are related to the popularity of the event.

The next prizes awarded were for the athletic events. These were 'amphoras of oil' – that is, Panathenaic amphoras.The amphoras were filled with oil and on the reverse side depicted the contest in which the athlete had competed. On the front they always depicted Athena Promachos between two colonnettes, on top of which were cockerels and, after the 4th c., well-known statues of the era. The inscription ΤΩΝ ΑΘΗΝΗΘΕΝ ΑΘΛΩΝ ('From the Games at Athens') alongside one colonnette denoted the provenance and content while advertising the games, whose political role was always significant. The prizes ranged from 30 amphoras for the winner in the boys' pentathlon to 70 such vases for the victors in the men's events; in every case, the competitor finishing second received

532

533

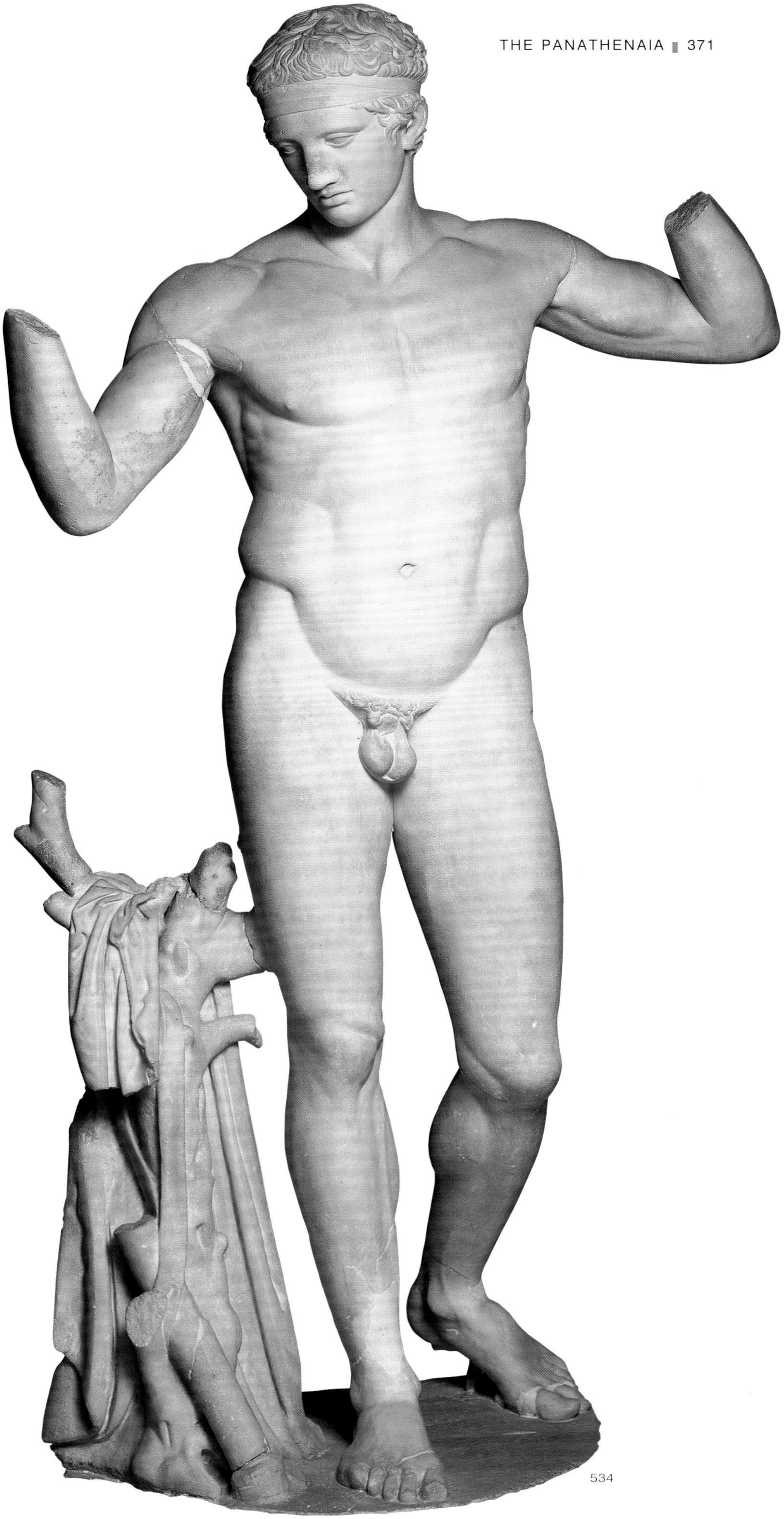

534

535. Athena Promachos is depicted on the earliest known prize from the Panathenaic games, an amphora dating from 566-560 BC. London, British Museum.

536. Scene of a young winner receiving his prize. The official has given the winner branches, which he holds in his hands, and now binds a ribbon about his head. Attic red-figure kylix dating from 490-480 BC. New York, The Metropolitan Museum of Art.

537-538. Two sides of a Panathenaic amphora, dated to 340/339 BC by the inscription referring to the archon Theophrastos. It was awarded as a prize to the winner of the apobates race at the Panathenaic games held in 338-337 BC. Los Angeles, J. Paul Getty Museum.

535

536

one-fifth of the quantity awarded as first prize. In the equestrian events, which are mentioned next in the inscription, the largest prize was 140 Panathenaic amphoras, which were awarded to the winner of the chariot race – an indication that this was the most spectacular and popular event of all. Given that in the 4th century, regular Panathenaic amphoras were about 0.60-0.70 m. high, with a greatest diameter of 0.35-0.45 m., it may be concluded that each vase held about 35-40 kilos of oil. The winner of the men's stadion, who received 70 amphoras, would thus have won about 2.5 tons, while the victor in the chariot race, with his 140 amphoras, would have won about 5 tons of oil.

Such enormous quantities of oil could naturally not be consumed by the victors themselves, and they were apparently allowed to sell it, particularly on the export market, where there was a huge demand for Panathenaic oil for athletic uses (oiling the body, etc.). It seems reasonable to suppose that the sale of the prize would have brought great financial profits to the victors. For example, if the winner of the chariot race sold all the oil he had won, he would receive an amount of money equal to at least 6 years of daily wages. With this, he could buy a large

537

538

house in the city or a flock of sheep or 15 slaves. Of course, to be able to afford a fast chariot team, he probably owned all of these already.

It should be noted, however, that the victors in the panhellenic games, including those at Olympia, received even greater material gains, even if their prize was only a simple wreath. For an Olympic victory was followed by so many honours and donations from the victor's native city that his life might be radically changed. Many cities, for example, offered large lump-sum pay-

539

539. The winner of a music contest at the Panathenaic games, wearing a crown, ascends the pedestal, surrounded by a seated judge and two standing spectators. Attic black-figure amphora dating from the last quarter of the 6th c. BC. London, British Museum.

540. The Autostephanoumenos is a relief dedicated by a victor in the sanctuary of Athena at Sounion. It depicts a youth placing a metal (gold?) wreath, as is clear from the holes in which it was fixed, on his own head (about 460 BC). Athens, National Archaeological Museum.

ments, dining rights for life in the prytaneion, exemption from taxes, honorary seats at all public events, and many other privileges. These benefits, along with the profit that victors made from their participation in games throughout the Mediterranean at which the prizes awarded could be converted into money, led to a rapid increase of both the glory and the personal fortune of the great athletes, particularly in later periods. Pindar was right, then, when he wrote in his first Olympian ode: 'He who is victorious at Olympia enjoys, for the rest of his life, the sweetest ease.'

After the equestrian events, the inscription recording the prizes awarded at the Panathenaia

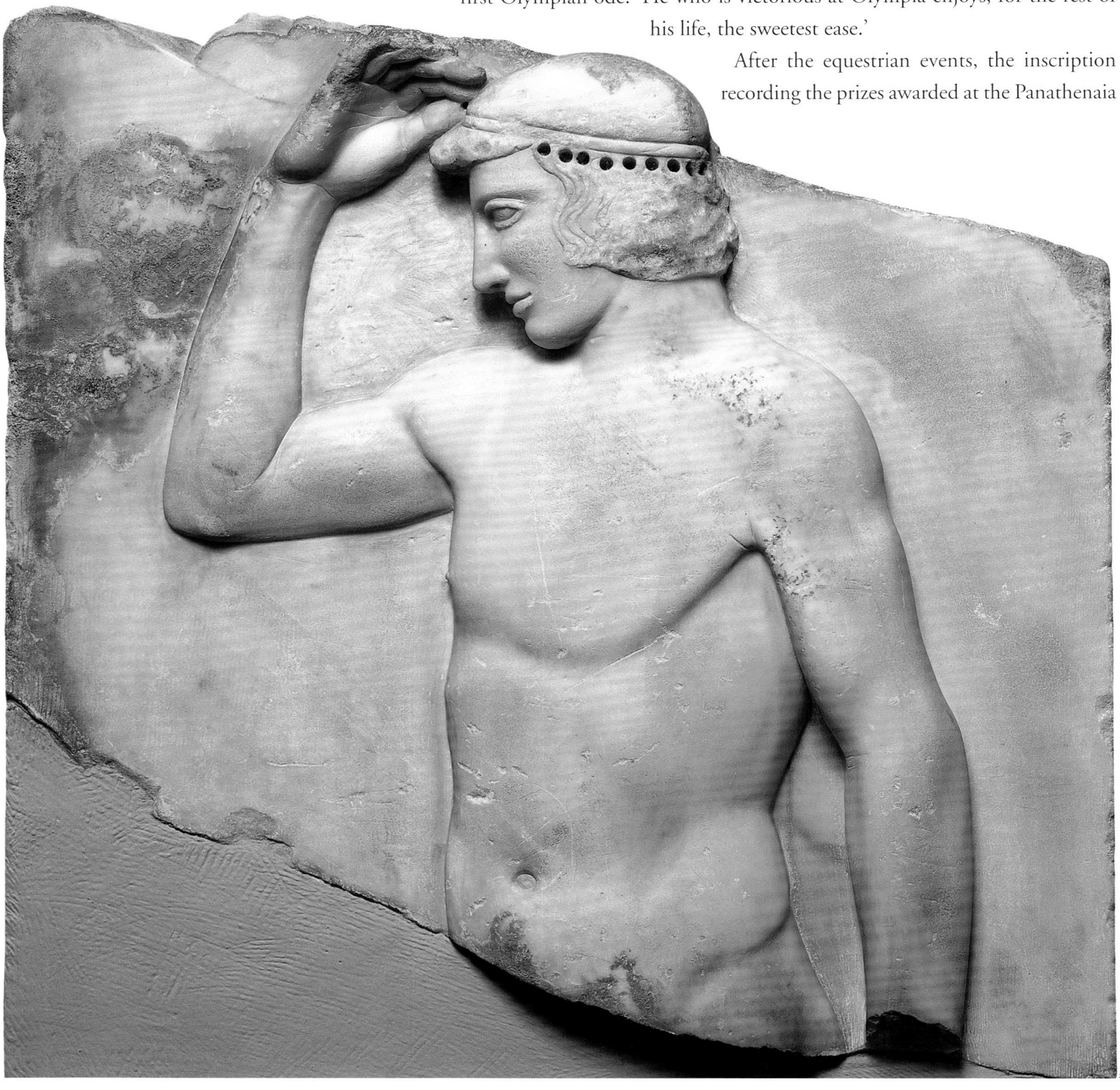

540

541. The awarding of prizes and depictions of victors were amongst the most popular scenes in ancient Greek art. Below, Victory prepares to tie a ribbon on the winner of the wrestling event taking place in front of her. Panathenaic amphora produced in the archonship of Charikleides (363/362 BC). Athens, National Archaeological Museum.

542. Bronze statue of an autostephanoumenos dating from the late 4th c. BC. Los Angeles, J. Paul Getty Museum.

541

542

lists those for the Athenian competitions, which were of far less value. It is indicative that the first prize in the javelin from horseback was 5 Panathenaic amphoras. In the team events, in which the participants competed by tribe, the prize for the winning team was 100 drachmas and an ox, which the victors presumably slaughtered and ate at the victory banquet. In the rowing contests, the victorious team received 300 drachmas, 3 oxen and 200 free dinners for its members. It is evident from the quantity and nature of the prizes in this category that the objective was to intensify the rivalry between tribes and give prominence to the sense of patriotism and devotion of their members to the old, splendid events of the Athenian tradition.

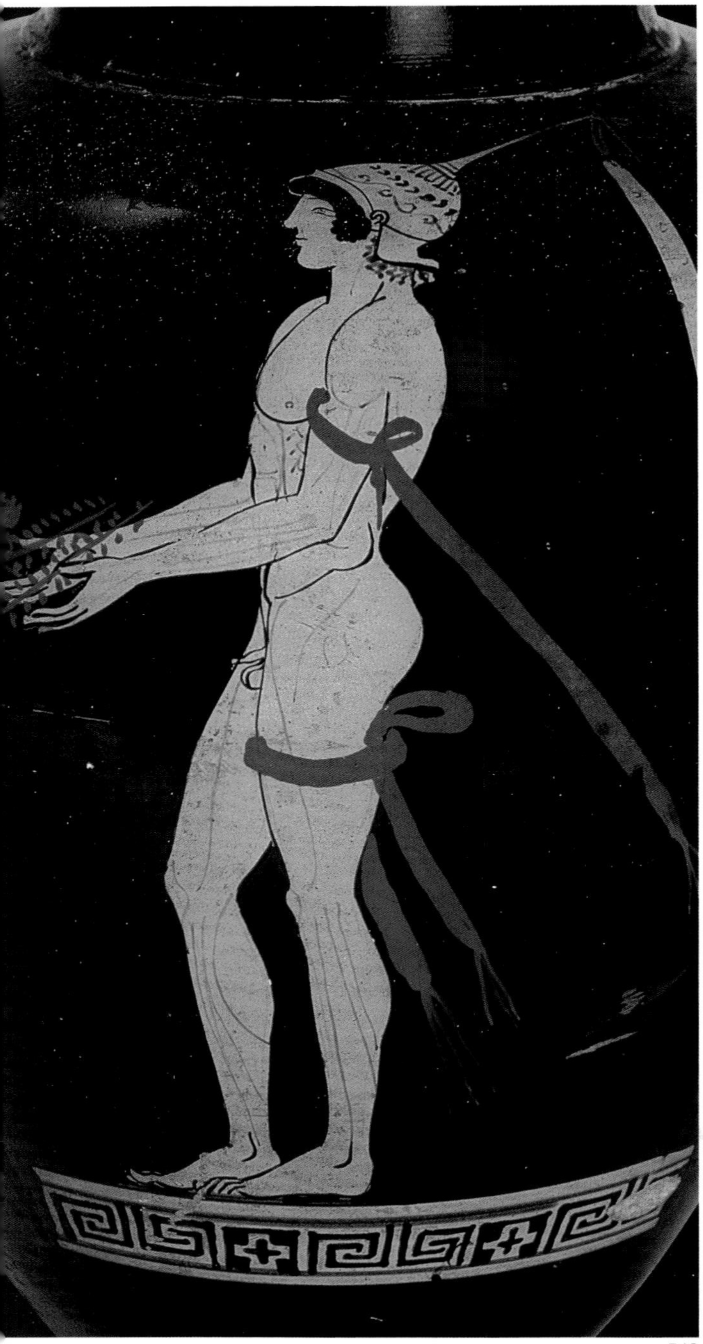

543

543. Below, a young victor holding branches in his hands, with ribbons tied to his body. He wears an unusual helmet on his head (490 BC). St. Petersburg, Hermitage Museum.

544

544. Attic red-figure kylix with a depiction of an official or a relative tying victory ribbons to the body of the young winner (490-480 BC). Munich, Staatliche Antikensammlungen.

Venues for the preparation and conduct of the games

545

Peisistratos's decision in the 6th century to institute the Great Panathenaia was accompanied by other measures designed to strengthen and develop athletics in Athens. The most important of these was the foundation of three gymnasia, in which the youth of Athens could exercise in an organised manner under the supervision of special officials. These were the first public gymnasia in the history of athletics; the ancient Greek word *gymnasion* derives from the adjective *gymnos* ('nude'), and has reference to the ancient practice of training completely naked. These gymnasia were outside, but not far from, the city walls, invariably near rivers and shady groves, which were often also cult sites. Their names are derived from the areas in which they were built: the Academy, Lyceum, and Kynosarges.

The earliest facilities in the gymnasia were very simple and made of perishable materials (wood, canvas, etc.), and the areas originally had a purely athletic character. Later, however, given the presence in them of a young audience, they began to be frequented by teachers of theoretical lessons, such as philosophy, and, in the Hellenistic and especially the Roman periods, these lessons

546

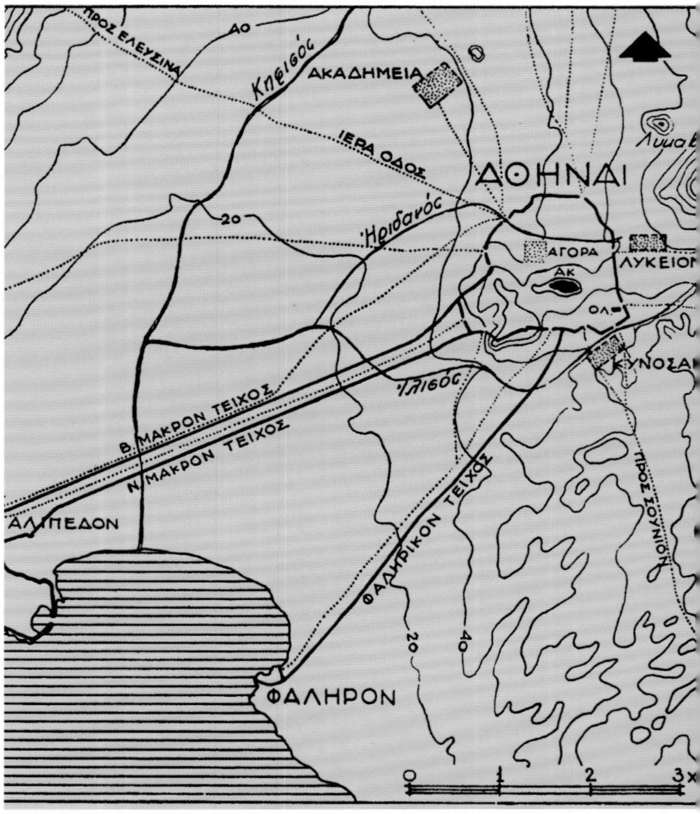

547

548

545. The responsibility for training and exercising the young in the gymnasia and palaestrae of Athens was borne by the kosmetai. *Seen here is a portrait of a kosmetes made about AD 225. Athens, National Archaeological Museum.*

546. General view of the remains of the palaestra in the Lyceum, as excavated in recent years in a building plot on Rigillis Street, Athens. Archives of III Ephorate of Antiquities.

547. The first gymnasia in the history of athletics were founded in Athens in the 6th c. BC. They were the Academy, the Lyceum, and Kynosarges, and they were located outside the fortification walls in groves and near the Kephisos and Ilisos rivers. The map of Athens and Piraeus shows the sites of the gymnasia around the fortified area of the city. Map by J. Travlos.

548. Team games were a favourite way of practising in ancient gymnasia. Here a game similar to modern volleyball, played by two teams of three youths. The one to the left is preparing to serve into his opponents' area (late 6th c. BC). Athens, National Archaeological Museum.

became predominant and displaced athletic activity completely. From this form of the gymnasium derives the use of their names in modern times to mean institutions of modern education. Gymnasium, lyceum, and academy are words that have found their way into many of the languages of the world.

The Academy lay in the northwest of the city, near the olive grove that, according to Athenian tradition, was descended from the sacred olives of Athens, the Moriai. The area is today known as Akadimia Platonos (Plato's Academy), since Plato first taught here in 387 BC, when he founded the school he called the Academy. Excavation has shown that the entire area covered about 450 by 300 m. next to what was then the bed of the river Kephisos. Various buildings associated with athletics and educational activities have come to light on this site. A large building with a rectangular peristyle courtyard and rooms on the north side has been identified as the palaestra. Square bases placed at regular intervals in the stoas have been interpreted as supports for the students' tables, and the use of the area for teaching purposes during later periods is suggested by the discovery of tablets used for written exercises. Another large building with a square ground plan, measuring 40 by 40 m., known as the Square Peristyle, certainly belongs to the Academy complex, though its specific function has not yet been established.

The Lyceum, a large grove containing a sanctuary in honour of Apollo Lykeios, lay to the east of the city, between what is now Syntagma Square, Lykavittos, the Ilisos and the Temple of Olympian Zeus, in the area occupied by the National Gardens. The gymnasium here had existed from as early as the 6th century and was a favourite teaching place of Socrates in the 5th century. Building remains of the palaestra, built in the 4th century by the orator Lykourgos, have been located by excavations conducted in recent years in a large building plot in Rigillis Street, behind the Armed Forces Officers' Club. About 335 BC, Aristotle established his school in the Lyceum and called it the Peripatetic School. His successor Theophrastos of Ephesos continued to teach there, as did other philosophers down to the time of Justinian, who issued an edict closing all the philosophical schools.

Kynosarges was on the left bank of the Ilisos, somewhere between the modern First Cemetery and the old FIX factory. Earlier and more recent excavations have uncovered the foundations of large structures, though these cannot be assigned with any certainty to specific buildings. In the 4th century the philosopher Antisthenes taught in this gymnasium, founding the Cynic school, so called after the place name. The most famous representative of the school was Diogenes (d. ca. 320 BC). According to one highly probably theory, the gymnasium of Hadrian mentioned by Pausanias is in fact a reference to the renovation by the emperor of the facilities at Kynosarges.

In addition to the three old gymnasia, which lay outside the city walls, the city founded other ones inside them in the Classical and Hellenistic periods. One of these, known as the Pompeion, was built around 400 BC between the two most important gates of the city, the Dipylon and the Sacred Gate. The building was used to store objects used in the Panathenaic procession, and probably also the Panathenaic amphoras, and there is some evidence to suggest that, at the same time, it served as a gymnasium, until it was destroyed by Sulla in 86 BC. The interior peristyle courtyard of this building recalls the form of later palaestrae, and the statue of Socrates and mural depictions of the three great tragic poets and Menander inside it are completely in keeping with its use as a gymnasium.

In the 3rd c. BC, two more gymnasia were founded near the centre of the city. One of these was the gymnasium of Ptolemy, which was probably funded by a donation from Ptolemy II Philadelphos, the king of Egypt. The other was the Diogeneion gymnasium, named after the leader of the Macedonian mercenary garrison that was stationed in Athens during the second half of the 3rd c. BC. The precise location of these gymnasia was a matter of dispute between scholars as early as the 19th century, when a large number of inscribed honorific stelai referring to them were found in the district of Plaka, near the stoa of Attalos. However, these had been removed from their original positions

549

549. The equipment taken into the gymnasia by youths comprised an aryballos (a small oil container), a sponge, and a strigil, to clean their bodies. In his grave stele carved in the shape of a small temple, Stephanos holds these objects in his hands as he goes to the gymnasium accompanied by his dog (early 4th c. BC). Athens, National Archaeological Museum.

550. A young athlete practises with a ball, watched by his young slave holding an aryballos and a strigil. Attic grave relief with a depiction of a relief loutrophoros (first half of the 4th c. BC). Athens, National Archaeological Museum.

551-552. Discus throwers and a jumper excercise under the supervision of a trainer to the accompaniment of the music of a flute. Two sides of a black-figure Panathenaic-type amphora (ca. 510 BC). Würzburg, Martin von Wagner Museum.

551

550

552

and reused as building material in the Late Roman fortification wall erected by the Athenians after the devastation of the city by the Herulians in AD 267, and it is therefore difficult to determine the site of these buildings with any certainty. A recent theory suggests that the two names refer not to two different gymnasia, but to the same complex, located in Plaka, to the east of the Roman forum, next to Kyrrestou Street.

553

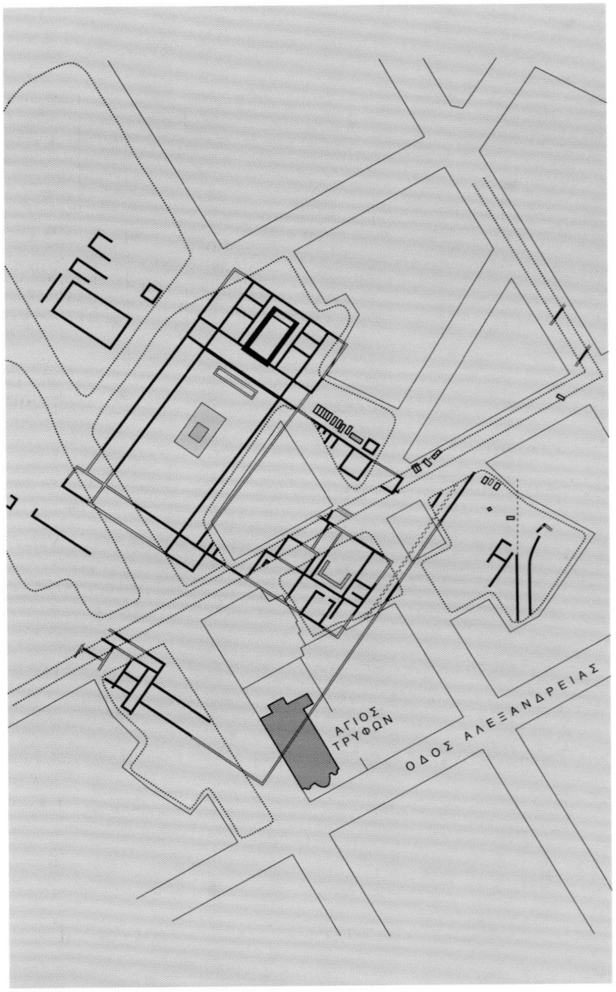

554

555

556

THE PANATHENAIC STADIUM

553. View of the court and rooms of the palaestra of the Academy. Archives of III Ephorate of Antiquities.

554. Plan of the buildings of the palaestra of the Academy in the area known today as Plato's Academy. Plan by J. Travlos.

555-556. The two kosmetai depicted here are Onasos of Pallene and Sosistratos of Marathon, who served in the gymnasia of Athens in the first half of the 2nd c. AD. Athens, National Archaeological Museum.

557. Marble throne known as the Elgin throne. The relief depictions on the side (table with wreaths and a Panathenaic amphora, olive tree) connect this sculpture with the Panathenaic games. According to one view, it was the throne used by officials in the Panathenaic stadium. Roman period. London, British Museum.

558. Panoramic view of the Panathenaic stadium from the east. The ancient monument was almost the same as the modern in terms of the cavea, but the track differed considerably: the lanes for the runners did not follow the perimeter but were parallel with each other along the main axis.

The venue for the athletic contests in the Panathenaic games was the Panathenaic stadium. This was built by the great Athenian orator and politician Lykourgos about 330 BC, in a natural depression in the embrace of the Ardittos hill, near the river Ilisos. In AD 140-144, the stadium was renovated at the expense of the fabulously rich Athenian Sophist Herodes Atticus, who covered the entire cavea with seats made of Pentelic marble. A few years later it impressed the traveller Pausanias, who described it as a marvel of craftsmanship. The stadium was renovated on the occasion of the games funded and organised by Herodes for the Panathenaia of AD 142/143. The Panathenaic ship used in the procession at this festival was placed on a long base on top of the hill to the north of the stadium. In return for this and his many other services to the city, the Athenians accorded Herodes the honour of being buried in the Panathenaic stadium. The ancient evidence for this is unclear, however, and it has not proved possible to find his tomb, which will either have been in the track of the stadium or, more probably, on the hill overlooking the curve, where the remains of sarcophagi have been discovered. In this case, we should expect to find a funerary monument like the one on Philopappos Hill. The stadium was excavated in 1870 by the German architect E. Ziller, who found only the earthen form of such a monument. All the marble from it had been converted into lime during the Ottoman period and above all during the early years after the liberation of Greece, to meet the building needs of the new capital. The Panathenaic stadium reacquired its marble form when it was reequipped with marble for the needs of the first modern Olympic games in 1896 and the so-called Inter-Olympics of 1906. The expenses for this were met by the national benefactor E. Averoff.

557

The track was 204.07 m. long and 33.06 m. wide. The cavea had a curve, and if this was its original 4th-century form, the Panathenaic stadium must have been the first stadium with a curve in the history of architecture. It seems highly likely that the idea of designing the narrow side of the stadium with a curve was inspired by the construction of the cavea of the Theatre of Dionysos a few years earlier. This new design not only created more space in this stadium, so that it held about 50,000 spectators, but also influenced the architectural evolution of the building down to modern times.

559. View of part of the orchestra and cavea of the Theatre of Dionysos. It was constructed for the drama contests at the Great Dionysia, but after 162 BC was also used for those held as part of the Panathenaic festival.

560. Many of the buildings that served the celebrations of the Panathenaic festival were built on the south slope of the Akropolis. Right, a panoramic view of the Theatre of Dionysos, with the Odeion of Perikles next to it. To its left are the stoa of Eumenes and the Odeion of Herodes Atticus.

ODEIA AND THEATRES

559

To house the music contests in the Panathenaic games, the first concert hall in the history of civilisation was erected. This was the Odeion of Perikles, built by the great politician just after the middle of the 5th century at the same time as the introduction, or more probably the revival, of music competitions in the Panathenaia. It is a large, almost square, building covering an area of 3,500 square meters on the south slope of the Akropolis, next to the Theatre of Dionysos. Its conical roof was supported on a forest of 81 wooden columns, which, according to the ancient literary sources, were made from the remains of the Persian fleet after the Battle of Salamis (480 BC). All four sides of the hall were occupied by seats for the audience, and there was a raised platform in the middle on which the musicians and singers performed. The Periklean building was destroyed in 86 BC during the siege of Athens by the Roman general Sulla and reconstructed immediately afterwards, with marble columns, by the king of Cappadocia, Ariobarzanes II. This Odeion was finally destroyed in AD 267 by the Herulians.

The renovation of the Theatre of Dionysos, which was now made of stone and acquired a tall proscenium, was probably associated with the introduction of drama competitions into the Panathenaia, probably in 162 BC. On this same occasion, a stoa was built next to the theatre at the expense of the king of Pergamon, Eumenes II, after whom it was named. It served as a kind of foyer to the theatre and a place in which the spectators could take shelter in the event of rain.

The donations made to the city of Athens by the rulers of the Hellenistic kingdoms were associated with their participation in the equestrian games of the Panathenaia, mainly by sending chariots. These gestures were made because the rulers in question had studied in Athens as young men and wished to thank the city that had endowed them with Greek education and culture. At the same time, the donations formed part of their propaganda programme, through which they sought to demonstrate that the Hellenistic kingdoms of the East were the successors of the Classical grandeur of Athens, the city that had disseminated the light of civilisation in earlier times.

560

THE ODEION OF HERODES ATTICUS

561. Before the construction of the Odeion of Perikles in the Classical period, the music contests in the Panthenaic festival were held in the open air, probably in the ancient Agora. Below, a young kitharode plays and sings before a judge, and is ready to receive the ribbons and prize vases held out by two hovering Victories. Attic red-figure pelike dating from the last quarter of the 5th c. BC. Athens, National Archaeological Museum.

562. Aerial photograph of the Odeion of Herodes Atticus on the southwest slope of the Akropolis. It was constructed by Herodes to house the music contests at the Panathenaic festival, and to adorn Athens with a fine monument of Roman architecture.

The latest building associated with the Panathenaia is the Odeion offered to Athena by Herodes Atticus, possibly the only ordinary mortal who, through the power of his money and his activities, managed to approach the status of an emperor.

Although the Odeion built by Perikles still served its original purpose in the middle of the 2nd c. AD, it appears not to have been in good condition. Herodes therefore decided to erect a new Odeion of Roman type on the south slope of the Akropolis, in which to hold music contests.

The building was dedicated to his deceased wife Regilla, who died in AD 160, the time at which the work of construction began. Pausanias saw the completed Odeion in AD 174, when he visited Athens. The multistorey facade, 28 m. high, would have been very impressive, as was the lavishly decorated stage building. The most striking architectural achievement, however, was the semicircular roof, 38 m. in diameter, which had no internal supports. Herodes' Odeion held 5,000 to 6,000 spectators and was used for over a hundred years, before being burned and destroyed by the Herulians, a barabarian tribe that invaded Athens in AD 267.

561

5

The end of the Panathenaia

The latest research suggests that the Panathenaia continued to be held until about AD 410 – longer even than the Olympic festival itself. The reason for this was that Athens and its philosophical schools and games were one of the last dynamic defensive outposts of the pagans against the new religion. This does not mean, of course, that the festival retained anything of its brilliant past at this period. We should imagine a small group of fanatical old men, the last believers in Athena, laboriously ascending the Panathenaic Way to offer an old piece of cloth as the new peplos to the goddess's statue, which may still have stood in the Erechtheion, a few years before this temple was converted into a Christian church. The formal end of the festival was possibly dictated by the

563. General view of the temple of Hephaistos (Theseion), which was converted into a Christian church in the 5th c. AD.

564. The conversion of ancient temples into Christian churches and the use of ancient statues in later buildings are two phenomena contemporary with the cessation of the games. Plan of the Erechtheion by J. Travlos. When the temple was converted into a church, the floor was dug up, thus marring its original form.

565. Statues from the facade of the Odeion of Agrippa, incorporated into the large Early Christian building in the ancient Agora known as the Giants' Palace.

563

564

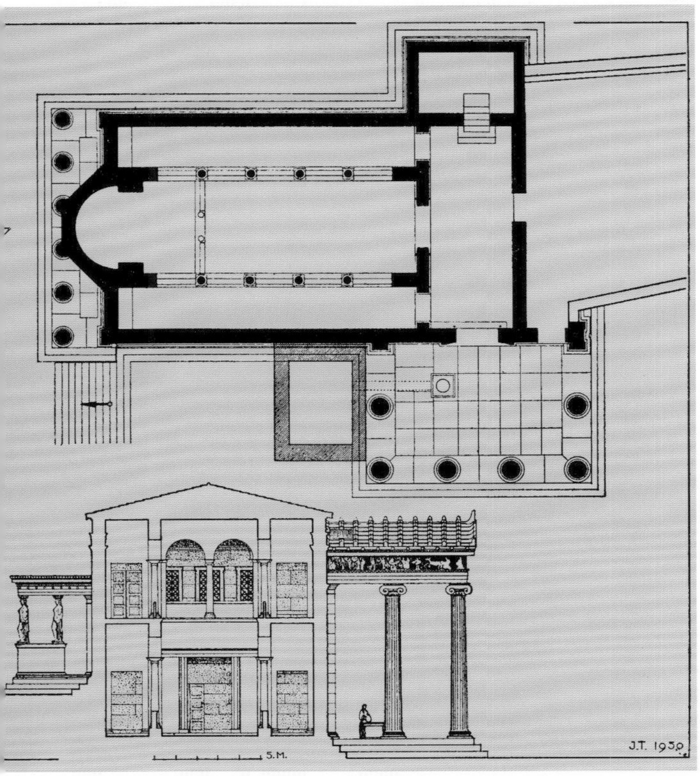

edicts of Theodosius II of 426 and 435, which demolished another bastion of the ancient world, the cult at Eleusis.

Within a century, in 529 BC, the edict of Justinian banning any activity connected with ancient religion led to the final closure of the illustrious philosophical schools of Athens, at which many of the great Church Fathers had studied, including Basil the Great (d. 379)and Gregory of Nazianzus (d. ca. 389).

As early as the second half of the 5th and the first half of the 6th c. AD, many of the ancient pagan temples, such as the Parthenon, Erechtheion, and the temple of Hephaistos (Theseion), were converted into Christian churches to serve the worship of the new religion.

It is certainly no coincidence that the final struggle between two religions and two worlds was played out in Athens. The result was, of course, predetermined: the old, ancient world, in which the supply of ideas had now dried up, was inevitably vanquished by the new message and the vigorous, robust world represented by Christianity.

565

Other Greek and Roman Games

Local games in Greece

567

Alongside the four great panhellenic games and the Panathenaia, a vast number of other games were held throughout the ancient Greek world. Almost all of these were *chrematitai* games – that is, games in which the prizes offered to the victors were sums of money or objects of greater or lesser value. The most common prize was a crown of precious metal, though other objects, characteristic of the locality of the games, were also awarded. At Pellene in Achaia, for example, the victors received chitons, at Tegea bronze objects, on Delos silver disks, and at the Lykaia in Arkadia and the Herakleia at Thebes bronze tripods.

566. Four bronze horses now in San Marco, Venice, where they were taken by the Crusaders after the capture of Constantinople in 1204. It was believed that they were brought to Constantinople by Constantine the Great, who seized them from a major ancient Greek sanctuary, and that they were probably connected with a four-horse chariot by Lysippos. Recent opinion, however, regards them as originals of the 3rd c. AD erected in the hippodrome at Constantinople.

567. Wreaths never ceased to be the most characteristic prize awarded at all the games in ancient Greece, even though prizes of another kind, consisting of money or valuable objects, were also awarded at most of them. Here is a gold wreath of Hellenistic date. Los Angeles, J. Paul Getty Museum.

568. Relief slab from Mantineia, Arkadia, probably the facing for a pedestal, depicting the music contest between Apollo and the Silenos Marsyas. The Skythian stands between the two contestants with his knife, ready to flay the defeated Marsyas (about 320 BC). Athens, National Archaeological Museum.

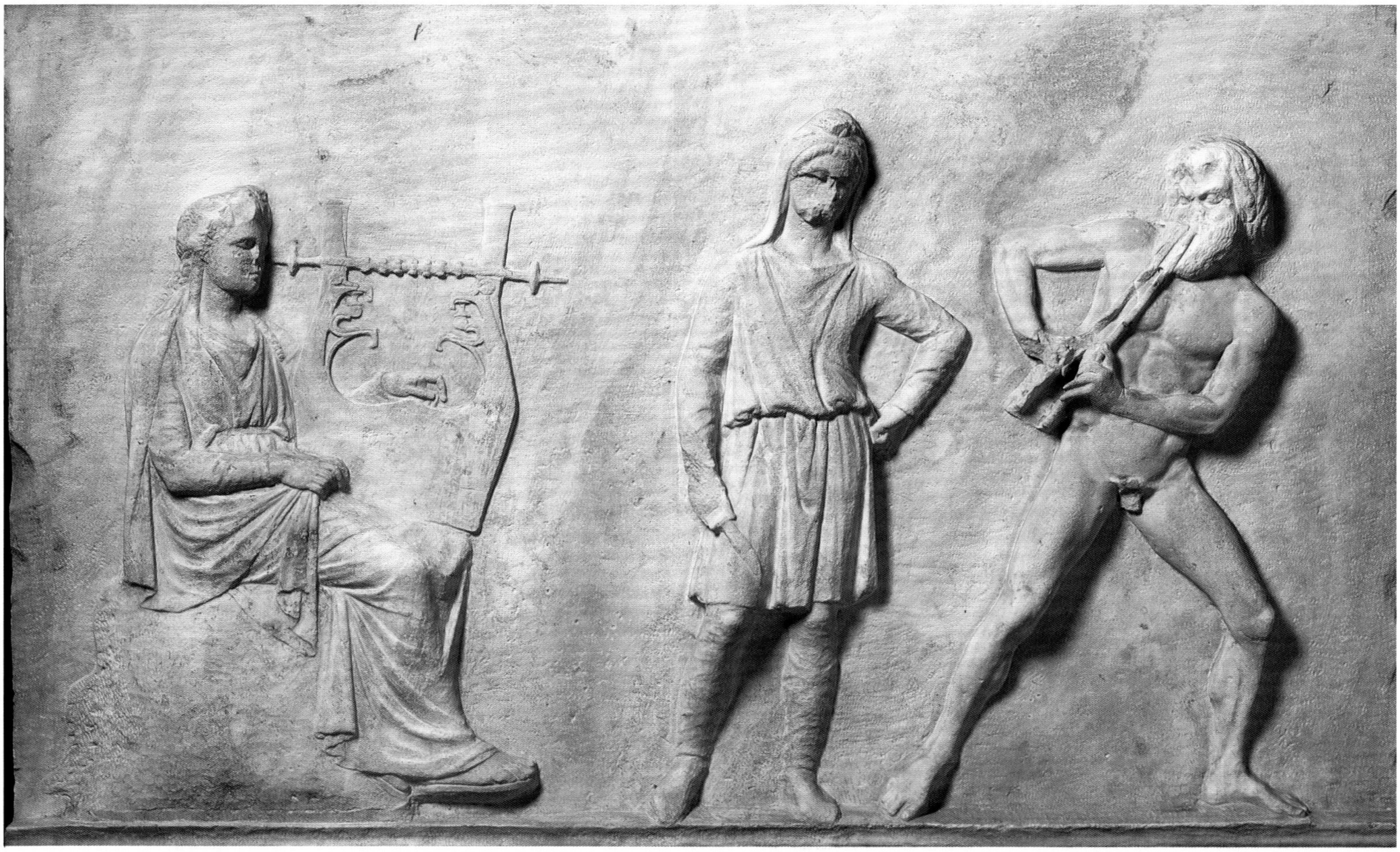

568

THE HERAIA AT ARGOS

The Heraian games at Argos were also known at some periods as the *Ἐξ Ἄργους ἀσπίς* ('shield from Argos'), since, in addition to the myrtle wreath and other prizes, the victors received bronze shields. The shield was the symbol of the festival and the games and was carried at the head of the sacred procession from the city to the sanctuary of Hera by the most worthy youth of the city, who was probably selected by winning a contest. This procedure is the source of the Argive maxim *ἄξιος εἶ τῆς ἀσπίδος* ('You are worthy of the shield'), meaning you are worthy to carry the shield.

A prize awarded at the Argive games – an inscribed bronze tripod – was found together with other valuable grave offerings in the tomb of Philip II of Macedonia. It dates from the second half of the 5th c. BC, about 100 years earlier than the tomb, and it was apparently placed inside as an heirloom owned by the Macedonian royal family. One of Philip's predecessors, possibly King Perdikkas II (454-413 BC) competed at the Heraia and won it. The object acquired added symbolic value in light of the claim that the Macedonian royal family traced its descent to the Argive Temenids.

569

GAMES IN MACEDONIA

In Macedonia itself, athletic activity is first found as early as the 6th c. The discovery of Panathenaic amphoras in many areas of Macedonia is evidence of the early interest taken by Macedonians in athletics. The earliest games, called the Olympia, were held from the 5th c. onwards at Dion, the great Macedonian religious centre at the foothills of Mount Olympos, in honour of Olympian Zeus. In addition to athletic events they included drama and music contests. From the 4th century on, games were also held at Aigai, the old capital of the Macedonian kingdom.

570

The most important architectural complex connected with athletics in Macedonia has been excavated at Amphipolis. It is a gymnasium complex with a long stoa for foot races, a palaestra with a peristyle courtyard, baths, and probably sanctuaries of Hermes and Herakles. It was probably founded in the Hellenistic period and remained in use until the middle of the 1st c. AD. The most important of the small finds is an inscription with 139 lines, dating from

569. Bronze tripod, a prize from the Heraia at Argos, found in the tomb of Philip II at Vergina (second half of the 5th c. BC).

570. Decadrachm of Syracuse (first half of the 4th c. BC). Athens, Numismatic Museum.

23/22 BC. It is the text of an ephebic law containing a vast amount of information regarding the education of ephebes, offices, the social structure of the city, and so on. A similar ephebic law has been found in the area of Veria.

571. Part of a mosaic floor from Larisa with a depiction of Victory crowning Contest. Roman period. Larisa, Archaeological Museum.

572. One of the two ancient theatres at Larisa, built on the south side of the Phrourio hill at the end of the 3rd c. BC. In the Roman period it was used as an arena for gladiatorial combats.

THE GAMES AT LARISA

The panhellenic games held at Larisa are worth noting here, since they included not only the well-established contests but also many new events. These were archery, either standing or from horseback; *aphippolampas*, a nocturnal torch race on horseback; and *aphippodromia*, in which the riders dismounted and remounted their galloping horses. The great interest shown in equestrian events at these games, especially those requiring great skill in the handling of horses, reflects the character of Thessaly as a horse-breeding region, whose riders were famous throughout the ancient world.

The most intriguing event at these games was the *taurotheria*, the object of which was to subjugate a wild bull. The first stage of the event involved the bull being pursued by a horseman for a very long time, until it tired. After this came the crucial point of the event: the horseman rode his steed alongside the bull and jumped on to its back, seizing it by the horns. When the bull

571

572

was thoroughly exhausted, the rider jumped off, seized it by the horns and, twisting its neck, stuck them in the ground. This marked the end of the contest, indicating that the athlete had defeated the bull.

The taurotheria was a very spectacular and popular contest and, despite its local character, endured for a long time. The earliest evidence for it are depictions on the coins of Larisa dating from the second half of the 5th c., while the latest is provided by the very lively descriptions by the poet Heliodoros in his poem *Aithiopika*, in the 3rd c. AD. The Romans adopted these contests from Larisa and spread them throughout the West, where they became very popular, especially in Spain. However, the Thessalian taurotheria was more like an American rodeo event than a modern Spanish bullfight.

573

574

575

THE ASKLEPIEIA OF EPIDAUROS

573-574. Coin issued by the people of Larisa, with a horse on one side and on the other the critical phase of the taurotheria event, with the athlete seizing the bull by the horns (c. 460-440 BC). Athens, Numismatic Museum.

575. Reconstruction drawing by A. Defrasse of the sanctuary of Asklepios at Epidauros. From left: the tholos, abaton and temple of Asklepios and part of the temple of Artemis. Paris, École Nationale Supérieure des Beaux-Arts.

These games were held already in the early 5th c. in the famous sanctuary, and took place every four years, nine days after the Isthmian games. From the end of the 4th century on, the music, drama and poetry-recital contests were held in the theatre, which was renowned for its architecture and excellent acoustics. The theatre was also the venue in which the plays of the great tragedians were staged, down to the end of antiquity, for the entertainment and edification of the thousands of pilgrims, most of them sick people, who converged on the sanctuary of the healer god. There can be no doubt that the theatrical performances at Epidauros were associated with the cult of Asklepios and the need to provide psychological help, daily support and comfort for the patients. The athletic contests were held in the stadium at Epidauros, which was also constructed at the end of the 4th c., and, like that at Olympia and Nemea, had a subterranean vaulted passageway through which the athletes made their entrance; prominent seats for the games officials and important spectators; and stone seats inscribed with the names of donors. The hysplex in this particular stadium is of great interest, not only on account of its mechanism, but also because of an incident recorded in an inscription. Philon of Corinth, who had contracted to build it, was punished with a fine of 500 Alexandrian drachmas by the agonothetai, because he did not deliver the work by the agreed date.

576. Athletic games spread to the East along with the dissemination of Greek culture. Here, a bronze group of wrestlers from Alexandria (2nd-1st c. BC). Athens, National Archaeological Museum.

Games in the Hellenistic East

576

From the time of Alexander the Great onwards and throughout the Hellenistic period, the expansion of Greek culture to the East was accompanied by the wide dissemination of athletic games. The promotion of the values of Hellenism and the adoption of the Greek way of life by the entire world led to the building of new cities, including the erection of resplendent buildings for contests – gymnasia, stadia and theatres – which became the centres of athletic competition. These games were founded by the rulers of the Hellenistic kingdoms, who frequently named them after themselves – the Ptolemaia, for example, at Alexandria, the Eumeneia at Sardis, and so on. Other games continued to take their names from the gods to whom they were dedicated: the Asklepieia on Kos; the Halieia on Rhodes, honouring the patron god of the island, Helios (Halios in the Doric dialect); and the Leukophryenia at Magnesia ad Maeandrum, in honour of Artemis Leukophryene. Yet other games were founded on the occasion of military victories, such as the Nikophoreia at Pergamon, celebrating the great victory of the kings of Pergamon over the Gauls in 235 BC.

To secure the prestige of the panhellenic festivals for the new games, their founders sought permission from responsible officials, mainly of the Olympic and Pythian games, to imitate their contests and use them as models, following the programme and regulations in minute detail. In these cases, the new games were described as *isolympia* ('equal to the Olympics') or *isopythia* ('equal to the Pythia'). And to elevate the new games to the level of their models in practical terms, the founders ensured that they were *stephanitai* games – that is, material prizes were not awarded, at least not openly, but only a wreath (*stephanos*). In their celebrations, these games usually copied the corresponding celebrations of a panhellenic festival. The Leukophryneia, for example, which imitated the Pythian games in all three spheres, are referred to in inscriptions as *ἀγὼν στεφανίτης ἰσοπύθιος τόν τε μουσικὸν καὶ γυμνικὸν καὶ ἱππικόν* ('games for which the prize is a wreath, equal to the Pythian games with regard to the music, athletic and equestrian contests'). Other founders, however, were selective: the Nikephoreia copied the music contests of the Pythia and the athletic and equestrian contests of the Olympic games and are accordingly described as *ἀγῶνες στεφανίται, τὸν μὲν μουσικὸν ἰσοπύθιον, τὸν δὲ γυμνικὸν καὶ ἱππικόν ἰσολύμπιον* ('games for which the prize is a wreath, equal to the Pythia in the music contests and equal to the Olympic games in the athletic and equestrian contests').

577. Games were held as early as the 6th c. at the great festivals in the sanctuaries of Asia Minor. Here, a silver tridrachm of Kos with a depiction of a discus thrower, issued on the occasion of the games organised by the Dorian hexapolis at the sanctuary of Triopian Apollo near Knidos. The tripod depicted was the prize for the winners (480-450 BC). Athens, Numismatic Museum.

578. Aerial photograph of the stadium at Rhodes after the restoration work carried out by the Italian Archaeological School. There was probably a stadium from the very foundation of the city of Rhodes in the late 5th c. BC, but it was renovated in the Hellenistic period as the games expanded.

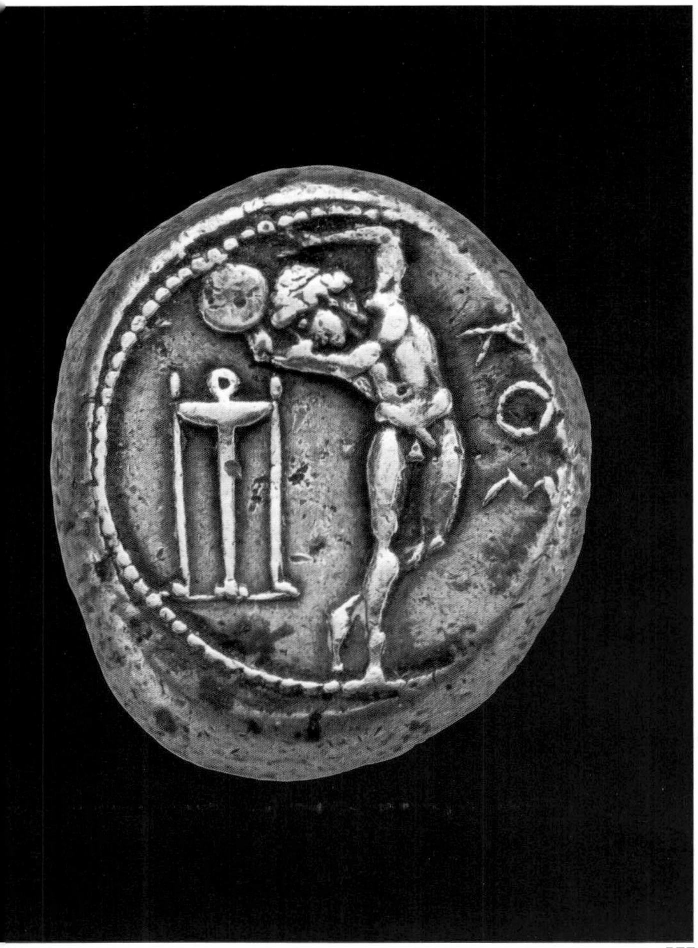

577

578

At this same period, many games were founded in Asia Minor that imitated the Panathenaia – yet another example of the prestige that still adhered to the old cultural capital. Such games are noted in Ilion and Priene as early as the late 4th c. BC, and are attested epigraphically at Pergamon from the period of Eumenes I, in the middle of the 3rd c. BC.

Very interesting evidence for the organisation and form of some of the games of the period may be derived from inscriptions in which all the celebrations are recorded in great detail. We learn from a 2nd-century inscription from Aigiale on Amorgos, for example, that a wealthy citizen had bequeathed a large capital sum, the interest on which was to be used to finance a two-day festival with games in honour of his dead son. All the inhabitants were invited to the festival, including women and foreign visitors. On the first day, there was a public meal in the city gymnasium, at which beef and pork were served, with bread, olive oil, 300 litres of wine, and fruit. Provision was also made for decorating the area with flowers. On the second day, after the appropriate honorary celebrations and the sacrifice before the statue of the heroised dead man, the athletic contests and torch race were held. In the heavy events, the pankration did not take place, and the dead man was declared to be the winner. This arrangement suggests that he had been a pankratiast in his lifetime and probably died during the course of a contest. At the end of the festival, all the athletes taking part had to place a wreath on the statue of the young man.

579

580

The games and the Roman emperors

Rome, Queen of all kingdoms,
your fame will never perish.

Inscription from Ephesus

579. In the games of Late Antiquity, it was the equestrian events, particularly the chariot races, that came to the fore. Here, a fragment with the horses of a chariot, from a mosaic floor in Thessaloniki (3rd c. AD). Thessaloniki, Archaeological Museum.

580. A metope from the temple of Athena in Troy depicts Helios driving his four-horse chariot. The great festival on Rhodes was dedicated to the sun god, the patron god of the island, and was called Halieia in the Doric dialect (300 BC). Berlin, Staatliche Museen zu Berlin-Preussischer Kulturbesitz, Antikensammlung.

581. Chariot races were the most popular events in Roman Italy and the West in general. Here, a wall painting with a scene of a chariot race from a house at Pompeii (45-79 AD). Naples, Museo Archeologico Nazionale.

The keen interest taken by Roman emperors in the games was not confined solely to supporting the games that already existed in Greece, but also extended to the founding of new ones. This was because the Romans became aware very early that one of the most effective ways to control the different peoples in their vast empire was to maintain existing institutions that had a cohesive character. At the same time, spectacles were a favourite pastime for the Roman populace and were in keeping with the hospitable climate.

A variety of new games was therefore organised on various pretexts in many parts of the empire, including Italy itself. Augustus was the first. In order to make propaganda capital out of his victory over Antony and Cleopatra at the battle of Actium in 31 BC, he founded the Actian games in Nikopolis, the new city that he built near the area of the battle in Epiros. These games were held on

581

September 2, the anniversary of his great victory, and responsibility for their conduct was shouldered by the Lakedaimonians, the only Greeks who had fought on Augustus's side, with all the others supporting Antony and Cleopatra.

A few years later, in AD 2, the Sebasta Isolympica were founded in honour of Augustus at Naples in Italy; they were conducted in accordance with the regulations of the Olympic games and awarded a wreath of wheat sheaves as the prize.

In AD 60, Nero founded his own games in Rome, called the Neroneia, held on October 13, the anniversary of his ascent to power. Nero personally exhorted the young men of all classes to participate in them, thereby incurring the disapproval of the intellectuals of the day. The Neroneia included musical, athletic and equestrian contests, the victors received an oak wreath, and the emperor himself competed in most of them. The games were abandoned, however, as soon as Nero died.

In AD 86, Domitian also founded the Capitoleia (*agon capitolinus*), in Rome in honour of Zeus, which continued to be held until the time of Diocletian at the beginning of the 4th c. AD. They included the stadion, diaulos, dolichos and race in armour, the pentathlon, the three heavy events, and a women's race. They were held in a specially built Greek-style stadium on the Campus Martius, with an odeion for the music contests, the foundations of which have been excavated beneath the Piazza Navona in modern Rome.

To stress the importance of these games, the emperors incorporated them into the 'circuit,' along with the Greek games. In order to become a 'circuit-winner' (*periodonikes*) in the Roman empire, a competitor had to be victorious not only at the four old games but also at the Actia, the Capitoleia and the Sebasteia! Despite this, the number of Greek-style games (*ludi graeci*) remained very small in the West. This was not only because of the Roman preference for the bloody gladiatorial combats and the spectacular chariot races of the Roman hippodromes, but also because those emperors who instituted Greek games in Rome were often criticised by the Senate and their political rivals for attempting to dilute ancient Roman values with Greek elements.

582. A depiction of two wrestlers from the mosaic floor of a Roman villa. In addition to chariot racing, bloody sports, particularly boxing, were to the taste of the inhabitants of the Roman empire. This explains why they not only passionately reproduced them in Roman dedications, but also depicted them in their mosaic floors (ca. 175 BC). Los Angeles, J. Paul Getty Museum.

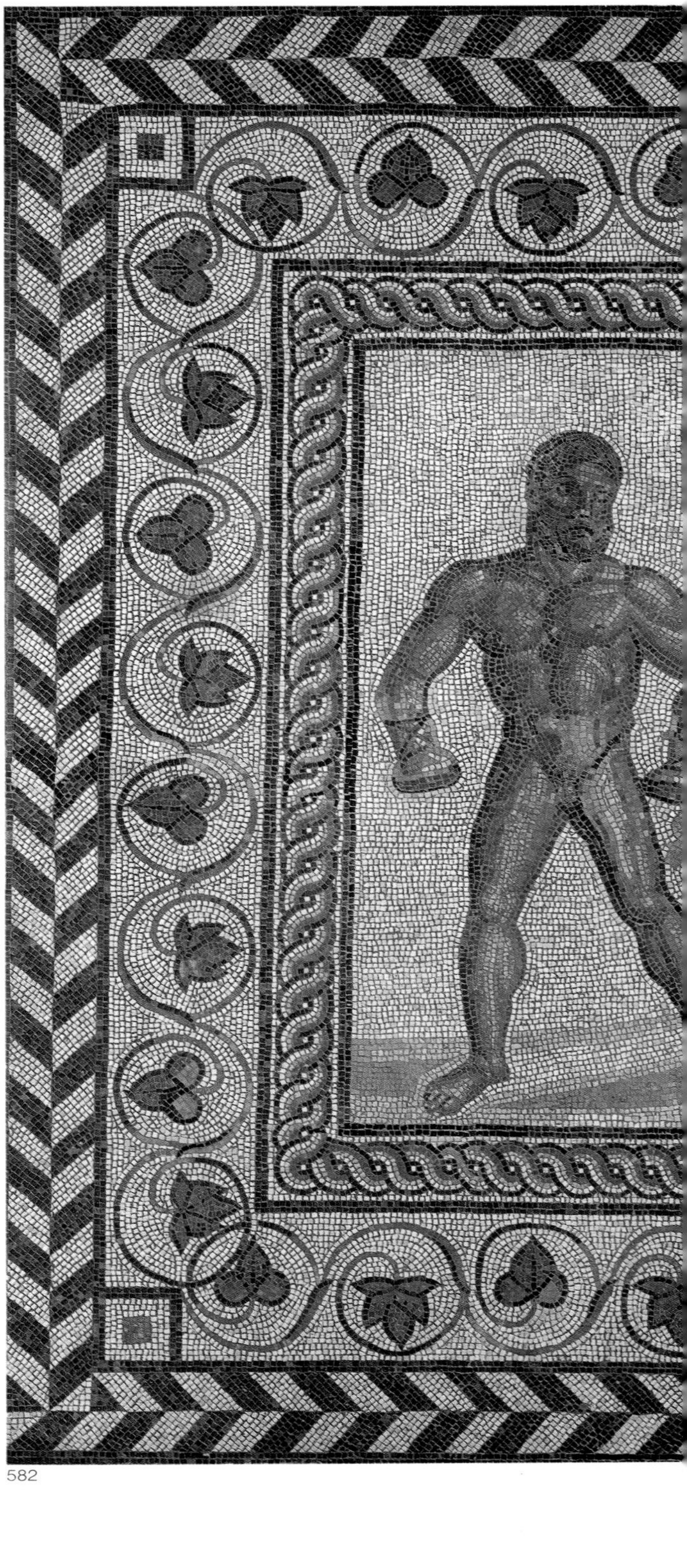

582

Games in the East in Roman times

The greatest explosion in the spread of Greek games occurred in the eastern part of the empire in the 2nd and 3rd c. AD, resulting in their number rising to hundreds. It is indicative that there is epigraphic and numismatic evidence for 30 different games in a single city in Asia Minor – Termessos in Pisidia.

Although these games were *isostephanitai* – that is, a wreath was awarded for victory – many very expensive prizes were nevertheless distributed. It should be recalled here that the amateur status of individual athletes had already been forgotten at a very early date, and from the Hellenistic period onwards they were organised into clubs. Under the Roman empire, these clubs acquired great power and exercised significant influence on the athletic affairs of the day through their relations with the emperor.

By this time, the request to Olympia or Delphi to be allowed to found new games was a mere formality. All decisions were taken by the emperor himself, who incorporated his own personal propaganda into the games in an attempt to strengthen his popularity. The names of the new festivals are revealing: Augusteia, Traianeia, Hadrianeia, Severeia, Gordianeia, Romaia, and so forth. It is interesting, however, that even at this period they still retained their religious character, though now the religious ceremonial served mainly the imperial cult, a major cohesive religious element in the vast empire, in which there were dozens of old and new cults (Isis, Mithras, etc.).

These new games were usually financed by wealthy citizens of the empire, who sought in this way to develop or maintain good relations with the imperial family. The festival of the Demostheneia at Oinoanda in Lykia, founded and financed by a wealthy local aristocrat, Gaius Julius Demosthenes, was characteristic of the period. Our knowledge of this festival is drawn from a long inscription of the time of Hadrian, in which all its features are described in minute detail. In order to found the festival, the emperor's permission and the formal ratification by the local council were required. Impressively, it lasted for 22 days and culminated in a sacrifice of 27 oxen. This yielded about 8,000 portions of meat, which gives us the rough number of participants. Twelve of the 22 days of the festival were given over to contests, mainly in music, the winners of which received large money prizes. In addition to the sacrifices and contests, the Demostheneia included many rituals devoted to the imperial cult, as well as other events, such as celebratory sessions of the council and popular assembly, a trade fair and a cattle fair. The economic element in all these events cannot be ignored, for the organising cities were filled with thousands of visitors (athletes, relatives, spectators). The attendant increase in demand for goods and services was met by the local economy, which thus made huge profits.

583

584

THE OLYMPIC GAMES OF ANTIOCH

The last games known in antiquity, which continued until AD 520, were the Olympic games held in honour of Zeus at Daphni, a suburb of Antioch. This festival was instituted at the time of the emperor Commodus (r. 180-92) by the people of Antioch, who paid a high price to the Eleians for the right to celebrate isolympia games for 99 Olympiads – that is, a period of 396 years. A major role was played in the foundation and celebration of these games by the emperor himself.

We learn from the great philosopher, orator, teacher and author of the period, Libanios, that the festival was celebrated every four years in July, and

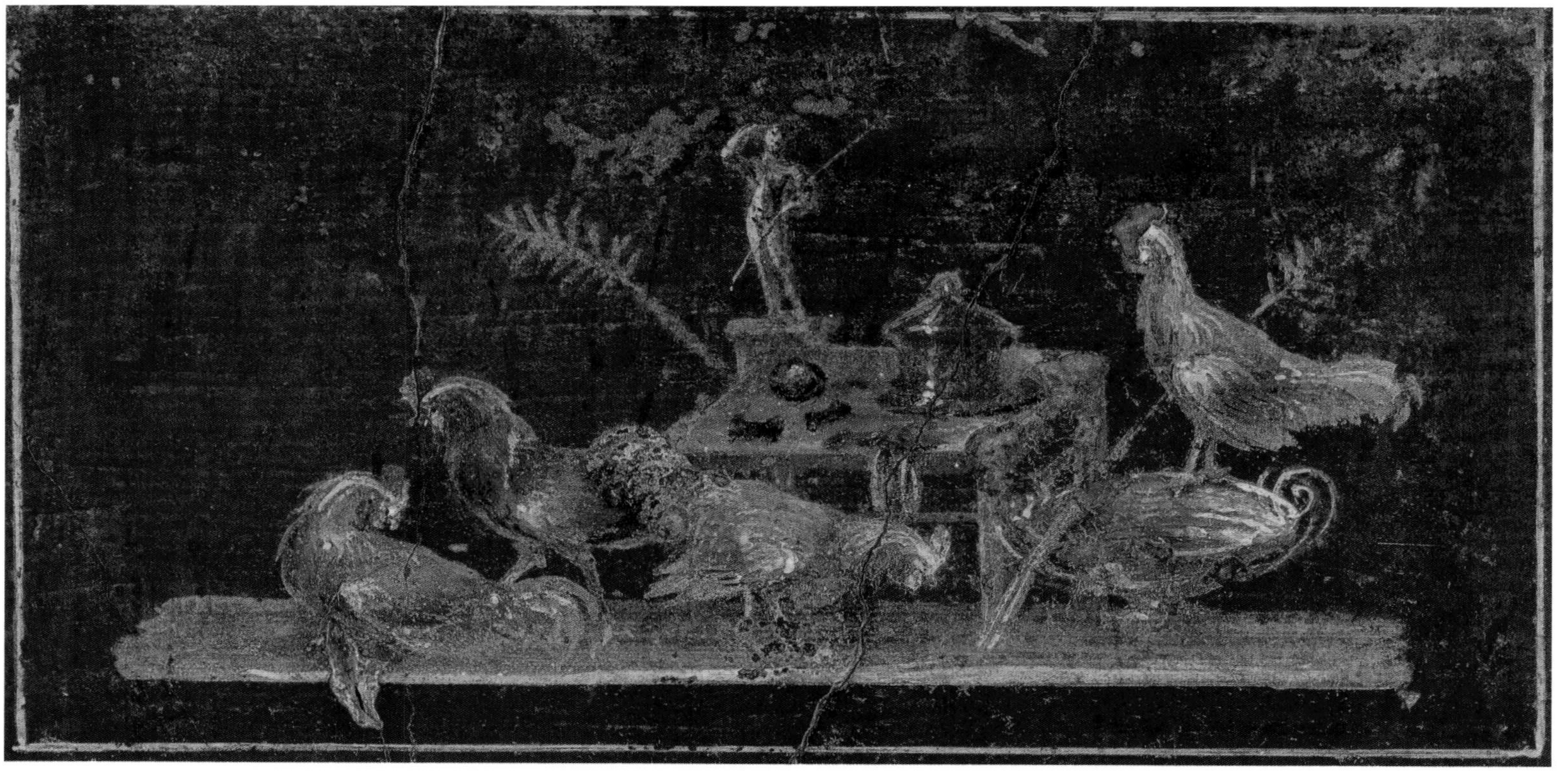
585

that both men and women had the right to participate, though they had to be pagan. This last provision indicates that at this period the early Christians did not look unfavourably on athletic contests, and that the enlightened Church Fathers characteristically urged young men to exercise and in general to exploit certain elements of the ancient way of thinking. The harsh, incessant preparation undergone by athletes was compared to the austere life of the early Christians.

The festival lasted for 30 days and included all the athletic and equestrian events held at Olympia, the prize awarded to the victors being a laurel wreath. The fact that these games endured until AD 520 is due to many reasons. Antioch was a wealthy city with a large pagan population, which increased considerably

583. Depiction of an athlete on a ring with a Carnelian stone by the seal-carver Epimenes from Ionia (500 BC). Such rings were possibly worn by athletes, who either dedicated them to sanctuaries or used them as tomb possessions. Los Angeles, J. Paul Getty Museum.

584. Statue of a victorious boxer on his pedestal, from a mosaic from the area of Pompeii. Impressive is the architectural frame. Beneath the statue is a cockerel, symbol of the boxing contest (1st c. AD). Naples, Museo Archaeologico Nazionale.

585. Wall painting, from Pompeii, depicting a dinner to celebrate victory. On the right, the symbolic victorious cockerel hovers above a gold vase, with the defeated contestants on the left. The entire scene is full of symbols of victory, palm branches and a statuette of a victorious athlete crowning himself (1st c. AD). Naples, Museo Archaeologico Nazionale.

586. Relief terracotta plaque of Roman date with the facade of an athletic facility, probably a palaestra. Amongst the columns can be seen a hermaic stele, a metal vase on a base (probably a prize) and a statue of a victor holding a palm branch in his hand. London, British Museum.

587. The Byzantine emperor Theodosios II holding the decrees by which he did much to bring an end to the ancient Greek games. By contrast, he supported the holding of Roman horse and chariot races. He is depicted here on one side of the base of an obelisk he erected in 390/391 in the hippodrome of Constantinople, watching chariot races together with his family from a special box. Constantinople, Atmeidan Square.

when many pagans converged on the city after the closing of the old sanctuaries. The games reached the height of their fame at the time of Julian the Apostate (r. 361-63), who took many steps to strengthen pagan institutions in an attempt to revive the ancient religion.

The survival of the games after the 4th and 5th c. AD, despite the ban imposed by Theodosius I and Theodosius II, appears to have been made possible by a very practical reason. The people of Antioch refused to abandon them because they had spent considerable sums of money to acquire the right to hold them, which had not yet expired. Presumably the Byzantine emperors found their argument reasonable and, unwilling to enter into conflict with the large, vigorous pagan population in the region, permitted them to continue to organise the games regularly, even though they were banned in other regions.

The end came inevitably in 520 with a decree of Justin I, a few years before the decree of Justinian in AD 529, closing the philosophical schools of Athens and putting a final end to all things pagan.

586

The end of the ancient games

The ancient Greek games had begun as a religious celebration in the context of the great festivals in honour of the Olympian gods. And although they had been renewed, had developed and had been accommodated to the many world-shaking changes that occurred in antiquity, they died out with the death of the ancient religion. Despite their vitality, and despite the human, archetypal ideals to which they gave expression, they were obliged to yield to the dynamism of Christianity and the fanatical opposition of some of the emperors and many of the religious leaders of the day. Their revival in modern times was quite independent of their original religious context, and this helped them to regain almost at once the human, global character they had already acquired in ancient times. And they continue, and will continue, to be held every four years, undaunted and thriving. Though now held in the new economic and social circumstances of the modern world, they will never cease to express the great, ancient, human ideals of competition, victory and reward.

THE EVENTS, RULES

588. The events at the four major panhellenic festivals and the dozens of lesser games held throughout the Greek world were virtually the same. This was due to the fact that all the games initially copied the events of the earliest and most important of them, the Olympic games, and later gradually adopted all the innovations and changes imposed at Olympia. There were naturally minor differences and deviations to be found everywhere,

588

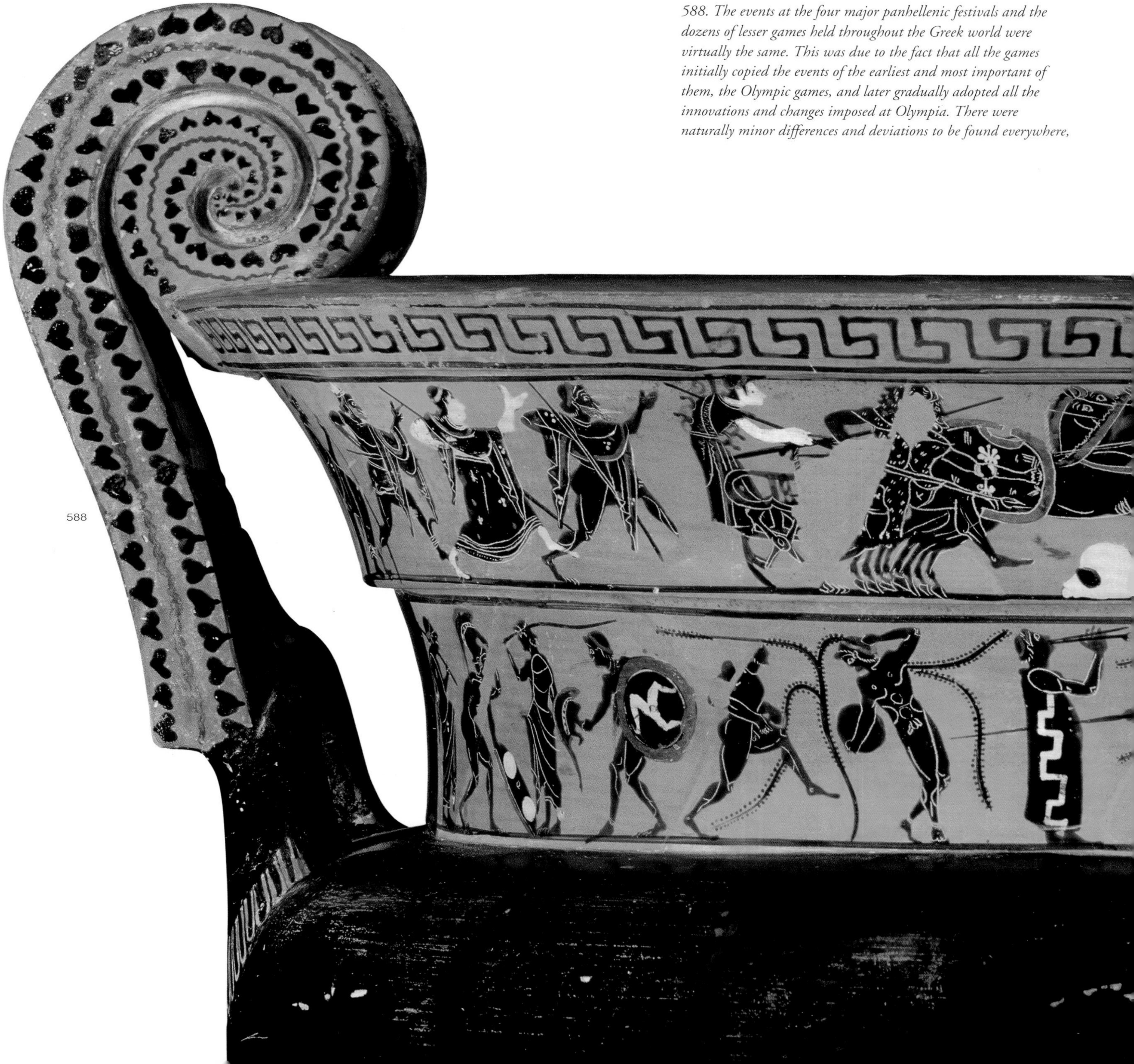

AND GREAT CHAMPIONS

depending on the particular features of each festival, but these were never enough to significantly modify the basic core of athletic contests. Almost all the athletic and equestrian events known in ancient Greek sport are depicted in two zones on the rim of the vase illustrated. Attic black-figure volute krater of the Leagros Group. Los Angeles, J. Paul Getty Museum.

Running

589

Running is a primeval activity. People ran in warfare and in hunting, and fleetness of foot was always an important attribute. The earliest evidence for running events are to be found in Mesopotamian and Egyptian sources, and these events made their appearance in the Aegean during the Mycenaean period. A Cypro-Mycenaean vase dating from the 13th c. BC offers the first undisputed representation of a race. Homer includes races amongst the events held by the Achaians in honour of the dead Patroklos (*Iliad*, XXIII, 740); the winner of the event was Odysseus.

Running is said to have been the oldest event at the Olympic games and, according to tradition, was established by Herakles himself. The particular event was the sprint, which was called the *stadion* by the ancient Greeks. In this race, the athletes had to run a distance of 600 feet, or about 192 m., which was the equivalent of one of the basic ancient measurements of length, the stadion, or stade. It is no coincidence that this event gave its name to the building in which athletic contests have been held from ancient times to the present day. For the first thirteen Olympiads, the stadion was the only event. The *diaulos* – a race over two stadia (about 400 m.) – was introduced at the fourteenth Olympiad, and the *dolichos* ('long'), the distance of which varied from 7 to 14 stadia, depending on the games and the period. In the race in armour, which was introduced in 520 BC, the runners covered a distance of 2 or 4 stadia, wearing helmet and greaves and carrying a shield. From the middle of the 5th century on, this event was made easier by dispensing with the greaves, and, after the 4th century, the helmet, too, was abandoned and the runners carried only a shield. Pausanias (5.12.8) states that 25 shields were kept in the Heraion at Olympia for the use of the runners in this race. Finally, the Isthmian, Nemean and Panathenaic games included a race called the *hippeios*, over a distance of four stadia (about 750 m.); the name of this event probably derives from the fact that in the chariot race the horses had to cover the length of the hippodrome four times.

The starting mechanism for the running events consisted of a long stone *balbis* with two parallel grooves, in which the runners placed their toes, thus ensuring a fair start. Vertical posts were set at one-metre intervals on the balbis, indicating the positions of the runners. Lines marked on the track in white

589-591. Various scenes connected with running.

589. Drawing of the earliest certain depiction of a race, on a Cypro-Mycenaean krater dating from the 13th c. BC. Nicosia, Pierides Collection.

590. A stadion contest, depicted on a black-figure skyphos dating from 540 BC. Athens, National Archaeological Museum.

591. Young athlete in the starting position, on a red-figure vase of the early 4th c. BC. Athens, National Archaeological Museum.

590

591

592. Bronze statue of the winner of a foot race, found in the Aegean Sea near the coast of Aiolian Kyme and dating from the Hellenistic period. Smyrna, Archaeological Museum.

593. The dolichos race is depicted on this Panathenaic amphora dating from 320 BC. The runners are shown with their bodies upright and their fists clenched, unlike the sprinters in the stadion who are rendered with their bodies leaning forward and their hands open. Los Angeles, J. Paul Getty Museum.

paint seem to have started from these posts, defining the lane in which each runner ran from start to finish.

In the 5th century, an artificial obstacle called the *hysplex* was devised to prevent false starts. This consisted either of individual barriers for each runner or, later, of a continuous horizontal rope stretched in front of all the runners, which fell when a special mechanism was operated by the starter, allowing the start to be perfectly synchronised. The finishing line for the stadion was at the other end of the track. For the diaulos, in contrast, the finishing line was also the start, since the runners covered the stadion twice, turning through 180 degrees at the end, around wooden posts, which are known for this reason as turning posts. In the long-distance race, the dolichos, the competitors did not run in a circle as they do today, but went up and down

592 593

594. One of the finest depictions of the stadion race depicted on a Panathenaic amphora dating from 530-520 BC by the Euphiletos Painter. New York, The Metropolitan Museum of Art.

595. A scene of a race in armour. On the red-figure kylix from Larisa, dating from the late 6th c. BC, the hoplite is preparing for the race. Athens, Archives of III Ephorate of Antiquities.

596. On the Panathenaic amphora dating from 344/343 BC, the contestants in the race in armour stand ready at the starting line. Athens, Archives of III Ephorate of Antiquities.

597. A statue of a victor from Eleusis. The slender proportions of the figure's body have suggested that it depicts a runner (early 4th c. BC). Athens, National Archaeological Museum.

the track, turning round individual turning posts near both ends, before finishing at the starting line.

Obviously, for events in which there were more entrants than positions on the starting mechanism, preliminary heats were held, called taxeis by the ancient Greeks. The number of positions varied from stadium to stadium: in Priene in Asia Minor, there were positions for only eight runners, at Epidauros eleven, at Miletos twelve, at Nemea thirteen, at Isthmia sixteen or seventeen, and at Olympia twenty.

One interesting feature connected with track events in the ancient world recalls the modern phenomenon of 'making' athletes in certain countries. During the period 588-488 BC, covering 25 Olympiads, athletes from Kroton in South Italy won 12 victories. In one contest, indeed, the first seven to finish were Krotoniates, giving rise to the mocking observation that the last Krotoniate was better then the first of all the other Greeks. Runners from Alexandria were also very successful, winning the stadion race a total of 18 times between the years AD 93 and 221, covering 32 Olympiads.

594

595

Our knowledge of impressive performances by individual athletes who won several victories comes mainly from lists of Olympic victors. It is known, for example, that the same runner won the stadion at two successive Olympiads on thirty occasions; the corresponding figure for the diaulos is eight occasions; for the dolichos four; and for the race in armour only two. Of the most famous runners mentioned in the literary sources, we may note Phanas of Pellene in Achaia and Polites from Keramos in Karia who, in 512 BC and AD 69, respectively, won all three foot races, the stadion, diaulos and dolichos, on the same morning. At the three Olympiads between 488 and 480 BC, Astylos of Kroton won both the stadion and the diaulos. The achievement of Leonidas of Rhodes, however, is completely unmatched: he was the victor in all three sprint races (stadion, diaulos, and race in armour) at four successive Olympiads from 164 to 152 BC, earning a total of twelve victory crowns.

596

597

The pentathlon

The pentathlon is the first multiple event in the history of athletics, and is thought to have been devised in Greece and indeed at Olympia, since the earliest evidence for it goes back to its introduction at the 18th Olympiad in 708 BC. It involved the following five events: jumping, discus, javelin, stadion race and wrestling, the last two of which were also held as separate events.

At the Olympic games, the events in the pentathlon were held on a single day, one after the other without a break. It was therefore a tough event demanding remarkable endurance, and this may account for the fact that the boy's pentathlon, introduced at Olympia in 628 BC, did not survive and was held on only this one occasion. In contrast, the pentathlon was held at the Panathenaia for all three age groups: men, 'beardless youths' and boys.

Although a considerable quantity of evidence is provided by the ancient literary sources, the sequence of the pentathlon events is not known with certainty. The jump seems to have been held first and the wrestling last. The method by which the winner was decided, an issue that has given rise to much scholarly debate, is also unclear. All that can reliably be said is that if anyone won the first three events, he was declared victor. If not, those who had finished in good positions in the first three events continued to the second stage, while the rest were excluded. Those who qualified competed in the fourth

598. Pentathletes were depicted in ancient Greek art by rendering only the javelin, discus and jumping events, since the other two (running and wrestling) were also held as events in their own right. Black-figure kylix from the workshop of Lydos depicting pentathletes amongst other youths wearing himatia (ca. 550-540 BC). Athens, National Archaeological Museum.

599. Pentathletes practising the discus, javelin, and jumping under the supervision of a trainer. Panathenaic amphora by the Euphiletos Painter dating from 530-520 BC. Amsterdam, Rijksmuseum.

598

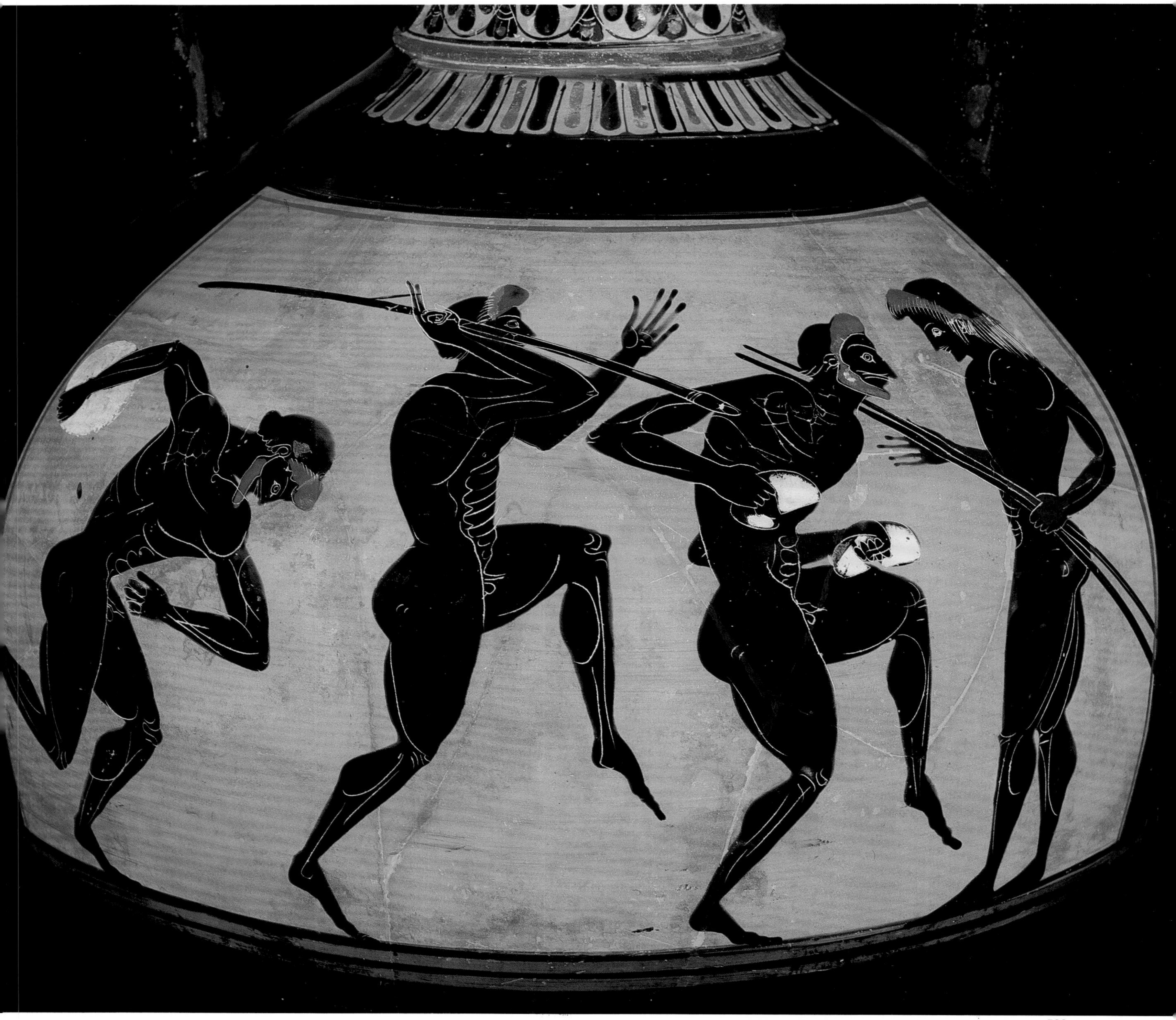

599

event, the stadion, the result of which was used as a basis for determining who should proceed to the wrestling, which produced the final winner.

The pentathlon was so demanding, requiring a combination of speed, strength and endurance, that the competitors were unable to repeat their victories. References to pentathletes who won at two successive Olympiads are confined to four cases: the Spartan Philombrotos (676 and 672 BC), Theopompos from Heraia (484 and 480 BC), Aelius Granianus of Sikyon (AD 137 and 141) and Demetrios of Salamis on Cyprus (AD 229 and 233). The last two also won the stadion race at the same games, a feat achieved for the first time in 464 BC by Xenophon of Corinth and celebrated by Pindar (*Olympian Ode* 13, 29-31).

600. Two pentathletes (a javelin thrower and a jumper) train in the gymnasium under the strict supervision of the trainer. Red-figure column krater by Myson (480 BC). Los Angeles, J. Paul Getty Museum.

601. Attic red-figure kylix, with a depiction of a jumper preparing to make his jump, holding weights in his hands (ca. 480 BC). Athens, Ancient Agora Museum.

602. Two stone halteres (weights) of different type, like those held by jumpers. The date at which their use was introduced is unknown, but the earliest are dated by votive inscriptions on them to the 6th c. BC. Athens, National Archaeological Museum.

600

JUMPING

The only ancient jumping contest was the long jump, which differed from the modern event in two respects. First, it was accompanied by music, in order to give the athlete's movements harmony and rhythm, or possibly to define the time during which he had to finish, for each athlete made a series of five jumps. Second, in the ancient event, the competitors held *halteres* (jumping weights) in their hands. These were specially shaped stone or lead weights weighing from 1.5 to 2 kilos each, which they swung in such a way as to give the body a forward impulse and achieve better results. The role of the halteres is disputed by scholars. Some assert that they helped to produce better performances, while others say that their purpose was to secure a steady landing with both feet, which was a requirement for a valid jump. Experiments recently conducted at Manchester University showed that the use of halteres led to an improvement of about 6% in the performance. Many halteres have been found in archaeological excavations, some of them bearing votive inscriptions by the victors. A characteristic example is a *halter* from Olympia dedicated by the Spartan pentathlete Akmatidas in the late 6th c. BC, on which the inscription tells us that he won the pentathlon *akoniti* ('without getting dusty') – that is, without a rival. Victories of this kind were not rare at the various games, and occurred when one athlete was so

601

602

superior to his rivals that no one dared compete against him. The word *akoniti* is thus used with pride in ancient victory epigrams.

Two famous jumpers were Phayllos of Kroton and Chionis of Sparta; references to jumps by them in excess of 16 m. have caused some scholars to posit the existence of a triple jump. There is no other evidence for this, however, and the figure probably refers to the sum of their five successive attempts. It may also be simply a question of exaggeration, which was quite common with regard to the great athletes of ancient times, to whom many almost mythical achievements were attributed. The ancient proverb 'to jump beyond the pit' is associated with Phayllos, who is said on one occasion to have made such a huge jump that he landed outside the sandpit.

a603. A jumper holding the halteres flies through the air during his jump. He is accompanied by a musician playing the diaulos and watched with interest by the judges and his fellow athletes. Attic red-figure kylix (480 BC). Munich, Antikenmuseum.

604-605. Scenes of discus throwers winding up for the throw, as captured by ancient vase painters.

604. The final movement before the release, in a superb view from behind. Attic red-figure kylix dating from 480 BC. Athens, Ancient Agora Museum.

605. The initial movement, with the hand still held low, on an Attic red-figure amphora by Euthymides, dating from 515-510 BC. Los Angeles, J. Paul Getty Museum.

603

DISCUS

Throwing the discus, the second event in the pentathlon, was also devised by the ancient Greeks and is mentioned by Homer in the athletic contests described in the *Iliad* and the *Odyssey.*

The stone or bronze discuses were lentoid in shape, like their modern counterparts, had a diameter of 17-32 cm., and weighed 4-5 kilos. Pausanias (6.19.4) states that three discuses were kept in the Treasury of the Sikyonians at Olympia for use in the pentathlon. In the discus, the competitors established a rhythm, roughly as in the modern event, and had five throws, the longest of which counted. There is no agreement amongst scholars as to whether they also rotated their body as they do today. The various views are based mainly on the

604

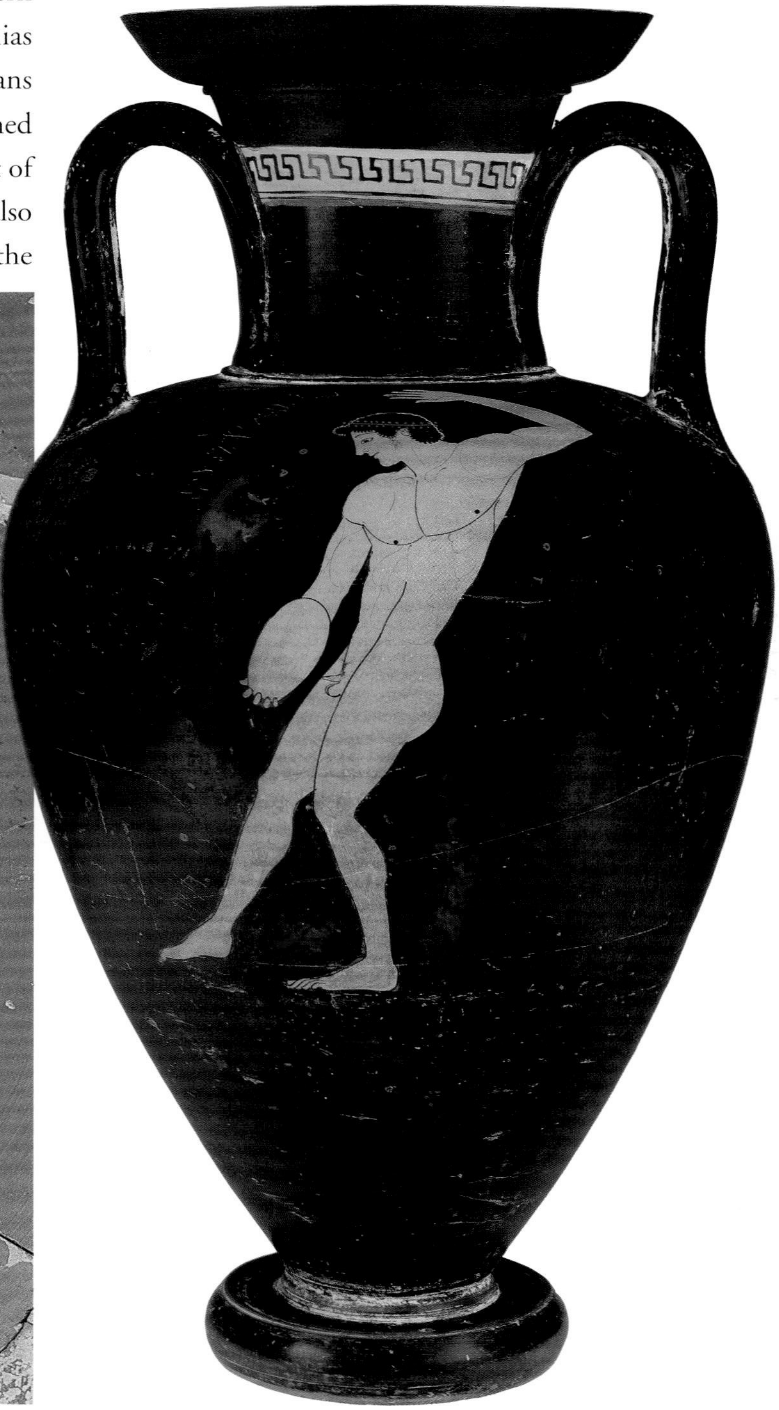

605

many depictions of the event in vase painting and sculpture, the main pieces being marble Roman copies of the famous Diskobolos by Myron. We do not know where the original statue, a bronze of the middle of the 5th c. BC, was erected but it was, presumably, a dedication from a victor in the pentathlon held at one of the major games.

Although we have no direct evidence as to precisely where the starting line for the throws was in the stadium, it can only have been at one end. The spot where the discus fell was marked by a small peg, called the *sema*, and the distance was measured with the aid of poles. None of the performances of the ancient athletes in this event are known, since they were not recorded anywhere. Popular tradition has preserved the memory only of the ones that were looked upon as great achievements.

The great discus throwers were Phlegyas, who threw his discus from one bank of the river Alpheios to the other, and Protesilaos and Phayllos, both of whose throws were longer than 100 ancient feet – that is, about 30 metres.

606. This fragment of a grave stele found in the Kerameikos is one of the finest early Attic reliefs. The head of a young man is projected against the discus he holds in his left hand. The outstanding artistic conception was inspired by the athletic activity of young Athenians as early as the Archaic period (ca. 550 BC). Athens, National Archaeological Museum.

607. One of the many marble copies made in Roman times of the famous bronze Diskobolos ('Discus Thrower') by Myron. For the first time in the history of sculpture, the artist has grasped and frozen this moment from the athlete's swing (1st c. AD). London, British Museum.

606

60

JAVELIN

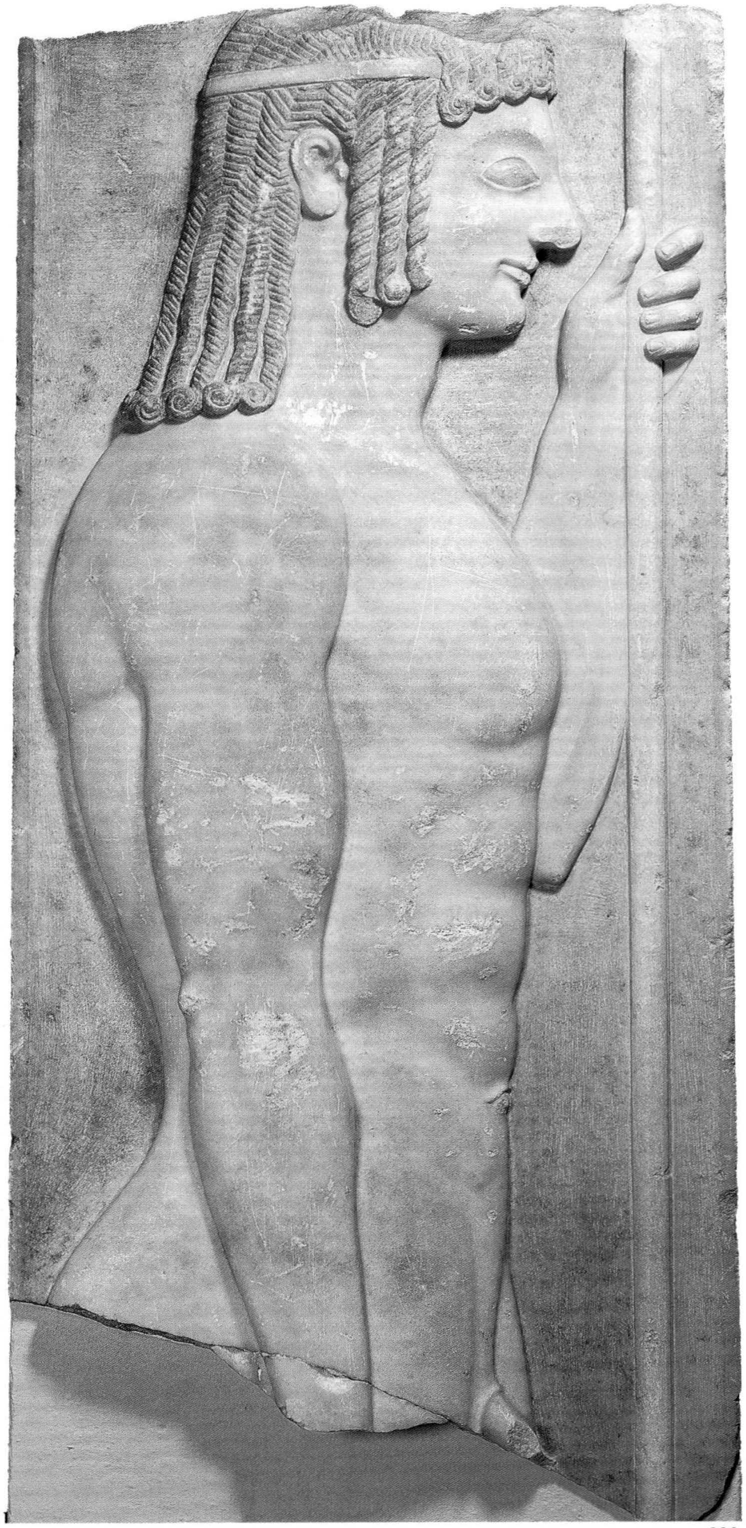

The origins of the javelin event were obviously in warfare, and Homer states that the Achaians at Troy and the suitors of Penelope on Ithake entertained themselves by throwing the discus and javelin. In the Greek games, there were two javelin events: the *hekebolos*, in which the winner was the one who achieved the longest throw; and target javelin, in which the competitors aimed at a target. Only the first was held at the panhellenic games, as one of the pentathlon events, while the second was found only at the Panathenaia, mainly in the form of javelin from horseback. In this, the javelin was thrown by riders on galloping horses, a feature that points clearly to the military origins of this event.

The javelins were made of wood and were 1.5-2 m. long; they were lighter than military javelins and probably lacked the bronze point. The technique of throwing them was roughly the same as today, except that a leather loop (*ankyle*), 0.40 m. long, was bound at the centre of gravity of the javelin; the thrower placed two of his fingers through this loop and held the javelin with the other three. At the point of the throw, the athlete released the javelin and then pulled hard on the loop in a forward direction, giving the implement a greater impulse. Of the javelin throwers famous in ancient times, mention may be made here of Mithridates, who is said to have thrown the javelin from the temple of Artemis in Ephesos for a distance of over 1 stade (180-190 m.).

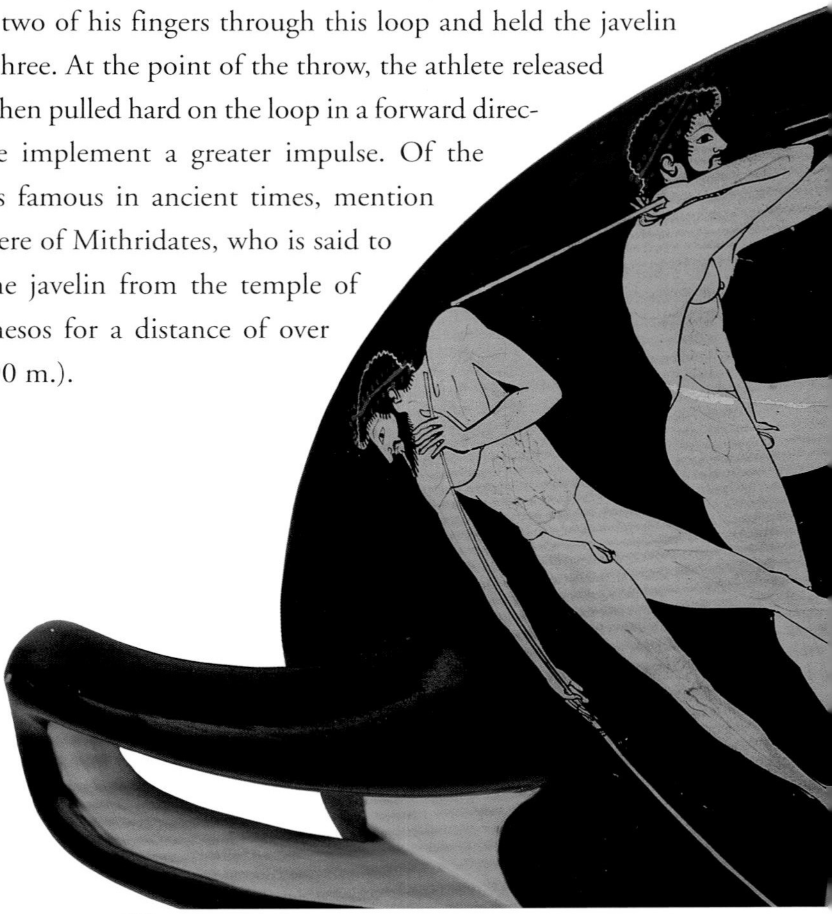

608

609

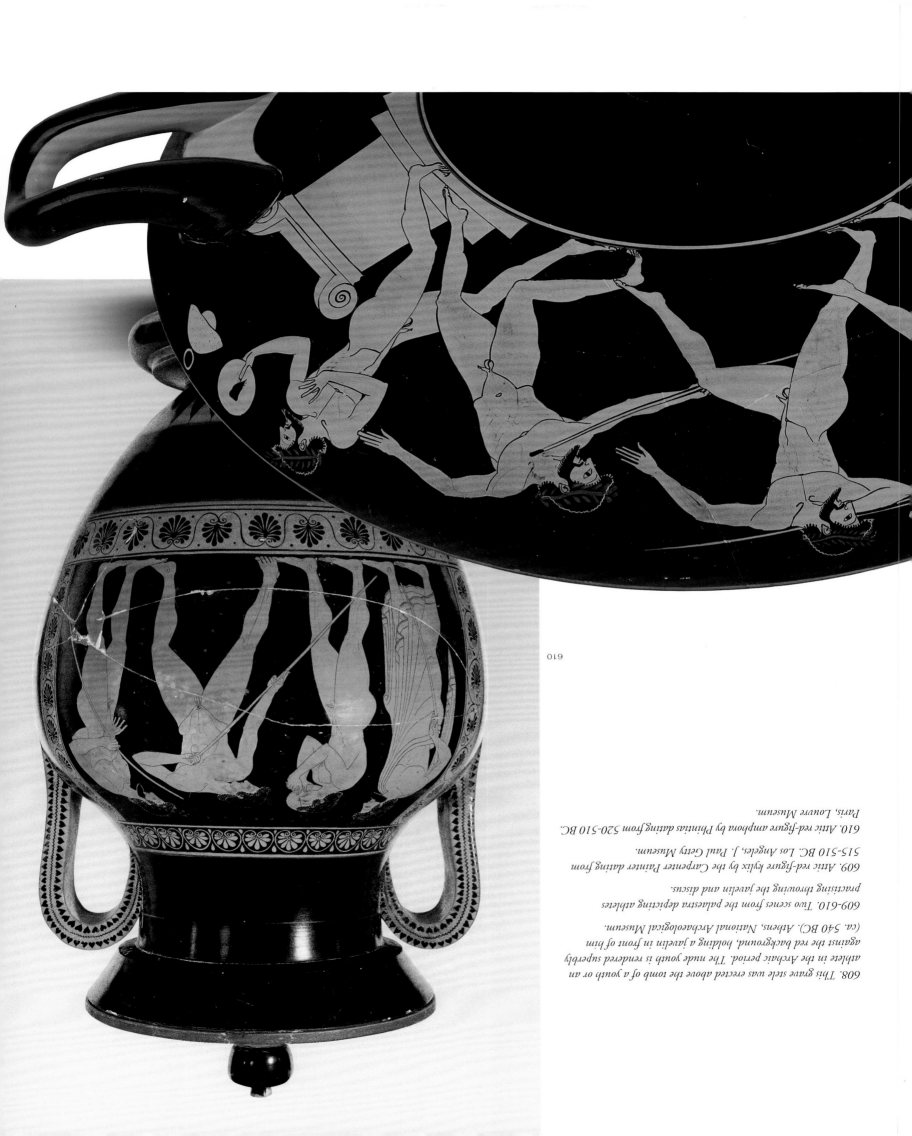

608. *This grave stele was erected above the tomb of a youth or an athlete in the Archaic period. The nude youth is rendered superbly against the red background, holding a javelin in front of him (ca. 540 BC). Athens, National Archaeological Museum.*

609-610. *Two scenes from the palaestra depicting athletes practising throwing the javelin and discus.*

609. *Attic red-figure kylix by the Carpenter Painter dating from 515-510 BC. Los Angeles, J. Paul Getty Museum.*

610. *Attic red-figure amphora by Phintias dating from 520-510 BC. Paris, Louvre Museum.*

610

The heavy events

The heavy events were wrestling, boxing and the pankration. They were known as heavy events (Pausanias 6.24.1) either because both the training and the events themselves were heavy and difficult, or because the competitors in them, the wrestlers, boxers and pankratiasts, were of heavy build, unlike the other athletes. In ancient times the competitors were not divided into weight or other categories. Apparently, therefore, at an early point in time a special regime was devised especially for these events that gave the athletes a suitable physical build and made them heavier. Combined with special exercises and training, this gave those who had the right psychological makeup hopes of winning.

The heavy events were held in the stadium, in a special area called *skamma* (*skapto*, dig), since it consisted of soft soil that was constantly renewed by digging it over. None of the excavations of stadia to date have succeeded in detecting the precise location of the pit, but it was probably in about the middle of the track, near the platform of the Hellenadokai, so that everyone could see. It is not impossible, however, that it was in the vacant area at the ends of the stadium, between the start of the track events and the cavea, though in this case not everyone would be able to see the event.

The pairings for the heavy events were determined by lot, and the loser of each bout was eliminated, until the final. If there were too many entrants for these events, some were regarded as *ephedroi*. The *ephedros* (reserve) was an athlete who was given a bye into the next round. Even though the bye was purely a matter of chance, we often encounter athletes in victory epigrams who are proud that they have won without having received a bye.

611

WRESTLING

612

Wrestling, a very ancient event known from Middle Eastern civilisations, is not depicted in Greece before the Geometric period. Strikingly, it makes its appearance simultaneously in vase painting and the Homeric poems (*Iliad*, XXIII, 700ff.), where Odysseus wrestled with Telamonian Ajax at the games held in honour of Patroklos. Wrestling was an event of great importance

611-612. One of the most characteristic scenes from a wrestling match, with the two opponents locked together symmetrically, seen here in two representations separated by about 200 years.

611. Relief from the base of a kouros statue dating from the late 6th c. BC. Athens, National Archaeological Museum.

612. Drawing from a Geometric vase dating from the late 8th c. BC. Argos, Archaeological Museum.

to the ancient Greeks and played a major role in the athletic education of the young. The main part of the ancient gymnasium was therefore called the palaestra (wrestling arena).

In both the panhellenic and the local games, wrestling was an independent event and also formed part of the pentathlon. At Olympia, it was introduced at the 18th Olympiad in 708 BC, while the boys' wrestling was first held in 632 BC. It was divided into two kinds: 'upright' wrestling, in which the winner was the one who threw his opponent to the ground, and 'rolling' or 'ground' wrestling (*alindesis* or *kato pale*). In the latter, the opponents started in the standing position, but then continued on the ground until one of the two opponents submitted. There is also a view, however, that upright wrestling was the only event held at the official games, and that all the scenes of alindesis found in art in fact depict the pankration.

The rules for wrestling in ancient times were not very different from the rules of Greco-Roman wrestling today. The contest began in the standing position, with the opponents facing each other. They are often shown bent over, with their foreheads touching, a stance compared by poets to fighting rams. All holds were allowed in the contest, except those involving the genital organs, but it was forbidden to use the fists or bite and, of course, to come to grips outside the pit. Since the winner was the one who threw his opponent three times, the winning margin could be 3-2, 3-1 or 3-0. In the last event, the winner would boast that he had won *apiptos* (without being thrown) – a phrase often used in victory epigrams.

There were many famous wrestlers in the ancient world, most of whom won several victories at many of the panhellenic games and at successive celebrations of them. In contrast with the other events, competitors in the heavy events could stay fit and repeat their successes over many years. The Spartan Hipposthenes won the boys' wrestling in 632 and five successive events in the men's wrestling at the Olympiads from 624 to 608 BC. His son Hetoimokles continued the family tradition with five victories (604-588 BC). Chairon of Pellene won at four successive Olympiads (356-344 BC), and Tiberius Claudius Patrobius was the last man to win three successive victories, at the Olympiads of AD 49, 53 and 57.

No one ever approached the achievements and fame of the legendary Milon of Kroton in southern Italy, one of the greatest athletes in the ancient world, who dominated the event for decades. He was winner six times at Olympia (once in the boys' wrestling in 540 BC, and five times in the men's event), seven times at the Pythian games, nine times at Nemea and ten at Isthmia, and he won countless victories in lesser games. His successive victories at the four great panhellenic games made him five times *periodonikes*. An epigram has survived that adorned the base of one of his statues, possibly the one at Olympia: *Μίλωνος τόδ' άγαλμα καλού καλόν, όςποτε Πίση εξάκις νικήσας ες γόνατ' ουκ' έπεσεν* ('This beautiful statue is of beautiful Milon, who won six times without being thrown').

613. Bronze statue of a wrestler (or runner) staring his opponent in the eyes before they come to grips. Roman copy of a Hellenistic original dating from the late 4th c. BC. Found in the Villa of the Papyri at Herculaneum. Naples, Museo Archeologico Nazionale.

614. Representation of Herakles wrestling with the giant Antaios. The Trikoupis kylix, donated by the great Greek politician (ca. 500 BC). Athens, National Archaeological Museum.

615-616. Scenes from successive phases of a wrestling match, as depicted around a situla dating from the last quarter of the 1st c. AD. Los Angeles, J. Paul Getty Museum.

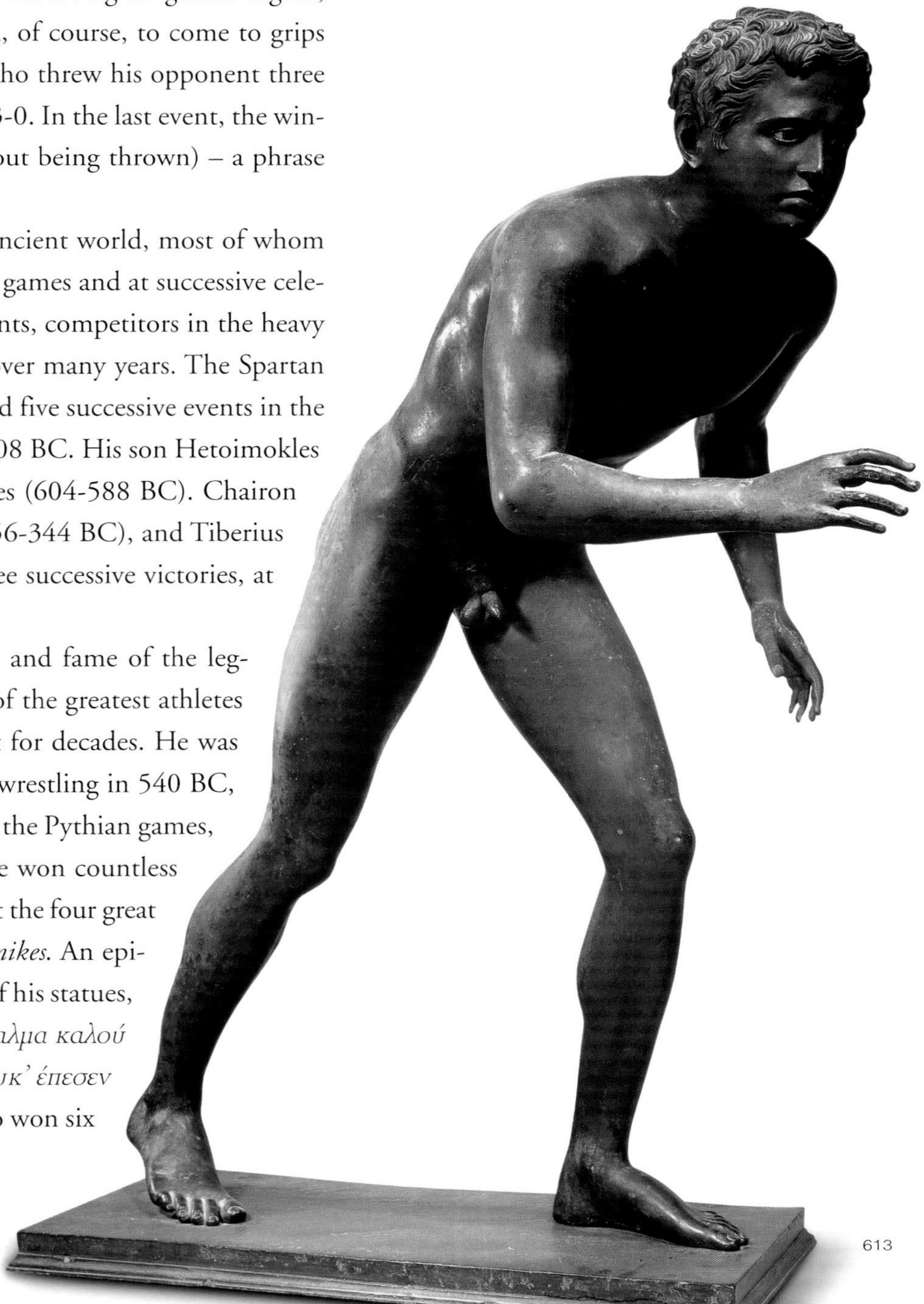

613

614

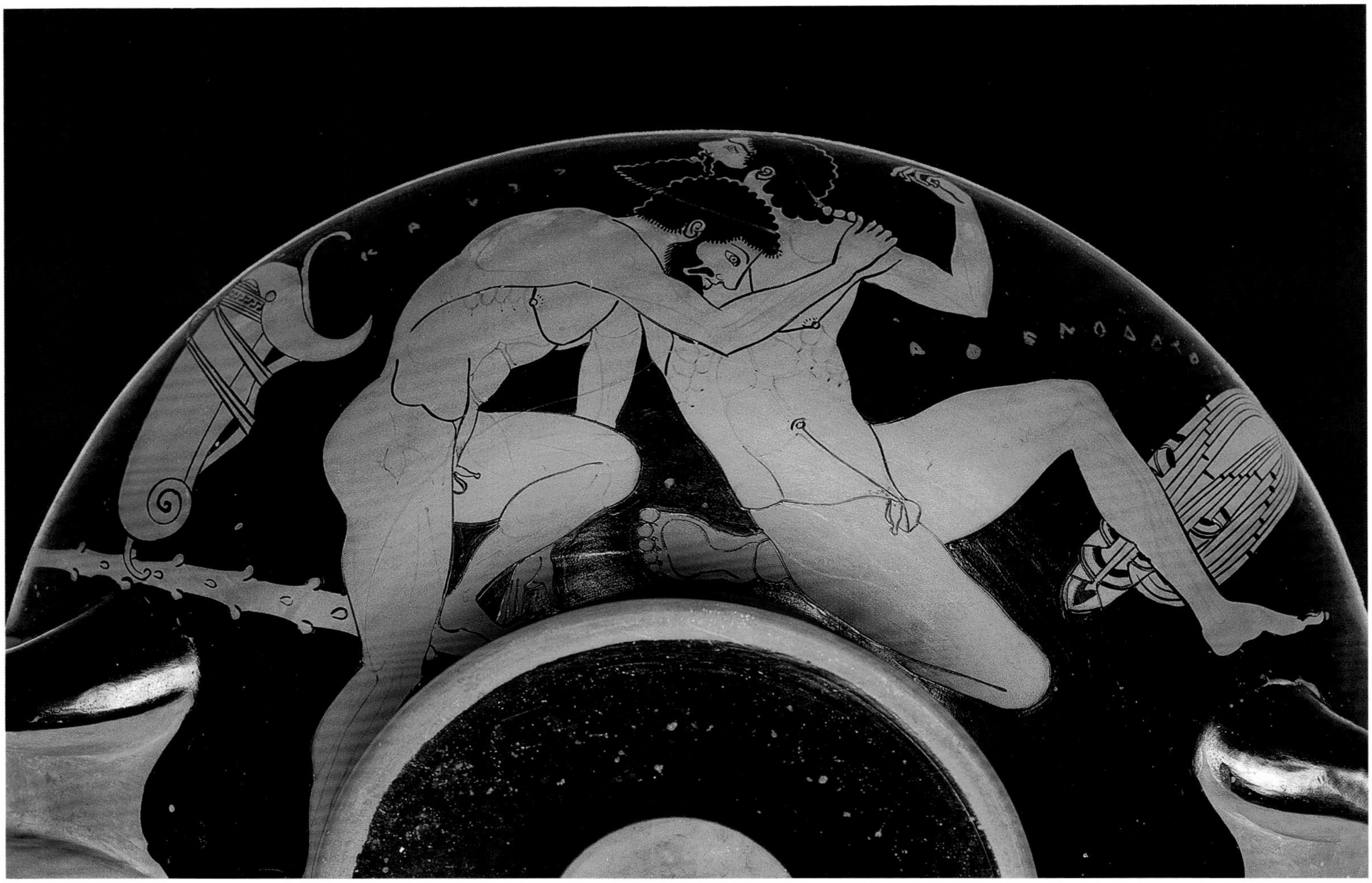

615 616

617

BOXING

Boxing is another very ancient event that makes its appearance in the Aegean civilisations in some very fine works of art, such as the stone rhyton from Ayia Triada in Crete and the famous wall painting of the Boxing Boys from Santorini, both of which date from the 16th c. BC. There is an interesting depiction of the event, in which two boxers are tied together by a rope, on a Cypro-Mycenaean krater of the 12th c. BC. In the boxing contest described by Homer (*Iliad*, XXIII, 681ff.) Epeios, son of Panopeus, defeated Euryalos and received a mule as his prize. Boxing was introduced as a men's event in the 23rd Olympiad in 688 BC, and the boys' contest was first held in the 41st games in 616 BC.

The most important development in ancient Greek boxing was the use of thongs, which the ancient Greeks bound around their fists. Already known at the time of Homer, they were strips of ox-hide leather 3 m. long which were wound around the palm and wrist to make the punches harder and also to afford protection. Sharp thongs were introduced in the 4th century: these were

618

reinforced with hard leather and stuffed with wool in places. Under the Roman empire, the *caestus* made its appearance, in which the thongs were reinforced by metal balls, making the punches fatal.

The contest began with the two opponents facing each other, holding out the left hand for defence and the right for attack. The tactic pursued in the contest was to direct the punches mainly at the face and upper body of the opponent until they knocked him out or obliged him to submit, which he did by raising the index finger of one hand. There were no limitations of space or time in ancient boxing, and the athletes were not divided into weight classes, nor were there rounds, points, or victories on points. Holding, punching to the genitals and kicking were forbidden.

619

617-618. Boxing is an event depicted fairly frequently in the prehistoric art of the Aegean, as on this Cypro-Mycenaean krater dating from the 13th c. BC, and an expanded drawing of the entire scene. Nicosia, Pierides Collection.

619. Characteristic depiction of a boxing match with the competitors hitting to the head with their left hand and defending themselves with their right. The contest is watched by a Victory and an athlete, who is tightening the thongs around his left hand with his teeth (336-335 BC). London, British Museum.

If the contest went on for a very long time, the 'climax' came into operation: the two boxers took it in turns to punch the other on the head, without making the slightest attempt to avoid blows or defend himself. The order was determined by lot, and the winner was the one who managed to knock out his opponent. Although this was a very tough event, especially the 'climax', very few cases of death are recorded. The best-known story involves Kleomedes of Astypalaia, who killed his opponent Ikkos of Epidauros in the final of the 496 BC Olympiad; the Hellanodikai stripped him of his victory, and Kleomedes went insane. Another very interesting anecdote is preserved on the grave stele of the boxer Kamelos of Alexandria, which dates from the 3rd c. BC and was found at Olympia. Kamelos, who was 35 years old, had won at Nemea and wanted to end his sporting career with a victory at Olympia as well. However, the inscription tells us that 'Here he died in the stadium, during the contest, having prayed to Zeus either to win or to die.'

The event naturally left many marks on the boxers, most commonly wounds to the face, cauliflower ears and broken noses, themes that often appear in ancient Greek literature and art. One satirical epigram for a defeated boxer says that when he returned home after the contest, his friends and relatives didn't

620

621

622

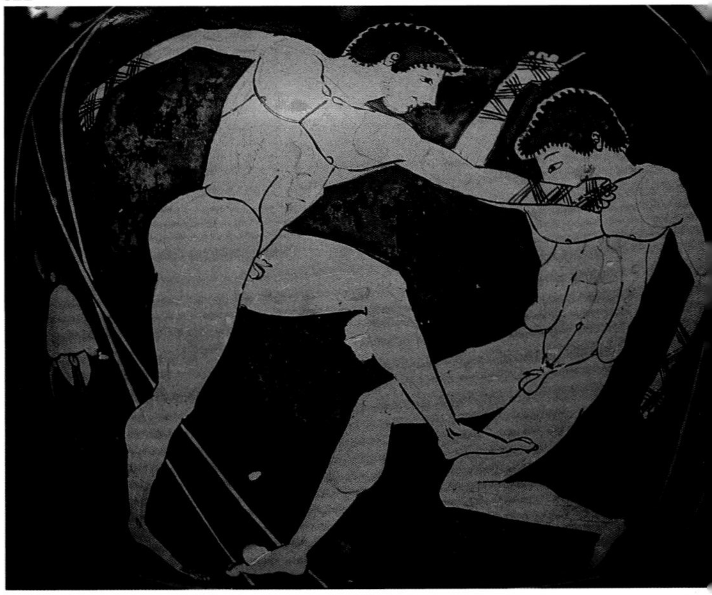

know him because of the wounds to his face. On the other hand, it was a great honour for a boxer to finish the contest unscathed, as in the case of the Eleian Hippomachos, winner of the boys' boxing in 300 BC, and Kleoxenos of Alexandria, who was periodonikes about 240 BC. Dio Cassius makes a similar statement regarding the handsome, unassuming Melankomas from Karia in Asia Minor, who lived at the end of the 1st c. BC. He became famous for the way he boxed: he did not punch his opponents, and didn't let them punch him. He achieved this by using delicate, airy movements of his body and limbs, which made his opponents so angry that they gave up the fight.

Other famous ancient boxers include Tisandros of Naxos in Sicily, who won many victories, including four at the Olympic and Pythian games between 572 and 560 BC, and Euthymos of Lokri in southern Italy, who won the Olympic event in 484, 476 and 472 BC. The greatest of them all, however, was Theagenes of Thasos, with 24 victories at the great panhellenic games (2 at Olympia, 3 at the Pythian games, 9 at Nemea and 10 at Isthmia). We learn from an epigram found at Delphi that he won a total of 1,400 crowns from games held throughout Greece, at which he competed in both boxing and the pankration. He was twice a periodonikes, and one of his victories at the Pythian games was *akoniti*. After his death, Theagenes was worshipped in his birthplace as a hero, and healing capacities were attributed to his statue. Pausanias tells us that he was worshipped in various regions even in his own time (2nd c. AD). According to one view, the famous Terme Boxer in Rome depicts Theagenes and was one of his cult statues, since there is some

620. Part of the grave stele of a boxer found in the Kerameikos, Athens. The man depicted is identified as a pugilist not only by the thongs wound around his hand but also by the broken nose and cauliflower ears (560-550 BC). Athens, Kerameikos Archaeological Museum.

621-622. Two depiction of boxing matches in which the boxers on the left are annihilating their opponents, who raise their index fingers to admit defeat.

621. Attic red-figure kylix dating from 500 BC. Athens, Ancient Agora Museum.

622. Red-figure amphoriskos dating from the early 5th c. BC. Athens, National Archaeological Museum.

evidence to suggest that it was displayed in a public place and the wear to it is consistent with cult practices.

Another famous boxer was Diagoras of Rhodes, a tall, statuesque man who, since he always competed without guile and bravely, became an idol and a model for all the ancient Greeks. Pindar composed his 7th Olympian Ode in his honour. Diagoras, who himself was victorious at Olympia in 464 BC and won many other events at panhellenic and local games, had the good fortune to see his three children and two grandchildren win at Olympia. One of his grandsons was the son of his daughter Kallipateira, who was famous as the only married woman to attend the Olympic games, disguised as a man, in order to see her son compete and win in 404 BC. Diagoras is also famous for the following reason: he had the good fortune to see his two sons, Akousilaos and Damagetos, win on the same day, at the 83rd Olympiad in 448 BC, the former in boxing and the latter in the pankration. His sons put their victory crowns on his head and then carried him proudly on their shoulders in the stadium, making a lap of triumph. There, cheered by all the spectators, he received the greatest triumph that fate could reserve for a mortal.

623

623. Bronze statue of the seated Therme Boxer. He is shown weary at the end of the match, with deep marks from the blows to his face and body (1st c. BC). Rome, Museo Nazionale Romano.

THE PANKRATION

The pankration (meaning 'with all one's strength') was a combination of wrestling and boxing. It was a tough event in which anything was allowed (holds, punching, kicking) except for biting and gouging the eyes. It was first held as a men's event in the 33rd Olympiad, of 648 BC, while the corresponding event for boys was introduced much later, in the 145th Olympiad, of 200 BC, when it was the last new event to be introduced into the Olympic programme. In other games, such as the Panathenaia, however, the pankration for youths and boys was held from at least 420 BC.

As in the case of wresting, there was *ano* and *kato pankration*, and the contest ended only when one of the two opponents gave the signal of submission with his finger, thereby acknowledging his defeat. These conditions made the pankration the toughest and most dangerous event in ancient athletics. Nevertheless, there were very few cases of death or serious injury, which says much for the ethics of ancient athletics. The most striking example, narrated by Pausanias (8.40.1), occurred in the final of the event at the 54th Olympiad in 564 BC. In this contest, the pankratiast Arrichion of Phigaleia found himself in a very difficult position, in the grip of a fearful hold by his opponent,

624. Depictions of athletes training for the heavy events, which was carried out in the palaestra. Left, a pair of boxers and right, a scene from the pankration, in which an athlete attempts to damage the eye of his opponent, provoking the immediate intervention of the judge. Attic red-figure kylix dating from the first quarter of the 5th c. BC. London, British Museum.

625. Characteristic scene from the pankration, showing more clearly than any other representation the combination of wrestling and boxing in this event. One of the athletes has put a hold on his opponent, immobilising him on the ground, and punches him. Marble group dating from the 3rd c. BC. Florence, Galleria Uffizi.

624

who was almost strangling him; with all the strength he had left, he grabbed his opponent's foot and dislocated the ankle. The terrible pain caused his opponent to submit, but, at that very moment, Arrichion died. In the end, the Hellanodikai declared the dead man the winner, because his opponent had admitted defeat by giving the signal to submit.

The fact that the pankration was very popular, like all the heavy events, despite the violence, injuries, blood and danger inherent in it, is an indication that the ancient Greeks were very tolerant of violence and found events involving wrestling and conflict very exciting.

One of the most famous pankratiasts in the ancient world was the third son of Diagoras of Rhodes, Dorieus, who won the event at three successive Olympiads and was also a periodonikes, since he won 8 times at Nemea and 7 times at Isthmia, and one of his victories at the Pythian games was akoniti. Another fine pankratiast was Sostratos of Sikyon, who had 17 victories at the panhellenic games, 3 of them at successive Olympiads (364-356 BC), 2 at Delphi, and a total of 12 at Nemea and Isthmia. He was given the nickname *akrochersites* ('the hands man'), because it was his practice to grab and crush his opponents' hands to oblige them to give up the contest. Polydamas from Skotoussa in Thessaly was also famous. He won only a single victory in the pankration, in the 93rd Olympiad, in 408 BC, but afterwards became famous throughout the world for his wide range of feats, in which he liked to imitate Herakles: he killed a lion with his bare hands, captured a wild bull and stopped a four-horse chariot moving at full speed with one hand. The base of his statue, made by the workshop of Lysippos, has been found quite badly damaged at Olympia; on it are preserved fragments of his feats, particularly a scene in which, in the presence of Darius, he dispatched three of the Persian king's 'immortals.'

625

Finally, the case of Marcus Aurelius Asklepiades of Alexandria, an athlete of the Roman period, is striking. A long inscription found in Rome describes all his achievements in detail: he acquired the title of periodonikes by winning at the games organised by three peoples (that is, of Greece, Italy and Asia Minor). His successes brought him honours in various cities, and he acquired the rights of citizenship in six of them. The end of the inscription states that he was obliged by the jealousy of his opponents to retire at the age of 25, after a sporting career of a mere six years. However, he succeeded in making a triumphant comeback fourteen years later, winning the pankration at the games held in his native Alexandria.

Equestrian events

The chariot was invented by the peoples of the Near East in the 2nd millennium BC and adopted in Greece during the Mycenaean period, first appearing on grave stelai from Grave Circle A at Mycenae (16th c. BC). An amphora of the Late Mycenaean period (13th c. BC) provides us with the first certain depiction of a chariot race. There is a striking description of a chariot race in Homer's account of the games in honour of Patroklos, and it is indicative of the importance attached to the event that of the roughly 600 verses of book XXIII devoted by the poet to the games, 391 relate to the chariot race.

Despite the fact that horse and chariot races were very ancient aristocratic events, they were introduced into the Olympic programme at a relatively late date – a circumstance that has puzzled scholars. The race for the four-horse chariot was introduced at the 25th Olympiad, in 680 BC, and between that date and 256 BC seven more equestrian events were gradually introduced, distinguished by the sex and age of the horses and the kind of chariot they pulled.

626-627. The first certain depictions of chariot races are to be found on Mycenaean vases dating from the 13th c. BC.

626. From a fragmentary krater from Tiryns. Nafplion, Archaeological Museum.

627. Chariot race on an amphoroid krater from Cyprus. Nicosia, Pierides Collection.

628. A charioteer urges his horses. Black-figure amphora. Athens, Ancient Agora Museum.

629. The beginning and end of a horse race: three young jockeys ride their horses to the starting line; the horse in the middle is given a final caress by the slave looking after him. Attic red-figure kylix dating from 480 BC. St. Petersburg, Hermitage Museum.

630. Depiction of the end of a horse race and the reception given to the winning horse, crowned with a wreath, and his rider. Men wearing official himatia and holding olive branches wave vigorously to express their delight. Panathenaic amphora dating from 530-520 BC. Nafplion, Archaeological Museum.

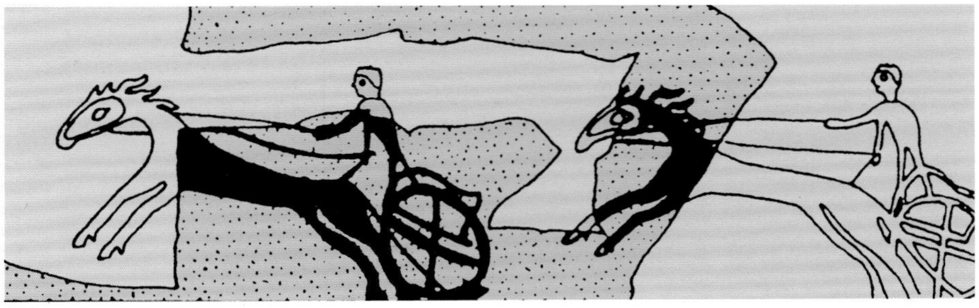

626

627

628

629

630

THE RACES

Chariot races were divided into events for the *tethrippon*, a chariot drawn by four horses, the *synoris*, which was drawn by two horses, and the *apene*, a cart pulled by two mules. There were also chariot races for foals (*poloi*). Horse races were divided into events for mature horses and foals, and there was an event for fillies called the *kalpe*. In the tethrippon, the chariots had to complete 12 laps of the hippodrome, a distance of 72 stades, or about 14 kilometres. The synoris for mature horses and the tethrippon for foals involved 8 laps, and the synoris for foals 3 laps (about 3.5 kilometres). In the horse race for *teleioi keletes* (mature horses) the horses ran the length of the hippodrome six times, a distance of about 2.3 km. The length of the course for the kalpe is unknown, but we do know that at the last turn, the jockey dismounted from the mare while it was still running and ran along with it to the finish, reins in hand.

631. Preparation for a chariot race. The charioteer, wearing a white chiton, and his two assistants yoke the four horses to the chariot. Attic black-figure hydria dating from 520-500 BC. London, British Museum.

632. Chariot race in progress. The vase painter has cleverly exploited the shape of the lid of the vase to show the chariots rounding the turning post. Black-figure amphora (520-510 BC). New York, The Metropolitan Museum of Art.

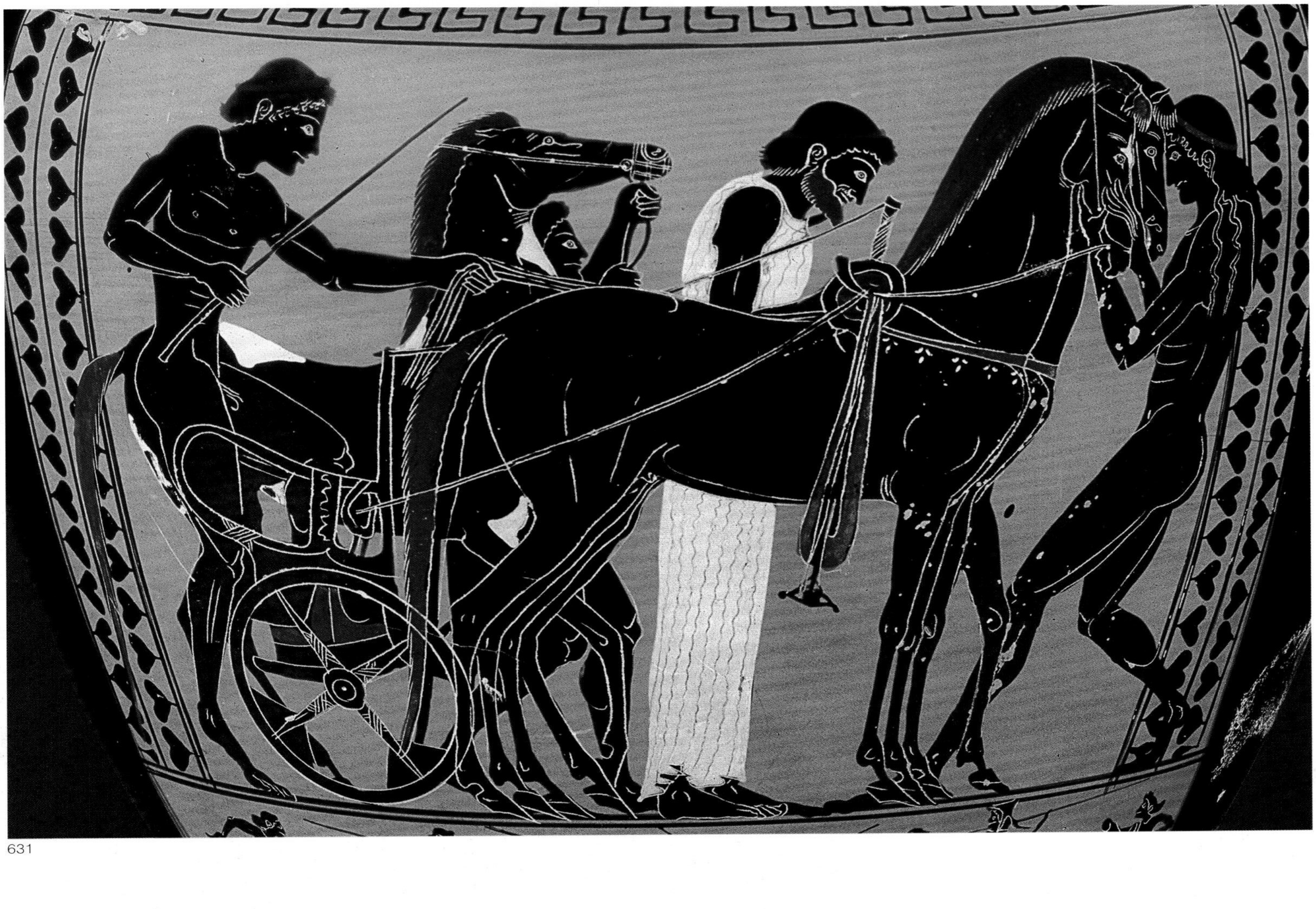

631

63

Famous Owners and Charioteers

635

The charioteers and jockeys were not the horses' owners, who were usually wealthy persons who hired these quasi-professional athletes to compete in the event, so as to protect themselves, the members of the ruling class, from the risks of the events. They might also cast the blame for defeat on the charioteer, though victory invariably redounded to the credit of the owner, who accepted the victory crown and all the privileges (fame, power, wealth) it showered upon him. There were very few owners brave enough to ride their horses and chariots themselves, one of them being the Roman emperor Nero.

This accounts for the emergence of women Olympic victors in the equestrian events, the better known of them being Kyniska, daughter of the Spartan king Archidamos, who won two victories, in 396 and 392 BC, and Belistiche, the concubine of Ptolemy Philadelphos, the king of Egypt. The number and names of the famous winners in the equestrian events are impressive. They include Kimon, grandfather of the famous Athenian general, who won at three successive Olympiads (532, 528 and 524 BC) with the same tethrippon. The tyrants of the Greek colonies in southern Italy and Sicily – Gelon, Theron, Hieron and Anaxilas – as well as the tyrant of Cyrene Arkesilas all won repeated victories at many of the panhellenic games in the first half of the 5th c. BC, for which Pindar composed victory odes.

It is characteristic of the wealth and ethos of Alkibiades that he entered seven four-horse chariots in the Olympiad of 416 BC, and finished in first, second and fourth place. The rich, haughty Athenian, who was also leader of the Athenian delegation at this Olympiad, celebrated his victory by giving a lavish dinner for all the spectators at the games, of whom there would have been about 50,000. Later, during an apologia before the Athenian people, he boasted that this action had increased the prestige of the city to a much greater extent than any other initiative, purely political

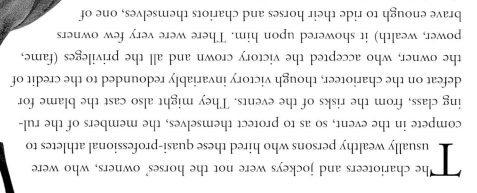

FAMOUS OWNERS AND CHARIOTEERS

635

The charioteers and jockeys were not the horses' owners, who were usually wealthy persons who hired these quasi-professional athletes to compete in the event, so as to protect themselves, the members of the ruling class, from the risks of the events. They might also cast the blame for defeat on the charioteer, though victory invariably redounded to the credit of the owner, who accepted the victory crown and all the privileges (fame, power, wealth) it showered upon him. There were very few owners brave enough to ride their horses and chariots themselves, one of them being the Roman emperor Nero.

This accounts for the emergence of women Olympic victors in the equestrian events, the better known of them being Kyniska, daughter of the Spartan king Archidamos, who won two victories, in 396 and 392 BC, and Belistiche, the concubine of Ptolemy Philadelphos, the king of Egypt. The number and names of the famous winners in the equestrian events are impressive. They include Kimon, grandfather of the famous Athenian general, who won at three successive Olympiads (532, 528 and 524 BC) with the same tethrippon. The tyrants of the Greek colonies in southern Italy and Sicily – Gelon, Theron, Hieron and Anaxilas – as well as the tyrant of Cyrene Arkesilas all won repeated victories at many of the panhellenic games in the first half of the 5th c. BC, for which Pindar composed victory odes.

It is characteristic of the wealth and ethos of Alkibiades that he entered seven four-horse chariots in the Olympiad of 416 BC, and finished in first, second and fourth place. The rich, haughty Athenian, who was also leader of the Athenian delegation at this Olympiad, celebrated his victory by giving a lavish dinner for all the spectators at the games, of whom there would have been about 50,000. Later, during an apologia before the Athenian people, he boasted that this action had increased the prestige of the city to a much greater extent than any other initiative, purely political

633. Superb perspective rendering of a four-horse chariot during a chariot race. Everything in the scene contributes to the intensity of the contest. Panathenaic amphora (late 5th c. BC). London, British Museum.

634. Bronze statue of a horse and its young rider, in a race, retrieved from the bottom of the sea near Cape Artemision. The realistic treatment of the youth's face and of the anatomical details of the horse is an impressive achievement of Hellenistic art (2nd c. BC). Athens, National Archaeological Museum.

634

In the horse races, the jockeys rode bareback and naked, holding the reigns in one hand and the whip in the other.

With regard to the rules for the event, we know that after the start, every charioteer strove to take the inner track of the hippodrome, so as to run the shortest distance. The drawing of lots for positions, which were regarded as the result of divine intervention, was of very great importance for the final outcome of the event. The most dangerous point of the event was the moment when the horses rounded one of the two turning posts placed at the ends of the long axis of the hippodrome. The horses had to pass very close to them without hitting them, and had to do this 24 times in the case of the four-horse chariot race.

In these circumstances, one can imagine the tension, passion and fascination of the event. Accidents happened, of course, with jockeys falling from their horses, chariots colliding, and competitors getting entangled. All this made the event even more exciting and increased the emotions of the thousands of spectators in the hippodrome.

THE RULES

The equestrian events were the most spectacular and therefore the most popular events at the Olympic and other games. This can be appreciated from the astonishing descriptions of them preserved in ancient works of literature, from the superb depictions in works of art, and from the size of the money prizes awarded to the victors at some of the *chrematites* games, such as at the Panathenaia.

The chariot was occupied only by the charioteer, who held the reins in his hands and also a long rod, which was either used as a goad or had a little bell hanging at the end, the sound of which stimulated the horses during the race.

633

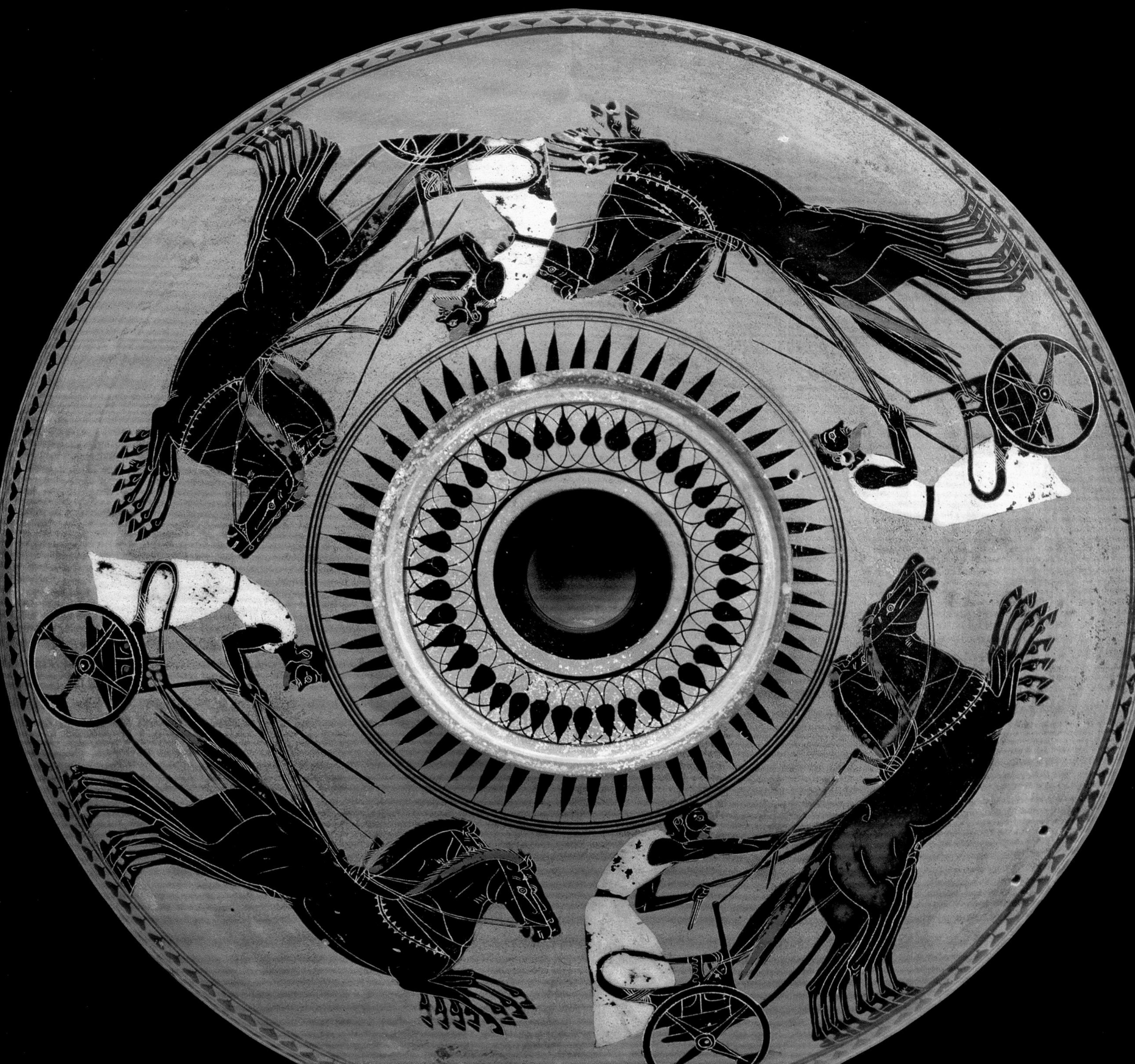

or military, taken by his fellow Athenians. We should not forget Philip II of Macedonia, who exploited his participation in the equestrian events at Olympia for purely political purposes. Finally, almost all the rulers of the Hellenistic kingdoms, including the Ptolemies of Egypt, the Attalids of Pergamon, and others, as well as, later, several Roman emperors or members of their families, competed in the equestrian events at the panhellenic games and the local games held in their own regions.

The last known winner of an equestrian event at Olympia was the Athenian T. Domitius Prometheus, who won the four-horse chariot race at the Olympiad of AD 241. After this time, the equestrian events went into decline at the Greek sanctuaries. They lost their appeal in the face of enormous competition from the games in the Roman hippodrome, which were now predominant throughout the whole of the Roman empire.

635. Side view of the Charioteer of Delphi. The group was dedicated by Polyzalos, brother of the tyrants of Syracuse, who won two successive victories in the chariot race at the Pythian games of 478 and 474 BC (ca. 470 BC). Delphi, Archaeological Museum.

636. The most difficult point of the chariot race, which revealed the true ability of the charioteer, was when the chariot rounded the turning post. All the racers tried to take the inside line of the arena, so as to cover the shortest distance. This moment is rendered excellently on the sharply curved surface of an Attic black-figure oinochoe dating from 500 BC. Athens, National Archaeological Museum.

636

BIBLIOGRAPHY

The bibliography on ancient Greek athletics is vast. For over 160 years, the issues that have concerned many Greek and foreign experts have been the subject of books, articles and conferences and have made a substantial contribution to a fuller knowledge of ancient Greek culture. I confine myself to listing here the most recent and readily accessible works that contain authoritative texts and a wealth of illustrations.

Titles in Greek

Ιστορία του Ελληνικού Έθνους της Εκδοτικής Αθηνών, Vol II (1971), pp. 472-507.
N. Yialouris (ed.), *Ιστορία των Ολυμπιακών Αγώνων* (1982).
J. Mouratidis, *Ιστορία της Φυσικής Αγωγής* (1990).
O. Alexandre (ed.), *Το Πνεύμα και το Σώμα* (1992).
E. Spathari, *Το Ολυμπιακό πνεύμα. Από τη γένεση μέχρι την αναβίωσή του* (1992).
E. Kefalidou, *Ο νικητής αθλητής. Εικονογραφική μελέτη με έμφαση στην αγγειογραφία* (1995).
P. Valavanis, *Άθλα, Αθλητές και Έπαθλα* (1996).
X. Arapoyianni, *Ολυμπία. Η κοιτίδα των Ολυμπιακών Αγώνων* (2002).

Titles in Other Languages

J. Jüthner, *Die athletischen Leibesübungen der Griechen* I (1965), II (1968).
N. Bengtson, *Die Olympischen Spiele in der Antike* (1971).
H.A. Harris, *Sport in Greece and Rome* (1972).
R. Patrucco, *Lo Sport nella Grecia Antica* (1972).
M. Finley and H.W. Pleket, *The Olympic Games: The First Thousand Years* (1976).
S.G. Miller, *Arete: Ancient Writers, Papyri and Inscriptions on the History and Ideals of Greek Athletics and Games* (1979).
D. Young, *The Olympic Myth of Greek Amateur Athletics* (1984).
V. Olivova, *Sport und Spiele im Altertum* (1984).
D. Kyle, *Athletics in Ancient Athens* (1987).
M.B. Poliakoff, *Combat Sports in the Ancient World: Competition, Violence and Culture* (1987).
W.J. Raschke (ed.), *The Archaeology of the Olympics: The Olympia and Other Festivals in Antiquity* (1988).
D. Sansone, *Greek Athletics and the Genesis of Sport* (1988).
W. Coulson and H. Kyrieleis (eds.), *Proceedings of an International Symposium on the Olympic Games, Athens, 5-9 September 1988* (1992).
D. Vanhove, *Le sport dans la Grèce antique: Du jeu à la competition* (1992).
J. Neils (ed.), *Goddess and Polis: The Panathenaic Festival in Ancient Athens* (1992).
D.G. Romano, *Athletics and Mathematics in Archaic Corinth: The Origin of the Greek Stadion* (1993).
D. Vanhove (ed.), *Olympism in Antiquity* (1993).
S.G. Miller, *The Ancient Stadium at Nemea: A Self-guided Tour* (1994).
F. Rausa, *L' Immagine del vincitore. L' atleta nella Statuaria greca dall' eta arcaica all' Ellenismo* (1994).
W. Decker, *Sport in der griechischen Antike* (1995).
M. Golden, *Sport and Society in Ancient Greece* (1998).
P. Valavanis, *Hysplex: The Starting Mechanism in Ancient Stadia. A Contribution to Ancient Greek Technology* (1999).
U. Sinn, *Olympia: Cult, Sport and Ancient Festival* (2000).
J. Swaddling, *The Ancient Olympic Games* (2000).
P. Badinou, *Olympiaka: Anthologie des Sources grecques* (2000).
S.G. Miller, *Excavations at Nemea II: The Early Hellenistic Stadium* (2001).
H. Kyrieleis (ed.), *Olympia 1875-2000: 125 Jahre Deutsche Ausgrabungen* (2002).

Illustration Credits

MUSEUMS – ARCHIVES – COLLECTIONS

ATHENS: Photo Archives: Kapon Editions: figs. 4, 9, 301, 302, 331, 375, 492, 559, 560; Moses & Rachel Kapon: figs. 61, 63, 65, 73, 83, 84, 87, 107, 114, 118, 129, 134, 146, 164, 165, 167, 169, 171, 177, 178, 182, 183, 185, 194, 196, 210-213, 264, 270, 277, 278, 281, 295, 299, 304, 305, 307, 313, 325, 328, 330, 335, 343, 344, 348, 350, 351, 357, 361, 364, 365, 369, 371-374, 384, 407, 416, 417, 419, 429, 430, 432, 433, 437, 440, 442, 448, 462, 463, 467, 468, 470-473 476-478, 484, 498, 500, 509, 553, 555, 556, 563, 565, 572, 587; G. Kitsios: fig. 139; D. Benetos: figs. 17-20, 22, 23, 25, 29, 46, 70, 110, 216; G. Fafalis: figs. 38, 75, 126, 180, 232-238, 241, 245, 251, 253, 273, 275, 287, 294, 300, 314, 317, 319, 308, 309, 332, 362, 366, 386, 388, 389, 391, 393, 394, 395, 403-406, 413, 420, 423-425, 435, 449-453, 455, 464, 486, 506, 533, 545, 635; G. Fafalis (photographs from publications of the German Archaeological Institute): figs. 12, 41, 43-45, 50, 55, 57, 66, 79, 80, 128, 133, 141, 150, 151, 152, 160-163, 166, 168, 186, 184, 187, 190, 215; Chr. Iosifidis – G. Moutevellis: page 11, figs. 31, 39, 266, 608 ■ T.A.P.A.: figs. 5, 32, 33, 34, 40, 48, 49, 51, 54, 59, 67, 69, 71, 76, 90-101, 109, 135, 140, 148, 154, 158, 159, 188, 189, 244, 246-247, 252, 262, 280, 282, 286, 288, 289, 290, 293, 318, 329, 338, 341, 342, 352, 353, 354, 356, 359, 360, 363, 390, 571, 621; G. Fafalis: fig. 634 ■ French Archaeological School: figs. 250, 263, 271, 291, 310, 311, 312, 320, 322, 323, 324, 326, 327, 339, 355; Philippe Collet: figs. 240, 283, 284, 376 ■ German Archaeological Institute: figs. 41, 58, 68, 88, 89, 105, 106, 179; Romaides (1875): figs. 43, 52, 60, 115, 117 ■ G. Giannelou: figs. 16, 21, 56, 62, 74, 78, 86, 119, 153, 172 ■ P. Valavanis: figs. 102, 381, 546, 554 ■ N. P. Goulandris Foundation, Museum of Cycladic Art: fig. 480 ■ National Archaeological Museum: fig. 135 ■ Archaeological Society of Athens: fig. 306 ■ ICOM—Greek section, Athens: figs. 227, 490 ■ Photographic Archives of Prehistoric and Classical Antiquities: fig. 142 ■ I Prehistoric and Classical Antiquities, Dr. H. Partidas: figs. 254, 321 ■ G. Kouroupis: figs. 230, 345, 380, 382, 387, 412, 414, 466, 474, 578 ■ S. Mavrommatis: figs. 502, 513, 519, 520 ■ Benaki Museum: figs. 2, 379, 385 ■ Numismatic Museum: figs. 104, 242, 570, 573, 574 ■ S. Stournaras: figs. 24, 147, 175, 400, 595, 597, 601, 602, 636 ■ Studio, N. Kontos: fig. 518 ■ T. Tloupas: pp. 24, 29 (base), figs. 260, 261 ■ Hellenic Institute for the Preservation of Nautical Tradition, T. Tzalas: fig. 259.

AMSTERDAM: Rijksmuseum van Oudheden: fig. 599.
BALTIMORE: Johns Hopkins University: fig. 195.
BASEL: Antikenmuseum Basel und Sammlung Ludwig, Clare Niggli: fig. 603.
BERKELEY: University of California, Nemea Excavations Archives: fig. 465.
BERLIN: Staatliche Museen zu Berlin–Preussischer Kulturbesitz, Antikensammlung: fig. 223; Ingrid Geske-Heiden: figs. 336, 346; Johannes Laurentius: fig. 337; Jürgen Liepe: fig. 580 ■ Dr. H. R. Goette: figs. 85, 193, 402.
COPENHAGEN, National Museum: fig. 13.
DILBEEK: Miel Verhasselt: figs. 72, 426, 457, 528.
FERRARA: Archaeological Museum: fig. 226.
FLORENCE: Sopridenza Archeologica per la Toscana: figs. 35, 479, 526 ■ Scala Archives: figs. 11, 36, 257, 334, 398, 566, 625.
LONDON: British Museum: pp. 9, 10; figs. 1, 81, 113, 131, 132, 197, 205, 267, 333, 383, 443, 445, 494, 535, 539, 557, 586, 607, 619, 624, 631, 633.
LOS ANGELES: The J. Paul Getty Museum: figs. 593, 600, 615, 616; Ellen Rosenbery: figs. 124, 191, 192, 203, 495, 537, 538, 542, 567, 582, 583, 588, 605, 609; Bruce White: fig. 198.
MUNICH: Staatliche Antikensammlungen: figs. 125, 446; Koppermann: fig. 544.
NAPLES: Archivio dell' Arte, Luciano Pedicini: fig. 201, 303, 581, 584, 585, 613.
NEW YORK: The Metropolitan Museum of Art: figs. 268, 269, 536, 594, 632.
PARIS: Réunion des Musées Nationaux: fig. 397; Hervé Lewandowski: figs. 14, 204, 206, 207, 499, 503, 505, 529; Chuzeville: fig. 610 ■ École Nationale Supérieure des Beaux-Arts: figs. 15, 145, 285, 296, 297, 298, 378, 493, 496-497, 501, 511, 512, 575 ■ PHO.N.E.: fig. 221 (eagle, left: Albert Visage; eagle, right: François Gohier).
ROME: Alessantro Vasari: fig. 120 ■ Ministero per i Beni e le Attivita Culturali – Soprintendenza Archeologica di Roma: fig. 623.
SMYRNA: Archaeological Museum: fig. 592.
ST. PETERSBURG: Hermitage Museum: figs. 224, 543, 629.
TARQUINA: Foto Soprintendenza Beni Archeologici per l'Etruria Meridionale: fig. 176.
VATICAN: Photographic Archives of the Vatican Museums: figs.157, 228, 229, 347.
WASHINGTON, D.C.: Smithsonian Institution, Museum of American History: fig. 144.
WÜRZBURG: Martin von Wagner Museum der Universität Würzburg, K. Oehrlein: figs. 218, 418, 551, 552.

BOOKS AND CATALOGUES:

Fuilles de Delphes, École Française d'Athènes, Paris (1902): figs. 272, 292, 340.
Mind and Body, Ministry of Culture, Athens (1989): G. Fafalis, figs. 6, 30, 47, 121, 136, 138, 143, 173, 174, 199, 200, 202, 265, 370, 396, 399, 401, 411, 439, 441, 444, 447, 454, 481, 482, 485 507, 521-525, 527, 531, 534, 541, 548-550, 561, 568, 576, 577, 590, 591, 598, 604, 611, 614, 620, 622, 628, 630.
The Gold of the World, Kapon Editions, Athens (1997): figs. 248, 249.
The Human Figure in Early Greek Art, Ministry of Culture, Athens (1987): G. Fafalis, figs. 26, 243, 447, 524, 530, 540, 606.
Olympia Bericht IV: fig. 181.
A Stage for Dionysos, Kapon Editions, Athens (1998): figs. 349, 562.
Ο Χαρίλαος Τρικούπης και τα Δημόσια Έργα, Kapon Editions – Lydia Tricha, Athens (2001): figs. 421, 422.
Sculpture in the National Archaeological Museum, Athens, Kapon Editions, Athens (2002): fig. 458.
Πολεοδομική Εξέλιξις των Αθηνών, I. Traulos, Kapon Editions, Athens (1993): figs. 510, 547, 564.
Ο ναός του Διός στη Νεμέα, Benaki Museum, Athens (1983): fig. 461.
Άτλας για τις ταξειδιωτικές σημειώσεις του Β. Νταβίντωφ από τα Ιόνια Νησιά, την Ελλάδα, την Μ. Ασία και την Τουρκία, St. Petersburg (1839): fig. 460.
Parthenon, the Elgin Marbles, National Mortgage Bank (1989): figs. 514-517.
Ελληνικός Πολιτισμός. Μακεδονία, Το Βασίλειο του Μεγάλου Αλεξάνδρου, Athens (1993): figs. 255, 256.
Guide to the Archaeological Museum of Thessalonike, Kapon Editions, Athens (1996): figs. 532, 569, 579.
Το Πνεύμα και το Σώμα. Η αναβίωση της Ολυμπιακής Ιδέας, 19ος-20ός αιώνας, Ministry of Culture, Athens (1989): fig. 558.
Αρχαία Τέχνη της Κύπρου στη Συλλογή Γεωργίου και Νεφέλης Τζιάπρα Πιερίδη, Cultural Institute of the Bank of Cyprus, Athens (2002): figs. 589, 617, 618, 627.
Δελφοί, K.-V. Petrakos Editions, Athens (1977): figs. 274, 276, 279.

INDEX